HIGH
TIMES
HARD
TIMES

Also by George Eells
The Life That Late He Led
   A biography of Cole Porter

Hedda and Louella
   A Dual Biography

Ginger, Loretta and Irene WHO?

Merman, An Autobiography
   With Ethel Merman

HIGH TIMES HARD TIMES

ANITA O'DAY

WITH GEORGE EELLS

With an updated discography compiled by

Robert A. Sixsmith and Alan Eichler

OCM18D50968

Limelight Editions

An Imprint of Hal Leonard Corporation
New York

Limelight Editions (an imprint of Hal Leonard Corporation)
19 West 21st Street, New York, NY 10010

Published by Limelight Editions
Fourth printing, 2007

Printed in the United States of America

Library of Congress Cataloging-in-Publication Data

O'Day, Anita.
   High times, hard times.
   Discography: p.
   Includes index.
   1. O'Day, Anita   2. Singers---United States---
Biography.   I. Eells, George.   II. Title.
ML420.03A3 1988   784.5'0092'4[B]   88-17896

Limelight ISBN-10: 0-87910-118-0
Limelight ISBN-13: 978-0-87910-118-3

www.limelighteditions.com

Graham Young, Leonard Feather, Maynard Sloate, Elizabeth Pettet, Earl Clark, Hal Brown, Dale Thorpe, Angie Oger Ridgeway, Al Lyons, Sam LiPari, Maury Stein, Bill Dohler, Tut Soper, Bert Lawrence, Carl Hoff, Mike Gould, Shorty Sherock, Remo Biondi, Rajah Bergman, Danny Bramer, Alvista Perkins, Ron Kinney, Joe Arden, Jane Gaylor, Norma Jasper, Frank Liberman, Ray Forman, Elaine Poole, Natalie Schafer, Dr. David Boska, and Mark Sendroff have our gratitude for the help they have given.

In addition, special thanks to Robert Sixsmith Jr. and Alan Eichler for providing the detailed discography; to Tom Clapp for advice and encouragement; to our indefatigable literary agent Gloria Safier; to John Poole for his excellent memory and unending patience; and to Mel Zerman for giving this book a new life.

To Emily,
my small canine friend

CONTENTS

FOREWORD

(Excerpt from a broadcast of *60 Minutes*, June 22, 1980)

This is a story about a woman who wanted to be a jazz singer and refused to let anything stop her. She started singing at the age of twelve for coins thrown on a dance floor. She just barely made enough money to pay the rent as a band singer—a "canary"—in the forties. She had two bad marriages and was a heroin addict for fifteen years. She survived all that to become one of the world's great jazz singers just at the time the world turned its back on jazz and flipped over rock and disco. It's the story of Miss Anita O'Day, who, at sixty, is at her peak and is now beginning to get a little recognition and make a little money as the disco fad begins to fade and jazz makes a comeback.

Anita started singing forty-six years ago, and, right from the start, it was not easy. She met bandleader Gene Krupa at a Chicago tavern, and a year later she became the Krupa band's canary. A canary, some of you will remember, was the pretty girl in the bouffant dress who spent most of the evening sitting on a chair in front of the big band, snapping her fingers and bouncing a little in time to the music. "Thanks for the Boogie Ride" and another song she sang with the Krupa band, "Let Me Off Uptown," were big sellers. Anita's name began appearing on music magazine lists of most-popular singers. She had hit the big time and was making all of $40 a week.

Anita moved on to other bands, and then, as the big-band sound lost popularity, to small jazz groups, still not making any money to speak of but learning to make the transition from canary to jazz singer. Then, in 1954, she got hooked on heroin. She stayed on it for sixteen years, through several arrests. Anita has sort of blocked the heroin years out of her mind. She tends to gloss it over, make it seem unimportant. All she remembers is she kept singing.

Anita insists she was working constantly during the heroin years, but friends and musicians who knew her say she lost a lot of weight and was ill a lot and had serious bouts of depression. During one of those she took a big overdose and was declared dead at a California hospital. As soon as she got out of the hospital, she went to Hawaii and broke the heroin habit. Cold turkey.

She returned from Hawaii singing better than ever; more important, singing jazz better than most women ever have. But Elvis Presley and the Beatles had changed her world. Rock was in. There were no jazz audiences. So as usual, there was no money for Anita.

Now there may be a lot of big paychecks on the horizon. She recently sang in Carnegie Hall. She plays Marty's in New York several times a year and clubs in Boston, Chicago, Los Angeles and Japan. She's very popular in Japan. And it's not just nostalgia buffs out there in the audience; the young people are out there, too.

If you're interested in jazz, consider this: Billie Holiday is dead, and Anita, Sarah Vaughan, Carmen McRae and Ella Fitzgerald are getting on. The real sad thing, according to [critic] Leonard Feather, is that there are no young singers coming up to replace them. Jazz takes too much time and discipline, and there's not enough money in it.

So this is the story of Miss Anita O'Day. She got hurt and scared and confused along the way and put a kind of laughing lid on her emotions. When she finally got herself off heroin, she says she avoided getting back into trouble this way: when her old drug buddies tempted her, she would walk on by. She walks on by a lot of things, except music. In a way that the old cliché never meant, she lives not only for her music but in it. And if she could do it all over, there's not much she would change.

—Harry Reasoner

PREFACE

Joe Glaser, who was my booking agent for many years, used to say, "Anita, you've got a million dollars' worth of talent and no class."

That's exactly the way I felt on the morning of March 4, 1966. I was really strung out when I went to the American Guild of Variety Artists to meet Dee.

"Hi, Anita," she called from behind her desk, signaling she'd scored. "Let's go for coffee."

Before leaving, she slipped me a packet of heroin and lent me her outfit. I locked myself in the ladies' latrine and prepared to cook up.

Until he took a job in Hawaii, John Poole, my true friend and drummer, had always put the needle in my arm. Now I had to rely on myself. I tied off and tried to hit one of the veins on the outside of my arm. I missed. I tried again, and again I missed. The third try I hit, drew out blood, waited, plunged it back in, withdrew it and plunged it back again for an extra zing. For a moment, I felt this glorious surge of warmth beginning deep within my stomach and spreading through my body. It was heavenly. I thought, Gee, this is good! This is the most! What a ding! Pow!

And after that—nothing.

It was lucky for me that one of the girls in the office wanted to use the latrine. When you shoot up, the trick is always to have somebody around in case you OD. You have to be found right away. That's the difference between Lenny Bruce and somebody like Stan Getz or me. Lenny had a roommate, but his roommate didn't come home for six hours and that did Lenny in.

As Dee told it, this broad waited about ten minutes for me to come out. Then she complained, "Why don't your friend rent a room? What's she doing? She's been in there long enough to have a kid."

"How long?"

"Who counts? Ten, fifteen minutes."

Dee panicked. She jumped up, ran over and rammed the door like a bulldozer. The door gave and she saw me crumpled on the floor with the hypodermic needle still in my arm. She pulled it out and hid the outfit in her dress.

"Heart attack! Heart attack!" she began yelling.

One of her hip coworkers had already called the Beverly Hills Fire Department Rescue Unit. They took Dee with me to the nearby Beverly Hills Emergency Hospital at 10:45 A.M. As a confirmed junkie, Dee started planting confusion during the ride over. She gave them 9124 National Boulevard as my home address and claimed my first seizure took place there. (I hadn't been near the place in weeks.) When Dr. Bayer entered "possible overdose" in the space behind "Nature of the Complaint," Dee pretended she was indignant, but Dr. Bayer went ahead and gave me 50 milligrams of Megamide IV before having me transferred to the UCLA Center for Health and Sciences.

I was out cold. Both pupils in my eyes were unresponsive. My breathing was rapid and shallow, but Dee kept up such a steady stream of conflicting chatter about my background that she managed to rattle the doctor so much that on the official report he recorded my temperature as 36, my pulse 110 and my respiration 16. The first page of the report places my "attack" at home. On the reverse side is a notation that I'd been found "unresponsive in the bathroom of a ladies' clothing store." Apparently Dee planted both stories in case the police got involved and my defense attorney needed those discrepancies to discredit the medical report. She also managed to see to it that the AGVA office went completely ignored.

* * *

At the UCLA Medical Center after I began to come around, Dee told me that at one point the doctors could detect no heartbeat and were just drawing the sheet over my face—in other words, I seemed to be dead—when a young doctor ran in with some contraption which he used to get my heart started again.

"I guess they figured you were legally dead so they had nothing to lose," Dee told me. "Luckily, whatever that thing was it worked."

Strangely, when I recently obtained the UCLA Hospital records, no mention was made of the incident.

After I'd been installed in a room and begun to come around, Dee filled me in on the stories she'd told. She said she'd signed me in as a heart patient and warned me to stick to that story because the doctors suspected an overdose. Then she cut out before somebody got the idea of connecting her with my problem.

During my stay at the hospital, treatment included various examinations, an electrocardiogram "showing no acute changes," a stomach wash and IVs. When the doctors realized I was conscious, they tried to get me to admit to them what I'd taken, but I wasn't talking. On his report, Dr. Rose noted that I firmly denied using drugs during the past eight years and insisted I'd collapsed because of lack of food and sleep.

Under "Impression," on the Radiological Consultation Report, the doctor wrote, "Negative chest."

The Psychiatric Report noted that I'd been brought in "five hours previously . . . requiring resuscitation procedures . . . relates for the past two weeks suffering flu-like symptoms, and since breaking off with a boyfriend drinking heavily unknown quantities of whiskey, wine and beer daily, eating and sleeping poor, moving from place to place until on the day of admission finding herself without money or lodging."

Under "Mental Status" the psychiatrist noted: "She admits to 'I drink because I'm depressed,' but denies suicidal intentions or attempt. Appears mildly depressed. There is no evidence of recent or remote memory loss. Intellectual functioning appears within average range. Judgment is unimpaired."*

*For full report, see Appendix.

Apparently the only people taken in by our alibi were Dee and me.

When John Poole, in whose apartment I was sitting out the lease, called from Hawaii and couldn't get an answer at any time of the day or night, he wigged out. He was sure the police had nabbed me or I'd OD'd. He frantically started calling friends to find out whether they knew what was coming down. But the situation smelled of trouble to most of those cats who were no strangers to it. Nobody wanted to go to the landlady to inquire about me and have the police tailing them or to go into the apartment and find my body on the floor with all that would involve. Nobody was willing to get involved in any way.

Nobody except a tall, lanky drink of water who had earned his living with his funny voices and guitar playing. He'd toured the country with musical tab shows and been featured as one of Al Pearce's Gang on early radio before hitting the uptown taverns in Chicago where I met him. Eventually he landed in California where he worked as a comic emcee in burlesque bars. When they faded, he opened a Mr. Fixit shop with the slogan, "If we can't fix it, throw it away."

Al Lyons both had character and was one. He'd been a tea smoker until grass became illegal in 1933, then he switched to alcohol. But high or drunk or sober, he was a stand-up guy who was my mentor and loyal friend. We first met on a particularly sad day for him. His sister had died and he adopted me immediately as a substitute sister which ain't bad. It's a big world out there when you're alone.

And in 1968, he was the only one of all the cats I called "friends" who wasn't hung up on drugs and had nothing to fear from the police. Al went to the Pooles' apartment where I'd been living and to see Dee, who gave him the heart attack story.

Meanwhile, back at the hospital (to coin a phrase), I got out of bed and started looking for my clothes. A nurse came in and hustled me back to bed. "You've had a heart attack," she said. "Now stay there."

I couldn't tell her I was as good as I was ever going to get. How could I explain that I'd been in on an evening when some friends brought Stan Getz around after an OD. And when Stan saw some of the guys cutting up a packet of smack, he hollered, "Hey, man! Save a little taste for me."

That's not as unusual as it might seem. Because scoring is always uppermost in any junkie's mind, even after he's OD'd. Me, all I knew was I had to split before the chemical got counteracted or wore off and confirmed what Dee had said the doctors originally suspected.

Stymied, I began beating the pillows in frustration. No matter how upset I am, I hardly ever cry. I believe the only thing crying accomplishes is to make you sick.

After a few minutes of my carrying on like this, a familiar lanky figure, carrying a television set, appeared in my doorway. It was Al Lyons and he wanted to know what was going on. I told him I'd fainted and the dumb doctor thought I'd had a heart attack. "All I need is some nourishing food and rest," I said, trying to con him. "Get me out of here and take me to your place."

Al later told me he knew the score, but he didn't press me because he believed forcing people to face up to their problems might cause them to commit suicide. He just agreed that if what I wanted was to sign myself out of the hospital, I could stay with him and his mother until I was okay again.

Now I knew Al's mother wasn't going to be happy about the idea, but I was desperate. Once, years before, Al told her he thought he wanted to marry me. She let out one long "Nnnyaaaaaannnhh!" and hit the floor in a faint. Al thought she was having a stroke or a fit and backed out of his marriage proposal which was all right with me. He was—and is—a nice guy, just not my type. But I was sure nobody could convince his mother of that, and I wouldn't be exactly welcome at their home out on the corner of Lankershim and Victory in the San Fernando Valley.

Mrs. Lyons was a big woman and she saw to it the only time I got to spend alone with Al was when she went to the bathroom— and even then I'm not sure she closed the door tight. She had been a concert pianist and they still owned a beautiful grand piano. It was beautiful to look at, but by now both she and Al were quite deaf. If they'd tried to de-tune the piano, they couldn't have made it sound any worse. Still, she entertained us by playing all the classical compositions without hearing one false note, which was a blessing for her at least.

It jangled my nerves and I wanted to get away. Al was an eccentric who didn't believe in banks. He kept his money stashed around the house and had a pile of postal money orders two inches high. Almost any time I asked he would lend me three or four hundred bucks, which I always paid back. But when I hit him for plane fare to Hawaii he refused to let me have it. I suspect the reason was that he didn't like John Poole's influence over me.

So I lay around, eating his mother's cooking and getting a lot of sun until John called me from a pay booth in Honolulu. He told me again that the word was out on the grapevine that the cops were set to bust me. His best advice was: "Go tell your landlady that you'll be giving up the apartment in a week or ten days when the rent is up. She'll believe that because she knows you're broke. But get out of Southern California *now*."

I had Al drive me back to the apartment. I told the landlady that I was sick and wanted to get my TV set fixed so I could lie around and watch it while I got well. Then I took the TV set and sold it for a hundred bucks to one of my doctor's nurses.

In those days, a one-way ticket to Hawaii cost $83 or $84. I picked up one and got a reservation on the red-eye special. Then I went back to the apartment, threw together a bag of essentials and split in the middle of the night. I took a taxi to the airport and breathed easier after my plane took off. When I set foot in Hawaii, I had exactly sixty cents in my purse.

John, who had broken his habit a year earlier, was at the airport to meet me. But it seemed there was a slight complication in that his wife didn't want me staying with them. So he had hocked some of his drums to raise enough bread to pay my rent for a month. He said that if I sincerely wanted to kick my habit, I now had the opportunity. It was up to me.

I told him I'd think it over. I thought about the alternatives and decided to try. My OD had scared me. I concluded that the price of being a hip, swinging chick eventually had become too great to pay. I'd almost had to die to take the first step in learning how to live.

CHAPTER I
EXCESS BAGGAGE

Getting pregnant while she was single was something I don't think my mother ever got over. That was really a heavy situation in 1919. Girls killed themselves, became prostitutes or got married and carried the guilt with them all their lives. Mom took the last route.

Mom's unmarried name was Gladys Gill and early pictures show an outdoorsy girl with devilish eyes and her own kind of prettiness. There she is crouched in the crotch of a tree holding a rifle and the squirrel she's just bagged. Or, on another occasion, she's astride a horse, wearing a jockey suit at a time when most women didn't wear pants. But by the time I became old enough to remember her, she was solemn, if not downright grim.

Mom and Dad were both from Kansas City, Missouri. Mom had a half-sister, Aunt Belle, whom she was closer to than anyone else in the world. Aunt Belle stepped in and took care of her after their mother died until Mom was old enough to go to work in the box factory. That's where she met Dad whose name was James Colton.

Dad was an only child, a happy cat, a personality kid. He was tall, slim, with dimples and a delicate bone structure, all of which I inherited. He was also handsome, sandy-haired, and he drank a lot. He was a real ladies' man and wound up having ten marriages and nine wives before he was fifty.

He must have had a great line to get Mom to "go all the way," as they said back then. Anyway, he did what nice guys did when Mom told him she was pregnant. He married her.

Too bad he couldn't have been a cad. Too bad for her. Too bad for him. And too bad for me.

As soon as they were married, Mom and Dad moved to Chicago where no one was going to be minding their business. Mom always told me that I was born at Michael Reese Hospital on December 18, 1919, but when I needed a birth certificate to get my passport for the European tour with Benny Goodman in 1959, I was stunned to learn I'd bowed into the world as Anita Belle Colton on October 18, 1919. That was about six-and-one-half months after they cut out from K.C. Finding out about my real birth date put a lot of things into focus for me that had bothered me all my life.

I couldn't explain it, but I'd always felt that in some way I was to blame for whatever was wrong. Eventually I could see that Dad had done the "right thing" in marrying Mom, but as soon as they moved into an apartment in the uptown district of Chicago, Dad abdicated.

He got a job as a printer when they came to Chicago and worked for Cuneo, the biggest outfit in the city. He made good money, but, like a lot of other people, he'd drink up his check on the way home on payday. During my earliest years, I don't have any memories of him at all. Between the time I was a little over a year old and when I reached seven, he just wasn't around.

I can't say the same about Mom. She looked after me, but there used to be a popular phrase, "excess baggage," and that's what she made me feel like.

Not that she ever complained. Not Mom. She was a straitlaced, old-style martyr who pitied herself because she had to work and was left with a daughter to raise. I didn't realize it at the time, of course, but she made me feel I was keeping her from living her life. She worked hard all day, took me to the baby-sitters, picked me up after work, cooked dinner and went to bed.

I guess she was tired, but I couldn't understand why she never cuddled and kissed me as I saw other mothers do with their children.

From the time I was two years old, I was sent off to Kansas City to visit my grandparents on my father's side each summer. They were churchgoing people and it was there that I began singing. I enjoyed Sunday School for that reason, but when I'd get adjusted to life with Grandpa and Grandma Colton, they'd take me back to Chicago or Mom would come down and get me. I don't think I had any clear idea where I belonged and I suppose I interpreted those changes of locale as some kind of punishment.

Mom liked music and after I returned from Kansas City and sang a little song, she seemed very pleased. I must have been starved for attention because after she started me in kindergarten at four and a half, I really enjoyed learning little songs. At five, I took the leading part in a Christmas play in which I sang and danced. It was one of the few times Mom showed any pride in me when I was a kid. I was so proud I almost popped my buttons.

When I first started to grade school at Stewart, I did okay because we talked our lessons and I could remember whatever was said. But I began floundering when we got into identifying printed letters and numbers. I don't know why nobody thought it strange that I couldn't learn to read and that I printed so much larger than other kids. Me? I thought I was dumb. Mom? She just sighed and accepted it as another burden for her to bear.

I guess teachers then didn't give much thought to why a kid had trouble learning to read. I know that none of them ever sent a note suggesting that I have my eyes checked. So I tried to make myself invisible to escape getting called on and making some stupid mistake in front of the whole class. In my mind, I wasn't worth a whole lot and nobody went out of the way to make me feel good about myself.

Then when I was seven a wonderful thing happened. My dad started showing up at the apartment again. He laughed and joked and won me over the same way he must have won the heart of any woman he went after. To be honest, Dad never looked after me and he contributed very little to my support, but even so he probably gave me more love than Mom.

I don't think I was aware that he and Mom had divorced because of his drinking, gambling and chasing pretty girls, but after he began coming by more often, Mom began to bloom. After a few weeks of this, they had a long private talk. When it was over, they told me they were remarrying and we'd all be living together again.

I guess the short period that followed was the happiest of my childhood, and it came about in a strange way. It seems Dad had been shooting craps and had cleaned this other cat out of cash. His opponent was one of those never-say-die types who put this seven-room West Side apartment against Dad's money. Dad accepted the challenge and won. So you might say that Mom and Dad's second marriage depended on the roll of the dice.

I was at an age where Mom felt I needed a father and I did, because Dad really knew how to make a girl's heart flutter. He got me a dog, Kayo, who was really something. You could send Kayo to the store with a note in the bag ordering anything, even hamburger and he'd bring it back untouched. For a while I don't know whether I loved Dad or Kayo most. Certainly Mom wasn't in the running.

About a week after we moved into the apartment, a piano was delivered. Dad told me he'd bet on a horse named Anita, a long shot that paid off, and he'd used his winnings to buy a piano. Who knows whether it was the truth or just some of Dad's blarney? True or not, it really made me feel good.

That piano was intended to play a big part in our home life. Mom felt that if Dad couldn't or wouldn't give up drinking, at least he could do it at home. With the big apartment and piano for music, they could have his friends in for parties. So Dad mixed a batch of home brew which he put in the pantry. And it wasn't long before the yeast began to work and caps were popping off the bottles in the middle of the night.

In the beginning, the piano provided entertainment for everybody. Mom would sit down and play songs like "Moonlight and Roses." She'd sing tenor, Dad would sing the third part pretty good and I'd put my fingers in my ears and learn the melody. I guess those sessions are the most satisfying memories I have of our family. Of course, I didn't realize then that music was going to be such a large part of my existence.

Once the home brew had worked, the parties started. Dad's crowd turned out to be poker-playing hard drinkers. The get-togethers Mom had encouraged turned out to be drunken brawls and even so they didn't stop Dad from going out on payday and showing up at home on Sunday night or Monday morning empty-handed.

But Mom was determined to play it home style so she'd try to be out at the Cuneo plant to catch Dad as he left on payday. I don't think she caught him more than once or twice so even though he was earning a hundred bucks a week—not bad for the time—money was always scarce at our house.

Finally Mom gave up on reforming Dad. She went out and got a new position as comptometer operator at Armour's packing plant and when Dad came home she had the door bolted from the inside. They had terrible fights, screaming at one another through the door, blaming each other, while I cowered in one of the back rooms, praying, as my grandmother had taught me to do, that they wouldn't hurt one another. And my prayers were answered because Dad would always eventually disappear.

Mom found a one-room-and-kitchenette and gave up the seven-room apartment. We sold the piano and used the money to move and that was the last I saw of my father until I was grown and out on my own. I never let Mom know how much I missed him or the pain I felt that he didn't care enough to come around and see me when she wasn't there. Like a turtle, I developed a hard shell to protect myself. I might be vulnerable, but I learned how to hide my pain with a flip remark or a hard-boiled attitude.

Dad might be gone, but that didn't mean I didn't hear a lot about him. Every time I did something that rubbed Mom wrong, she struck up the same refrain: "You're just like your father! You're no good! You'll grow up just like him." Have that dinned into you long enough and it's bound to happen.

I knew one thing for sure. I'd do anything not to be like her. Mom had no friends that she visited or who visited her. She never went anywhere except to the ball game on her day off, which happened to be the day ladies were admitted free. She didn't drink or smoke at a time when the whole world was smoking and drinking. When I look back, she seems to me exhausted, uptight, unable to express emotion and filled with self-pity. Given a choice, I wanted to be where the action was. If that made me like my father, okay. He was out there with interesting people.

The irony is that even today it's difficult for me to talk about my deepest feelings. Even when I'm hurt, I'll make a joke or tell you off, but I'll never cry. By repeating that I was just like Dad, I think Mom caused me to imitate him. I guess I felt it was hopeless for me

23

to be good so I became incorrigible as I got older. But I wanted her approval too, and I worked for it. Maybe that's why I ended up with the worst of both of them. No, no, that's a joke, folks.

Music was really our only bond. Mom kept the radio going constantly. A new song would appear and we'd have something to get excited about. Not that we agreed. She was crazy about "Beyond the Blue Horizon" and "Cryin' for the Carolines" while I tried to get her interested in "Exactly Like You" and "On the Sunny Side of the Street" which she thought were just a lot of noise.

She tried not to miss Horace Heidt and His Musical Knights or Shep Fields and His Rippling Rhythm. But it ruined her day if she missed Wayne King's broadcast, especially a new hit he had around 1932 called "The Waltz You Saved for Me."

She kept the radio on after I went to bed, so I used to go to sleep to the strains of the *Lady Esther Serenade*, as Wayne King's program was called. That was certainly going-to-sleep music. Nytol!

Seriously, I loved listening because the Wayne King Orchestra often played just down the street at the "beautiful Aragon Ballroom" which was located on Lawrence not too far from us.

Those memories may not sound very intimate to you, but they were about as close as Mom and I got. I think that for a long time after she and Dad split up, her emotions were frozen. I don't remember her ever kissing me or even smoothing my hair affectionately. I can understand all that now, but at the time I kept trying to figure out what I'd done that made me so unlovable.

I suppose the Depression worried her, too—the possibility of losing her job—but it didn't really change anything much for us. Where we were it was always Depression times. Mom gave me fifteen cents for lunch. During the worst times, maybe she cut that to a dime, but a dime went a long way back then. I didn't suffer. I still wore the same kind of gingham wash dresses. We'd never had any money. So how could we lose what we'd never had?

But when I was around twelve years old, all the kids began getting bicycles. One of my friends let me try hers and after a couple of failures, I found the secret of it. Nobody had to hold the bicycle or help me keep my balance, I was a natural. I rode along feeling the wind against my face and running through my hair and I thought this is really neat. I began picturing myself whizzing along the streets waving at my friends, dazzling them with my fancy circles, figure eights and the classic "Look, Ma, no hands."

I knew what Mom was going to say if I broached the subject to her. She'd tell me I had no more sense about the value of money than Dad, that she worked long and hard to keep a roof over our heads and food on the table, then she'd go on about how hard it was to keep me in dresses and shoes and the upshot would be that there just wasn't enough bread for something silly like a bicycle.

I knew she'd parade out all those clichés, but I couldn't get that red bicycle with silver trim out of my mind. I really believed that if I could have one that was all I'd ever want in this world. So finally one night I blurted out my request. And Mom responded as if I'd written out the speech for her.

I didn't cry or beg. I just looked at her defiantly and said the thing I knew would bug her most: "Okay, I'll ask Dad."

"You just do that," she told me. "See which comes first, his whiskey or you."

That night I couldn't sleep thinking about the red and silver bicycle. I kept seeing myself whizzing along, like wow!, causing people to turn in wonder at this vision of speed and grace.

I *had* to have a bike so a couple of days later I stole one. It didn't have any silver trim, but it was a boy's red bicycle. I saw this kid ride up, get off and lean it against the wall outside the corner drugstore. I stood there staring at it, my insides feeling like jelly. I looked around. There was nobody in sight so I hopped on and pedaled away as fast as my legs would take me.

I knew I had to paint it. It hurt me to do it, but I'd already learned that in this world you can't have everything. If I went riding around on the bike with its original red paint job, the kid would spot it and recognize it. So I took it home and painted it black. I hated black, but it covers red better than any other color. When I'd finished, I looked at it and thought, Yeh! Now I got my own bike! and I put it away to dry.

Mom never even noticed or, if she did, she must have thought some friend was letting me borrow it.

About the third or fourth day, I was really getting expert at wheeling it around. I went to the park and was riding around showing off a little, hoping some of my friends would see me and tell everyone what a great rider Colton was. Instead, the kid who owned the bike saw me. I wanted to zoom off, but I figured then he'd know what I'd done so I pretended not to notice him and hoped the black paint would fool him.

No such luck. He came up and wanted to know where I'd got my bicyle.

"Aw, I had it a long time."

"What if I told you it's mine?"

"You're goofy. Your bike's red."

"How'd you know that?! It is my bike! You—"

I sped off, but he found out my name and where I lived from the other kids. That night he brought his father over to talk to Mom. They had the serial number to identify the bike and I found out right then you have to do more than slap a little black paint on something to get away with stealing it.

It broke my heart to part with that bike and I was embarrassed at being caught, but what humiliated me most of all was to hear Mom apologizing and telling these strangers she didn't know what she was going to do with me; I was becoming just like Dad.

With Mom, punishment never fit the crime. It was always the same whether she caught me in a fib or stealing a bicycle. She knew that the high point of the day for Uptown kids came after our evening meal at 5:30 P.M. By 6:00, we'd gather and hang out around the corner. When it got dark, we'd go home. Big deal! But I had to be sick or out of the city to miss being there.

After I stole the bike, Mom said, "No going to the corner to-night."

"Aw—"

"Not even off the front porch for a week! You understand? Once you're home from school, you're grounded. You're going to learn right from wrong beginning here and now!"

I felt as if I were in prison. Mom would barely speak to me. For a while I just sat. Then I remembered that summers when I was visiting Grandma and she took me to Sunday School, the teacher said we were to pray to Jesus for guidance when we were bad. I prayed for him to show me the way and tacked on a request that He would find a way for Mom to get me a bicycle.

I must have appeared very forlorn or, I thought, maybe Jesus had spoken to Mom about my prayers, because not long after, her heart softened. She took me to Sears and picked out a red-and-chrome

26

girl's bicycle. She paid twenty-five cents down and twenty-five cents a week. It was all she could afford.

It was probably the biggest thrill I'd had up to then. I not only got the bicycle, I looked on it as proof Mom did love me even if she didn't make a big thing about it.

It wasn't until later it occurred to me maybe Mom was just being practical. I'd almost finished at Stewart and it was going to be too far for me to walk to Senn Jr. High. Certainly the Sears' weekly payment was less than a week's bus fare. Was that why she'd bought me the bike?

I was never going to impress anybody with my grades, but I shone in gym and music, especially during the Friday afternoon homeroom programs. These were impromptu, volunteer happenings. There were tap and acrobatic dancers, a dramatic reader, a few singers (a boy with a high tenor voice was very popular), chalk talks—anything any of us could do or dream up. I'd usually volunteer near the end. My specialty was novelty songs with audience participation. One I remember was "All the King's Horses." It went:

> The King's horses
> And the King's men,
> They march down the street
> And they march back again.

Up front, I'd have my classmates primed to ask, "Who?" And I'd sing:

> The King's horses
> And the King's men.

I'd heard that number on the South Side one night when George Beiber and I competed in one of the lindy hop contests they were holding around the city.

George was a big, fat, twenty-five-year-old who was really light on his feet. He had perfect coordination, a great sense of rhythm and such acrobatic skill he could make it look as if I were flipping him over my head. Mom trusted him because when he promised to have me home by midnight he always did.

People ask me when I first smoked grass. Well, I smoked it before it became illegal in 1933, although it really wasn't legal for me to smoke anything then. But before going into our dance, George and I would share what we called a reefer. It was no big deal when I was twelve or thirteen. If you lived in the Uptown district, you could buy a joint at the corner store, if not nearer. I never read the newspapers so I didn't know when pot was outlawed and beer became legal. One night I asked George for a hit on a joint and I thought he was going to flip out. "Do you want to get us arrested?" he hissed. Then he told me what had come down. It didn't make sense. One day weed had been harmless, booze outlawed; the next, alcohol was in and weed led to "living death." They didn't fool me. I kept on using it, but I was just a little more cautious.

George and I usually won in our category. In fact, we became sort of unofficial lindy hop champions around Chicago at the time. First prize in most contests was ten bucks. I'd let George keep seven since he was so much older, and I'd take three home to Mom. George couldn't understand that. I'm not sure I did myself. I told him I pitied her and didn't want to be a burden. But maybe giving her that money was my childish attempt to prove she was wrong. I wasn't like my father who hardly ever gave us a penny. I was a giving person like she was.

George wasn't my boyfriend. We were both natural dancers and made an eye-catching team. I did get interested in a boy named Steve about this time. He was the type I almost always went for in later years: curly blond hair, blue eyes with a devilish glint, and a good physique. He was my first big crush. Years later when I was appearing in Las Vegas, he came by to see me. He owned a little circus. Time seemed not to have touched him. After he left, I wondered what my life would have been if I'd stayed in school, we'd kept going together and maybe married.

Well, we'll never know, will we?

With the arrival of spring I was already feeling restless when my advisor called me for a conference. He pointed out my grade average had dropped so that Commercial Geography was the only subject I could hope to pass. I promised to apply myself more, but all the way home I kept thinking how hard Mom worked and what a disappointment my report card would eventually be to her. I decided to give her a break by forgetting about school and visiting my grandparents. It wasn't exactly running away. I was just moving up the date for my regular summer visit and saving Mom bus or train fare.

The next morning, after she left for work, I threw a few things into a handkerchief—I think I'd seen too many B movies—and went to the intersection near our house where I asked some sharp-looking dude the way to Kansas City. He told me which city bus to take to reach the edge of town and which highway led to K.C.

I thought, "Well, now there you are! How hard can it be?" What I didn't realize was that the trip was around five hundred miles and would take four nights and five days.

One thing to remember: This was Depression time. Some people felt lucky to be living in piano crates. Another homeless child more or less wasn't anything for anyone to get excited about. There were lots of them roaming around the country. People were too busy keeping a roof over their heads to bother a mature-looking twelve-year-old who seemed to know what she was doing.

Lots of truck drivers stopped to give me a lift. Most of them were kindly family men; some of them were scum. One thing I got hip to very quickly was not to get in with any driver whose rig sported a "No Riders" sign. That guy invariably had other ideas about the kind of ride I needed. The worst of these picked me up on my second night out. I was tired and chilly and the warmth of the heater quickly made me drowsy. I was half asleep when I realized the truck must have stopped. You know, like I didn't feel the vibrations anymore. But I did feel the guy was beginning to mess with me, whispering, "Wake up, honey."

"Are we in Kansas City?" I mumbled.

"No, baby. On the side of the road. Just you 'n' me."

Him and me! I felt my slacks being unbuttoned. Suddenly I was wide-awake. All I knew about sex then was what I'd heard from the kids on the corner. Mom and I would have been embarrassed to talk about anything so intimate. But instinct took over. I let him have a knee where it would hurt most, wrenched open the door, jumped out and ran toward a bright area down the highway. The lights came from a roadside café. Nothing fancy, a place where truckers stopped.

I sidled in and got up nerve enough to approach the counterman. "Can I sit here until dawn?"

"How old?"

"Sixteen," I said, thrusting my front to show how I was starting to bloom up there.

"What're ya doin' here?"

"I hitched a ride with a trucker. He's very nasty and I don't want to be where he can get me."

Upset as I was, I didn't feel like crying, but I managed to squeeze out a tear or two for effect.

The counterman must have realized I was really only thirteen or fourteen, and I guess he pitied another loser because he took the trouble of lining up a ride with a nice family man who also happened to be a trucker. This man drove me into the downtown area of Kansas City and helped me look up Grandpa's address in the telephone book. When I finally got to the house, there was no one home. I sat on the steps until the lady next door recognized me and wanted to know what I was doing there.

"Waiting for Grandma."

"Annie's at church on the corner," she said.

I might have known. We always spent a lot of time at that church during my visits. What I learned there supplied me with some much-needed strength to see me through the rough hours of my addiction later.

I'd enjoyed my first night's sleep at Grandma's when Uncle Vance showed up looking for me. Uncle Vance was a traveling salesman for a pots-and-pans organization, but he was a pretty straight cat. He explained that Mom had been frantic when she called him. Why she hadn't called Grandma I have no idea, but hearing that she really was concerned about my welfare made me glow inside. Maybe I wasn't just excess baggage after all.

After Uncle Vance pressed a bag of goodies into my hands and put me on the train headed for Chicago, I spent most of the trip dreaming of all the things Mom and I would say to one another when I got back. If they sounded suspiciously like soap opera, maybe that was because those radio dramas and an occasional movie were the only places I ever heard people talk about love and loneliness and the need for one another. Nobody at our house expressed feelings. Anyway, the emotional bath that I imagined would take place when Mom and I saw one another again would have made Mother Monahan, that sentimental old busybody on "Painted Dreams," seem like a cynic.

As the train pulled into the station, my heart was pounding and I could hardly wait for the doors to slide open. I rushed out of the railroad coach and ran along the platform, ready to hurl myself into Mom's arms. As I took the steps two at a time, I could see Mom standing there by the train gate, just as Uncle Vance had said she'd be. My stomach knotted as I looked at her. She wasn't smiling; she didn't even look as if she was glad to see me. I started taking the steps one at a time. I guess I'd always really been hip to the fact that she'd never tell me any of the kind of stuff I'd imagined on the trip. But any sign she felt something toward me would have been welcome, from a kiss on the cheek to a slap.

Of course, that wasn't Mom's way. I can still remember her exact words as I climbed the steps: "Hurry up, Anita. For heaven's sake, dinner's going to be late enough as it is."

CHAPTER II
CUTTING LOOSE

When I was fourteen years old, Mom's half-sister came to live with us. I adored Aunt Belle. I could talk with her in a way I'd never been able to with Mom. For a long time, Aunt Belle's life had been as satisfactory as Mom's was unhappy. Aunt Belle loved her husband and he treated her nicely. They had no problems about money either. He made a good salary, doing whatever he did. Aunt Belle worked, too. She earned $16 a week and saved $10 of it for their old age.

But when she got to be fifty-two or fifty-three years old, her husband came home one evening and announced he was in love with a young chick. Nothing else mattered. He wanted a divorce so badly she could have the furniture and the money they'd saved—which was what Aunt Belle had earned over the years anyway. But she knew she couldn't fight this young stuff. So she agreed to let him go.

She wasn't happy, but she still had her job to keep her mind off her troubles. After the Depression hit, the bank where she had her savings account failed. The company where she worked declared bankruptcy. She had some nice furniture, but it and her diamonds were sold for rent and food. Finally, there was nothing left except a few clothes and some photographs. All her belongings fitted into one suitcase and a cardboard box.

Uncle Vance wanted to take her in with them, but he was having domestic problems and his wife objected. So Mom was the only one Aunt Belle could turn to. Uncle Vance sneaked her money for bus fare from K. C. to Chicago where Aunt Belle hoped she could find another bookkeeping job, but nobody was hiring fifty-two-year-old women.

So she did Mom's housework and laundry, looked at her photos of happier days and encouraged me to try to be something in this world. She thought I ought to pay more attention to school, to try harder, but I had other ideas.

I'd become an avid fan of the Walkathon, a twenty-four-hour-a-day endurance contest at the Arcadia Gardens Ballroom just a few blocks from our house. And after George Beiber and I won first prize with our lindy on the Amateur Night and second prize in the amateur elimination feature called the Dynamite Sprints, world champs Marion Kirk and Mike Gouvas made my scalp tingle by telling me, "Kid, you could do all right in these things."

They showed me a copy of *Billboard*, the bible of small-time show business then. On a page devoted to Walkathons, promoters were advertising for contestants, including two shows scheduled to open in Muskegon, Michigan. One was to be promoted by Major General Hugh Talbott. Marion and Mike wrote a note recommending me to the Major General and I went home to explain to Mom that I was too dumb for school so I was going to enter the Walkathon. "They feed you seven times a day and see that you get free medical care. Even if I don't win, I ain't gonna do bad with the money I'll make dancing, singing and selling pictures of my partner and me."

Mom's objection was that she couldn't spare the bus fare, but I brushed that aside, saying I'd hitchhike like I had to Grandma's. That did it. I guess it had been a strain supporting Aunt Belle and me. This way she'd have me off her hands and would still know where I was. Knowing I was with the baby-sitter or out dancing with George Beiber was always important to Mom. She seemed to feel that as long as she knew my whereabouts, I wasn't likely to get into serious trouble. And if I was on a Walkathon floor, she believed I'd be supervised and she'd have nothing to worry about. Just to make sure, the first weekend I was in Muskegon, Mom rode half the night on a Greyhound bus from Chicago to visit "The Palace of Wasted Footsteps," check on the situation and meet the Major General, who assured her he'd keep an eye on me, which was good enough for her.

In that way I began the two years I spent drifting around the Midwest as a professional Walkathon contestant. It seems unbelievable now, but there were once fifteen thousand people—promoters, emcees, floor judges, trainers, nurses, cooks, janitors, cashiers, ticket-takers, publicity agents, promotion men, musicians, contestants and even a lawyer—whose main source of income over a number of years came from endurance shows. Whatever I said to Mom, it was all a big adventure when I arrived in Muskegon. It certainly beat sitting behind a desk at Senn Junior High as far as I was concerned.

It wasn't hard to enter. A doctor took my blood pressure, listened to my heart and then sent me behind a screen with a "nurse" who checked me out for lice, crabs and other body vermin. When I objected, asking her what kind of a bum she thought I was, she said, "Listen, sweetheart, it's for your own protection. The regulars welcome it. Everybody's in close contact in a jackpot like this."

I passed and got teamed up with a patent-leather, black-haired guy who looked like an economy model George Raft. He'd been a professional marathon dancer since 1932. His name was Sam LiPari and he always built up a big Italian following: "Only I don't sing and they're musical. You Italian?"

"No. Irish. Anita Colton, but I call myself O'Day," I said and went on to explain I'd decided O'Day was groovy because in pig Latin it meant dough which was what I hoped to make.

Sam taught me to sing the "Onion Song" phonetically in Italian, but before he could build a following he quit the show to enter a bigger one.

Unlike the Chicago contest which had emphasized entertainment, the Muskegon spectacle sold misery. The Major General ordered the floor judge to chain each couple together after 572 hours and the crowds immediately increased. So he turned on more heat:

34

TRAINING QUARTERS ABANDONED
NO MEDICAL ATTENTION
NO ASSISTANCE

the newspaper ads blared.

GOODBYE, FOREVER!!!

We'd been in chains for nine days. About June 11, I was eliminated during a twelve-hour grind. Truthfully, I don't remember much about the Muskegon show except my disqualification ceremony. You always got one if you lasted over five hundred hours in a contest.

"Ladies and gentlemen, seven hundred eighty-two long, tedious hours have passed since this sporting classic got under way," the emcee announced. "Now one more plucky little girl, Miss Anita O'Day, has fallen by the wayside. All her efforts go unrewarded. Here there's only one winner, folks. The rest are losers.

"But in tribute to this little girl's gallant spirit, the remaining contestants will pass, one by one, to bid adieu to a little girl whose courage and fortitude only they can appreciate.

"So dig not into your pockets, but into your hearts and let's hear the silver ring as it hits the floor. It will be her only buffer against cold and hunger."

My partner stood behind me and I buried my face in a towel as the Walkathon songbird sang the official elimination song:

Oh how we'll miss you tonight,
Miss you when lights are low.
Oh, how we need you tonight,
More than you'll ever know.
You did your best on the floor,
Now you're not here any more.
Though your poor heart is aching,
Now our hearts are breaking.
Old pal, how we miss you tonight.

The coins showered to the floor and when added to what I'd made singing and selling pictures of my partner and myself, it came to ninety-five bucks which may not seem like much bread

35

today but it wasn't as bad as it sounds. A nice breakfast cost fifteen cents then. A tuna salad sandwich went for seven cents, a coke for five. A fried perch dinner set you back thirty-five cents or you could splurge fifty-five cents for either a tenderloin steak or half of a barbecued chicken with all the trimmings.

From Muskegon, Wayne Dooley, another contestant, wired Leo Seltzer, the Barnum of Walkathon promoters, about the show he was opening in Kankakee, Illinois. Seltzer accepted Wayne and partner. I was "and partner."

I now considered myself a professional Walkathoner. But if anybody had asked me whether the first contest was on the level, I couldn't have answered. Sometimes when the nurse said our fifteen minutes of rest were up, I'd feel as if I'd been there a long time. But as to whether I'd been given extra sleep, I was too dingy to ask anyone and the pros weren't about to tell me.

Some customers used to heckle us, saying the whole thing was "just a put-up job," "a racket." All I knew was I was getting thick calluses on the balls of my feet and my ankles swelled, and when I fell out, I was exhausted.

In Kankakee, I was still an outsider. The main thing that happened was that Erskine Tate's Recording Orchestra, which played for the show, gave me musical help. Until then, the pianist would find my key and I more or less sang the melody without fooling around. But with Tate, I began thinking of myself as an entertainer—not trained, but an entertainer. Tate helped me work up a couple of songs. In that way, I took my first stumbling step forward. I dimly realized what I wanted in life: to be a singer.

The Springfield, Missouri, Walk-A-Show was housed in the beautiful, midtown Shrine Mosque. Opening night, promoter Jack Steinel livened up proceedings by sitting ringside and tossing quarters, half-dollars and silver dollars to professionals who could sing, juggle, eat fire, dance or otherwise entertain.

Steinel rated the entertainment value by the size of the coin he threw. The best got a silver dollar. I can still remember the shiver that went up my spine as two big silver dollars clattered to the floor after I sang "Is It True What They Say About Dixie?"

That was definitely a *kip* show. Kip is a yiddish term for sleep or sack out. And kip shows were more entertaining because contestants weren't tired all the time. The winners were those who could run fastest and longest in the sprint, not those who could drag around the floor the longest. How did we get our sleep? If anyone missed a contestant and asked, he was getting a pedicure or a haircut, she was having her physical or her hair set.

I'd also got hip that each promoter carried several flash teams with good wardrobes. These were people who could run and entertain. The promoter guaranteed them sponsor money and gave them the "breaks."

The best team got first chance for one of them to be "frozen alive." The contestant would enter a fifteen-hundred-pound tomb of ice wearing a one-piece bathing suit and shoes and carrying a towel to place under the head and shoulders to prevent ice burns. He/she carried a flashlight to signal everything was all right as suspense built. If possible, the promoter had an ambulance stationed at the front door and a resuscitator prominently displayed beside the ice tomb.

Why would anyone do it? Money. The shoes, towel and padded bathing suit prevented discomfort and the sponsor paid a dollar a minute encouragement money plus whatever audiences tossed on the floor.

"Sweetheart couples" were popular, too. I knew one handsome guy and a cute chick whose act was to enter the show separately, team up, fall in love, get engaged and have a public wedding. They did it in contest after contest, always collecting carloads of shower and wedding gifts.

There were others who had a mysterious something that appealed to audiences. People such as Louis Meredith, Hughie Hendrixson, Margaret Goudy and Jayne Moon couldn't compete with Frank LoVeccio (Frankie Laine) or Jean Reid (June Havoc) in terms of talent, but they brought as many or more customers to the box office.

From what I've told you, you're probably hip that a lot of the boys weren't ex-Eagle Scouts and many of the girls weren't the kind I'd have met in Grandma's Sunday School. Was I the type I'd have met there? At that point, yes. But I suppose some things I did later shocked people who'd shocked me then. But in Springfield I was only fifteen and acted like Miss Priss.

I wouldn't talk to the boosters who hung around the edge of the floor, took orders, stole the merchandise and delivered the hot goods for a fraction of the real cost.

I steered clear of a pretty prostitute who made jokes about dancing shows until her feet got tired, then going into a house until, to quote her, "my ass gets tired."

And I was really shocked when the older of two brothers gave the younger a flourishing whorehouse for his twenty-first birthday. Wanted him to be financially secure, I guess.

But there were also solid, upright citizens among us. Earl Clark was accepted, even admired as a "square john." He palled around with some of the toughest characters, but he never smoked grass, never drank hard liquor and hardly ever smoked a cigarette. He'd been a Golden Gloves boxer and also had made All-State in Nebraska football as left halfback. He had blond hair and gray-blue eyes and took care of his athlete's body which was really a body to take care of. But we were just friends. He was married to a beautiful girl who took tickets. Anyway, I might not have been his type.

In our chitchats, Earl never urged me to stop smoking tea, but I realized he wished I would.

Earl and a lot of other people really dug a nothing song, "The Lady in Red," that I did. He admitted having no talent, but he said he could recognize it and he didn't want me squandering mine. He also warned me not to get involved with my partner, Dick LeNac. "He's a buddy of mine," Earl said, "but he's playing the rail and from that it's just a step to pimping." Earl needn't have worried. I was only fifteen and just mildly curious about but not really into sex.

Shortly after, LeNac cut out with this redheaded railbird he'd been romancing and I teamed up with seventeen-year-old Dale Thorpe. A few days passed and one morning Dale woke me and said, "Look, honey, you're spread all over the front page!"

Sure enough! LeNac and the redhead had been gunned down by her irate husband. There was a picture of LeNac sprawled on the floor of the club—dead. Beside it was a cozy team picture of him and me. The editor gave great play to LeNac's former connection with the Walk-A-Show, ending the caption, "The girl in the photo has no connection with the tragedy."

I came in second at the end of the show but neither the murder nor my prize money were as heavy as something that happened after Dale quit. Most of the audience had gone and many of the contestants were sleeping. Lights had been dimmed. My new partner, Charlie Loeb, was talking to some girl over the rail. I'd dug my hands deep into the pockets of my slacks and was shuffling along. Maybe it was fatigue. Kids often got squirrelly during those quiet moments. I've seen some picking bouquets and chasing butterflies that didn't exist and taking uppercuts at partners who did. So what happened could have been a dream, a hallucination—who knows?

Maybe I *was* squirrelly, but I truly believed—and I still believe—I was walking around alone and then all of a sudden I wasn't alone anymore. There was this Presence, this Person beside me. He wore all white clothes, shoulder-length hair and a beard. (Remember, this was long before anyone had heard of the Beatles, gurus or hippies.) In my mind, there is no doubt it was Jesus.

In a very quiet voice He asked me how I was feeling or something to that effect. It was an easy come-on. I wasn't startled to find Him at my side. It was almost as if I'd been expecting Him.

"What are you going to do in this world, Anita? What is it you'd like to do?"

I thought how I'd wanted to be a printer like Dad, even talking a girl friend in junior high into signing up for printing class. Later I got interested in becoming a beautician to help make the world a prettier place. But when He asked, I didn't hesitate: "If I had my wish, there is only one thing I'd like to do: sing."

"You've got it. That will be it," He said, or words to that effect.

I didn't tell anyone then or for a long time, because people would have called me squirrelly. But nothing else—family, lovers, husbands, children, a home—could compete with my need to express myself musically after that. I didn't kid myself about having a great or even pretty voice, but I wanted to give music a shot, to learn how to use what I had to contribute to the world's enjoyment.

Very quickly after encountering Him, things started moving up for me. The publicity man put out a dope sheet, dishing out Walkathon gossip. In the very next issue, he noted, "Ozarkians are taking in a big way to Anita O'Day's brand of song selling." Then, in the December 6 issue of *Billboard*, a correspondent wrote:

> . . . Many skits are interspersed with endurance and a large staff of stooges headed by "Pistol Pete" Wilson, Red Oleski, Joe Solar, Charlie Loeb and Jimmy Kelly give fans plenty of laughs. Freddie Nevola and Mary DiRosa have fans gaga over their dancing. Anita O'Day and Andy Lynch hold top spots for their singing . . .

Something like that always made me think of my mysterious visitor and thank Him. If I ran into a setback, my faith might waiver, but when I began doing well again, I'd be convinced He had really visited me.

"Daddy" Fox's Race of the Nations Walkathon at the Surf Ballroom in Racine, Wisconsin, was a flop and I was a little el dingo. But my singing had improved noticeably and I'd learned to play an audience. I was *in* enough to be built up as half of the sweetheart couple by emcee King Brady. The novelty was that the other half wasn't a contestant but another emcee, Hal Brown.

Hal and I remember the details differently today, but since this is my book, Hal is getting only a couple of lines for his version. He claims he came down with mumps, causing me to conclude he'd been chippying around and had caught a venereal disease, so I gave him the gate. That's his story.

The way I remember it was as a box office gimmick. It was never meant to be anything more than a mock wedding. But there'd be the engagement party presents, the shower presents, and the wedding presents. I thought it was nifty.

It was at the shower that Mom put in her appearance, as Brady had persuaded her to do, and demanded the wedding be stopped. She said I was not yet eighteen and lacked her approval. Brady flashed a paper giving my age as eighteen. Mom stormed around the emcee's stand, threatening to have everyone hauled off to the pokey if the marriage took place.

I have to hand it to her; she put on quite a show before allowing Brady to gradually persuade her to go along with it because of the expense involved in making the cellophane wedding dress and the bridesmaids' gowns. Everything about the wedding was to be real except that Brady would substitute for an actual minister. Back in quarters, Brady reimbursed Mom for her bus fare and gave her a ten-spot for her cooperation.

Man, talk about a materialistic society. Everything about the wedding was some kind of a promotion. Merchants stood in line to offer services and presents in return for publicity. Bakeries and florists? Okay. But a funeral home? A loan company? A doctor who donated Wassermann tests? Even some preacher eager to build his flock sent a wire offering to officiate at the real wedding when I became of age. I will say that the cellophane was the most elaborate of my three marriages, even if it wasn't a *real* one.

It was after the wedding that the Foxes ran off, stranding us. Hal saved everything with his "Real Live Baby Raffle." Naturally, such a promotion stirred up women's clubs, churches, the Humane Society and movie interests, resulting in his arrest.

By 6:00 P.M. on the night of the raffle, fans were lined up halfway around the block by the time Hal was sprung from jail. The house was packed when he took the stand, quieted the rowdy crowd and copped a plea, raising the censorship issue. Did the fans want the contest run off to determine a winner even though there was no money to pay the prizes?

They did.

One by one, through treadmills, grinds, duck waddles and sprints, we dropped from thirteen contestants until only Jack and Penny Gurgeson and Al Gilbert and I remained. The Gurgesons nosed us out during the ten o'clock period and were crowned champs. For a fleeting moment, I felt sad. Then I shrugged it off. Win or lose, what difference did it make? This wasn't my mission in life. I was going to make my contribution singing. I believe it was there in Racine that I began thinking of quitting the endurance business and getting on with my mission in life.

After the baby raffle, which turned out to be a live baby piglet much to the audience's delight, we contestants sang "Auld Lang Syne" as the fans left the building. Then Hal asked everyone connected with the fiasco to line up along the bleachers and he passed out "getaway" money. As my "husband" reached me, I gave him a friendly peck on the forehead and he gave me a five-spot, the same as everyone else.

I didn't see him again for forty-odd years. A few months after Racine, I read in *Billboard* that he'd married Norah, one of the beautiful Branch sisters who were dancing in a contest in Rockford, Illinois. When I ran into him at the track in 1980, they were still married, which I'm sure wouldn't have been the case if we'd tied the knot in Racine.

From Racine, a carload of us pooled our money for gasoline to get to Springfield, Illinois, where I was back with the Major General. Once again, newspaper ads read like a medical report:

BUNIONS, CORNS, BLISTERS, FALLEN ARCHES,
AND STILL THEY GO.
THRILLS! CHILLS! SPILLS!
DANCERS, SINGERS, COMEDIANS
100 ATHLETIC ENTERTAINERS
HOW LONG CAN THEY LAST?

Ninety-seven days we were there, covering 4,656 miles in 2,328 hours. I came in second again.

By now you're probably wondering why we put ourselves through all this? People were so persistent with that question that a lot of us signed our photos, "For no good reason. . . ."

But we were putting fans on. We did it for money, for shelter and food. On its own level, too, the Walkathon was a form of show business. Trendy thinkers bemoan the sadism of the crowd and the masochism of the contestants. But there was talent developing there.

Actress June Havoc, singer Frankie Laine, comedienne Cass Daley and stripteaser Lili St. Cyr made their marks after leaving the endurance business. Red Skelton worked as an emcee. So did hipster comedian Lord Buckley; Frankie Little, featured with Spike Jones; radio comic Johnny Morgan and game show host Randy Merriam. Helen Forrest sang with her brother's band at a contest in Atlantic City. Betty Hutton was an intermission singer on several shows. Jazz great Jay McShann had the orchestra on at least one contest. B.S. Pully and partner, H.S. Gump—those initials stand for exactly what you think—were stooges in Walkathons long before Pully thought of Broadway or Hollywood. Nellie Roberts and Bennie Rothman were featured on Broadway with Olsen and Johnson doing their Walkathon ballroom routine, and

Tiny Epperson went from a Rockford, Illinois, contest into Cole Porter's *Panama Hattie*. Choreographer-director Charlie O'Curran and choreographer Nick Castle succeeded in Hollywood—and the list goes on. It was a training ground that many looked back on fondly. Reminiscing once, Nick Castle said, "We didn't make as much money, but we had a helluva lot more fun."

Those marathoners who made it big and those who succeeded less publicly were all cats who were not content with the security of a place on the assembly line, waiting tables or driving cabs, even if such jobs had been available. Sure, some of them ended on Skid Row, but so did a lot of other people. We marathoners wanted our places in the spotlight. We wanted to be where the action was.

I got well financially in Springfield, Illinois, and went home. But life with Mom and Aunt Belle was awfully quiet. I still bought *Billboard* to check out my old pals, and one week I spotted an ad placed by a doctor looking for four girls of varying builds for his traveling educational symposium.

I called for an appointment and the doctor told me to come right down. He was a tall, silver-haired, impressive man, who wore a white medical smock and had a mellifluous voice that made even his "hello" ring out poetically. He explained that prior to his lecture, an educational film was shown. It was during the lectures that the four young ladies served as models to illustrate his anatomical points.

I was such a naive fifteen-year-old in spite of my experiences during the past two years, I had no idea he was selling sex. I was slightly surprised when he called the lecture his "performance." But then I thought, "I'm just a kid. What do I know? Who am I to criticize a doctor?"

I was still more surprised when our first booking for this "educational venture" was at the Gayety Burlesque Theater in Milwaukee.

Doc still wore his white medical smock. We four girls sat on a platform under bright lights, draped in gauze and nothing else. While Doc lectured, I looked out front during the first show and wondered why none of the men had brought his wife.

One by one, each of us girls stepped forward and struck various poses while Doc used a wooden pointer to direct the audience's attention to various parts of our anatomy and related our builds to the four basic female figures.

The girl before me was short and plump with stocky legs, big buns and big, firm breasts. Like the rest of her, her face was wide.

I was the last. Doc made a big thing over the fact that I combined characteristics of various types. My legs and arms were long and slim. My waist was small and my face narrow, but Doc directed special attention to my big boobs, uncommon in a girl with my build.

As I stood there, I wondered how well the gauze covered me.

The second show again brought no couples, but there was a full representation by the newspaper-over-the-lap brigade. I realized then what they were doing and concluded there wasn't anything educational about the presentation. We were in a burlesque scam, just one step above the carnival lot. I decided I'd go back to the endurance field for one more show while I figured out what to do next.

As soon as I saw the ad for the Arcadia Gardens contest, I rushed to sign up. What did I have to lose? Plenty, though I couldn't foresee it. I goofed, but I can't say I regret it. Because I met and worked with Dick Buckley, the chief emcee, and Red Skelton, the Midnight Maniac.

Both were highly talented in totally different ways just as they were completely different human beings. Skelton was so success-oriented that nobody interested him unless they were of some immediate use to him. Edna Stillwell, his ex-contestant wife, was a gifted comedy creator who was always busy developing new characters and material for him. Red learned Edna's routines, performed them over and over until he'd perfected them and then cherished them. He used them in Walkathons, nightclubs, vaudeville, adapted them for radio and when he got to be a big TV star, he was still doing some of the same bits. He was like a singer who learned the melody and never varied his performance once the song had been mastered. I absorbed a lot watching him, and I don't feel I'm detracting from his stature when I say that, skilled as his timing and slapstick clowning were, I never felt that he had a natural creative genius.

Skelton wanted great commercial success so badly I think he'd have climbed a ladder of razor blades barefoot to get to the top. Acclaim and money were his gods. If he was also an artist, it was in spite of himself. And I happen to think that as a pantomimist he brought his work to the level of art. But he was a hard person to feel close to. I think that's why very few of the Walkathoners felt he was one of us.

The self-ordained Lord Buckley, in contrast, viewed all people as princes and princesses, lords and ladies, counts and countesses. Half-American Indian, half-British, the athletically inclined Buckley would climb the high skeletal structure above the contest floor and clown around, half-stoned, with slips and trips that would have spelled curtains for him if he'd made a miscue. You could only conclude that someone was watching over him. For that I was eventually thankful, because Dick Buckley was very rhythmical and he took a special interest in my singing.

Unlike Skelton, Buckley performed for the joy of creating. If it hadn't been in a Walkathon, it could have been for a small crowd on a street corner or for his own amusement alone in his room. He was so much his own man, nobody, but nobody could control him. Bread? It was something to spend, a convenience, but not a necessity, not important enough to lead to compromise.

Yet as unwilling to compromise and as incorrigible as Buckley's attitude toward authority was, he eventually managed, because of sheer originality and artistry, to headline at top nightclubs, make movies and guest appearances on TV with Milton Berle and Ed Sullivan. A faint echo of Buckley's genius can still be heard on his recordings, "Euphoria" and "Hipsters, Flipsters and Finger-Poppin' Daddies, Lend Me Your Lobes."

So I was really enjoying myself at the Arcadia where we were selling entertainment instead of misery. It was here, too, that I first met Frankie Laine. It took him fifteen years of scuffling before he made it. But Frankie never considered giving up any more than I did, even though he was reduced to sleeping on his agent's desk at times.

One night a couple of weeks after the show had opened, I looked into the audience and my pulse began to race. I wanted to grab my partner and hide my face in his shoulder, but it was show time and would only have drawn attention to me. So I could only hope that

I'd matured enough that this man wouldn't recognize me.

No such luck. As we left the floor for our rest period, a flunky told me the manager wanted to see me in his office. When I entered, the man I'd spotted in the audience was waiting for me. My truant officer!

What could I say? I gathered my belongings and let him drive me to Mom's apartment. When he identified himself to her, Mom uncharacteristically became hysterical and began babbling about not sending me to reform school, a possibility nobody else had mentioned. She promised she and Aunt Belle would see to it I attended school.

That's how it happened that at fifteen years and seven months of age, after roaming the Midwest unchaperoned, hitting the front pages as a bystander in a murder case and participating in a mock wedding, to mention only a few of my adventures, I suddenly found myself forcibly returned to a desk at Senn Junior High.

As one of the Walkathon emcees used to sing, courtesy of George M. Cohan, "Life's a funny proposition."

CHAPTER III
UPTOWN

Senn Junior High had my body between 9:00 A.M. and 4:00 P.M., but my mind was wandering the taverns of the Uptown district. In 1936, Chicago was still a toddlin' town. In addition to the big clubs and theaters in the Loop that used stars, there were a lot of funky Uptown hangouts such as the Barrel of Fun, Liberty Inn, Warm Friends, and, of course, the 5100 Club where eventually Danny Thomas was to make his name.

At school, the only time I felt I was living was during Friday afternoon entertainments. I was obsessed with music and Fridays I'd let it all out. The rest was zilch. The way I looked at it was I had to serve my sentence.

On December 18, which I *thought* was my sixteenth birthday, I split again. That night I sneaked out the window of our apartment, as I'd been doing since the truant officer got me, went over to the 5100 Club where a lot of kids hung out on the street, listening to Fletcher Henderson's brother Horace blow. Horace had a terrific band. On this particular night, I fell into conversation with a cat named Redd Evans, who played the sweetpotato* with Horace

*Ocarina.

Heidt and His Musical Knights. He and I got to singing and I really felt alive, as if I was where the action was at last.

"I like riffs, don't you?" Redd asked.

"Riffs? What are they?"

He sang one, then explained it was a repeated musical phrase. I really dug that. Riffs became the center of my world. I went around working out riffs all the time. So Redd had an influence on me from the first time we met.

That night he invited me to go in and see the show. I accepted, not to see the show but to hear that Horace Henderson band without the accompaniment of street noises.

Since it was my birthday, I celebrated by ordering my first alcoholic drink.

Would you believe—a Pink Lady?

I was confident I could walk into one of the Uptown taverns and land a singing job right away, but I was in for a rude awakening. Finally, I got a dancing job at the Celebrity Club. A character called Blondie ran the joint. The girls in the line had to sit with the customers and drink. By the end of the second night I'd fended off enough propositions, and I told Blondie I wasn't born to be a B-drinker. The customers aside, I might have reacted better if the drinks had been real champagne and whiskey instead of ginger ale and cold tea.

I walked off the job, went over to the Vanity Fair a few blocks away where they needed a replacement in the six-girl line. That's the kind of town Chicago was then. There was plenty of work for anyone with a little experience. Not that you had to be very skilled. At the Vanity Fair, we performed the same simple routine in three different sets of scanty costumes during each show. These taverns could get away with that kind of thing because everybody got so drunk they didn't notice. In fact, that's where I learned to drink—which led me hither and thither.

I hadn't been there long when the producer came backstage one night and asked, "Can any of you broads sing? Our canary's got laryngitis."

"I can do 'I Can't Give You Anything But Love, Baby,' " I told him. He thrust a costume into my hands, told me to get dressed and go on.

When I finished singing, the audience wouldn't let me go. The problem was that the piano player and I only knew that one song in the original key. So we repeated it exactly the way I'd done it the first time. I was just singing melody that night. The customers still hadn't had enough. So I sang it the very same way a third time. People were there to have a relaxed time and they went along with it as if I were Jessica Dragonette.*

The Vanity Fair's "canary" had flown the cage, so I kept the spot. Oro "Tut" Soper, the piano player, worked out three or four tunes with me in the next day or two and I became more convinced that I had a real shot at becoming a singer.

One night as I came off stage, Tut suddenly grabbed me and kissed me. As he let me go, he said, "I'll never forget that. I saw stars! But I'll never do it again."

I wondered why, but he didn't, even though most nights he walked me to Mom's apartment after work. The very fact that he wasn't trying to get me in bed was enough to separate him from most of the other guys around taverns. He explained that he was delving into the occult and belonged to a group known as The Mystic Brotherhood of Tampa, Florida. One of their tenets prohibited sexual relations. Not outside of marriage. Prohibited them. *Period.* Tut said he was having a hard time living up to that rule and envied another one of the Brothers. His name was Don Carter and he was more ascetic. Carter was working at the Vialago and Tut suggested maybe Carter, who understood counterpoint and harmony, could write some arrangements for me.

I was all for it, but the following day I ran into Dick Buckley, who suggested I call in sick and work a tryout with him and Al Lyons at the Planet Mars. I jumped at the chance and that decision changed my life. I became a protégée of Buckley and Lyons. Lyons, you remember, later rescued me from the UCLA Hospital in 1968 after I'd OD'd.

The Planet Mars, at 1117 Wilson Avenue, had a regular show, as regular as any show laid out and emceed by Dick Buckley could be, because Dick was an anarchist at heart. If, after five minutes on

*a popular operatic type radio star of the thirties

49

stage, he decided the audience was square, he'd boom out, "That's all, folks. The show has been concluded."

Dick was always in trouble because he refused to play Casper Milquetoast with the bosses. The owners could work him over, give him his lumps, but he still ran things his way. The only way they could have controlled Dick would have been to kill him. A couple of them wanted to, but they weren't about to do that because wherever he played, he did business.

Dick wanted nothing written down. Even the most far-out comics had routines at that time. I remember Bill Dohler, who played alto sax and loved jazz, telling Dick how much he admired his comic improvising. "But everybody has a certain underlying form to work from," he said. "Even the great masters have to have that."

"Not I," Dick announced, drawing himself to his full six feet two inches. Dick was the forefather of Professor Irwin Corey, Lenny Bruce and such Chicago improvisors as Mike Nichols, Elaine May and Shelley Berman who made it big twenty-five years later.

At the Planet Mars, Dick's acrobatics were even wilder than they had been at the Arcadia Gardens. The stage was slightly elevated and tables were scattered around the room. Dick would be up there on stage sipping gin, smoking tea or popping pills as casually as if he were in the privacy of his home. In the midst of a low-key bit, he'd let out a war whoop, sprint to the edge of the stage and leap into space, barely clearing the heads of the customers with his arms and legs as he sailed beyond the tables.

There were all kinds of wild scenes at the Planet Mars which made me feel if I could keep my cool there, I could perform anywhere.

The cast never knew what to expect. Once, when everything was quiet, the audience heard a shriek. Suddenly, Al Lyons dashed through the crowd, wearing only a red cap with a tassel and a pair of shorts. A couple of seconds later, Dick sprinted after him with a long loaf of Italian bread sticking out of his pants like a huge penis. Seconds later, Dick's Great Dane, with a pet monkey on its back, pounded out, pursuing Dick. It was just an Olsen and Johnson kind of thing, but naturally, with Dick, it had to have a sexual connotation.

I admired Dick because he was, like, the action and my aim had always been to be where it was. I suppose to most people these were just dull little taverns, but I came from a very dumb, one-room-and-kitchenette scene so the taverns seemed glamorous to me.

On the other hand, Dick always lived in spacious quarters supplied him by a real estate man who was a Buckley fan. He got Dick a series of apartments where all Dick's friends were welcome at any time of the day or night. If, temporarily, you didn't have a pad, you could sleep there as long as any floor space remained. What's more, Dick supplied all the food and other goodies to keep the party going from morning to night.

His first wife, as far as I know, was Angel Rice, but she soon cut out after he took up with a tall blonde with a lovely complexion whom everybody called Peaches. Now Dick and Peaches generally received in the nude. Friends were free to bring their friends, too. Often they'd bring along somebody who was semi-legitimate, only to be met at the door by a stark naked Peaches. I knew her quite well, but I don't believe I ever saw her except in the buff.

Guests were also invited to leave their clothing by the door. But those of us who didn't want to shed our clothes didn't have to. Whatever way you chose to play, it was all right with Dick. That was your game.

One thing I want to make clear. This was no sex orgy. Dick just felt it created a free atmosphere in which he'd tell stories, play good music, whatever. He developed the Amos 'n' Andy bit which became his best routine at home, using naked friends.

Eventually, he elevated himself to Lord Buckley, but at this time he was playing a Greek king or a Roman emperor and he modeled life in the apartment on their customs. For instance, when he'd be lying on the couch, he'd signal Peaches, who'd immediately fetch a bowl which he'd urinate into.

At the time, I thought, "Well, that's the way Dick plays it." It was okay with me. What did I know? I was just a kid.

For the show at the Planet Mars I sang only "Mr. Paganini" and "It's De-lovely," but Dick wanted me to develop my potential. "You can sing and dance and have an extremely rhythmical understanding," he told me. What he felt needed improvement was the quality of my sound. It wasn't pretty, but if I worked on that quality I could turn the roughness into an asset.

Originally, he'd been a fan of Bix Beiderbecke's clarity of tone. So when he heard Louis Armstrong's trumpet, it seemed rough in comparison. But he listened to the records over and over until he finally began to dig what Louis was blowing. "You can do the same thing," he said. "Even though you haven't got much chops, you have other qualities to create excitement."

He asked Al Lyons, who was the only one of our crowd who owned a phonograph, to work with me. Al, who regarded himself as a musical missionary, gladly agreed. Every afternoon we'd go to his trailer, sit down and he'd play records over and over for me. He'd start a recording, interrupt to point out, "That's true tone. Listen!" He'd play it again. "Dig?" Or he'd say, "That's the beat. Hear it?"

I heard a lot and learned a little. After he played Mildred Bailey, who was singing long before Billie Holiday, I realized she was in a wonderful category as far as sound was concerned. What was most useful was discovering how she sang consonants instead of vowels the way most singers do. Then he put on Billie Holiday, telling me to listen to the way she wedded her high, wailing voice to the story, holding notes, sharping and flatting for effect. We also studied Ella Fitzgerald's sly, little-girl quality and her scatting.

He played records people like me and my friends had never heard: "After Hours," and Paul Whiteman's "Garden of Weed," a far-out instrumental in which you had to imagine the tempo as you went along. First there was a beep from way out there somewhere, like, say, Mars. Gradually it grew and grew, and the effect was *fab-u-lous!* Al used to try it on musicians to sort out the weed heads from straight cats.

During intermissions at the Planet Mars, Al played six-string chords on his guitar at a time when most taverns had ukelele-style singers and players. Often I'd join him and try to incorporate some of the things I'd heard. It was a nice setup and I learned such tunes as "Dreamin' Time, Just Dreamin'" and "You Showed Me the Way."

"You Showed Me the Way" was a real go-tune with simple harmony. Green as I was, Al made me see that you had to do it in exactly the right tempo or you didn't get it. It was like betting on a horse. You got it and won or you didn't and you lost.

The lady who really showed me the way more than working with Al or listening to Bailey, Holiday or Ella Fitzgerald was Martha Raye. When I saw her in *Rhythm on the Range* at a third-run movie house in 1937, Martha turned my thinking around.

Previously my favorites had all seemed to be big, hefty ladies. Martha was slim like me. She danced and used her body as well as her voice to help put across her songs. She was a presentation singer. She gave me the idea that I could sing jazz and still perform.

To this day, when she sings, the back of my neck begins to creep. She's that *natural* who comes along every now and then. She doesn't pretend to know music, even though she was married to David Rose, a musician, and has associated with music people all her life. She's rhythmical, a very good tap dancer, a show business gal. She doesn't think of herself as a singer; she just sings.

I took whatever I could use from wherever I could find it. The thing that bugged me was that I couldn't take more because I had very little tone. I might never have figured out the reason, but Al did. When he asked why I didn't have a uvula, I thought he was talking dirty. How should I know a uvula is a small tongue hanging down where the roof of the mouth meets the throat? When most people sing, they use the vibrations of the uvula to produce tone. I finally found I hadn't had a uvula since I was seven when a careless doctor sliced it off while he was removing my tonsils.

So I can't get a sound with the air back there because there is nothing to vibrate it. That's the reason I got into singing eighth and sixteenth rather than quarter notes. Instead of singing, "Laaaaaaaaa," I'd sing "La-la-la-la-la-la-la-la," etc., to keep it moving. People would hear me and say, "There she goes again," but necessity explains my style. Whether June Christy and Chris Connor had the same doctor and lost their uvulas too, I don't know, but they push that tone forward.

After I'd been at the Planet Mars a couple of weeks, I went with Dick and Al to the Ball of Fire for the 5:30 A.M. breakfast show. There, the entertainers who worked at the host tavern put on a program for people working other clubs in the city. For some reason, the Ball of Fire's emcee couldn't be there so Dick substituted for him.

I don't remember who was on the bill except for a torch singer, a kind of Queen Bee of the Northside taverns. Her beauty compared favorably with Hedy Lamarr's. She had long black hair framing her pale white face, naturally pink-tinted cheeks, pale blue eyes and perfectly proportioned features. Not only was she a knockout, she had a good voice, wonderful tone, and when she sang a ballad like "My Bill," she had everyone in the place crying.

She and the Ball of Fire crowd did their show, then they sat back while Dick called people from other spots out of the audience to perform. Eventually he got to me. I sang a jazz arrangement Al had worked on with me, "A Hundred Years from Today," and I was a big hit. If they had allowed encores, I'd have got one.

After I'd finished, I headed for the bar. Shortly, this black-haired, blue-eyed beauty came up to me and said, "My name is Betty Hall, but they call me Trilby." (At least that's what I think she said. Over the years it was Betty Hall, Trilby Hailey, Elizabeth Rogers, Betty Rogers and Elizabeth Pettet. And who remembers what else?)

"Oh? I'm Anita O'Day."

"I never heard of you before."

"Oh?" I said. "I never saw you until tonight either."

She told me later that her feathers were ruffled because, while a lot of gal singers had floated through the Northside, none of them ever before had received a reception equal to hers. What especially bugged her was that she didn't dig jazz. But as we kept chitchatting, it turned out she was a protégée of Buckley's the same as me.

Dick came over to say he was glad to see we'd met because he had an offer to open at the Ball of Fire. He wanted to use us both: Betty as The Mysterious Trilby and me as The Princess of Swing.

Trilby and I got to be great friends. Don't ask me why. We were both seventeen, but nothing alike. She was a torch singer. I sang swing. She didn't dig it. She drank beer. I preferred pot or cognac or scotch. Trilby was a lovebug, in and out of love every week. I was my own woman. She thought I was a little cool and calculating because I put my career ahead of any guy I met. She loved singing but longed for a white cottage surrounded by a picket fence.

Trilby and Lea Roberts became my best friends. Lea worked mostly as an intermission singer. She was five feet eight, weighed two hundred pounds and had a good voice with a nice tone. It was a trained voice. She didn't sing opera, but would choose pieces such as "Smoke Gets in Your Eyes" and other show tunes. She looked down on Dick's slapstick, but off stage she was out for a good time just like the rest of us. We were like the Three Musketeers. For example, one morning after we'd finished our shows, we changed clothes, had breakfast and went out to Riverview Amusement Park. We spent all day riding rides, having funny photos made, whatever, and came back exhausted.

Lea went to her job. Trilby and I arrived at the Ball of Fire without a wink of sleep. It was 6:00 P.M. and the first show didn't go on until 8:00P.M., so we crawled under a couple of tables with long white cloths on them to rest for an hour. The next thing I knew I heard the band playing the overture of the show. Didn't we scramble!

A lot has come down since those happy days. Lea died in 1979 and over the years Trilby and I have had our disagreements, but we've stayed friends. When she heard I was doing this book, she couldn't imagine what on earth I was going to write about.

"You haven't had a hard life," she said. "The only bad thing that happened to you was that you got on dope, and you did that to yourself."

From her point of view, I guess that's true. I had a mother. She didn't. "I grew like a weed," she used to say. When she was sixteen, she had a baby that her father forced her to give away. The love of her life was Doc Cassidy, the doctor who altered Dillinger's appearance. He'd get jealous and beat her. She was terrified of him, but madly in love with him, too. "You never thought more of anyone than yourself. With you, Anita, your career always came first," she often said.

She was right. Singing came before all the nice guys and certainly before the Doc Cassidys of this world. He combined a sodium pentathol habit with a liking for anything alcoholic. Now that didn't make for the most stable cat in the world. The fact is that one night he blew his head off right in front of his mother, his sister and Trilby.

Trilby's best shot romantically and professionally was Phil Yordan who wrote *Anna Lucasta*. Phil got her a screen test at MGM.

The studio offered her a contract, but Trilby walked out on it to return to some musician in Chicago. He turned out to be tangled up with a forty-five-year-old broad.

"God, when you think back on those things! I wasn't really a bad girl," she said, "but, you know, I've thought about it a lot and I made the same mistake over and over. I thought if a man wanted to have sex with me, he loved me instead of the other way around."

"So you're really like me."

"How? You weren't a lovebug."

"Right," I said, "but all the bad things that happened to us we brought on ourselves."

She thought about it for a second.

"Right," she said, and we both began laughing because at sixty we could recognize the truth of what we had really shared.

Looking back, I also realize I was always alone, fending for myself, doing the best I could without the family support a seventeen-year-old ordinarily gets. Smoking pot, drinking, playing it cool were my ways of hiding the pain and deprivation I wouldn't let myself recognize.

Think about it. Dad abandoned Mother and me. No big deal the way I played it. Mom was a strange, complex woman who must have loved me in her way if we judge people by what they do instead of what they say. Otherwise, why would she have struggled to keep me with her? But she never expressed love. And when she'd do something nice, she'd tell me how inconvenient it had been before I even got a chance to feel grateful or thank her. Now, I know Aunt Belle loved me, but she had had so many disappointments and problems she didn't have the energy to give me what I needed.

So I drank, got high, learned to cover up my feelings of pain beneath a hip, swinging-chick personality I'd carefully developed. When I went on stage and sang "It's De-lovely" or "Organ Grinder's Swing," I got the love I craved. I didn't need anyone. For me, music equaled love.

I can't recall exactly where we were playing, but one night this man came in and asked me how I'd like to sing at the Vialago with Floyd Towne's band. How would I like it? Towne's band had seven pieces; we had four. Towne would provide a lot of harmony. I felt I was really about to get moving.

Trilby and I ran over to the Vialago between shows. Everything was mirrored—the walls, the ceiling, even the posts that held up that ceiling. The dance floor was made of glass and different colored lights rotated slowly beneath it. I loved it.

I remember Paul Jordan was on piano, Bill Dohler on alto sax and there were some other sharp cats in the band. But the one who caught my eye was a tall drummer with pale blue eyes, naturally blond hair and *yellow* skin. He was more than handsome. He was pretty. He looked terrific, a kind of Oriental sex object.

Talented? He played like an angel—drums, vibes, cymbals, timpanis, bells, the whole bit. Bells! Nobody played bells then. Musically, this guy's ideas were very advanced. He almost played a tune during his drum solos, doing stuff I'd never heard anyone do before.

I felt a musical rapport with him immediately. But what really blew my mind was that this was the drummer Tut Soper had told me about, the ascetic one who belonged to The Mystic Brotherhood.

I started going to the Vialago between sets to dig him. After a while I noticed he focused his attention on one post so intently that people danced by it to see what he was looking at. He was looking at himself, admiring his movement and technique in the mirrored post.

At first I thought, "Strange cat." Today people would say, "What a narcissist!" Not me. I'd never heard of that Greek dude who stared at himself in a pool until he turned into a flower.

Don and I never talked, but when I'd finish work, I'd run down to the Vialago to catch a glimpse of him. And that was all I got because he cut out as soon as the show was over. He never hung out, had a drink or played cards with the other fellows. He was evasive, withdrawn, a loner.

He'd take off on foot and I'd follow at a distance until he reached the apartment he shared with his mother. Then I'd stand across the street watching the building and thinking about him. You could say I'd been around, but really I was still just a teenager with a crush on an older guy. He was twenty-seven or twenty-eight and I was sixteen.

Finally, one night I went in and found somebody else occupying his chair. I thought he'd taken the night off. But when he was missing the next time I dropped in, I asked Floyd Towne what had happened to Don.

"Carter's got yellow jaundice," Towne told me. "He'll be back in a few weeks."

I certainly hoped so. Because I *had* to get to know him.

When I learned Don had returned to the Vialago, I began running over there after the show again. Don couldn't avoid me, but he didn't make any friendly moves either. I finally got up enough nerve one night to say, "Bye."

"Good night."

He obviously wasn't an outgoing personality. But I kept talking to him. I mentioned Tut. No response. I kept suggesting things, but he was the most "no" person I'd met up to that time. He didn't drink, like bike riding or going to the beach. When I asked what he did with himself, he said he worked on arrangements. That sounded good. I told him Tut thought he could write some for me. Don smiled and said maybe someday.

After that, I began picking out effects he'd created and asking him about them. When he saw I really was engrossed in music, he began discussing techniques with me. I tried to memorize what he said, because to me he was *the* best.

You're probably thinking, "She was in love with this cat so naturally she'd say that." Not true. Recently I had a friend contact several Chicago musicians who knew or worked with Don—Gene Krupa, Davey Tough, Chick Webb and whoever. I sent my friend because I didn't want these guys to say what they thought I wanted to hear.

Bert Lawrence first remembered Don from a ballroom at Washington and Pulaski in 1927 or '28. "All Chicago musicians went to hear him, including Krupa, who admitted he learned from Carter," Bert said. "Krupa had the showmanship. He milked the crowds for applause and knew which side the money was on. Carter achieved equally difficult effects and made them look easy. That's why Krupa was *Krupa* and Carter just went on demonstrating his impeccable technique."

Bill Dohler, a legendary wild man who played with most of the white drummers around Chicago, remembered Don as an innovator. "He showed the way," Dohler recalled.

He was getting double sound on a single bass drum with his hand and foot long before Ray McKinley featured double bass drums or Louis Bellson made them famous. I happen to have an affinity for the rhythm section—the bass, drums and piano—because that provides the harmonic structure. Don would play with his hands, feet and have sticks in his mouth for chimes and bells. He was truly incredible. Compared to him, Krupa sounded like he was banging two frying pans together.

Tut Soper described Don as "potentially the greatest—as a drummer and arranger." His only reservation was that Don smoked grass which Tut felt made him erratic. (I don't personally agree with that, but it's Tut's opinion.) "When he wasn't stoned, his drumming was smooth, polished to perfection. He understood dynamics and when he could throw off his inhibitions, he produced some fantastic results. Looking back, you can only say, 'What a waste.' "

So there you are! Those Chicago cats felt the same way about Don's talent as I did. Why didn't he make it? Maybe that wasn't his goal. Maybe he was too much of a perfectionist.

I don't know whether most people can understand this, but my two deepest emotional commitments grew out of musical collaboration rather than romantic or sexual attachments. The first was to Don. Oh, maybe I hoped he'd come on with me at first, but when he didn't, it was no big deal. I was only seventeen and not really into man-woman relationships.

Anyway, I can tell you now that musical intimacy is on a completely different plane—deeper, longer-lasting, better than the steamiest sexual liaison. Passion wears out, but the longer you work with a really rhythmical, inventive, swinging musician, the closer you become.

Don could talk musical concepts for hours. *That* stimulated me. He taught me to play the piano by 1-3-5-7-9-11-13 instead of a-b-c-d-e-f-g. *That* thrilled me. Because I could now pick out the notes of a song I wanted to learn. He dug helping me. Me! Man, I was living and learning.

Gradually I began babbling about personal problems. I was still living at home and working gigs at various joints in the Uptown district. Usually Don either didn't respond to my outbursts or just grunted. But one day when I complained that Mom was bugging me to get in earlier when the joints I worked didn't close until 4:00 A.M., I almost wigged out when he quietly suggested I move in with him.

"But what about your mom?"

"Mother understands the business," he said.

I don't remember his mother's first name because I never called her anything but Mrs. Carter—which tells you something about where I was coming from—but I do remember wondering whether she'd welcome me. Don's dad, a cornet player, was long out of the picture. And Don had such a reputation as a mama's boy that Trilby suspected a little incest might be going on. But a father's absence seemed normal to me.

Mrs. Carter was a tall, stunning woman with hennaed hair, pale blue eyes like Don's and an affected way of speaking that entertainers used to call stage diction. She was somewhere in her fifties, and when she walked, she glided along with the stateliness of an old Rolls-Royce. Everybody assumed she'd been in show business, but nobody knew which branch.

The first time we met, she said, "You're talented. And I hope my son helps your work."

She'd always been nice to me, but when Don invited me to move in, I felt uneasy and told him he'd better clear it with her.

My mom didn't object and Don said his didn't either. The Carters lived in half of what had once been a six-room, floor-through apartment. It had been divided into two flats, each with a living room, bedroom and kitchen. The day Don moved me and my belongings in, I met a different Mrs. Carter. In spite of Don's reassurances, she looked at me as if I were a waterbug who'd managed to crawl under the door. I'd never been clothes-conscious, but the going-over she gave my cheap little sweater, skirt and the knee-high socks I wore to keep the winds that blew off Lake Michigan from freezing my legs chilled me.

"Donald, are you sure this is what you want?"

Don answered, "Wait until you hear her sing."

"I've heard her," she replied. "I know she can sing." Then, without pausing, she said to me, "Of course, you realize your being here entails additional expenses."

"Oh, I told Don I'd pay eight-fifty a week."

That was above average for those days and seemed to satisfy her.

Moving in with them was a bold thing to do in 1937 even though his mother was present. The first week I slept on a couch in the living room. Every night Mrs. Carter dragged out a folding army cot for herself. Don slept in the big double bed in the bedroom.

Living with someone, you find out a lot about them. Don had always looked immaculate and he should have. Whenever I wanted to get into the bathroom, he was in there, taking one of his six or seven baths a day. He had a thing about water. When it rained in the middle of the night, he'd get dressed and go for a walk. When he'd come back, by a system he'd worked out, he'd write down the rhythm of the raindrops on the umbrella. The next night he might use that rhythm in his gig or he might put it in the drum book he was working on.

After I'd been at the Carters for a week, right out of the blue Don surprised me by suggesting we go to City Hall and get married. It was as matter-of-fact as if he were asking me whether I'd like a hit off the joint he was smoking. He didn't tell me he loved me. So, even though I worshipped him, I didn't tell him how I felt either. He didn't buy me a ring and I didn't get a special dress. No friends went along to stand up with us. After the ceremony both of us came back to the apartment and got ready to report for work as usual.

On our wedding night, he kissed me on the forehead before we climbed into the big double bed. I waited for him to make a move, thinking maybe he wanted to make sure his mother was asleep, but he stayed on his side of the bed, and, after a little while, he turned over and went to sleep.

Believe it or not, I wasn't upset or really disappointed. I knew the tenet of the Mystic Brotherhood against sex. Truthfully, maybe I hoped he might break it, but when he didn't, it was okay with me. I loved him, but I realized he wasn't into physical relationships. So I accepted what he had to give. Besides, I was inexperienced and still a little uneasy about sex myself.

Don and I lived with his mother for almost a year. I really didn't push for us to get our own pad. Mrs. Carter did the work and the living was easy.

When Don was working on his music, I'd go out to ride my bike along Lake Michigan. I didn't have much to talk to his mother about and it never occurred to me to ask her to teach me to cook, clean or even make a bed properly. In my mind, mothers did those things. That was their contribution. I was going to be a famous singer and entertain the world. Jesus had promised me and I'd already come a long way.

The times I really was happiest were when Don gave me lessons on his drum practice pad or would have other musicians in. Mrs. Carter always made them welcome and I felt I learned a lot. Art Hodes, Bill Dohler, Paul Jordan and Maury Stein were a few of the guys. Art, who played fine Dixieland piano, was the first visitor. He and Don decided to teach me "Exactly Like You." That's when I realized I needed to know a lot more than Erskine Tate and Al Lyons had taught me. But Art and Don showed me how the song went and when I finally sang it, Art said, "Hey! What about the kid? She learns fast and she sings pretty good, huh?"

Hearing such praise from Art Hodes made me so proud I felt like I was going to be sick. I had to get out of there. I thanked him and scurried out to ride my bike in the fresh air. (That happened in 1938 and in 1975 I recorded "Exactly Like You" during my tour of Japan.)

Gradually the Uptown scene was falling apart and our crowd began drifting away. Dick Buckley went on smoking pot and popping pills. But Al Lyons gave away the pound of grass he had and took up serious drinking. Trilby cut out from Uptown and got a job in Russell's Silver Frolics. I took gigs wherever I could get them.

At about this time, Maury Stein, brother of Jule (who'd changed the spelling to Styne), took practically the whole Vialago crew, including Don, into his band for an engagement at the Chez Paree, then Chicago's top nightclub.

Maury had high regard for Don's talent and developed tolerance for his eccentricities. He had to. Don hadn't been with him long when he began complaining that the band needed more good music. Duke Ellington had given Don twenty songs, but he needed paper to make arrangements. So Maury bought him fifteen hundred sheets of paper.

Very quickly, Don brought him the introduction to a thing called "Grievin' Granddaddy." The fellows tried it. It sounded great. Don gathered up the parts and took them back to finish his work.

62

Shortly he brought in the intro to "Jingle Bells, a Cubolic Fantasy"—seven bars. "Don's 'Jingle Bells' sounded like a lit-up Christmas tree," Maury once said.

A few days later Don showed up with the intro to "Mood Indigo," which was just brilliant. In all, Don brought in over fifty sensational intros, but he never completed any orchestration.

Maury began to get impatient. Finally Don showed up with the arrangement for Irving Berlin's "Blue Skies." Maury couldn't wait for the band to play it. Don passed out the music. His hands were empty and the piano and bass had no charts. He had forgotten to write them. He shrugged. "I could have sworn I finished them," he said.

"That finished his arranging for us," Maury said. "But there still wasn't a better drummer around."

Trilby's spectacular beauty and great way with ballads earned her a shot at the world-famous Kitty Davis', located at the end of the Loop down by Jackson and Wabash.

I felt everybody was moving up in the world and my turn was sure to come. Trilby promised to see what she could do.

Kitty, who was already known as Kay Kane, actually fronted the joint which was run by her husband, Danny. Their gimmick was claiming all employees were college graduates. Cornered about that, Kitty's stock reply was, "They sure are! Graduated from the College of Hard Knocks."

This was a big-time club for me. It was a two-story affair. There were no B-drinkers during my time and the clientele was less rowdy than in the taverns. On the ground floor as he stepped through the door, the first thing the customer saw were all these beautiful "26" girls scattered around the room. "Twenty-six" is a dice game similar to "21." At Kitty's, the prize was a coupon book for free drinks. But that bunch of pretty girls in low-cut, slit-skirt gowns were a big attraction for any guy who wandered in. Periodically, a dice girl would leave her station to go to the microphone to sing or dance. There was continuous entertainment. Dice girls, waitresses, bartenders, busboys—they all entertained.

Trilby had Lea and me drop in to case the joint. If we liked what we saw, she said she'd try to get us hired. We loved it and Trilby introduced us to Kitty, a kind of wild orchid of a woman who was about forty-five and beginning to frazzle at the edges. Her hair was perfectly done—which impressed me since I'd never been in a beauty shop—and she wore spangled gowns. If you wanted to cast anybody for the role of a madam, Kitty was the one. Not pretty, but not plain. A lot of lipstick, big-busted and tough as any man that came down the pike, that was Kitty. But she did her game well and was definitely someone people wanted to know. Chicago was a conventioneers' town and Kitty ran a twenty-four-hour continuous operation.

She chatted with Lea and me briefly and said she'd arrange for us to talk with Danny. Lea wanted to think it over. The next day she announced she was going to marry the guy who'd been proposing to her for six months and give up show business. Shortly after, she went to work for Marshall Field and remained for the next thirty years.

Danny Davis was a crumb who had mob connections. He told me that everyone at the club earned $22.50 a week. All tips we collected had to be deposited in a can. Anyone caught withholding on the house could expect to be fired on the spot.

Danny insisted on total honesty, but apparently he wasn't too bright, because after I'd left his employ, he double-crossed the mob. They let him off—just closed down his joint. So he and Kitty went to Florida where they opened Kitty Davis' Airliner. It was a big spot. But apparently Danny didn't learn easily. He double-crossed the mob again and was found with half his skull blown away.

That night, before he hired me, he had me get into one of their shortie dresses with black net stockings and sing. After I finished, he said he'd have me broken in on the "26" game right away and I'd start working the noon to 8:00 P.M. shift next day. Getting that job was a big event in my life. I felt, *She's coming up in the world!*

But after about a month on the dice game, it really bored me. I didn't like having to sit in one place all the time, smiling at customers and playing "26." The only chance I had to move around was when it was my turn at the mike. That was three or four times in an eight-hour period, with maybe an encore if there was a big tipper in the house to decorate the mahogany bar with green stuff.

I told Kitty I really didn't dig my assignment so she spoke to the

64

floor manager who asked, "Would you really rather break your ass hustling drinks?"

"I'll try anything once, mister," I told him. "Whatever, it has to be better than this."

So I went upstairs where they gave me a skimpy apron to match my short skirt. The routine was simple. I'd take the order, give it to the bartender who mixed the drink, handed it to me, and I served and collected for it.

Beauties came on like beauties. I never came on like that because I never considered myself a pretty girl. Instead, I was vivacious. Tips were good. Unless somebody was just off the farm, he never left less than a dollar. Five bucks was fairly common and once I hit the jackpot with a hundred-dollar bill. Which was no thrill because it went into the box which we turned over to the floor manager at the end of the evening. It didn't bother me. I was just interested in the music side because the piano player was an exceptional musician nicknamed Dick Pockles, who helped me master a few more of the technicalities.

I must have been at Kitty's six or seven months when this guy came in one day. He was dressed in a suit and tie and looked like a young businessman. He ordered a drink and when I brought it, he said, "Would you sing a tune for me? Do you know 'I Can't Get Started'?"

"Of course, I know it. Do I know it!" If you don't feel pretty, be enthusiastic anyway.

The tip was ten bucks. Shortly, I got to the mike and did the number. Afterward I ambled over to where he was sitting.

"I did your song. Did you like it?"

"I loved it," he said. He decorated the mahogany with another ten bucks and asked me to do another number.

The floor manager knew when he had a good thing going and signaled for them to put me on again right away. When I came back to where the guy was sitting, he said, "I'm Carl Cons, an editor of *Down Beat*. I'm opening a club in the Loop. Are you signed to this place?"

I told him I wasn't.

"Would you like working for me? Three sets between ten P.M. and four A.M. A hundred and twenty-five a week."

"Where do I waitress?"

"You don't waitress."

"A hundred and twenty-five and I don't waitress? Where?"

"The Off-Beat Club. Under the Three Deuces, 222 North State. We're remodeling. You'll be on the opening bill."

I could hardly wait to get off work. By 8:00 P.M. Don would already have left for the Chez Paree, so I hopped the elevated and went up to tell Mom and Aunt Belle that I had a job where I wouldn't be on my feet eight hours or do any waiting on customers.

"Besides, I get a raise," I said, "so you can count on an extra two dollars-and-a half a week from now on."

I still hadn't learned that no matter how much money I gave Mom, she was never going to be able to give me the affection I craved.

I waited up for Don to tell Mrs. Carter and him my news. Word had spread among musicians about Cons' partnership with Sam Beers, operator of the Three Deuces. They were hiring hot new talent the public hadn't noticed yet. Don got so excited he picked me up and waltzed me around the room. Mrs. Carter's face set.

"Aren't you going to congratulate Anita?" he asked.

"Congratulations," she said and went into the kitchen.

Poor Don was torn between sharing my excitement and rushing after his mom. He said he'd be back in a minute, but for a long time they were at the kitchen table talking between themselves. I realized then that she'd never take me into the family. It would always be them in the kitchen and me in the parlor, bedroom, whatever.

I was disappointed and hurt and damned mad. I decided to make my stand. I went to bed and fought off sleep, waiting for Don. When he crawled into bed, I said, "Don, this isn't going anywhere."

"We'll talk about it later."

"No. Either you're my husband or her son. I think we should try living together without your mother.".

"There's nothing to do about it tonight."

"When?"

"I'll take care it it."

I didn't expect any action. But the next night after work, Don and Mrs. Carter talked a long time in the kitchen. I was so angry I almost got up and went over to Trilby's. When he came to bed, I pretended to be sleeping.

Next morning, he said, "Okay, Mom's leaving."

My first reaction was how wonderful, then, very quickly, I began feeling scared. I'd forced the issue and got what I wanted. I should have been happy, but it suddenly hit me that I didn't know how to cook or wash or take care of the apartment.

Several days later, Don said Mrs. Carter had a housekeeping job and would move the next day. The first night she was gone, I was careful not to muss the bedclothes too much so that I could make the bed in the morning. I switched shifts at Kitty Davis' to make it possible for Don and me to be together more.

About three days later, we were out of the food his mother had prepared before she splilt. Now Don, who had been used to specially prepared meals, was getting things dumped from a tin can into a heating pan and from there onto his plate. What did I know about cooking?

Then one day he said he was getting low on shirts. Panicsville. I managed to wash a load of clothes. Bleach? Starch? Forget it. Worse still, I didn't iron too well. In fact, I'd never ironed at all. The situation got chaotic. I was upset. Don was upset. What made it worse was that I'd gotten his mother out of the house hoping our marriage would be consummated, but in our agitated states anything of the kind was impossible. I thought it over and decided to admit I'd been wrong.

"I'm sorry, " I told him, "but I don't know how to do these things. You'd better get your mother back."

He agreed.

"Maybe now she'll understand we're together."

"Maybe." He didn't sound convinced.

And she didn't accept him and me as a couple. Now she made me feel a total outsider. Don? How could he allow it? I wondered. In his dealings with musicians, he had, like, a noble attitude. But for me? I never could be sure he loved me. After his mother had been back a little while, I decided seducing him was the only thing that would change the balance of relationships.

That night, when he finally left his mother, I wasn't completely on my side of the bed. He kissed me on the forehead and whispered to move over and give him room. I moved an inch or two.

"Anita? Are you asleep?"

"Not now," I said, pretending he'd awakened me. I threw my arm over his chest.

"Anita, I have an offer from Joe Marsala for the Hickory House in New York. Mother and I are going —"

"What about me?"

"We'll send for you as soon as we can."

"I've got the fare and—"

"Not until we're settled, honey."

I took my arm off his chest and moved to my half of the bed.

"Congratulations," I said, unconsciously echoing his mother.

"It'll work out better all around. You don't want to miss opening Cons' new club."

"Right."

"You always say music comes first."

"Right."

He was forcing some hard decisions on me. I'd been able to accept our relationship because I knew music was everything to him, too. What I'd counted on was a musical partnership. It seemed I wasn't getting that. He was walking away just as Dad had. He wasn't any more demonstrative than Mom. Why did people who supposedly loved me treat me like this?

I didn't beg or cry or let him know how let down and furious I felt. I kept reminding myself that he'd taught me a lot about singing, drumming and picking out pieces on the piano, whatever. I didn't speak until I could play it supercool, chitchat about his wonderful opportunity with Marsala's outfit and mine at the new Cons club. I felt abandoned, rejected, but he wasn't going to know it.

The day the Carters left, I moved into the Chelsea Hotel, which, from the viewpoint of an ambitious, eighteen-year-old singer, was the only place to be. The Chelsea, at Wilson Avenue off Sheridan Road, housed 100 musicians in its 150 rooms—to say nothing of gamblers, expensive call girls, boosters, chorus girls, etc. There was a party going on somewhere twenty four hours a day. Three practice rooms were sites of almost continuous jam sessions and the bar downstairs operated twenty-two hours out of twenty-four.

Only twenty to twenty-five minutes from Loop theaters, clubs and hotels, the Chelsea's price was right at $5 a week. Of course, I missed being with Don, but I dulled the ache by smoking grass in my tiny room and sitting around the bar cutting up jackpots with cats who hung out there.

Was Benny Goodman jealous of the cats he hired? What about Harry James' new outfit? And Billie Holiday's telling off Artie Shaw? How good were the Dorseys' latest releases? And what effect would the defections have on Red Norvo's band? Was Mildred Bailey right in butting in and telling off Red in front of the band? And while we talked, I tried to drink up all the cognac in the place.

Eventually I got a few letters and a picture postcard of the Radio City Music Hall from Don, but he never suggested my joining him and his mother in New York so I marked time waiting for the Off-Beat to open.

CHAPTER IV
WALKING ON THE WILD SIDE

I bought a January issue of *Down Beat* when I got to the Loop and took it to work with me. There was no difficulty in finding the announcement of the January 18 premiere of the Off-Beat Club. It was right there on page one, along with Carl Cons' statement of policy and the names of the opening attractions—Max Miller's Quartet and Anita O'Day. Me!

Kitty Davis spotted the paper on my make-up table and advised me not to give notice until I was sure the Off-Beat was going to open.

"I hear rumors," she said ominously and rolled on out of the room.

After work, I beat it over to the Three Deuces. I'd been there earlier to hear Roy "Little Jazz" Eldridge and his group. Now I wanted to find out how work on the new room was progressing, hoist a few and dig the show. I think it was singing pianist Julia Lee and that roly-poly little novelty drummer Baby Dodds. They worked the long, street-level bar that catered to drop-in trade.

I flashed my ID to the manager and asked whether I could case the new room. He led me down a flight of wide, steep steps and into this big area where I almost flipped my wig. The painters were still daubing the walls and there were no interior decorator's doodads in sight. First night was only ten days away. I decided to follow Kitty's advice and withhold my notice until I heard from Carl Cons.

HEP CATS TO GET NEW DEAL WITH MINIATURE SWING CONCERTS, NEW TALENT, RIBS AND JIVE ON TAP, Down Beat promised when I got around to reading the issue I'd bought earlier. What Cons hoped to do was to go New York's Onyx Club one better. The Off-Beat would provide Chicago musicians and the in-crowd with a chance to catch jazz instrumentalists and promising swing singers before the general public rocketed them to stardom.

On the eighteenth, Cons finally called to say he'd definitely be opening the doors on January 25.

Would this delay damage business?

No, Cons assured me. It had increased interest. The phone girl had reservations for a full house opening night. So many callers had asked to be placed on standby that he was offering Opening Night II on the twenty-sixth. That was already nearly full, so he was dramatizing the Off-Beat's appeal by staging Opening Night III.

Never before or after have I heard of a joint kicking off with three premieres, but the Off-Beat did. That kind of launching gave the spot a momentum that fed upon itself. Nightclub reporters ran preopening items and photos that generated interest among people who generally weren't into the music scene. So contagious was the enthusiasm that the editors of both the Herald-Examiner and the Evening–American made reservations on the morning of the twenty-fifth, making it necessary to add extra tables to accommodate them.

Cons had a lot of far-out ideas for his time. Entertainers and musicians, whether neophytes or veterans, black or white, were to be picked from the most adventurous bands, instrumentalists, singers, whether or not they were commercial. The audience he counted on for steady patronage was to be made up of musicians and swing fans.

"We want it known," he said in Down Beat, "it's to be a spot where the boys can drop in before or after work without worrying how they're dressed or if they've got folding money, and have a beer or a round of drinks with one another."

Up to that point I might have thought I'd died and gone to heaven. But in the last paragraph, the writer ended the story— and as an editor, Carl Cons did not alter the paragraph— by describing Max Miller's Quartet as ranking with the Benny Goodman and Adrian Rollini groups "for real musicianship and originality." Me? I was "the young chirper whom Teddy Wilson, on hearing one of her records, swore was Billie Holiday—although Miss O'Day had never heard Billie up to that time." Max was the equal of Goodman. I was apparently a Billie Holiday clone, although in those days we'd have said "carbon copy."

The kicker was I'd never made a recording.

On opening night, Max Miller's dazzling quartet had hardly got out the first couple of bars of their opening number when people streamed from the tables and the small bar onto the dance floor and the most sensational jitterbugs in the city energized the whole room. Arms, legs and bodies were flying through the air in a pyrotechnical display that set me bouncing and wanting to join them.

Max had broadcast regularly over radio station WIND so he had a following in Chicago. He played vibes and piano and, more important to me, he was a swing, or 4/4 player.

Before 1935, Dixieland, with its 2/4 beat, dominated jazz. Then along came Benny Goodman who ushered in the Swing Era with those wild Fletcher Henderson arrangements with the 4/4 beat, and that was for me. (After Swing came Bebop and Cool Jazz, Progressive Jazz, whatever, but I'll get to that later.)

Max was a nice guy and he drank. I don't think that's exactly why I liked Max, but it made it easier for me to relax with him. Whatever, he scored astonishingly with everyone there that night. I was happy for him—and scared for myself.

I had reason to be. Here I was, going on before an audience made up of people who could tip the scales, influencing my whole future in Chicago music circles. Cons had promised us rehearsal time. Last minute decorating made that impossible. Miller didn't need rehearsal except to test the acoustics. He and his men were accustomed to working together. So they scored and I was petrified.

I had twenty-four minutes to fill and very few tunes to fill that time with—five numbers. Forty years later I can only recall three of the titles: "Jeepers Creepers," "Oh, Lady, Be Good!" and "Blue Moon." On the tunes I knew I could do five or six different versions of the chorus; I'd begin with the melody and end with the melody and what went on in between depended on what hit me while I was up there singing.

That night I did "Jeepers Creepers" and the other three tunes. I saved "Oh, Lady, Be Good" as an encore.

At the point where the bridge comes to the second chorus, I needed an idea from somewhere. I saw a polka dot blouse. So I developed that chorus as a bagful of polka dots. To keep the version going, I searched for new ideas. Where was I going to get my inspiration? I looked around the room and that gave me the idea of singing the structure of the room—long wall, short wall, long wall, short wall. That gave the frame for that chorus. I turned to the band. Five men. So I put it into a five rhythm. Anything that I could get an idea from, I put to work to fill out my time on the stand. I did it that way because technically I was not knowledgeable about music. I needed to get the thought behind the sound going, and I took it from wherever I could find it.

In all, I did twelve choruses of "Oh, Lady, Be Good!" and when I finished, the place exploded. People shouted, stamped, applauded, whistled, stood on their chairs and cheered. It was the response you dream about, made sweeter by the fact that it came from people who understood what I was doing. I was a success beyond my wildest expectations.

I wasn't just the toast of Chicago night life; I was the toast of all the hep (hip came later) musicians and hepcats in the city.

The February *Down Beat* had a huge picture of me sitting on a stool, wearing a dark jacket, striped skirt and black patent leather pumps. My legs were crossed to emphasize their shapeliness and the skirt was short enough to show a hint of thigh. My right elbow rested on my left knee and my right hand cupped the right side of my chin lightly. My slightly opened mouth, painted-on eyebrows and pageboy bob gave me a sophisticated look far beyond my years and experience. The caption read: SHE SCORES WITH CHICAGO MUSICIANS. In the unsigned news story beside the photograph, the writer noted: ". . . Anita O'Day—the little girl whose singing style is comparable only to a combination of Bailey and Holiday—panicked the house as she took the stand for a dozen encores with Miller's quartet kicking out the accompaniment."

I must have done "alreet" because both Max Miller and I were hired for ten days. When his ten were up Max moved on. I stayed for the next four months as the house singer on a week-to-week basis; then an early hot spell late in May caused Cons to close the club until September.

Each Monday between 1:00 and 5:00 P.M., Cons held auditions. It seemed to me as if every girl singer in Chicago—novelty or torch, sweet, swing or Dixieland—tried out for my spot, but I hung in there.

Jimmy McPartland and his band followed Miller. McPartland played cornet, not trumpet, and he played authentic Dixieland. Musically, his style of Dixieland was the best you could get with the exception of Satchmo's, because Bix Beiderbecke was already dead. It was great, but not for me. I'd sung Dixieland occasionally before swing came in, and I've done it infrequently over the years, but at this point, I considered myself strictly a swing singer, 4/4 all the way. Period. So when I came on, McPartland left the stand and I used his band playing a 4/4 beat.

It wasn't an ideal setup so Cons hired Darnell Howard and His Off-Beat Quartet as the house band. I also worked with them when Wingy Manone came through as a single. Wingy was a New Orleans cat who had lost his right arm in an accident, but that didn't stop him from putting that trumpet through some fancy paces. Nor did it make him any less of an extrovert. He referred to his false arm as his "iron wing." There were a million stories about him because he was a character spelled with a capital C and he loved to tell tales on himself.

He used to recall how Jack Teagarden had heard him with Bing Crosby on the *Kraft Music Hall* radio shows. Jack wired Wingy, "If you can read, come on."

Wingy wired back, "Can read. Am coming."

At the first rehearsal they tried 'Waitin' at the Gate" four times. Wingy couldn't cut it.

Jack called him over. "Why did you wire me you could read? You can't read."

Wingy replied, "Man, I can read." Using his iron wing, he pointed to a piece of music. "Now here goes Wingy, " he said. "That's an F, that's a G, that's a C-sharp, that's a D. I can read 'em; I just can't divide 'em."

I think Wingy was the first person I ever heard compare improvising to a horse race. It went something like this:

"We're all lined up at the startin' gate, " he said. "Now we're off. In the first couple of bars, right at the start Wingy's got the lead. I keep the lead for about twelve bars, then the tenor saxophone overtakes me for about six bars, then I go back into the lead again for the last eight bars. We go into another chorus where the trombone takes the lead. I'm behind all the time, on his tail all the time, and in the last chorus I get the lead but the damn piano takes me down and in the last eight bars of the tag, Wingy takes it over and the winner of the race is—Wingy Manone!"

Later, when I got deeply into improvising, that's the way I thought of each number, as a horse race. Only Wingy's race was written out like it had been fixed. When I improvise, I put myself on the line. Sometimes I win, sometimes I lose, sometimes it's too close to call. But I got the basic thought from Wingy.

Even though more often than not I worked with Darnell Howard, I was being exposed to all these different groups, mostly black, with their individual styles. Jay McShann's piano playing really swung when he wasn't devoting himself to boogie-woogie—and it still does. Stuff "I'se A Muggin'" Smith was phen-omon-able! I had never cared for violins, but when I heard those jazz riffs, it opened my ears to the possibilities of a hot fiddle or any other instrument when it falls into the right pair of talented hands. Then, as a bonus with Stuff, we had Jonah Jones, who was billed as "Gabriel of the Trumpet" and lived up to his billing. Muggsy Spanier, who appeared a couple of times, played strictly Dixieland. For some reason, whenever he appeared, he brought out an entirely different clientele than usually showed up. But all those guys were a kick to me because I got exposed to a variety of sacred harmonies and at that time I still looked upon myself as an apprentice.

After I'd caught the acts at the Off-Beat, I got into the habit of going upstairs to the Three Deuces to hear Baby Dodds. Baby was a genius. This was in the days before the sock pedal. All he had was a big bass drum, a snare drum and a little top cymbal. He'd sit there shaking his little shoulders, doing his military precision-like rolls on the snare drums, and swinging so hard it scared you. Usually the other act was a singing pianist. Julia Lee played there several times. Lil Armstrong, an ex of Louis', came through, and so did "The Chi-Chi Girl, " Rose Murphy, with her chirpy little voice. Listening to her gave me the idea of how to handle "Honeysuckle Rose." I also learned from her that you can entertain with no chops. I was no Sarah Vaughan, but I didn't have to be.

They also started bringing in male piano players. None of them made too much of an impression on me until this one cat turned up. He just played, never sang. After each of my sets that first night, I climbed the stairs to check this guy out and hear him do whatever he was doing because he was really something, the best ever. When I finally got his name, it turned out to be Art Tatum. Guys like Art and Baby Dodds could play. Nobody can play that well anymore. Oh, maybe a few in a modern way, but it's not the same.

Even before the Off-Beat opened, Carl Cons went after musicians who were appearing at spots located in the hotels around town which were required by law to close at 2:00 A.M., or in theaters which closed even earlier. He wanted them to drop by our joint, which was open until 4:00 A.M., to hear our music and, if they felt so inclined, to sit in with the group. Paul Whiteman was the first big name to come in. He was a guest of Wingy Manone. Soon all the cats around town were dropping by when they weren't digging Earl "Fatha" Hines at the Blackhawk.

Of the music men visitors, by far the most important to me was Gene Krupa, who had sat in on jam sessions in this very room below the Three Deuces with such cats as Benny Goodman, Bix Beiderbecke, Tommy and Jimmy Dorsey, Eddie Condon and others. That was when he was just a kid scuffling around Chicago, long before he went to New York where he eventually joined the Benny Goodman band and established his own. Early in March, Remo Biondi brought him around after they'd finished for the night at the College Inn. Gene had a good band, but it still hadn't reached its potential. He was the handsomest bandleader of the era, but I went for sandy hair and blue eyes so I wasn't flipping over him personally. It might have been just another night if Remo hadn't come over after I'd finished my set and said Gene wanted to meet me.

After we'd expressed our mutual admiration, Remo told Gene that I played drums, too. When I mentioned Don Carter had taught me, Gene really flipped. Because what he hadn't learned from black drummers around the city, he'd picked up from Don and Davey Tough, then added the Krupa flair.

Gene also talked about my special sound and my improvising. He really dug it in a totally low-key way. By that I mean he didn't say he had to have me in the band or that I was the greatest thing he'd ever heard. What he did say, very quietly and sincerely, was, "Anita, I never fire anyone, but if my girl singer ever quits, you've got the job."

Remember, I was only nineteen years old and Gene Krupa was telling me he'd like to hire me. He was offering a chance.to sing in the big ballrooms, the top theaters and on the radio. That way lay fame. I'd have a chance to make my contribution. I managed to thank him and got away from the table. I was so high on life I was afraid I'd flip out if I stayed. It never occurred to me that before I heard from him a week, a month, a year, seven years might pass. Or I might never get the call. I was too excited to conceive of such a downer. That night I remembered to thank Jesus for the promise he'd made in my Walkathon days.

Not all swing musicians dug me as much as Gene. Some didn't dig me at all. Later that year, Benny Goodman, "The King of Swing," was playing the Chicago Theater. Somebody heard he was looking for a girl singer and I hurried over to audition.

When my turn came, I handed this nothing song they'd assigned me to the audition pianist. He played the intro and I took off. During my months at the Off-Beat, I'd learned a lot. I paid my respects to the melody to make sure I was keeping in touch with my listeners, then I began to play around with the chord structure and the beat, returning to a bit of melody at the end.

Benny jumped up, obviously annoyed. "What was *that?* You didn't sing the melody."

"I don't sing the melody on songs like this one," I informed him. "Everybody already knows the melody."

"In my band, the girl singer sings the melody," he said.

It was his band. I couldn't argue. I didn't say anything. I just turned on my heel and walked out.

The next girl who auditioned I think was Helen Forrest, who had a warm, musical voice and got the gig. I wasn't devastated. Benny and I weren't meant for one another, musically speaking. He wanted me to sing the melody and I don't always feel that.

One alligator at the Off-Beat Club was convinced he and I were meant for one another. An alligator is a jive term that was coined by Cab Calloway in the 1930s. His definition of an alligator is a person who listens to music, follows music, but doesn't play an instrument. All of that applied to Carl Hoff.

This Carl Hoff was not the orchestra leader, but the golf pro at the Biltmore Country Club in Barrington, Illinois, a suburb about forty miles from the Loop. And an unlikelier customer for the Off-Beat would be hard to imagine. Festivities didn't get under way until 9:30 or 10:00, and the room closed at 4:00 A.M., while Carl was due on the golf course as early as 6:00 A.M., teaching early-bird millionaire enthusiasts. Since he also had a pro shop, he occasionally drove into the Loop for supplies.

That's how he happened to turn up at the club. He parked his new Plymouth in the lot beside the Three Deuces and went shopping. Meanwhile, a rainstorm hit and he ducked into the upstairs alcove where he spotted a picture and a sign reading "Anita O'Day—Appearing Nightly." Afterward, he always claimed he immediately fell in love with my photo. He decided to have a beer and check me out. Believe it or not, the double whammy was that as he came down the stairs, I was singing "My Heart Belongs To Daddy".

Carl didn't make any attempt to meet me, but he stayed until almost closing time. The next day he called his best friend, Ray Forman, and asked Ray to come to see the girl Carl said he was going to marry. That night they came into the club and when I appeared, Carl nudged Ray. "That's her."

I finished my set and went to the Three Deuces. Ray was puzzled that I hadn't come over to the table.

"Aren't you going to introduce me?" he asked.

"I can't," Carl admitted. "I haven't met her yet myself."

But he never doubted he would eventually marry me. In spite of his 6:00 A.M. work schedule, Carl began driving to the Loop and coming into the Off-Beat for an hour or two a night. But I didn't pay much attention. Everywhere I worked people turned up who followed me around.

Carl was about five feet eight, trim, athletic, with blue eyes and sandy hair. Doesn't he sound like my type?

Well, he seemed like a man from Mars to me. He came from a typical middle-class family. His father was a CPA and Carl had had an education. He had what, for the time, was a middle-class attitude toward women; he idealized them. Didn't drink, except a beer or two. Didn't smoke. Tea? He only knew about the kind you brewed. Grass? That was a covering for the golf course. Does he sound a little square for hip-flip me? Not to me, he didn't. Maybe I was ready for that kind of guy after the wheeler-dealers I'd met in the Walkathons and in the Uptown district.

Instead of hanging out in taverns, he golfed with millionaires every day. He had good manners, could talk with anyone. Who cared if he wasn't a musician? At least he liked jazz and was making ten or twelve grand in seven months—pure money because he had no living expenses. It felt nice to know somebody who was a solid citizen.

Pretty soon he began staying at the club until I got off work so he could drive me home. He raved about my voice, my long legs, my slim waistline and my big boobs. It was obvious what was on his mind.

"Flattery will get you anywhere but *there*," I told him.

But he was a gentleman! He waited three weeks before asking, "May I kiss you good night?"

There were a couple of steps behind me. To cool him down psychologically, I moved to the upper one so that I was a little above him. "Okay, you can kiss me good night."

He took me in his arms and gave me a very brief, warm, tender kiss which seemed to make him very happy. It also made me happy. Then he sped off into the night.

On his day off, he'd come by in the afternoon and we'd sometimes hang out at a place across from the Chelsea. He'd have a beer and I'd have a rum and coke and we'd play the juke box, especially Harry James' "Ciribiribin" and Benny Goodman's and

Martha Tilton's "And the Angels Sing." I never did "And the Angels Sing" because to me Martha had made that tune her personal property.

Other times Carl would take me to Riverview Amusement Park and goof around. Best of all was when we'd go to the Biltmore in Barrington. He lived at the club and had a terrific phonograph and all the new records, especially jazz.

When the weather got warm, he taught me to play golf. I was athletically oriented, agile, but I didn't know anything about hitting the ball, so I started with 10 or 12 strokes a hole, shooting 180 or 190. But Carl was such a kindly, patient teacher that by the end of the summer I was shooting under 90. He told me I could become a terrific golfer if I really got involved—and I loved hearing it.

(I'm getting ahead of myself, but the next season, even though we weren't married, we played in the Mr. and Mrs. Open for a couple of weeks. Carl regularly shot 64 at the Biltmore, which got the buck, but his 71 on a strange course didn't get it and my upper 90s was laughable. Still, it was fun to hang out with the country club crowd.)

To backtrack, by the time in late May when the heat caused Carl Cons to close the Off-Beat Club, Carl Hoff was in love and urging me to marry him. Reminded I was already married, he bugged me to go to New York to find out where I stood with Don. I didn't have the money, so, as I recall, he helped me raise some cash for the trip.

On the train to New York, I didn't sleep at all. All I could think of was Don versus Carl. I made lists in my mind, cataloging their good points. Carl won. I cataloged their faults. Don won. But I felt happier than I had in months and I couldn't deny it was because I was going to be with Don again.

When I reached the Hickory House where he was appearing, I was so exhilarated I could hardly control my legs. Just being there excited me and looking forward to seeing Don doubled the excitement. When I spotted him behind the drums, he was more than handsome. He was pretty. I couldn't wait for the set to finish. For once, I didn't concentrate on the music. Don was all there was room for in my mind.

The group finished the set and I rushed over and threw my arms around him as he came off the stand. I could feel him tense and pull away ever so slightly. At that moment I began to be sorry I'd come. He didn't even give me his special, impersonal forehead smooch. I could have been a stranger.

"How'd you get here?"

"Hitchhiked," I teased.

He looked shocked.

"The train, you idiot. You didn't send me the fare so I came on my own."

"Where are you staying?"

"With you."

I couldn't resist tormenting him a little. He looked so uneasy, I laughed.

"Don't worry. I've got a hotel room."

"Good." He relaxed a little. "We can get together tomorrow." With that, he just more or less walked away.

"Hey," I said, "I made a long trip here. You're my husband, remember? We're partners, aren't we?"

He didn't answer.

"Come over to my hotel after your gig."

"I can't. I have to get home."

It reminded me of the days when I'd first known him and he was always running off the minute the last note was hit at the Vialago. But he gave me the address and told me to come to breakfast the next morning.

"I want to talk to you alone."

"We'll do that at the apartment."

Next morning I went to the Carters, knowing in my heart the marriage was over. They lived in a brownstone where they had a floor-through apartment. A strange, elderly man answered the door and motioned toward the living room without saying a word. I wondered if Mrs. Carter had remarried.

Don and his mother were in there.

"Who was that that answered the door?"

Mrs. Carter was icy as ever, explaining it was their roomer.

"My replacement?" I asked lightly.

Nobody smiled.

There was nothing left for me to say or do—except thanks for everything. Don had helped me musically and, in spite of what he was doing now, my heart went out to him. I didn't even bring up the possibility of our getting together again. Or even seeing one another alone. I didn't cry. When there's nothing left, there's no use crying.

Fluffed off by Don, I got right onto the next train and headed for Chicago late that afternoon. I was now more confused than ever. My partnership with Don, which I'd always counted on, was out the window and even though I had a slightly empty feeling, a few belts from the brandy flask in my purse put me into an up tempo mood as I began to think of Carl.

Carl could now be considered without the shadow of Don falling between him and me. Here was a cat with class. When I couldn't make up my mind whether I loved him or not, he'd hung in there. "Take your time," he'd said at first. "Take your time," he'd repeated coolly, long after most cats I knew would have backed off.

Who else had liked me just because I was me? Dad had never stuck around to assume any responsibilities. And even if Mom loved me, she made it seem like a duty. When I got hung up on Don, all the moves had been up to me.

Looking back, I didn't regret the relationship with Don. I was into music and he was like a mountain peak among people around the Uptown tavern scene. It was easy to see why I'd flipped over him. But why had he gone along with it? Because, I finally admitted to myself, in his spaced-out world, a kid—which was what I was—with a kid's minimal demands—which were what mine were—was all he was prepared to handle. Don couldn't have cut it if I'd insisted on more than a musical partnership. And I'd been idealistic enough to think that we'd work together and develop together and then eventually—presto! change!—we'd be in love the way other couples were. Presto change! When that time came, he cut out with his mother and I'd been klutz enough to believe that he was going to send for me once they got set in New York.

Okay, so Don was out and over. Instead of torching for him, I took another hit off the flask in my purse.

When I got back to Chicago, Carl would be waiting. There was no doubt how he felt about me. Why hadn't I seen it from the beginning? So he wasn't a musician? So what? The more drinks I had the less important that seemed.

What was so great about music? And what was so bad about the country club scene? From the time we'd met, he'd helped smarten me up. Coming from a blue-collar, low-income, one-room-and-kitchenette background, what chance had I had to know there was something else?

Carl had loved introducing me to big-name stores and restaurants and he'd taken me out to the Biltmore in Barrington where nobody talked like a page out of *Down Beat*. When I came on with my hip chick lingo or made a social boo-boo, he took it in stride. Sometimes he thought it was funny. Sometimes he gently and privately corrected my grammar and manners.

What would be so bad about having a husband who made more than ten grand a year? I wasn't into show business to make a million or become a big star. I wanted to be song stylist, an artist. Couldn't I just do that for Carl and myself? The rest of the time I could learn to cook and keep house, be his wife and play golf—he thought I had the potential to be a super golfer. Who said I had to go on working and waiting to hear from Krupa?

As the train rushed on through the darkness and the lights in the coach were turned off so people could sleep, I sat there dreaming about the wonderful life Carl and I were going to enjoy together. Even if he wasn't a musician, he followed music. And he was a good man. I felt waves of love for him and his goodness, his consideration and sacrifices. There was no reason in the world for me not to marry him.

Throughout the twenty-two-hour train trip, I was on cloud nine, thinking of Carl and me, looking forward to what our life would be. I'd boarded the train in New York, my emotions a shambles, my ego lower than a fallen arch, and here I was, on top of the world. I wanted to wake everybody in the coach and shout, "I'm in love again."

Instead, I unscrewed the cap of the bottle and had another hit off my brandy.

Came the dawn, as they used to say in silent movies, and as I began to sober up, everything wasn't so simple. Had I really felt this way about Carl all along or was I grasping at him on the rebound? Sure, it would be great for me if I got a divorce and married him. But as long as there had been a ray of hope with Don, I'd never for a moment considered it. I knew that even if I leveled with Carl about this, his ego would cause him to think that once we were married, I'd completely forget Don.

So, instead of going back to the Chelsea and calling Carl, I moved in with Mom and Aunt Belle. Carl, I told myself, would have every right to press me about marriage now. I wasn't sure I wanted to be married to anybody.

That's when I started going around with a different crowd, playing a different game. Up to that point, I hadn't thought much about how most people in the world I was living in were going to bed with anyone who appealed to them. My mother and I had never discussed sex. Whatever I'd picked up came from overhearing people around me talking. I was curious, but I didn't ask questions because I didn't want anybody to know how naive I was. Anyway, I didn't think about it much. In the Walkathons and during the tavern scene, I'd guarded my virginity as if it were eighteen-karat gold.

Now I was in a different frame of mind. I felt I was old enough to check out this thing called sex. Not with Don or Carl or anybody who was in love with me, but just somebody I dug. No strings attached.

One night I was in the Chelsea bar when this attractive blond, blue-eyed fellow came in. Somebody said, "Anita, you know Earl Nutter."

Earl said, "Hi, Anita. How you doing?" or something equally memorable. I don't know what I said, but when I saw him, my heart went flutter. Flutter rhymes with Nutter. Immediately, I knew what I had in mind.

He began coming on to me. We had a few drinks and talked music. He was a trumpet player. Good. I'd always been strange for horn men. He had a big collection of *old* Louis Armstrong 78 rpm records in his room. I didn't wait for him to make the suggestion. I said, "Why don't we go listen to a few?"

The room was very small and his phonograph was very small, but he had a lot of recordings. The only place to sit was on the bed. We sat there drinking and I kept thinking how much he looked like my very favorite movie star, Gene Raymond.

Well, music will take over. He made his move and I was receptive. I wish I could tell you that that first time I saw roman candles,

84

shooting stars and that the earth moved. Not so. But when anyone has asked me, I've always said that I lost my virginity to the accompaniment of Satchmo's raunchy horn playing.

Now the second time—well, that was different. I wasn't in love with Nutter. It was just the best kind of an affair because I was so strongly attracted to him physically and he was a master of the game.

By the third time, I began looking forward to meeting him after work every night. We'd climb the steps of the elevated, our arms around one another's waists, snuggle together on the elevated train to Wilson Avenue and go to the Chelsea bar for a quick drink. We'd say hello to other musicians and then rush to his room.

There our lust was played out to the accompaniment of Louis Armstrong, backed by the terrible musicians he invariably chose to work with. But it was neither his trumpet nor the inept backing that fascinated me. What fascinated me was Satchmo's singing. *That* was inspiring. His timing was impeccable. He phrased in unexpected ways. Most interesting to me was that he had no tone at all. That was encouraging to a girl who had lost her uvula at seven. In Nutter's room at the Chelsea every night, I learned almost as much about song styling from Satchmo as I did about sexual ecstasy from Nutter.

Earl was a player who'd been out there a lot, I found out later. I guess the girls he went around with didn't need to be told about contraception. Soon it was too late. I was pregnant.

I may have been dumb enough to get pregnant, but I wasn't goofy enough to think Nutter would want to hear that I was. So I never told him. Or maybe I was afraid he'd do the honorable thing. Guys sometimes still subscribed to the old code in 1939. Truthfully, when I found out that I was pregnant, I couldn't bear the thought of having him around me. So I told him I was beginning to get hung up on him and it would be better if we didn't see one another for a while. (We didn't. He didn't come around again until I was doing the *Anita* album with Buddy Bregman in December 1955.)

My problem was to find an abortionist. It was no great moral crisis with me any more than if I'd used some kind of birth control. There was no peer disapproval. Girls I'd been working with were always getting abortions so there was no disgrace connected with it. Also, I didn't, and don't, believe that the baby has a soul of its own until the umbilical cord is cut and the baby breathes on its own.

So I started inquiring. One of my girl friends knew about a dumb place upstairs on the West Side where this midwife did an unusual type of abortion for five bucks. She worked in this old tenement on the fifth floor back. There was no furniture except a couple of tables and some basins. The midwife, whatever, was a human icicle, but for five dollars, what can you expect?

The old woman washed up and told me to undress and get on the table. She warned me I'd feel some pain because as soon as she finished, I had to leave. So no anesthetic was possible.

The procedure was to insert chemical-soaked cotton packs in my vagina and leave them for a couple of days. How I made it out of that office and back to Mom's apartment, I'll never know. But when I got home, I just crawled into bed and stayed there. Aunt Belle didn't bother me the first day, but the second day Mom didn't go to work so she was around the apartment and she was more curious than Aunt Belle. I told her I had cramps, which was true. Cramps and spasms. I'd get them and then they'd go away and then come back again. Something like mild labor pains, I guess. I'd imagine the process must have been something like having a baby with induced labor, only in the most unnatural way.

I became frightened. Not only that Mom would find out, but also for myself. Finally, when I could hide my fear and pain no longer, I did a very strange thing for me. I confided to Mom what was going on. I don't know what her first response was because I passed out, but when I came to, Mom was holding this little thing up to the light, studying it. I freaked out. I screamed for her to take it out of my sight and she scrambled out of there. I do remember Mom said later the fetus wasn't far enough developed to tell what sex it was.

Surprisingly, Mom didn't hassle me about what I'd done. She played it very cool and mumbled something about my being supposed to have had a brother, but . . . .

In other words, she'd done something similar at some time. Whether she told Aunt Belle or not, I don't know, but afterward, the episode was never mentioned by either of them. I lay around, weak and depressed and scared, for several days. That's when I made up my mind to stop playing around.

CHAPTER V
OH, FOR THE LIFE OF A GIRL SINGER

I'd stuck to my resolution not to call Carl. The way I was feeling, I'd end up hurting him or myself. So I played it cool. Then I got a gig at the Bar of Music on Howard Street, the dividing line between Chicago and Evanston. Evanston is the home of Northwestern University and the Woman's Christian Temperance Union. Because the WCTU has kept Evanston dry, all kinds of spots catering to college kids had sprung up along Howard Street. The collegians had ears for musical experimentation and I loved working to them. Business was so good at the Bar of Music that the management advertised regularly in the Chicago papers.

Naturally, Carl saw my billing the Sunday before I opened and he was on hand for opening night. I had no idea what he'd say about the fact that I hadn't gotten in touch with him, but Carl was one cool alligator. I told him a lot of things had changed. I started to tell him about Nutter, but he stopped me, didn't want to know about it. I also said I had to have time to sort out my feelings. He thought that was reasonable but showed every sign that he was going to pursue me until I agreed to marry him.

He almost got lucky. The relationship might have faded shortly after that if my first engagement as a big band singer had worked out and I'd gone on the road. The way things came down, I got word that Raymond Scott and "His Superb Orchestra," as it was modestly billed, was auditioning girl singers at the Sherman Hotel and someone had recommended he check me out.

So I got myself all gussied up for the occasion and went to the hotel to meet Scott. Instead, I was ushered into a room containing nothing but a piano and a lot of electrical transmitting equipment. Scott, I learned, was ensconced in his private suite, having the voices of all the would-be vocalists piped in to him. That way he felt he wouldn't be swayed by visual appeal. Great! I believe what you hear is more important than what you see, too.

Apparently Scott dug the sounds I sent out because shortly after, I got a call to join the band immediately.

Ray Scott had had great success as an arranger and the leader of a sextet on CBS radio before he decided to take to the road with a big band. And even though he was now out there before the public, he still carried a studio musician's attitude with him. Of course, he wrote his own arrangements and you were expected to blow it exactly as he'd put it down. He was a martinet, a perfectionist, a hard man to feel any warmth toward. His whole approach produced perfection without feeling. Even though he hired good musicians, his attitude soon reduced them to something like wind-up toys who did everything the same way night after night. The result? Tedium. Perfection can be boring too, you know.

When I turned up, Scott was impatient when he found I didn't sing most songs in the key they were written in. But, in going through his book of arrangements, we found "Blue Skies" and another standard I knew.

Naturally, I'd rather have sung with a swing band, but I was just a neophyte and happiness to me had always been singing, so I was giving it my all. Scott was a name band and I planned to stay until Krupa made good on his offer.

My opening gig was a three-day engagement, four shows a day, at the Orpheum Theater in Madison, Wisconsin. I wasn't feeling too secure and Scott's unyielding attitude didn't give me much support, but still I enjoyed playing to thousands of enthusiastic people each day.

After the last show the second day, Scott thrust a piece of music in my hand.

"This is your key," he said. "How fast can you learn it?"

I told him that depended on how the situation fell. If I got inspired, I could learn a song in a few minutes. But sometimes I couldn't ever catch it.

"We'll do this the last show tomorrow night," he said and walked abruptly away.

I looked at the arrangement and thought, "Yeah, this is a cute novelty." I read it through several times and took it to bed with me. Then I worked on it during breakfast and got to the theater early so the pianist could play it for me. In my dressing room, I worked some more.

By the last show the final night in Madison, I felt fairly confident I could do it. I heard Scott say, "Here's a new novelty that just came out and Anita O'Day's going to sing it for us. Here she is!"

There was a ten- or twelve-bar intro. I counted the bars as I took my place at the microphone and opened up and, could you believe, I couldn't remember another word? Not one! I scatted the first chorus, danced the next two and came back with:

Wah-da-da-da-big-a-doo-doo
Da-da-do-dee-bang!

and made my exit.

I thought I'd covered very nicely and the audience was going wild, yelling for more. I took an extra bow. I was sorry I'd muffed the words, but felt, everything considered, I'd carried it off okay. I could cut it the next time Scott called it.

When the show ended, one of the guys said Scott wanted to see me. I went toward his dressing room, expecting a compliment on how I'd handled a tricky situation or at least a little reassurance. I knocked on his door and he called for me to come in.

"Hi, Mr. Scott. I'm sorry—"

The sight of his face, distorted with rage, stopped me mid-sentence.

"What were you doing out there tonight?" he snarled. "I hired a vocalist. You give me a lot of gibberish and a dance."

"Mr. Scott—"

"You're not working some Chicago dive now. Pick up your check and get out!"

I couldn't believe it. We'd never really got anything together.

So whenever people ask how many big bands I was with, I say four and a half. Guess who's the half.

Carl called the theater just after I left so when I got to Mom's, he was there waiting. After he heard about the Scott fiasco, he asked how a Florida vacation sounded. A fellow from the Biltmore, an heir to the Jewel Tea fortune, aspired to be an amateur golfer. He'd invited Carl to drive to Miami in his new Mercury. Since Mr. Jewel Tea was taking along his wife or girl friend—I don't recall their legal status—Carl called Mr. JT, told him about my bum luck and this cat suggested Carl invite me, too.

It sounded sensational. I'd never been to Florida. The four of us set out, looking forward to a nice, relaxed trip. JT received a monthly stipend of some kind and he assured us he would take care of everyone in high style.

The trip down was a gas. We ate and drank and stopped at all the posh places and JT grabbed the tab. "Not to worry," he'd say, or, "My pleasure," as he picked up checks. Finally I was living the way I'd always dreamed of.

JT found a lovely old Florida stucco house off Biscayne Boulevard at about Sixty-third Street in Miami proper. The four of us had settled in for a relaxed winter with no worries when JT put in a duty call to his mother. That turned our dream vacation into a nightmare. His mother cut off all funds and we were practically penniless. (I guess it must have been JT's girl friend who was with us. If it had been his wife, his mother would hardly have cut off his allowance. Unless, of course, she was another Mrs. Carter.)

Carl and I thought the situation was hilarious for about ten minutes, then we realized the gorgeous, fully furnished house we'd rented had a bare cupboard.

"No big deal," I said. I was used to being broke. "We'll get jobs."

"Me?" said JT. "I don't know how to do anything."

"Me either," said his girl.

"You don't work," he announced.

"You can," I told him. "You can bus dishes at a cafeteria. You don't have to be an expert for that."

"Me?" he howled. "I'm too uncoordinated."

Carl said that since JT had provided the transportation and the house, he'd get a job.

"Great. What will a golf pro pull down a week down here?" I asked.

"Honey, I'm a golf pro in Barrington. In Miami Beach, I'm an auditor. I know how to keep books and one of the guys at the Biltmore has hotel interests here. I'll call him."

He did and the member got him on as night auditor at the Nautilus which was then one of Miami Beach's poshest hotels.

"I'll get a gig," I volunteered. "There are plenty of spots."

"And I'll be your manager," Carl said. "It's not dignified for a girl formerly first-featured with, quote, Raymond Scott and His Superb Orchestra, unquote, to go from *boîte* to *boîte* hunting a job. I'll book you."

He grabbed the phone directory and began studying clubs. I threw him the amusement section of the paper.

"Call me if you get me into the Five O'Clock Club," I said. "I'm going out back to pick some grapefruit and some coconuts from the trees in front. At least we won't starve."

We practically lived on them until Ray Forman, who was in Miami working as an exercise boy at the track, came around with some hungry friends who wiped out the remaining grapefruit in one afternoon.

Luckily, one of Ray's pals knew the owner of a joint near the Five O'Clock Club who was looking for a group. This dude told us he'd try to get us in if I could line up a small combo.

Next morning, Carl drove me downtown where Ray Singer, president of the musician's union, gave me a line on four journeymen musicians who were as hungry as I was. We worked up a few numbers. Carl came up with the name "Four Knights and O'Day" and we went out to audition. That's how I landed at the El Chico. Considering the circumstances, we weren't half bad.

Since Carl and I worked nights, we were free to spend our days on the beach with JT and his chick. It was as carefree a time as I'd ever had. Carl couldn't have been more attentive and I worked up new numbers while dreaming of getting a smooth, dark tan to cover my freckles. Instead, the sun brought out the freckles until I looked like a spotted leopard. Even so, life was so idyllic I began wondering whether I really wouldn't prefer being Carl's wife and living it up with the country club crowd instead of working with Krupa.

That question was quickly answered when I read in *Down Beat* that Irene Daye was quitting Krupa late in January 1940 to marry Jimmy Blake, one of Tommy Dorsey's trumpeters. To me that meant one thing: Krupa would be phoning. At last all those daydreams I'd had since that night at the Off-Beat were about to become a reality. I was going to get my chance to do my stuff with a really swinging outfit. I'd been fooling myself to think there was any question of choice. Whatever heaven is, it can't be any more blissful than the future I looked forward to as Krupa's canary.

When we got back to Chicago, Carl and I took a one-room apartment at the Chelsea, taking our meals in the coffee shop. After all, it would only be a matter of days, or weeks at most, until the call to replace Irene Daye.

A month passed and still no word. My relationship with Carl swung from highs to lows. We were either way up in the ether or way down in the pits. In addition to our contrasting temperaments, the apartment was so small we were always stepping out of each other's way.

Since there was no word from Krupa, we decided to do a very daring thing for 1940—take an apartment together. Living together is so common now, even a president's children can do it, but it was a bold move back then. Anyway, we rented a big, furnished apartment on Bryn Mawr: large living room, bedroom, dining area, kitchenette and bath. And what a difference a little space makes. Our relationship was still stormy, but if I didn't feel like living Carl's well-ordered, neatly scheduled life, I could go off by myself without bothering him.

But whether we were at the Chelsea or in my apartment, there was a lot of friction because Carl had begun offering advice on the best way to build my career. I was a swing singer and an uncompromising one. Carl thought I ought to take a more "professional attitude," which translated into "Go the way the money is best." If the call didn't come from Krupa, then I should tie up with one of the sweet bands. He couldn't understand that I didn't worship money. (I didn't know then that it is a monetary world.) He'd been making ten and twelve thousand dollars for each term at the Biltmore and he thought everyone was into money. Much as he liked jazz, he couldn't understand that artistic fulfillment with an obscure jazz group was more important to me than singing with a

Mickey Mouse band for a lot of bread. It was one of those arguments which nobody wins.

Months went by. Carl returned to the Biltmore and I spent a lot of time in Barrington with him when I didn't have a gig at some small club. Cold weather arrived and Carl moved back to Chicago with me. I'd just about decided I'd better give up waiting and pursue some other big band leaders when Krupa's manager, Frank Verniere, located me with great news. Irene Daye was marrying not Jimmy Blake but Corky Cornelius, and they were joining the Casa Loma Orchestra following Gene's February 1941 date at the Chicago Theater.

I was in the clouds *and* the depths. I'd missed my period and had begun getting morning sickness. How unlucky could I be? My feelings toward Carl had deepened. If he wasn't exactly my white knight, he was kind, sweet and thoughtful. He worshiped and waited on me, even rinsing out my panties and knee socks before retiring. He had made himself a part of my life. When I told him about the call from Verniere, Carl danced me around the room, whooping with joy. Then I had to spoil the moment by telling him I was pregnant.

"God, Anita!" Carl was suddenly glum. He assured me he wanted to marry me. He'd love to have a child, but he knew what this gig with Krupa could mean to me. He felt I deserved the opportunity to become what we both felt I was capable of becoming. Because of an "accident," he didn't believe I should be burdened with a child. We were hardly in our twenties. There would be plenty of time to start a family later. He couldn't let me pass up what I'd waited so long to get and then would resent him for later.

I started to cry. It was the first time I could remember anyone considering what I'd feel. He must really love me.

"Listen, this is a time for celebrating. Let's go out on the town," he urged. "We'll manage to take care of your problem tomorrow."

The Wilson Avenue scene had been going on for a long time and if you had the connections, you could get whatever you wanted there. I inquired among some girl friends and found another midwife—a fifteen dollar one.

Carl was scared, but he stood behind me and I kept telling

myself that the way I'd been raised, I should never take responsibility for another life. There were too many children on earth who hadn't been given a chance already. Why should I add another? So Carl drove me to within half a block of the address and waited in the car, just as he'd been told to do.

The building was similar to the first one, but this time the apartment was only three flights up. The midwife had dyed blond hair capping an angelic face, but when she opened her tight little mouth, she spewed venom. Once she got my fifteen dollars, she ushered me into another of those bare rooms with only a table, some pans and a sink. While she washed up, she indicated I was to undress and climb on the table. The next thing I knew she was inserting this clamp. I moaned softly. She started scraping and I let out a loud yelp.

"Any more of that, you can dress and take your problem with you," she said. "You want to stir up the neighbors?"

I promised to be quiet, but as she went about her work, a low moan escaped in spite of myself. She looked up and said, "Well, you got it in you, honey. It's gonna hurt to get it out."

After that I bit on my handkerchief. I didn't want to do anything to stir up any more philosophizing. These old women, in their dumb walk-up apartments, performing their services without anesthetics, were the only places most girls had to turn to in 1941. In those days, reputable doctors wouldn't consider involving themselves in such an operation on any single or most married women. Even though things still aren't as relaxed as they should be, it is hard to remember what a poor female who got pregnant had to go through to correct her carelessness back in the 1940s. Anyone lucky enough to find even a doctor who'd lost his license to practice had to have more bread than most of us girls could raise. Luckily, this pregnancy was caught before the placenta was formed so that only a curettement was necessary.

After a couple of days, I felt well enough to leave the apartment and Carl took me to the Chicago Theater to see and hear Krupa's organization. My head was jammed with the wildest kind of dreams about the future as we sat there; I didn't even know what the film was. Soon I'd be criss-crossing the country, playing ballrooms and theaters, doing radio remotes and making records. It looked as if Jesus was really going to make good on the wish He'd granted that lonely dawn in Springfield, Missouri.

Gene had made a splash as Benny Goodman's drummer in the band that inaugurated the Swing Era in 1935 before striking out on his own in 1938. He was a star, whether with Benny or on his own. In forming his band, he wanted the ensemble work Benny had plus arrangements that allowed him and his talented sidemen great freedom. Now, in 1941, Gene was trying to change the band's direction. And who was joining at exactly that moment? Me. That's who.

The end of the picture jolted me back to the theater. I could hardly wait for the stage show to begin. Then the curtains opened and the platform holding the Krupa aggregation moved forward with the spotlight hitting Gene.

Gene was as magnetic as a movie star, filled with wild exuberance as his raven-colored hair, flashing brown eyes and black suit contrasted with the snow-white marine pearl drums that surrounded him. His gum-chewing, facial gymnastics, tossing of broken sticks to the audience and general flamboyance visually complemented the Krupa sound that incorporated rolls, flams and paradiddles that reverberated throughout the theater.

His was the first big-time band to spotlight the drums in a Balaban-Katz style presentation featuring the drummer. When Gene played "Drum Boogie" or "Drummin' Man," there was no mistaking that he'd incorporated the best of the Chicago drummers (such as Baby Dodds, Chick Webb, Don Carter, dozens of black drummers from the South Side) plus sounds of the Belgian Congo to create the Krupa style. He was loud, but musical. And when, for no good reason, he'd yell, "More pork chops and lyonnaise potatoes," it perfectly complemented what you heard and saw.

I'll never forget the sight and sound of him as sweat popped from his forehead, ran down his face, dripped off the tip of his nose, moistened his flying hair and came through his shirt as his arms flailed in twenty directions to produce different musical sounds. Nobody described it better than Gene who said he was "grunting and sweating like a steel mill."

People who bad-mouthed him as only a showman with a faltering beat were dead wrong most of the time. When he was paying attention to business, he had a driving beat that propelled the band.

As the featured musicians took their solos, I flipped at the idea I was soon to join them. Now, most big bands owed their success to some black arranger or arrangers. Benny Goodman had Fletcher Henderson. Gene had several. The most talented, as far as I was concerned, was Elton Hill. Little chills ran up the back of my neck as I realized he'd be writing charts for me.

Irene Daye was a good singer, but secretly I always *knew* there was a different kind of contribution for me to make. She was a singer. I was a song stylist. As I listened, I realized I didn't have her range. She sang the songs in the keys they were written, while I was a fourth down or a fifth up—whatever.

But sitting there in the Chicago Theater, riding my musical high, I felt certain Elton Hill was already working on two or three arrangements to get me through the first few weeks on the band. I'd heard Gene was making changes, trying to improve the band's quality. He knew that some of the cats didn't read too well, that often the band played out of tune, and that a lot of the time it just didn't swing. I guess he wasn't sure why these things were true.

If he'd asked me, I'd have told him the key to his problems probably lay in what happened when Carl and I went backstage after the performance in Chicago. Gene and Frank Verniere weren't into getting me set musically. They didn't know where I was at—after all, it had been almost two years since Gene had caught me at the Off-Beat—but all I did was scat a couple of numbers with the piano player. Gene drummed lightly on the top of the piano and said, "Okay."

I wanted to let his arrangers hear me, but none of them were around and no appointment was set up while I was waiting around Chicago for the theater engagement to end.

What Gene and Verniere were concerned with was settling on a hairdo I could manage for myself on one-nighters and sending me to be fitted for stage costumes—dainty embroidered sweater tops, colorful long skirts and peekaboo sandals. They also wanted to schedule a photographic session for Gene and me with Maurice Seymour, the photographer favored by show business royalty passing through Chicago. Seymour went in for dramatically lit, heavily retouched glamour shots.

When the sitting took place, Seymour posed Gene and me for several of these, then did some shots of me gazing soulfully into the lens of the camera. I did what he ordered, but at the end of the sitting, I suggested a shot of me at the drums and Gene watching.

96

After all, I hadn't been married to Don Carter for nothing. They went for it.

Encouraged, I had the idea of slipping off my sandals and getting on one of the floor tom-toms for an action shot of Gene playing a snare and me clapping out the rhythm. Both Gene and Seymour went for that, too, and the picture captured a fresh playfulness that pleased promoters and newspaper editors everywhere.

I should have realized then that with big bands, business always came first. Then, if there was time, art was taken care of. But I was too starry-eyed to analyze.

Around 11:30 P.M. on February 13, 1941, a friend of Carl's drove him and me up beside the Krupa special bus, which was parked in front of the Capital Lounge next to the Chicago Theater. Carl told him to wait while he got my costumes hung on the rack in the back of the bus along with the band uniforms. My luggage was stashed in the outside compartment.

Carl kissed me tenderly and I got on the bus, really feeling more in love with him now that we were parting than at any time when we'd been living together. I looked outside and there he was, still hanging around, smiling. When he saw me, he blew me a kiss and my heart welled up at what I read as the pride he felt that his chick was the featured female vocalist with one of the most popular bands in the land.

About then, Verniere showed up. He told me Gene was assigned seats one and two. As the only girl on the band, I drew three and four which would give me room to lie down to sleep on long jumps. I told him I didn't play girl-boy, I played human being. If the guys got one seat, that was enough for me.

"Wonderful." Verniere smiled. "That solves a problem."

He went to the door and yelled, "Okay," and a couple of minutes later Carl bounded into the bus, smiling, and everybody was yelling, "Surprise!"

It seems that since Carl was classified 1-A and about to be drafted into the army, out of the goodness of his heart, Gene had okayed Carl's traveling with us so he could be with me until his "Greetings" from Uncle Sam arrived. So I spent my first night with the band snuggled in Carl's arms.

And it was some night. When it came time for the bus to pull out, everybody started shouting, "Murph's not here," "Where's Murph?" "Anybody seen Murph?"—whatever. Norman Murphy, a trumpet player, was missing, so the driver shut off the motor and the band boy ran back to the hotel looking for the missing trumpet player. Half an hour later, he came trudging down Randolph Street carrying Murph over his shoulder, passed out drunk. The guys threw Murph on the back seat, piled the drums around him and we finally took off.

I was very glad Carl was there. Howard Dulany, who sang the ballads, got drunk on beer, and his cocker spaniel, Jerk, got unruly when Shorty Sherock, high on grass, and Dave Wagner, who was drunk, decided to play bear and wolf. Shorty, the wolf, would stand with his feet on the arms of two seats, straddling the aisle, and leap at the bear, attempting to knock him over. When the wolf failed, the bear would hurl him back down the aisle. It was bedlam.

After I'd looked over Irene Daye's charts to check out which ones I could use, I gave Gene the bad news that there wasn't anything except—just possibly—"Georgia On My Mind."

"What's this 'just possibly'?"

"There are two notes I'm worried about. But if you'll get me a little box to stand on, psychologically that will help me and maybe I can hit them."

From his reaction, I think Gene wondered whether he'd hired a kook, but all he said was, "Sing that until we get new charts. You'll have your box."

"I thought she already had one," one of the drunken cats in the back of the bus yelled. Everybody laughed.

I'd had a few belts myself and I wasn't about to let that pass, so I yelled, "Listen, I've got my tape measure and I'm going to take the measure of every cat on this bus, starting with you! So get unzipped!"

That got a bigger laugh. It was just a joke. After all, I was nestled in Carl's arms. But that's the way stories get started. Over the years, some of the guys insisted I acted out my joke.*

*I'm aware there are a lot of Anita O'Day stories out there, just as there are around any nationally known figure. There are sexual myths about everyone from Marilyn Monroe and Cary Grant to Wallace Beery and Martha Raye. Anyone in public life is fair game for fantasizers, except possibly Shirley Temple and Grandma Moses. And I'm not even sure about them. If some of you are wondering whether I've heard the one about me and every guy in the Kenton band, I have. Pure fantasy.

My first gig with Krupa was at the University of Michigan Jay Hop Ball in the International Building on Valentine's Day, February 14, 1941. I'd played to crowds before, but this was the biggest bunch of healthy, happy-looking alligators I'd ever encountered. Luckily, these were open-minded college kids who were receptive to "experiments." Because my entire repertory that night consisted of "Georgia On My Mind."

While the band played the first set of the evening, I sat uncomfortably at the side of the platform, trying not to wrinkle my skirt. When Gene announced me, I danced to the microphone, stepped onto the little box I'd requested and sang "Georgia." Then I acknowledged the applause and went back to my chair until the first break.

When we came back for the second set, I sat there until Gene announced me. Again I danced over to the mike, mounted the box and gave out with "Georgia." I did that same song three times that night and I never did sing it the same way twice.

Having Carl along these first few weeks eased the transition from singing in joints to being the center attraction of thousands of eyes when I took solo spots with a nationally famous band. Whenever I ran up against a situation that made me uneasy, Carl was there to guide me through it. He also kept me from getting lonely. And from the enthusiastic way he took to the business, coming up with some good ideas, I began to think that maybe it didn't have to be a choice between him and my career. It seemed possible that the chitchat he'd developed as a golf pro would serve him just as well in music management. So when he was finally drafted into the Army, I felt a fierce loneliness that made me keep myself half bombed most of the time.

Luckily, Gene was leading the band. He came from a background a lot like mine, a rough Polish neighborhood in Chicago. My dad was absent while I was growing up; his died when Gene was very small. With nine kids to support, Gene's mother had little time to pay attention to him. He was a poor student just as I was. *But* he had an older brother who took a job in a music store. Not that he was interested. It just happened to be the only place that would hire him. When Gene was old enough, his brother got him on part-time. Gene dug music. So he cased the cornets, saxophones, you name it. Drums happened to be the cheapest instru-

99

ment he could find. Gene saved until he got together sixteen bucks and bought himself a drum.

Grandma, on my father's side, saw to it I got religious grounding. Gene's mom wanted him to be a priest, but he was more interested in hanging around outside ballrooms listening to the music, digging the drummers. Neither of us had much time for religion until we got in trouble.

The first gigs Gene worked were in rough joints. One place he used to tell about always ended the evening with rival gangs battling each other. That was the way the dance ended. But Gene's flashy style made him such a hero to both of the gang leaders that when Gene was ready to leave he signaled them and a truce would be called. All these battling roughnecks would halt and part like the Red Sea to let Gene get his drums through. Then the melee would begin again.

So Gene didn't have any problems understanding my ways. In 1933 he'd married a telephone operator from the Dixie Hotel on Forty-second Street, when that was still a theatrical center and the Dixie was a glamorous spot. But Ethel, the girl he married, wasn't all that different from a girl from his neighborhood. She really loved him and couldn't believe she'd captured this handsome cat who was obviously headed for the big time.

By 1941 Ethel wasn't around much anymore. Gene had developed a roving eye. Once after Carl left, he even joined me in my extra seat one night. We chitchatted about music and this and that. He began to move in and very casually asked: "How would you like to have breakfast with me?"

"Sorry," I told him. "I never mix business with pleasure."

"Good girl." A few minutes later, he said he guessed he'd try to get some sleep. I never had any more propositions—if it was one—from Gene. I was glad. I liked Ethel.

Not that it would have made that much difference. Gene wasn't handling the temptations that go with success too well. In addition to the girls on the road, he had a little fling with Dinah Shore and then moved into the big leagues with Lana Turner. Dinah chose me as one of her ten favorite singers in a magazine layout. But I never was sure whether she admired my singing or just liked Gene and wanted to help by giving him a little indirect publicity.

Dinah had a nice figure and face that wasn't bad after the

experts got done fooling around with it, but Lana had a dynamite figure and Gene didn't call her "Dreamface" for nothing.

Lana and I were on a first-name basis without really knowing one another. She had to pass my dressing room to get to Gene's. When she'd go by, she'd call out, "Hi, Anita."

"Hi, Lana."

That was it.

She hung out with Gene, not with the hired hands, although she did come to my dressing room one time to ask if she could use my make-up mirror, comb and brush. I didn't ask any questions and she didn't offer any explanations on how she got disheveled.

Eventually, Gene settled $100,000 cash on Ethel in return for a divorce. He wasn't going to mess with any paltry alimony and in 1941 or '42, $100,000 was a sizable sum. Ethel accepted it and quietly faded from the scene. Gene's romance with Lana was in the words of a famous songwriter "too hot not to cool down." She eventually fluffed him off for someone else.

After that Gene drank more heavily and used a little pot, which eventually got him into serious trouble but made him a lot easier to work for.

When I'd been with the band a few weeks, gowns became a problem. Gene didn't supply any new ones. I wasn't making much money, but I picked up an attractive floral print in a thrift shop somewhere. The first night I wore it we played a ballroom that was sweltering and I perspired freely. When I removed the gown after the dance, I discovered why I'd got it so reasonably. I was the tattooed lady. Some defect in the dye caused it to transform me into a walking flower garden. I left the dress behind and decided I had to do something about the situation. What I did changed the fashion for girl singers on the road.

Big-band work is pattern work and Gene was pleased at my ingenuity in keeping within the pattern with my riffs. When he complimented me after a gig later in the week, I got up the courage to ask for special consideration even though I knew in my heart he regarded all girl singers as trinkets to decorate the bandstand. I explained how hard it was to keep the skirts looking fresh. I explained how I'd had to spend time learning how to carry and dance in them, even to sit in them.

"That's a problem all girl singers face," he said.

"But I'm not your ordinary peaches-and-cream band chick," I argued. "I don't come on as a pretty girl in ruffles who flirts. I'm not Balaban-and-Katz time."

"So?"

I warmed to my subject. "I want them to listen to me, not look at me. I want to be treated like another musician. I believe you remember longer and better what you hear than what you see. Agree?"

"Possibly."

"In theaters and hotel ballrooms, I'll wear gowns."

"And the rest of the time?"

"On one-nighters why can't I have a band jacket just like the guys, with a skirt to match and a shirt?"

Gene shrugged. "No reason, I guess."

It was as easy as that. I dodged dresses whenever possible. My uniforms became a kind of trademark and were eventually copied by a lot of band singers on tour. But after I invented the idea of wearing the uniforms, it produced a lot of rumors about my sex life. The story went around that I preferred ladies to men! No way! What does a jacket or shirt have to do with anyone's sex life?

Critics have written that the Krupa band took on a new spirit after Roy "Little Jazz" Eldridge and I joined. That's partly true. But if you want to know the real inside story, this is it.

I'd been on the road about five weeks and a lot of the time the band just was not swinging. Graham Young had come on only a week before I did and he was a little bit disappointed. He thought the trouble was that Gene had got leaderitis. Instead of staying at the drums, he'd turn them over to Graham, who didn't pretend to be much of a drummer, and get out front waving his hands.

Anyway, about my fifth week with Gene we played a Battle of the Bands date against Jimmie Lunceford. It was in Baltimore, I think.

Lunceford's band started and played forty-five minutes or an hour and, man, did they swing! Wow! It was just too much. They must have been out to show Gene, because when it came time for intermission, the first cat to quit was the drummer. He stopped and left the stage and the band went on swinging without him.

Then to rub it in, the bass, the guitar and the piano left the stage and the band still swung. Finally they finished the number and got off. When we took the stand, Gene was still shaking his head and the first tune he called was "Let's Get Away from It All."

That was the turning point. Whenever Graham Young and I meet we recall that night. Before that, Gene had been wanting to hire Roy Eldridge as first trumpet. But whoever was advising him gave Gene the word that it would be too controversial, because those were the days of strict segregation. Gene's advisors were worried about their ability to book an integrated band. This was not unusual. In those days there was not a white band that had a regular black member in it. Benny Goodman had Lionel Hampton and Teddy Wilson, but they didn't sit in the band. They came out as soloists or with the quartet or sextet. Teddy Wilson played piano, but Benny also had Jess Stacy or whoever. Teddy Wilson was not the band piano player.

Well, after Jimmie Lunceford drove us into the ground, I suppose Gene figured we needed all the help we could get and to heck with commercial considerations. The band wasn't going to make it commercially unless it could swing anyhow, so Roy joined a few days later.

Before agreeing to take the job, Roy made Gene promise that nobody else would be fired. Roy then accepted a position as featured soloist. In order to give him something to do, Gene took some of Shorty Sherock's solos and had Roy perform them out front. After a couple of weeks of this, Shorty approached Roy and said something like, "Hey, man, what's the idea of taking all my solos?"

Now Roy's never been anybody's Uncle Tom. Ask me and I'll tell you that. So after Shorty gave him a bad time Roy went to Gene and said, "Hey, man,* I'd like to come into the band."

The next day Roy was in the section, but the band still wasn't swinging. But once when Gene went out front to lead, he called out, "Hey, Jazz, get over there and play some drums."

What a wonderful coincidence that Roy's first instrument before he took up the trumpet had been drums. Roy wasn't a technical master of them, but he swung like mad and the band picked

*We all talked like *Down Beat* was written in those days. Remember when articles were continued, the editors asked us to "Modulate to pg oo."

up and sounded better than it had since I'd joined. Gene's eyes got like saucers. His jaw dropped and you could see the transformation take place. From then on, he decided to stay back with the skins and lay down some time. That's when the band caught fire—at that moment—and things began to change.

Arrangements started coming in within a week or two. There was a lot of experimentation. We were playing gigs every night so we could test arrangements to see whether they were going to jell or not before we took them into a recording studio. When you were working every night things happened that weren't written and the arrangements grew. They evolved and when they were ready, we recorded them. Sometimes things never fell into place and the arrangement was taken out of the book. Or, if it was recorded before it was ready, the record was never released.

The nice thing was that although Gene took lots of solos—and the crowd expected it—he left plenty of room for other people to shine. For a while his band became one of the swingingest, best bands of the time.

Reviewers picked up on it and began remarking on the new spirit that I mentioned earlier. One flipped out and called me the new "field general of the organization."*

Another thing that gave us a shot in the arm was that we were booked into the Meadowbrook which gave us nightly live broadcasts and then on April 21 we were to open Gene's first engagement at the famed Café Rouge of the Pennsylvania Hotel in New York.

Gene and Frank Verniere did some thinking too. Ever since Gene had been recording for Okeh, a subsidiary of Columbia Records, he had mostly confined himself to making cover recordings of other bands' hits. This guaranteed a certain medium-sized sale for the Krupa version of Tommy Dorsey's "I'll Never Smile Again" or Glenn Miller's "Moonlight Serenade," but rehashing other leaders' successes didn't inspire Gene's guys.

After Gene noted how well Roy's style and mine complemented one another, he began buying material especially suited to us. On that basis, he decided to go after some hit records on his own.

---

*Of course not everybody dug what I was doing. Barry Ulanov suggested in his *Metronome* review: "Anita O'Day should clear her throat."

I was set for five recording dates beginning March 12, 1941, before we opened at the Meadowbrook and running to June 5. My first recording had "Georgia On My Mind" on one side and on the other "Alreet," a novelty especially suited to my style. But we didn't break completely from the past. Howard Dulany and I sang Helen O'Connell's and Bob Eberly's "Green Eyes" which had been their big hit with Jimmy Dorsey. But the luckiest of the numbers from those first recording sessions was a song picked for me by my old friend Redd Evans, who had left Chicago and was now a New York music publisher. It was a written dialogue between two people and a trumpet. Naturally the trumpeter was Roy.

Redd was chiefly concerned with me. Roy had had plenty of experience. Redd wanted me to make the most of the opportunities provided by Elton Hill's arrangement. To make sure I didn't mess up, Redd came down to teach me how to sing "Let Me Off Uptown."

"Timing's the secret," he said. "It can make it or kill it."

Even though to me Uptown was my old Chicago neighborhood, to most people it meant Harlem. So I asked Waverly Ivy, the black band boy, to take me uptown to Minton's and some other swinging places after we finished work at the Hotel Pennsylvania so I could check out the atmosphere.

Finally, Redd was satisfied with everything about the way I handled the song except my singing of the word *town*. So I went to Miriam Spier, a famous vocal coach, a couple of times.

Ms. Spier showed me how to sing that word, but she wasn't at all impressed. She told me I'd never be a singer. She was right. I'm not a singer. I'm a song stylist. So I never went back to her.

We recorded "Let Me Off Uptown" at Liederkranz Hall in New York on May 8, 1941. Roy was a small, round-faced black man, but he seemed ten feet tall when he took those trumpet solos. "Let Me Off Uptown" was just bits of dialogue over vamping music followed by a chorus, more dialogue and then Roy's spine-tingling trumpet solo. Gene used to tell people that with the arrival of Roy and me he felt the whole band began to find itself and really move. He also said that "Let Me Off Uptown" was the biggest hit he ever had.

It was such a big hit Miriam Spier must have decided she'd taught me how to sing after all because she included my picture on

the dust jacket of her book on learning to sing and even placed an
ad in *Metronome*:

ANITA O'DAY
vocalist with

GENE KRUPA
Studies singing with

Miriam Spier   1307 Sixth Avenue
New York City

With that hit record, it seemed almost everyone's attitude toward me suddenly changed. I had taken a room at the Picadilly
Hotel (you didn't live at the Pennsylvania on $40 a week plus $7.50
a side for recording) and I'd got to know the guys who ran little
music shops along Broadway. They all got behind the record, playing it and recommending it to customers. Roy's name and mine
were both used in "Let Me Off Uptown" so suddenly everybody
was saying, "Hi, Anita." My privacy was gone. I'd go into some
dumb bar, as was my habit, to have a drink, and the first thing I
knew somebody'd spot me and want me to sign a matchbook or a
soggy napkin. I didn't mind. I loved it, gloried in it, basked in it! I'd
achieved my goal. I was entertaining people, making them happier, which was what I'd set out to do.

As Roy and I began working closely together in theaters and
ballrooms the audiences could dig the interaction between us and
they began to make assumptions. Because of our musical rapport
they assumed we were lovers, whatever. That's a dangerous thing
to do. You make your assumptions, you lose your money.

Roy and I were coworkers. I'd been a follower of his sound and
his 4/4 jazz playing since I'd danced to his group at the Three
Deuces while I was in high school. I still admired him. But we were
just musical partners, never lovers.

I did have a tight relationsip with one member of the band, Al
Beck, another trumpeter. We began as drinking buddies and it
developed from there. He was always around backstage. He had a
nice personality. He was short, round, a terrific guy. There was a
song "Mr. Five by Five" (made famous, I believe, by Jimmy Rushing), but I hung it on Al as a commemoration of our relationship. It
got more serious than I intended. That complicated things. Carl

had gone into the service and wound up in Fort Lewis, Washington. He was calling and writing me, bombarding me with plans for the future. He was thrilled by the recordings and the radio remotes. I felt a terrible guilt.

Finally, the band took a break. During my time off, I went to Tacoma, Washington, to meet Carl. I didn't want to go on double-dealing. I knew I had to tell him about Al. Carl had been able to maneuver a four- or five-day pass and had reserved a lovely room at one of the best hotels in Tacoma. In his mind, this was going to be *the big reunion*. Little did he know! I was so driven to confess that I felt ill waiting for him, knowing how crushed he was going to be.

Finally, he arrived with a big bouquet of flowers which made me feel all the worse. We didn't have ten good minutes together. I blurted out my story, told him in fairness to him I didn't think there was any point in continuing our relationship.

He didn't explode. He didn't slap me around. I could have dealt with that. He just looked sad and said that if this was the end of the line there wasn't any point in our spending time together. We weren't at the hotel more than a couple of hours before he was taking me to the railroad station even though I urged him not to. And when we parted, I don't think either of us thought we'd ever see one another again.

I went back to join the band, and except for a note saying that he had been accepted in the Aviation Cadet Program to become a pilot and was being transferred to Santa Ana, California, for preflight training, there was no communication. I felt guilty about what I'd done to him, but I kept telling myself it was best for both of us.

In August when we returned to my hometown to play the Chicago Theater, I was beside myself with excitement. The thrill of actually playing this theater wiped everything else out. To me, as as a kid scuffling around taverns, the Chicago had always represented entertainer's heaven.

Naturally I got royal treatment on home territory. At the risk of sounding like I'm boasting, I have to tell you I was gaining a reputation in music circles as being the best of the young band singers. Newspaper interviews spread that word to nonprofessionals.

People who'd never paid the slightest attention to me tried to get a tight relationship going with me, apparently hoping some of my magic would rub off. On the other hand, Aunt Belle and even Mom read the stories and began treating me different—special. I had to make a real effort to get them to behave naturally. I think that's the first time I realized that fame makes demands as well as bestows gifts.

One person didn't change. That was Dad. One day between shows a guy in the band was taking me over to Marshall Field. His mother clerked there and had volunteered to get me a twenty-percent discount on some decent luggage. The guy and I were just leaving when Dad showed up. Just looking at him, it was clear he'd hit the point where the only way for him to go was up. It broke my heart to see him wearing a threadbare old suit that looked as if he'd slept in it, a blue workman's shirt buttoned at the tieless collar. All I could think of was how dapper he once had been. But then I looked past the effects of constant boozing. I saw that he'd obviously made great effort to pull himself together and he was trying to toe the line, to show some signs of dignity out of respect for me. And I realized that the spark of caring was still there. What did I care what the guy, his mother or anyone else thought? I threw my arms around Dad and invited him along to Field's. He was my dad and—better or worse—I loved him.

Word leaked out that I'd divorced Don Carter and reporters were curious about it. I suppose they thought I'd used him and cast him aside. Naturally my pride wouldn't allow me to tell them the real reason for the split. So I assumed a brittle, hip attitude and told people who inquired, "Well, I'd learned everything about music he could teach me." The quote was picked up by the record reviewer of *Look* magazine and without the background of the "marriage" I don't think it did anything to soften my image as a wild, calculating chick.

While in Chicago, more recording dates were set. Roy and I tried "The Walls Keep Talking" but it didn't really do much for us in comparison to "Let Me Off Uptown."

Leaving Chicago, we set out on a series of one-nighters that would take us to the Hollywood Palladium for a four-week stand.

The band's popularity was growing and so was mine. I could tell that the longer we worked the more the crowds went for my singing style. When I first joined Gene and we'd gone east, I got hardly any requests for autographs. Once, as I was leaving the theater between stage shows in Newark, New Jersey, a teenager asked me to sign my name. I was happy to oblige. I took her book and wrote, "Best Wishes, Anita O'Day." As I handed it to her she smiled and thanked me. I'd taken a few steps when I heard her say, "Aw, she ain't Irene!" and I turned just in time to see her rip out the page, crumple and toss it in the gutter. That didn't happen anymore. Lots of people now wanted me to sign autograph books and recordings.

We completed our tour and settled in at the Hollywood Palladium beginning September 20 and closing October 5, 1941. Then we played the Orpheum in downtown Los Angeles, opening October 28.

I know the *in* thing has always been to put down the Hollywood of the 1940s, but then I've never followed the crowd. On that first visit, and every succeeding one until I finally moved out here, I'd see the sunny skies and pink buildings and think: Ah, Utopia!

On the Coast there were more recording sessions. Gene tried teaming me with Johnny Desmond, who had a real voice, on "Two in Love." The result didn't set the world on fire. Johnny was a good-looking, personable kid, but not exactly the typical Krupa cat. He vocalized before he sang, did things properly and took good care of himself—things I admired but never did. How he came to join Krupa, I never could figure out, because most of us were hard-drinking, high-living cats. Johnny didn't smoke, drink, or do dope and, as far as I know, he was true to the pretty wife he had at home. He was a straight cat in every way. It paid off. He's still out there doing his thing. But come to think of it, I did all the things he didn't do, had a lot of fun and I'm still out there too.

Our trip back east on the train in November 1941 was heavenly compared to the one-night-stand bus trip that took us west. This was the era when jazz and popular music were pretty much the same thing. When they stopped being the same thing is when jazz started taking a commercial nose dive. But this was the apex of swing and jazz.

Gene didn't pay as much money as Glenn Miller and a few others, but being with his band was more fun because he was as excited about what he was doing as the most inexperienced cat in the aggregation.

One of the things he really dug was the music of Frederick Delius. For this trip, he brought a portable phonograph and his Delius records. Coming back from California, he would turn on Delius in the men's lounge. Pretty soon Remo Biondi would show up in with his guitar. Then Sammy Musiker and Graham Young and some other cats would drift in. Pretty soon I'd join them to do a little scatting. All of us were stretching our talents, trying to learn, which was exciting. We entertained ourselves with the thing we worked with—music.

But it wasn't all Delius. We'd try *Body and Soul* in the key of E instead of B-flat. Do that and you produce something very different.

Even before Gene had left Benny Goodman he'd got deeply into the Dennis-Roosevelt Expedition Records. These men had taken early recording equipment with them into the Belgian Congo where they'd recorded the eight-foot-tall Zulus playing their drums. The natives played very intricate rhythms and Gene was fascinated. He began working on arrangements by laying out every part on the floor of his apartment. He assigned one rhythm to the trumpet section, another to the saxophones, etc. When the band began working on the arrangement, each music stand had a tom-tom attached. Every section played a different rhythm on their tom-toms and Gene played counterpoint rhythm to the background. The result was "Blue Rhythm Fantasy," "Jungle Madness" and "Tymp Boogie."*

Most of the trip from California east was spent jamming and I got a natural high. After I joined Krupa I was just out there every day to learn something from every job. I was always happy no matter what the working conditions were because I was performing my song styling. That was my life. Whatever else I did, music was my mission. The other things were relatively unimportant, if not really quite a bore.

*Years later, Ginger Baker did a drum solo for a rock group called Cream. He must have copied it from Gene—consciously or unconsciously—because it was identical to what Gene had done on "Blue Rhythm Fantasy."

By November we were back east playing such places as Cincinnati, Bridgeport, and York, Pennsylvania. I especially remember York because Gene got arrested for disorderly conduct when Bury's Restaurant refused to serve Roy and Waverly Ivy because they were black. Gene made a scene and we all walked out and got on the bus. The management must have called the cops because they arrived and Gene made a big mistake. The police were sympathetic to his stand against discrimination. But when they began hassling the bus driver over some minor infraction, Gene began to burn and out popped, "Let's get on with it!" That turned the cop's attention to him and another beef developed. I can hear the words as clearly as if they were spoken yesterday. Gene said to the officer, "I can buy and sell you." With that the officer hauled him off in a squad car and booked him. In the end he forfeited the ten-dollar bond. The press connected the arrest with the restaurant's discrimination and Gene emerged a hero.

Ironically, the day before this occurred Roy and I had hit the musical jackpot for a second time. The song that did it for us was "Thanks for the Boogie Ride." I don't know what Roy's deal with Gene was, but I received my customary $7.50 per side and Gene earned enough out of Roy's and my two hits to buy a house in Yonkers.

I can just hear you asking, "What was she? Double-dumb?" Maybe. Double-dumb and double-dedicated to doing my thing—entertaining the world.

I wasn't alone. Most girl singers didn't do much better whether working with a sweet or a swing band. There was no union for any of us. Wee Bonnie Baker's "Oh, Johnny," "Billy" and "You'd Be Surprised" made a name band out of Orrin Tucker's Mickey Mouse outfit, but she never got a dime extra for recording. And in 1939, Billie Holiday blasted Artie Shaw in *Down Beat*. "Artie never paid me for that record ('Any Old Time')," she told the interviewer. "Just before it came out, I simply got enough of Artie's snooty, know-it-all mannerisms and his manager's outrageous behavior and left the band. I guess Artie forgot 'Any Old Time.' I know he never paid me.

"With Basie I got seventy dollars a week, with Artie sixty-five dollars. When I make my own records I get one hundred and fifty dollars, that's another reason I left Shaw." That was from Billie at a time when she'd been in show business long enough to be well established while I had yet to win *Down Beat*'s new star poll.

Show business is like a cocoon. Doing a show, packing up, traveling, relaxing with booze or pot, sometimes getting in town just in time to freshen up before doing a gig, sometimes repeating that routine over and over blots out things that ninety-nine percent of the public is involved in. The war in Europe? I didn't read the papers or listen to the radio. It didn't make much of an impression on me. Not as much as the Depression, and the Depression hadn't meant all that much.

Later when people would cut up jackpots about where they were when the news came on December 7, 1941, that the Japanese had bombed Pearl Harbor, I never peeped. I guess I must have been on a bus somewhere in the east. I seldom read the papers in those days and the only news I listened to were bulletins that interrupted band remotes. So what war was going to mean to the band only began getting through to me when guys on the bus began debating whether it was better to wait to be drafted or to volunteer, and I began noticing fellows on the street in sailor, soldier and marine uniforms.

When Frank Verniere started talking about holding the band together as long as possible, worrying about gasoline supplies and the condition of our tires, it began worrying me. But then Gene or somebody got the word we were to keep doing our bit for civilian morale and we'd be told when there was any other way we could serve our country. So I took that to mean I should just concentrate on my job.

New Year's Eve 1941 found the band heading the stage show at the Times Square Paramount with Dinah Shore, the extra added attraction for the public and for Gene as well. The film was *Louisiana Purchase*, starring Bob Hope. We grossed $91,000 the first week, the most taken in by the theater at that point. With grim news from both fronts, people jammed seven and eight shows a day to forget their troubles. And I'm proud to say more than one of the cats in the band came around to tell me that I was just as good at the last show as the first and vice versa. While business didn't hold to the level of the first stanza for the next three weeks, it was good for the entire engagement.

But something not so pleasant was developing. In New York, Roy was really big. I was just the new kid. But he'd go uptown after our last show and everybody loved him. I guess some of them had kind words for me too, because he started watching me when we worked together.

While we were playing different theaters, I'd kept developing my part of the act. What was I to do? Stand there doing nothing? Or the same thing every time? That's not the way I live or think. So I'd embellished my part, thinking I was making something better of the show from the front. It seemed to me that Gene and Roy and I made quite a flashy group, one that audiences went for. But from Roy's point of view I got to dancing too much during "Thanks for the Boogie Ride" and "Let Me Off Uptown." He got upset and ordered me to stop. I couldn't understand his thinking. I was just trying to make my contribution. And I told him so.

One day Roy said to Gene, "Tell the kid to quit upstaging me."

He hadn't spoken directly to me, but I said, "Upstaging you! What are you talking about?"

He didn't answer.

I turned to Gene. "Don't you want me to dance when he plays? I thought I was augmenting. If not, just tell me. I'll sing and walk away or stand there like a wooden dummy."

Gene didn't want that because Roy's trumpet solos and my dancing were important as a front. He wanted to keep Roy and me happy. He couldn't say yes or I'd have stopped and he couldn't say no or Roy would have flipped out. So he talked about the up side and the down side without committing himself. Neither Roy nor I knew where he stood on the problem. Gene was very good at that.

Whatever Roy felt about me offstage, he was too great a pro to let the audience sense it. So they looked and they listened and they watched and they got their own ideas of what was going on between Roy and me.

Roy still kept nagging me to stop upstaging and I kept insisting I was only keeping things moving. We'd argue. He'd get uptight and tell me off. I couldn't understand it. I'd been doing these things before he joined, because Gene sometimes had to be behind the drums, not out front leading. And usually when I'd danced, he'd give me a nod so naturally I thought he liked having me do it.

Roy finally got to the place where he stopped talking to me offstage. I didn't care whether he talked or not. In fact, I was glad. If he was really pissed off, he'd say out of the side of his mouth, after he finished a solo, "See what I'm talking about" or "You're at it again."

During the second week at the Paramount, Roy began saying to Gene after every show, "She's upstaging me!" I insisted I was just trying to dance gracefully and quietly while he played the best trumpet solos in the world.

He wouldn't give in. I wouldn't cave in. It was a standoff between us and Gene couldn't, or wouldn't, take a side. I didn't understand Roy's attitude. I felt if he wanted to be mad at me for adding to the show that was his problem.

When we finally moved to other stands, "Little Jazz" kept complaining. Finally he must have concluded that as far as he was concerned he could do without this person—me—forever and he'd never speak to me again—which he didn't for several years. Not even when we worked together.*

But even when he was angry with me, my admiration for his talents never changed. Once we got on that stage it was a pleasure because he improvised and that's what I did and do. He hadn't studied trumpet and I hadn't studied singing. It should have been a perfect relationship—which it was on stage.

I didn't cry about what was happening offstage even though it gave me the blues. I learned young not to cry. When the woman my mother hired to look after me put me down for my afternoon nap, I used to scream for Mom. But this old bag would say,"Shut up! She'll be here after work. Bellering won't bring her any sooner." So I realized crying never changes things. It just stirs up your emotions more. If it makes you feel good, go ahead and cry, but the only person it will hurt or help is yourself. So I don't do it.

*By the late '50s or early '60s, Roy forgave me. I went into the club where he was working and he came up and said, "I heard you on the radio." I thought he meant a record. "No, a commercial. For Dr. Pepper," he said. "I told my friend, 'That's Anita. Nobody else sings like that.' " He was delighted I had my own sound and he could recognize it just as I can recognize him on any old tune. That recognition is the ultimate respect between our kind of musician.

CHAPTER VI
THE ROAD THAT LEADS TO FAME

What I would wish for everyone is the high I felt in 1941 and 1942, when the Krupa band was swinging and I was wailing my way to the top of the heap as the new star of the year in *Down Beat*'s 1941 poll. Life was good, full of promise in 1942 when the same magazine's top five girl singers were 1) Helen O'Connell, 2) Helen Forrest, 3) Billie Holiday, 4) Anita O'Day, 5) Dinah Shore. During this period Gene had a great band. Maybe the best in the land. Not everybody agreed we were that good, but we thought so and got our highs from the sense of fulfilling what we were put here for.

I was doing my kind of work with my kind of people, because that's what the Krupa band was made up of. And I was into playing "good buddy" instead of "girl singer."

What did that mean? Dressing sensibly and looking after myself. I wore knee-length socks way back then because they were more comfortable for traveling than a garter belt. Besides, silk was scarce and nylon not yet on the market. As for taking care of myself, after a gig there was usually time for a drink or a snack while the instruments were being loaded. I carried my own bags and paid my own checks. Gene used to put me down because of my diet, warning, "You'll never make it, O'Day. You don't eat right."

I was lucky to eat at all. Although my voice was coming out of jukeboxes and radios everywhere and thousands of people were coming to theaters and dances—presumably a certain percentage of them to hear me—I was being paid $40—four o bucks—every seven days. Even then Gene was always hitting me for two-bits for smokes, which was what a package of cigarettes cost then. Nor did he pay me back. But with all the good food, Gene's dead and I'm alive, going stronger than I have in years. So what does that prove?

As I think back, life was divided into the times when we were out there in front of the crowd doing our thing and receiving the love and adulation that helped us to flower. That was the A-side.

The flip side was the endless travel, the consecutive one-nighters spent on the bus, trying to sleep with lights flashing in our faces while being tossed around by the rough roads and the driver's sudden application of the brakes. Constantly tense, unable to relax, we traveled on our nerve.

Booze, grass or pills helped some of us through those nights. I smoked some grass, but I wasn't an every-dayer. It wasn't an issue. I hardly touched pills. If anything, I drank. When one of the boys needed a steadying belt, he knew my purse always contained part of a pint of cognac or Scotch. But booze was no issue either. I was succeeding in my work, and when you're succeeding you feel good about yourself and don't do things that will defeat you. I was trying to do the best I could, to stay up there and do a good show.

We all played it day by day. If we had only a short jump to make, we'd arrive early at the spot where we were appearing. We'd freshen up and walk around town. It kept us from feeling the depth of our loneliness. We'd meet people and often they'd show up at the dance that night.

If the jump was a long one, we slept on the bus and watched scenery or played games, especially poker. I was so good that on a very long trip I ended up $350 ahead. I thought, gee, I hate to see all that money get away at the bar. Because that was my style, to invite everybody to have a drink on me.

This time I spotted a fur sale advertised in the newspaper. I took my winnings and went down and picked out a jacket with twenty-six-inch full-length silver fox pelts. Ecologists hadn't started raising our consciousness yet and every girl singer thought she should have a fur wrap.

Except for the brief fling with Al Beck, I didn't get involved with anyone on the band. I'd thought when I told Carl about Al that day in Tacoma and then cut out that we were finished. Not so. No way were we through with one another. For a while there was silence on his part. Then I got a letter, followed by more letters and finally a phone call.

He was thinking of transferring from the Infantry into the Air Corps, and I think he was lonely and a little shaken up by the idea that he was well into his twenties while all the others were eighteen- and nineteen-year-olds.

I wrote back and I listened and tried to do what I could. Why wouldn't I? Carl had never been anything but a loving, stand-up guy with me so far as I knew. And I didn't blame him or myself for my getting involved with Al Beck. I was young and lonely, like a lot of other girls at the time. The only difference was they wrote their "Dear John" letters. I delivered mine in person.

I was glad to write and talk to Carl. I didn't expect our romance to go anywhere. But I was glad we could at least be friends.

While I was doing all this looking inward, the outward world was changing, fast. Guys would leave the band for some branch of the service. New cats would replace them, and before the new ones settled in *their* replacements had arrived. Johnny Desmond left and Ray Eberle came on briefly. To keep the band functioning, Frank Verniere kept a book filled with names of swing musicians and their instruments for every section of the country. Quality was up, down, up again.

As bus travel got harder to manage, Verniere arranged for us to do our bit by appearing at army, navy, and marine bases. Playing these gigs did something not only for the boys, but it also provided hard-to-find transportation to our next date, usually a week-stand, which allowed our bus driver an opportunity to get the bus worked on. A plane always seemed to be going in our direction and even though the seats were more like benches, it was comfort city to go zooming through the sky instead of bumping along the highway.

Some of the guys weren't crazy about flying. I was, most of the time. But late in 1942, we played some Midwest camp and were due at Sweet's Ballroom in Oakland, California, the next night.

The Army provided a DC-3 for the band and another for the instruments.

The trip began like any other. Some of the guys settled in, reading or trying to sleep. Quite a few of us broke out some whiskey and started a poker game on the floor to break the monotony.

Almost as soon as we were aloft, we hit a snowstorm, but that didn't bother us. The air pockets were a little more disruptive to our game, and we had to keep the bottle caps on because one minute you were okay and the next you'd feel as if both the floor and the pit of your stomach had dropped out.

On these planes they always issued parachutes, but after a few flights we looked on them as a part of the red tape and a lot of us never put them on.

This particular trip, we'd been in the air an hour or so. Buddy Stewart, our boy singer, had gone to the latrine. Suddenly the door leading to the pilot's cabin opened and a young captain came into our section.

I saw from the look on his face that something was up. He said we'd run into a bit of trouble. He didn't want to alarm us, but everyone should get into a parachute. You never saw a poker game break up so fast. I scooped up my money and stuffed the bills in my bra.

The captain explained the de-icers were malfunctioning and ice was forming on the wings. If the buildup continued, we'd have to abandon the plane.

In my anxiety to get ready, I managed to get my parachute upside down or backward. Everybody was yelling at me to get it corrected.

Just then Buddy Stewart emerged from the head, saw the confusion and heard the captain saying that we'd lost contact with the field because our radio had gone dead. Buddy keeled over. Stiff. I mean he didn't even bend when he hit the floor. Gene, who was normally a dark-complected fellow, had turned chalky white and was chug-a-lugging what was left in a bottle of whiskey. A couple of guys were praying.

The captain, who had made a quick trip to controls, returned with more bad news. We were losing altitude.

I piped up to ask, "Is that good or bad?"

Everybody howled except the captain. "A perfectly sensible

question," he said. "If we lose it slowly, the ice may melt enough to break off."

Pushing my luck, I asked, "Are we over land or water?"

His answer made little prickles run up the back of my neck and into my hair. "Land, we think. If we don't get rid of the ice, we have to ditch."

The guy across from me crossed himself. Gene finished his bottle, and poor Buddy Stewart looked as if he was going to pass out again.

Then suddenly the plane broke out of the low-lying clouds. Not more than one or two hundred feet below us was San Francisco Bay. The pilot pulled up fast and the right wing went by something. Close, too close.

"*What* was that?" one of the boys asked.

If I'd known, I couldn't have told him. I couldn't get any sound out.

We bounced around, climbed a little and looked for the airport as the ice disappeared from the wings. Finally the pilot got us onto the ground and I made it to the ladies' latrine before getting airsick. When I came out, the guys were standing around wondering what had happened to their instruments. Frank checked it out and learned the plane carrying them had turned back as soon as its wings had begun to ice up.

We went to the hotel, and I wondered what I was going to do with myself, having a night off in a strange town. I didn't know anybody. I was just about ready to head for the hotel bar and hang one on when there was a knock at my door.

When I opened it, there was this tall, handsome, blue-eyed, blond Air Corps cadet. Just my type, standing there smiling at me. "Come right in," I said.

It was Carl, who had managed to get liberty so he could spend the evening in Oakland and be around in the San Francisco area the next day. So I didn't have to worry how to fill my evening.

For some time prior to our reunion, Carl's letters had been downers as he worried about whether he could cut it if he was accepted as an Air Corps cadet. Most of the other candidates were callow eighteen- and twenty-year-olds who would have little trouble adapting to the physical and psychological demands that would be made on them. I hadn't been able to imagine the healthy, happy, perfectly coordinated golf pro I'd known and loved coming up inadequate. "He's psyching himself out," Gene had said, after reading a couple of Carl's letters. And as I saw him standing there, I knew I had no reason to worry.

Neither of us was very relaxed. The whole weekend we played it cool. Neither of us was making any commitments. But secretly I believe we both were deciding that there was still something there. We weren't just casual friends.

This was especially true after we went over to San Francisco, where we did all the dumb tourist things a soldier and his girl might do—rode the cable cars, held hands in the cocktail lounge that overlooked the city at the Top of the Mark and dined at an authentic Chinese restaurant in Chinatown before going to the Municipal Auditorium for the gig.

At the auditorium a handsome young sailor appeared carrying a metal-rimmed snare drum (during the war, most rims were made of wood). He offered to let Gene play it, but Gene gave him the standard fan treatment, signing the drum "To John, Best Wishes, Gene Krupa."

I was sitting there talking to Carl and Frank Verniere when the sailor approached and asked me to sign his drum, please. I'd had a couple of drinks. Not enough to make me drunk, but enough to put a little chip on my shoulder. I was trying to concentrate on the gig and didn't want to be bothered, so I said, "No. N.O."

The sailor looked crushed and walked away. I didn't know his name. I didn't want to know it. To me he was just another starry-eyed amateur. If anyone had predicted that for at least twenty-six of the next thirty-nine years he'd play an important part in my life, I'd have told whoever said it that she was gazing into a cracked crystal ball.

By the time we opened Krupa's six-week stand at the Palladium on November 10, Carl was into his fifteen-week preflight training program in nearby Santa Ana, California. The first weekend he had liberty he showed up at the Palladium and that, you might say, rekindled everything. He came in the following weekend too, and by now any doubts I had that I might not be the right wife for him vanished.

I talked to Gene about giving me some time off, not only for Carl's sake but also because I was groggy after the grueling schedule of one-nighters we'd followed over the past couple of years. I felt I'd earned a bit of rest and relaxation, the R and R that service cats were always talking about.

Gene agreed, and when he found a temporary replacement to join the band the first week in January, he granted me a month off. By this time Carl was into the first phase of flight training at one of the privately owned and operated schools that the government contracted with civilians to operate. This one was run by Leland Hayward, an ex-literary agent who was to make a name for himself as a Broadway and Hollywood producer and gain posthumous fame in his daughter Brooke's autobiography *Haywire*. The school was located in King City, California.

I didn't know what King City had been before the war, but it was nowhere when I hit town. All the fast-buck artists had opened up, giving the place the worst characteristics of a boomtown.

Finding an apartment was impossible. Renting a room was an exercise that required drawing on all my experience scuffling through life with the cards stacked against me. Dingy though it might be, the room I found was vacant and I grabbed it. Then I called the school and left word for Carl where he could find me.

After that I hurried over to a supermarket, bought some Lysol, soap, sponges and roach powder. I proceeded to give the room a thorough going-over. When I finished, I bathed and fell into bed even though I thought I was too tired to sleep. I wasn't. Carl woke me when he pounded on the door.

I let him in and he threw his arms around me, peppering my face and neck with welcoming pecks before our mouths locked. When I pulled myself away, my heart went out to him. My lithe golf pro in civilian life was an uptight Air Corps man. I decided he needed to relax. We shared a joint and talked about the Krupa band, my recordings and Gene. Carl wanted to talk about anything except life at the school.

After we'd gone out for a leisurely dinner, we walked about, Carl's arm around my waist, chitchatting before we went back to the apartment. Inside the door, he peppered my neck, lips and eyelids with little kisses, nibbled my earlobes, unbuttoned my sweater and cupped my breasts in his hands, whispering how deeply he loved me, how much he missed me, how he'd longed for me, and how happy he was going to make me.

And he did!

Before I went to sleep, he begged me to marry him right away. I promised to think it over.

How he managed without awakening me I don't know, but in the morning I found him bringing in a breakfast tray to enjoy in bed. Doing these things obviously gave him so much pleasure, I decided that if marrying him would help boost his morale enough to get him through training and into the air force, it was the least I could do.

My only hassle was over deserting Gene because my replacement wasn't working out. I agreed to go back for the engagement at the Panther Room of the Hotel Sherman in Chicago to give him time to find another girl. But first I'd marry Carl and go back to the band after he was sent overseas. Carl and I were married at the USO in King City on July 18, 1943.

Three days after the ceremony, Carl arrived waving a newspaper and saying, "My God, Anita, guess who's been busted!"

He didn't need to tell me. A wild-man shot of Gene at the drums and being hustled into a marked police car by some burly officers took up almost the entire front page of a San Francisco newspaper Carl had bought.

The story said Gene had been charged with possession of a controlled substance and contributing to the delinquency of a minor. The minor was his valet. His valet? Gene had no valet. But when I saw the name, John Pateakos, I realized this was the replacement for our regular band boy who had been drafted. Gene had hired seventeen-year-old Pateakos because most adult, able-bodied men were in the service or defense work.

As Gene later told the story, the regular band boy had wanted to give him a going-away present. But surveying Gene's fifteen wardrobe trunks with cashmere sweaters, silk shirts, Sulka ties and, well, you name it, the band boy went out and brought him some high-grade grass. Pleased at the thought, Gene thanked him and carelessly stuffed it into his coat pocket.

I'm not trying to convince you Gene didn't use grass on occasion. He did. But if it was a choice between grass and booze, booze won nine times out of ten.

Unfortunately, there was a headline-hunting Treasury department man in the area who found out about the gift. Knowing nothing grabbed bigger headlines than a popular star getting busted, he specialized in star-busting. So he and some local authorities showed up at the theater with a search warrant and shook Gene down. They came up empty-handed.

Gene knew that the next stop would be his hotel. So he slipped aside and quietly called the new band boy. He told him to take out the laundry and to make sure that he took the cigarettes in his coat pocket and flushed them down the toilet. Instead, the kid filched them.

So the authorities nailed Gene on both counts.

Of course, it took me a long time to find out what was coming down after I saw those pictures in the paper. My first impulse was to rush to Gene's side. Luckily, I called Frank Verniere, who told me the greatest favor I could do would be to stay away. It wasn't exactly unknown that I smoked weed occasionally, and when the headline hunter busted Gene, he wanted to know where I was. The implication was that I was on his list.

The first news report didn't seem bad. Roy Eldridge was taking over the band and trying to hold it together. Gene had hired Jake Ehrlich, probably San Francisco's top attorney, to represent him, unaware that the DA hated Ehrlich and would bear down twice as heavy on his clients.

Gene entered a guilty plea on the possession charge and drew a ninety-day sentence. He plead not guilty to contributing to the delinquency of a minor and was convicted. He appealed.

Graham Young's aunt, who held a high-up position in social work from San Francisco north, had met Gene before Graham was drafted. She visited him in jail and wrote Graham that Gene was such a basket case emotionally that he belonged in a sanitarium instead of a cell.

What has never been told until now is that a good thing came out of the arrest. Gene's ex, Ethel had never stopped loving Gene. When she read in the paper that the band had folded when headed by Roy and that Gene was about to lose his Yonkers home, she flew to San Francisco to visit him.

It wasn't easy at first. But after they'd both cried a little, Ethel asked Gene whether he remembered the hundred grand he'd settled on her at the time of their divorce. "You know, I didn't need that money," she told him. "I went back to being a telephone operator." Then she opened her purse and took out a check for $100,000 and said, "Gene, I want you to have this back. No strings attached."

I think that was when Gene grew up emotionally. He'd made his success very young and he hadn't been able to handle it. But when Ethel came to him in jail and laid that money on him, it showed real caring. He'd tossed her out, like old trash in the alley, and still she came through with that kind of devotion. I'm happy to say that Ethel's noble attitude was rewarded, because when he got out of jail he remarried her.

Eventually the Appellate Court reversed the decision on the contributing-to-the-delinquency-of-a-minor count. In fact, there was some evidence Gene might have been set up for one of the periodic clean-up-the-city drives. Because the seventeen-year-old band boy turned out to have been a juvenile delinquent and a possible police plant.

Gene was released on double jeopardy after serving eighty-four of his ninety-day sentence for possession. But once you have the reputation of being an addict, it's hard to shake. To this day, plenty of people believe Gene was a hard-drug addict. Untrue. He never touched heroin or cocaine. His use of barbiturates was limited to occasional sleeping pills. To gain his reputation as a "dope fiend" all he did was smoke a few joints and drink a lot of Scotch.

Unfortunately, the scandal forced Gene out of the band business. He retreated to his home in Yonkers where he fumed and raged against his fate until he broke out in a series of rashes. But finally, recognizing his impotence to do anything about his predicament, he once again embraced religion. So out of all the bad came a greater good.

Benny Goodman has never been one of my favorite people, but I will give him credit. He was one of the few to visit Gene in jail, and after Gene returned to Yonkers in such a hyper-state, Benny took his clarinet and went up to play with him. In November 1943 he asked Gene to join his band playing for the ice show at the New Yorker. It was an easy break-in, doing all those rolls for the skaters.

Gene left Benny to join Tommy Dorsey at the famous unbilled appearance at the Paramount, where the crowd gave him such a tumultuous welcome that when Tommy asked him to stand up Gene bawled like a baby.

It was while playing with Tommy that he developed what he later called his "Kostelanetz complex." In June 1944 he decided to organize a new twenty-five-piece band with—would you believe?—nine strings, seven brasses and four rhythm pieces. He called it the "Band That Swings with Strings." When I heard that I never expected to work with Gene again.

Like a lot of other girls in 1943, I devoted myself to being an army wife. I stayed in King City until Carl was transferred to Gardner Field for basic, which was the second phase of flight training. Gardner Field was near Taft, California. There wasn't an apartment to be had, so for a while I stayed in a little hotel in Taft.

It was probably in Taft that Carl asked me to help him with a song they sang every morning as they marched from the barracks to the hangars. I asked him how it went and he sang: "Off we go into the wild blue yonder. . . ."

I stopped him. "That's a terrible song. It only has one note."

"Oh, that's not the way it's written," he said. "That's just the way I sing it."

I investigated and he was right. It's a wonder that Carl ever appreciated music. He turned out to be a perfect-pitch monotone. After trying for a whole week, I finally gave up, advising him, "Just move your lips without making a sound."

Carl came into Taft whenever he could get off, but it was lonely and we decided it might be better for me to get a place in Hollywood. I took a flat at the De Longpre Apartments and started looking for gigs.

As long as he was at Gardner, he managed to spend a lot of time with me, but when basic was finished, he was transferred to Luke Field in Phoenix, Arizona.

That was a bad period for both of us. The training was so rigorous that Carl again worried about washing out, and since I hadn't been working steadily money was pretty tight.

I did open as a single at Charley Foy's famous Supper Club in the San Fernando Valley, backed by Johnny "Scat" Davis and a pickup band. After my closing, I was still scuffling for a good Hollywood showcase. I'd proved to myself I could cut it alone. Now I needed to have someone with power catch my presentation.

But I took time off to go to Luke Field when Carl got his wings and commission. He had a ten-day delay en route to his next station which was Randolph Field in San Antonio. I nearly popped my buttons when he told me he was one of seventeen picked out of the graduating class of single-engine fighter pilots to go to the Central Instructors School in San Antonio. He may not ever have got his singing off the ground, but he'd made it up there into the wild blue yonder. And what made me especially happy was that as an instructor he'd never have to go overseas. Besides, he was now drawing officer's pay. That meant there was more money available for me to drop down to San Antonio whenever he was free.

Anytime I was in Hollywood, I kept working toward getting myself organized as a single. When I wasn't doing that, there were two ways I really enjoyed spending time: going to the Broadway department store on the corner of Hollywood and Vine to shop, and dropping in at the Palladium. The bartenders all knew me from the times I'd played there, and both the music and drinks were good.

When I was especially missing Carl one night, I went to the Palladium. Walt and Sue Yoder, who lived in the same building I did, were there. Walt was a great bass player with Woody Herman's band. I joined them just about the time Woody came along and greeted me like an angel from heaven.

They were opening June 8 and I said I'd be there. I'd always dug Woody's stuff. He had a high-grade swing band. Just hearing him always picked up my spirits.

Woody wanted to know what I was doing with myself.

I told him I was between gigs, trying to get my single together.

He wanted to know whether I'd consider opening with him. His girl singer, Carolyn Grey, who had been with him for several years, had quit and he needed a replacement at once.

It was a class-A outfit, but I'd had it with big-band work and told Woody so.

"Pays good," he said. "Lots better than Krupa."

"How good?"

"One hundred and twenty-five dollars a week."

Fan-TAB-ulous! Not that I was that much into money. But it was almost twice again what I'd made with Krupa at my peak, and since Woody paid higher salaries all the way down the line, he naturally collected better musicians than Gene. Maybe not more talented, but older, more dependable.

Maybe I'd have accepted an offer from another leader. I don't know. I do know that Woody was alert to little changes in music and was constantly altering his approach to keep abreast with the times. That impressed me.

As a leader, he was a front man, not an arranger. But he was a good one. He was long on experience. Born in Milwaukee, Wisconsin, in 1913, he started appearing as a tap dancer by the time he was six years old. He began studying saxophone at nine and was on the road at thirteen or fourteen. He'd been with Isham Jones and when Jones quit, Woody and some of the other musicians formed a cooperative which he fronted. From there the road was up.

We worked happily together at the Palladium for four weeks. Then Woody was booked into the Orpheum in downtown Los Angeles. Sometime during the engagement, he mentioned what he had planned for me after we went on the road. I panicked. I had no contract with him, and I thought it was understood that I felt I'd gone as far as I could as a band singer. After those one-nighters with Gene, I never wanted to see the inside of another bus. I thought Woody was hip to that. I'd told him, and in every interview I kept yakking about the single I had planned. Maybe he thought I'd changed my mind. Anyway I screwed up my courage and told him that much as I admired him and his band and good as the money was, there was just no way I was going back on the road. Woody got very upset. We both said some harsh things, but I held firm.

He didn't forgive me for a long time, but eventually he forgot about it. I'm glad he did because working with him and his first

Herd was as groovy a six weeks as any swing singer could ask for.

While I was appearing at the Orpheum, I stayed with Mom who had come to California and taken an apartment on Bonnie Brae, which was located in downtown LA much closer to the theater and gave us a chance to see one another daily.

After I'd left Krupa and settled on the West Coast, Mom decided to move to Los Angeles too. Aunt Belle had died and as emotionally frozen as Mom seemed, she must have needed at least occasional contact with her nearest relative. Namely, me.

Considering all the years in which we had failed to communicate except on the most primitive level, she proved surprisingly open about her feelings during the two weeks that I was there.

What really caused me to flip was her announcement that she'd registered with Clara Lanes' Lonely Hearts Club. Mom?!!! Suddenly, I was warning her that people weren't always what they seemed, and she must be careful not to give out her home address and to avoid being alone with anyone who answered her ad until she could check his background.

She assured me Clara Lane did all that. In fact, she was already in touch with a fifty-five-year-old, lifelong bachelor, who owned a big house in Van Nuys. They'd had dinner three times, and Mom felt his intentions were serious. "He's nice enough, but I think all he wants is a free housekeeper," she said. "So I've written Clara to ask whether she has any more prospects."

She did. The second one's name was Sam Jones. That name alone would have scared me stiff. "Nobody's named that," I said.

"Well, he is," Mom replied calmly. "If anybody was makin' up a name, they'd choose something less common than Jones."

I conceded her point.

Jones was twenty-two years younger than Mom. He'd come to California from Tennessee to get into war work, but had ended up in, of all places, a box factory. I guess that stirred a lot of Mom's youthful memories, even though Jones was as nondescript as Dad had been attractive.

When I met Sam, I remember thinking he was a nice, quiet, not-very-interesting fellow who obviously worshiped Mom. So eventually they got married. That solved Mom's problem. About the only times I'd see them was on Sundays. Sam loved to drive and they scooted all along the California coast, occasionally dropping in on me.

Then the army got Sam and Mom was alone again, which was why I decided to stay with her during Woody's engagement at the Orpheum. She didn't seem unhappy. But how could you tell? She must have been born without emotions.

While Sam was in the service, he sent Mom practically his entire earnings and she deposited them in their savings account. After the war was ended and he returned to civilian life, they took his army savings and bought a brand new Ford in which they drove up and down the state having a wonderful time. It turned out to be the most eventful period of Mom's life, a payment for all the bad years, for which I'm very grateful.

Even though I was spending more time as a war bride than a singer, my short stint with Woody Herman kept me up there in both *Metronome*'s and *Down Beat*'s 1943 polls. In the former, the first five were Mildred Bailey, Billie Holiday, me, Betty Roche and Peggy Lee. *Down Beat*'s top five were Jo Stafford, Peggy Lee, Helen Forrest, me, and Billie Holiday.

After I left Woody, Carl got his first assignment as an instructor at Lemoore Field in Lemoore, California. I went up and we went to Hanford to look for an apartment. We found just what we wanted in one of those big old residences that had been converted into four apartments, two up and two down. Our next-door neighbor turned out to be Agnes DeMille, who had revolutionized musical-comedy dancing with her ballets in *Oklahoma!*, but in Hanford she was just the wife of one of the administrative officers at Lemoore.

She and I used to exchange pleasantries when we met, but I had a lot more in common with some of the cats around the Officers Club at the base. I used to flub around there singing my heart out and when Carl finished he always knew where to find me.

The pianist was a very shrewd guy called Skitch and we hit it off pretty well musically. After a while a lot of the alligators got into the habit of coming over to listen to Skitch and me and other musicians who happened to be on the base. Carl was proud of that.

Skitch was a college man who really knew music and turned out to be an excellent conductor. He also knew how to play the game for his advantage, something I never was very good at. So I wasn't at all surprised when Skitch Henderson turned up leading the band on NBC-TV for Jack Paar's *Tonight* show. I'd always known he was good.

I may have rated with the alligators, but I was far from the perfect army wife. While I was living in Hanford and hanging out at the base, Lemoore got a new CO. They scheduled a reception to honor him, and all the officers and their ladies were "invited." They said "invited" but they kept track whether you made it or not, so I went to the damn party.

We got there early. There was no receiving line yet. I headed for the bar to fortify myself against the misery with a couple of fast ones. There was a nice-looking, friendly colonel at the bar too, and we got to talking. Suddenly the room just seemed to fill up. The colonel noticed it and said something like, "Gee, this is certainly a fine turnout."

I looked at him as if he were crazy and said, "Well, it oughta be. It's a command performance!"

You guessed it! He was the new CO. I thought Carl was going to kill me. He was certain he was going to be at the top of the CO's list from there on.

While I was playing air corps wife, Carlos Gastel suggested that he'd like to manage me. Carlos was a big, burly guy, six feet, two or three inches, with a barrel chest and tiny feet that gave him a strange walk for a man of that size.

Basically, he was a manager who was on an artistic rather than a monetary kick. He'd hear a sound, fall in love with it and go after the artist. He heard Nat King Cole, said he wanted to work with him, and they were together until Nat died. The same thing happened with many of his clients. He heard them and set out to get them—Stan Kenton, Peggy Lee, Benny Carter, Mel Torme, and a female jazz accordionist. She never made it, but Carlos tried like crazy for her over a period of years.

He heard that I wanted to go out as a single and agreed to manage my career. For my first tour, Carl arranged for Skitch Henderson to do some arrangements for me. They were lovely. First class.

Carlos booked me into a string of theaters, but when I opened there were still things to be worked out. Nothing was really set. For instance, Carlos put me into a seven-minute spot on the bill at the Oriental Theater in Chicago, the first city where Variety had a reviewer who would be likely to catch me. My allotted time, seven minutes, gave me a chance to pay passing respects to "Shoo Shoo Baby," "Alice Blue Gown" and "Let Me Off Uptown." Orchestra leader Ray Lang refused to let me rehearse an encore. He said I'd only be allowed my bow, then the program would move right on to the next act. Who was I to argue?

On the first show of the day, the audience was small and Lang did just that. On the second, a bunch of jivesters had crowded in on the "31¢-before-1 A.M." special admission, and they were determined to get their money's worth. I sailed through my three scheduled songs and left the stage. But those hepcats weren't about to let me off without an encore.

Lang started the music for the next act, but these kids were stamping, applauding and yelling "More! More! More!" They kept up the din until I went out for another bow. Even then they kept whistling and hollering until I apologized for being unprepared for an encore. Then I called to Lang for "Pistol Packin' Mama." After a stumbling beginning, I did okay with the swing crowd, but according to Variety's man Morg, I didn't "quite make the grade" although he admitted I had "the ability to fill a certain niche in the stage and cafe field," even though I was "badly unprepared for my debut as a single." According to him, I even made an "awkward exit."

On the same bill was Morey Amsterdam as the headline comic. Now Morey is also a songwriter, and during breaks between shows we all used to get together and flub around. He said he had a couple of tunes he thought I might be interested in. I tried them and chose one called "Gotta Be Gettin'." The one I turned down was "Rum and Coca-Cola." You know what the Andrews Sisters did with that.

Nothing I did seemed to go right on that tour, although I felt I finally hit my stride finishing the year at Loew's Capitol in Washington, D.C., even though the bill was headlined by Harriet Hoctor, billed as "America's Prima Ballerina." Me? I was "Top Swing Songstress."

I spent the beginning of 1944 staying in Brooklyn with Nita Barnett, Krupa's secretary, and looking over the New York scene while Carlos lined up dates for a swing through southern theaters to get me back in California.

During my stay at Nita's, Carl's telegram celebrating our first wedding anniversary arrived:

ALL MY LOVE AND THOUGHTS ON THIS SPECIAL DAY. I WOULD DO IT ALL OVER AGAIN, DARLING. YOU HAVE BEEN WONDERFUL.
    LOVE,
    CARL

I was embarrassed that I'd been so involved with my career problems that I hadn't remembered the anniversary, hadn't even sent a card. So I called Carl at the Field and told him Carlos was finalizing my bookings, and one way or another we'd be together again in about six weeks.

This had been my first real foray on my own as a single, and it had inflamed a problem that has always plagued me. I'm a perfectionist about music. I have a vision and can't easily compromise as some commercial singers do. When the accompaniment doesn't satisfy me musically, I'm unhappy and I let whoever is responsible know it. And when I can't meet the goals I set for myself, I'm just as hard on myself. It's not my nature to smile and shrug off failure. Sometimes I've taken stands that I later discovered were flat-out wrong. But many times my instincts have proved to be correct. I've just been ahead of my time. So I've made it a practice to follow my instincts and let the chips fall where they may.

While I was visiting Nita, I was so down about working conditions on my first theater tour that I began toying with the idea of rejoining a big band. Thinking she was helping me, Nita planted a story in Down Beat that I was considering joining Teddy Powell's Orchestra.

Allowing that item to be published was a serious goof. Because when I got back to Los Angeles, Carlos began campaigning for me to go on the road with a band he managed—Stanley Kenton's Artistry in Rhythm. By the time I reached the West Coast, I'd recovered from my blues and didn't want to work with either Powell or Kenton. But Carlos was persistent. He felt it would be a good marriage because I was better known throughout the country and had had more experience.

"And just what's in it for me?" I inquired.

Carlos felt Stanley and his crew could provide me with further exposure with a proper band background. The fact that I was into one thing and Stanley into something altogether different musically didn't bother Carlos at all. "Two geniuses—you'll make it work," he kept repeating until I wanted to throw up.

Carlos had an enthusiastic supporter in Carl. Carl was a wonderful golf pro, a good flight instructor and, in many ways, a good husband. But being in the Air Force must have bored him, because more and more he got to dreaming of becoming my personal manager after he was mustered out of the service. At that point he couldn't understand why I didn't want to go with Kenton. "If he goes back on the Hope show and you're with him, you'll become a household word," he said. That was just what I didn't want to become—a product.

But finally, to please the two of them, I agreed at the time Dolly Mitchell turned in her notice to try working with Stanley for two or three months.

One thing I can say is that Stanley wasn't any more interested in pandering to popular taste than I was. He did drop the *ley* from his name, but he refused the opportunity to turn himself into one of Bob Hope's comic foils. Truthfully, neither he nor I would have been happy in the strait-jacketed timing required on weekly half-hour radio programs. So we were booked to tour.

In 1944 it wasn't totally true that if you didn't swing you didn't mean a thing. There were Dixieland bands, sweet bands, the Midwest's Million Dollar Corn Bands and all kinds of novelty orchestras. But swing was the thing and Stanley just wasn't into it.

Our first ad after I joined him on May 2 read:

THE ARTISTRY IN RHYTHM
OF
STAN KENTON AND HIS ORCHESTRA
Bob Hope's Great Radio Band
Featuring
ANITA O'DAY
Lovely Songstress
A BOMBSHELL IN MODERN MUSIC

We played the Fairgrounds in Tulare, California. Stanley was in the forefront of Progressive Jazz. He was looking for something, evolving, and eventually he found it in upbeats which made for great listening in theaters or anywhere else for that matter. But for ballrooms where presumably a guy brought his girl to dance, it wasn't so good. Much of the evening they had no choice but to gather around the bandstand and *listen.*

In swing or 4/4 time, everyone finds the downbeat—one—and goes from there. But for anything written in upbeats—say something such as Stanley's "Opus in Pastel" with its fabulous five-part harmony for saxophones—the band didn't come in on *one,* it came in on *one and* to create the upbeat sound.

Now that's great. New. Different. Whatever. But I defy you to tap your foot to it, because you can't tap *up.* And for me, singing to it was just as hard as dancing to it. I'd made my reputation as a swing singer and getting into Stanley's upbeats was tricky.*

I put together choreography for the stage so that he'd *see* what we needed to get the song over. He had to find *one* for the accompaniment to match my dancing. Otherwise, it didn't work. Well, he missed it consistently. When he did, everybody would go ha-ha as if it were a joke, but Stanley wasn't clowning around. He was coming as close to it as he could get.

He used to amaze me. He was so far out that when he came to the end of a tune, he'd cut it off at 6⅞ beats, which was taboo as far as I knew. I don't mean you *can't* do it. He did. But music is math and the idea is to find the logical thing so people can also find it.

Later, after we'd talked about it, he'd say, "You let me know when it feels like a good ending." He'd have his hand going and I'd give him the signal for the stick. When he'd manage to end on *one,* the band would just fall back on their chairs. Because he was likely to end on 6⅞. The funny thing is he really did want to learn to swing.

*In July, while Kenton was playing the Orpheum in Omaha, Lakeside Park in Denver, the Palace in Columbus, Eastwood Gardens in Detroit and other spots I'd appeared at with Gene, Columbia released "Bolero at the Savoy" and "Side By Side" featuring Roy Eldridge and me. We'd cut the sides back in 1941 and '42, but those cuts got a lot of newspaper space wherever we played. Unlike lots of leaders Stanley never complained about it.

My entire recording work with Stanley consisted of three California sessions and two brief ones in New York. Only three tunes had any commercial potential. The best was "And Her Tears Flowed Like Wine" which we did three weeks after I joined him. And I'm proud to say that with Stanley, just as Roy and I had with Gene, I gave him his first million-selling hit.

Before we recorded it, I said, "Stanley, person to person, you're great. But we can't cut it with that pan banger you've got. How about letting me bring in a good swing drummer just for the session?"

He agreed. So I went club hopping on Central Avenue. In this one joint I came upon Jesse Price, who had his own group and was really blowing. He and I came from the same school of thought, so when he finished the set I approached him to ask whether he'd consider sitting in on a Kenton session. He would.

We threw the session and when the record was released it went through the roof. It changed the Kenton band from an organization with a special limited following into a name band. To this day I believe the tune succeeded because Jesse was an affirmative drummer.

Stanley thought so too. In fact, he invited Jesse to join the orchestra. Jesse was black. Very dark. The only other black musician in the band was so light he could pass for Cuban and often did.

Which brings up the enigma of Stanley. Because the more you got to know about him, the less you understood him. He respected Jesse and he treated him well. Some crumbs in the band didn't, but Stanley told Jesse that as far as he was concerned, "a man is a man." His worship of Duke Ellington made him look upon Ellington as a minor god. But he also was prejudiced, and much as he admired Jesse, he didn't step in and put a stop to it when the crumbs got out of line, the way Gene would have. And long after both Jesse and I had left him, he stirred up a brouhaha in *Down Beat,* claiming that in jazz *white* musicians were the oppressed minority. He also eventually became an outspoken supporter of George Wallace's white supremacist policies.

If you're wondering why I'm belaboring the point, I'll tell you why. Around the early 1960s, Stanley hired a black singer named Jean Turner. And one night when they were scheduled to play Charleston, S.C., the promoter barred Jean from the hall, saying,

"No niggers are allowed in here." What did Stanley do? He said either Jean would be allowed to sing or nobody would play. Jean wasn't allowed to sing and the band packed up and went home. Now what do you make of a man like that?

Anyway, Jesse Price wasn't about to put up with any harassment and quit the band shortly after he joined. But strangely, he always defended Stanley, excusing him for not knowing "how to handle the problem."

Stanley was totally improbable and unpredictable. He was a right-wing jazz musician, which in itself is a contradiction. He was a gentleman and a bigot. He believed in home and family. Yet for various reasons his three wives unanimously thought he was a lousy husband. He didn't communicate with the daughter from the first marriage for years, and the two children from the second indulged in some bizarre behavior that climaxed when his son was arrested along with others from Synanon, the drug rehabilitation center, for putting a rattlesnake in the mailbox of an attorney who opposed the organization. It would take someone a lot wiser than me to understand Stanley as he was then or what he became.

In her biography of Kenton, Carol Easton portrays him as "super-square Stanley, who could barely bring himself to say *damn*" and me as "superswinger O'Day, whose favorite adjective was *fucking*."*

The truth is Stanley and I respected one another. He went out of his way to make me happy. But coming from such a different direction musically, I was never very happy working with him. Besides "And Her Tears," I recorded "Are You Livin', Old Man?" which came in like third and Morey Amsterdam's "Gotta Be Gettin'" with a pseudo-Ellington arrangement. It came in like ninth, with only seven horses running.

Many of the others weren't even issued. Why? My guess would be that even though nine or ten drummers came on after Jesse left, none of them were strong. Don't ask me who they were. I never heard of them before they joined or after they left. It would be nice to think my constant complaints had something to do with scaring

*It wasn't my favorite adjective. Just because I'd get drunk and use it while hanging out with the guys didn't make it a favorite word of mine. That's the way they talked, and I always figured I was part of the gang.

them out of a business in which they had no chance of succeeding. A small contribution, but a contribution nevertheless.

Stanley was really the hardest worker of anyone I ever met in the business. The word "workaholic" hadn't been invented then, but should have been for him. He never seemed to rest. After the last performance everyone else went home, but Stanley stayed on at the theater working on arrangements. He always had a cot set up in the basement. That's where he generally slept. He didn't go to his hotel room, shower, get dressed and have breakfast the way the rest of us did.

He took leading the organization very seriously, calling a meeting about once a week. Usually after we'd checked into a theater, we'd all have to come in and sit down. Then he'd function as "the boss." He'd discuss any plans or problems and try to boost morale and keep discipline. "Now a few of you are smoking marijuana," he'd say. "I'm aware of that. Others are drinking too much. I can't tell you how to conduct your personal lives. But just make sure you don't get so far out you can't come back in time for the gig or do anything to cause trouble for the band."

That was interesting to me, because Woody Herman never did anything like that during the few weeks I was with him and Gene never went in for any of it either. In fact, he was doing some far out things himself.

When I first went into the Midwest with the Kenton band, we were on Stanley's first go-round of the spots I'd hit with Gene. I was young and life was a kick, so I'd always cooperate with the publicity people and newspaper reporters. Most of the time they devoted as much space to me as to Stanley and the orchestra. I'll say this for him, he didn't complain or cut me down the way some leaders would have. Happily for him, after a couple of hit records everybody knew what an artist Stanley was and recognized what a unique organization he'd put together. Even better, he influenced a lot of arrangements for movies and TV, later on.

After a few months, the band got so hot we were doing seven shows a day. For Stanley, it was pressure, pressure, pressure. I tried to tell him he couldn't do that to his body. If I had worked hard for a while, I disappeared and rested to give my body a chance to come halfway back. Before I got into drugs, if I dissipated for a week, then I straightened out the next week. Not Stanley. I don't know what drove him. Once he hit with his style, people liked his music. It became more and more Progressive until it was *semi*-dance music, but the fans seemed to be happy with the result.

Because of the shortage of gasoline and tires we had to travel by train. Sometimes accommodations were primitive. One summer night the only free space was in a cleaned-up cattle car which we shared with two moo cows. It wasn't bad. In fact, it was kind of groovy sitting there, looking through the open spaces between the boards at the moonlit countryside as we rolled through the night to our next stand.

There were quite a few kicks to be had, but generally I was as much a misfit socially as professionally in this group. On long jumps I was like talking to myself. Because everybody else was reading books. Finally I started reading comic books. Big print. In self-defense I tried to learn bridge. *Bridge!* I wasn't any good at bridge. On the Krupa band, I not only sat in on poker games, I trounced the guys. That crowd had beer for breakfast. They had their chicks. They bet horses, wherever, whenever, whatever. They were also a jamming band. They were people I could feel comfortable hanging out with. Kenton's band wasn't my scene.

So after about eleven months, I thought, "Well, great for him! Not so great for me. He's going one way and I'm going another."

I had a talk with him about how I felt. He was cool, gentlemanly Stanley. "You want to leave? Okay . . . just don't leave me without a girl singer."

That was fair enough because his boy singer, Gene Howard, could handle only ballads. Shortly after we'd had our talk, the band went into the Chicago Theater. Up the street at the time was a big Chicago band led by Boyd Raeburn, who was working a Chinese Restaurant called the Shangri-La, located on the spot where the old Three Deuces had once been. I dropped in to catch the band. I had no front thoughts about finding my replacement, but when this cute blonde girl got up to sing I heard a familiar sound. She was flat, but I don't put any singer down for being flat. I know I'm not an on-tune singer, really, and with Stanley the girl did novelty tunes mostly.

So after the set I went back to the girl's dressing room and asked her name. It was Shirley Luster. I introduced myself and said I was across the street with Stanley. "He wants me to find him a girl singer. You want to be rich and famous, right? Come backstage at the Chicago Theater between the ten and eleven A.M. shows."

Over she came. She auditioned. She and Stanley talked, and he told me afterward I could leave upon finishing the January 1945 Los Angeles engagement.

By the time the band got to Los Angeles, I'd been voted *Down Beat*'s trophy as the "Best Band Singer" of 1944, which Stanley and singer Georgia Gibbs presented to me on the stage of the Orpheum Theater on January 15, 1945.

I knew Carlos wasn't going to want me to leave when I could capitalize on the *Down Beat* award. So I went up to his office and started discussing my contract with him. I reminded him I'd only promised to go out for a couple of months, but that I'd stayed for eleven. I told him even Stanley admitted I'd done my part. Carlos tried to con me into staying. But in the course of the conversation, I asked to see how my contract was worded. When Carlos took it out of the file and handed it to me, I ripped it up. "Two months— whatever, I have no contract," I told him, dropping it into the wastepaper basket.

I'm sure that contract was on file at the musicians' union, with Stanley, or somewhere. But from Carlos' point of view, a contract was of very little use if I was unhappy and didn't want to perform. What good is a piece of paper if the artist is unable, whether for physical or emotional reasons, to go out and do her best?

Still, it developed that there was going to be a delay in Shirley's joining so I went along with the band to Tune Town in St. Louis, where seventeen-year-old Stan Getz joined. Stan kept bugging me to get Stanley Kenton to let him take a solo. Finally he got one. The only thing he knew were eighth notes, but he went out and played the whole thing in eighth notes and everybody just fell off their chairs. There Patti Dugan took over until Shirley Luster joined.

Only by now Shirley had adopted the name she was to make famous—June Christy. Of course, June doesn't remember it happening my way. She claims she ran into Stanley at the GAC agency, played some tapes for him and got the job. Stanley's version didn't agree with either hers or mine. But, once again, since this is my book, you're getting my recollections of how it happened. Until June writes her book, you're stuck with them, like them or not.

Before he knew I was leaving, Stanley had written arrangements of several new songs. I left before I got a chance to learn "Tampico" and "Across the Alley from the Alamo."

About two months after I quit, I was singing with a trio at a hotel in Salt Lake City, where I was trying more ambitious songs, such as Hoagy Carmichael's "Skylark," in which I really had to find the tone and place it, as well as such novelties as "Are You Livin', Old Man?" or "Let Me Off Uptown," in which, if I got the lyrics out, the crowd was happy.

I was sitting in the coffee shop one day during this engagement when a waitress said, "Hey, I like your new release, 'Across the Alley from the Alamo.' "

I was startled. I told her Kenton had had an arrangement made for me, but hadn't recorded it.

"It's on the jukebox," she said, digging for nickels to feed the machine. "And the other one too."

"Tampico" came on and, sure enough, it was in my key, my range. I had to listen carefully to detect an added lift that tipped me off that these were June Christy recordings of arrangements Stanley had written for me. June sounded so much like me I was almost fooled myself.

Now that's nothing against what June did. I copied Billie Holiday's ballad style for years. Everyone would say, "Gee, you're great. You sound just like Billie Holiday." The only drawback was that nobody ever remembered my name. Consequently, I stopped listening to other singers and started playing the recordings of instrumentalists. So instead of thinking how Billie did it, I'd work out phrasing, emphasis, whatever, that took off from Stan Getz, Buddy De Franco, or Zoot Sims. Maybe I'd use a nasal approach with an open throat to get onto a different form, emphasize an unexpected word until I developed a style of my own.

Eventually June Christy, Chris Connor, and for a while Doris Day, as well as others, were tabbed by the press as part of my school until they worked out characteristics of their own.

Speaking for myself, I think my time with Stanley helped nurture and cultivate my innate sense of chord structure. Stanley's musical concept and thinking exposed me to another way of employing my voice and almost by osmosis I incorporated some of what I heard.

So I kept working out and embellishing my singing with things

I'd discover. If the result pleased me, I'd develop it. If it didn't, I forgot about it, but I always kept working, hoping to make my presentation a little better. I knew I didn't have any chops, but I also knew I had a lot of heart.

Heart? That's what Assault had. He won a stake race and then in the same year the Kentucky Derby. And he was a horse that had a clubfoot at birth. So almost anything is possible if you have a lot of heart.

Just a personal opinion, of course.

With World War II winding down, there was an upbeat mood among the crowds that packed clubs. The war in Europe was all but won and the optimism that victory generated, plus Allied successes in the Pacific, created a euphoric mood. People were open to experiments of all kinds. Dizzy Gillespie, wearing his tam and horn-rimmed glasses, and blowing bebop, could desert bands and form his own combo in 1945. People were broadening their horizons.

After leaving Carlos, I tried fronting a trio and became more skillful at improvising. Freed of the pattern work and Stanley's arbitrary regimentation, I couldn't imagine why I'd stayed in band work as long as I had. I was free to sing as I felt now. I was a headliner, not a band singer. Not just an extra added attraction.

Carl, meanwhile, had been transferred closer to Hollywood so when I left the Kenton band, we had taken another place at the De Longpre Apartments and he'd come in almost every weekend.

It now seemed just a matter of time before the war would be over, and he thought it would be a good idea to look for a house. We finally found just what we wanted at 5129 Goodland Avenue in North Hollywood. The problem was that the owners were asking $5,000 for it. Five thousand smackers! Who had that kind of bread for an acre with a house?

By combining what little we'd saved, Carl and I came up with about $500, then I sold my silver fox jacket and Carl borrowed some dough from Phil Yordan, Trilby's old boyfriend, who had become a successful Broadway and Hollywood writer.

On April 8, ten days before VE Day, our $1,500 down payment was accepted, the mortgage was approved, and we got the papers making us property owners. Carl worked out plans and whenever he got into town set about remodeling the place.

If anyone had even suggested that I'd leave that little house and go back on the road before getting a chance to enjoy it, I'd have thought they'd flipped out. But shortly after I quit Kenton, John Gluskin, who had taken over management of Gene after Gene's San Francisco bust, had begun calling me about rejoining the Krupa band. I told him there was no way I was going to leave my little nest and position as a song stylist to sing with a band, especially one with all those strings Gene was featuring.

Apparently the public felt the same way. Although I wasn't aware of it, the band just wasn't making it at the box office. Why? It was bland. Unexciting. Gene was playing too few drum solos.

That was the real reason. But some of the yellow press played it up as if the public wouldn't accept Gene, proving there was no place in the musical world for "reefer addicts."

That really bugged me. I'd been smoking grass since I was a kid without any terrible effects. *Reefer Madness,* now a camp classic, was still regarded as a cautionary tale of the evils worked by tea, muggles, mary jane, gage, hemp, marijuana or whatever you wanted to call it.*

Then one day John Gluskin called again to say Gene was going back to the old swing band. He was dropping the strings and wanted to hire Buddy De Franco on clarinet, Dodo Marmarosa on piano and, hopefully, me.

"Not this chick," I told John.

"He's learned strings and swing don't mix," he assured me.

"I couldn't cut those one-nighters anymore."

"This would be a theater tour. Week stands mostly."

"Gene can't afford me. I get a lot more bread now."

But John Gluskin had an answer for everything. "You mean more at the box office too," he said.

"Sorry. I've had it."

"Anita, *please.*"

I couldn't believe it. He couldn't mean what I thought he did. "Listen, John, I can't afford to buy his cigarettes," I bantered. John didn't laugh. "I've already mailed the plane ticket. I'll pay

---

*I've always felt that exaggerating the destructive effect of marijuana was a big mistake. The fact that people had used it for years without developing severe problems made it easier for them to discount the physical and economic problems created by use of hard drugs.

for the cigarettes out of his expense allowance." He also agreed to hire Carl to work for Gene as soon as Carl was mustered out of the service.

So, one way or another, I found myself rejoining the band. Some famous writer and a lot of other people say you can't go home again, but I beg to differ. The second stint on the Krupa band was better than the first. A lot of the old gang had rejoined by the time I arrived from the Coast and walked in on a rehearsal. Gene's back was toward me and when I saw him giving instructions with that familiar hand chop, tears came to my eyes.

I quietly said hello to a couple of old buddies who gave me a swig of cabbage juice to settle my nerves. Then I walked out into the rehearsal. When Gene spotted me, he ran over and hugged me. "Welcome back," he said.

"Great to be here."

Gene fumbled around in his pocket. "Dumb damn broad!" He pressed a quarter in my hand. A quarter! "John says I owe you this."

"Keep it." I smiled, dropping it into his shirt pocket alongside his cigarettes. "You'll just borrow it back tomorrow."

He laughed, then yelled: "Okay, okay, back to work. Just because Anita's here doesn't make it a national holiday!"

I'll always be grateful I let John Gluskin talk me into going back to Gene for that second stint. Stanley was a gentleman, but working with him was like wearing a tight girdle. Working with Gene made you feel relaxed as if you were lounging around in an old kimono.

Nineteen forty-five had promised to be a good year. Besides getting "Top Girl Band Vocalist" from *Down Beat* in January, in February I found I'd been voted "Outstanding New Star" by twenty-two jazz critics participating in *Esquire*'s poll. I'd done well as a headliner, but there was something magical about the reunion of Gene and me at the Astor Roof on July 16 shortly before VJ day. I'll never forget the reception given by both diners and dancers that night we were reunited.

For some reason, Gene wanted me to open with "Drum Boogie" which really wasn't my number. Irene Daye had originally sung and recorded it, but it showed him off well and was one of his most requested numbers so I didn't mind. And his instinct in using it for our opening collaboration proved to be right, because when I danced

143

to the microphone, the audience yipped, yowled, screamed, stomped, stood up, applauded, and exploded into a roaring welcome. The bedlam drowned out everything including Gene's drums.

What could I do? I opened my mouth as though to sing. No way. I smiled and nodded. Bowed. I threw kisses. I curtsied. They went right on welcoming me home. I signaled with my hands for them to quiet down and let us get on with the music. It was useless. After more than five minutes, they finally subsided into happy exhaustion. Of many memorable receptions, that one stands out.

Right after VJ Day, Carl got out of the service and John Gluskin and Gene hired him to become part of management. He did advance work, promotion, and road management of one-nighters, the whole ball of wax. When we closed at the Astor Roof, we worked our way to Providence, Rhode Island, back to the Capitol Theater in New York, and then a series of one-nighters up as far as Portland, Maine, and back to the Capitol in New York again.

While we were in the East, Carl and I took an apartment in a building just east of Forty-seventh Street and Seventh Avenue in the same building where Morey Amsterdam lived. It was a kind of fun time because Woody Herman and three or four other name bands were working around town.

Not only that, Carl turned out to be a very creative cat. Maybe some of you remember the bit where all the lights were turned down and you saw Gene's shadow swinging away on the back cyclorama. That was just one of Carl's creations. He had a lot of good ideas and I was very proud of him.

I loved having somebody on the band to look after me. I just turned my paycheck over to him, and if I needed anything I'd let him know. Say I needed a new blouse for my stage wardrobe. I'd pull the covers from over his head and tell him. He'd take me shopping and whatever I could find, he'd pay for. Because at that point I really wasn't interested in worrying about money.

The only shadow on our relationship was that people kept coming around and telling me who they'd seen my old man out with the night before. I didn't like it, but it wasn't too much of an issue because everything else was so right.

Finally, we headed back west doing the regular routine—mixing a few weekly engagements, the usual one-nighters and finally the

Panther Room in Chicago for a fan-TAB-ulous six-week engagement during which I gave more of myself than I could afford.

In Chicago, our old buddy Ray Forman came back into the picture. He'd had a very, very successful joint out in Morton Grove and had become quite a wheel in local politics. But his marriage had collapsed and the joint had burned down, so he was at a low point in his life. Carl suggested that he come to California where the three of us would open a club. Ray went for it. So while I worked my way west with the band, Carl did advance work and Ray drove several of the musicians' wives to Hollywood. While Carl and Ray were waiting for the band to reach the Palladium, they added a bedroom, walk-in closet and a bath to our house on Goodland. As a gag, they tied a big red ribbon around the house; that was my Christmas present when the band and I arrived.

Everything should have been working out. Our New York recording dates for Columbia Records in the late summer and early fall brought a big winner with "Boogie Blues." It had been written and orchestrated for me while I was still with Kenton. But since Stanley didn't swing, he saw no potential in it. Gene had dug it immediately and had a new arrangement made. It became one of our best efforts.

Sy Oliver's "Opus #1" didn't do badly either. And "Chickery Chick" and "Hop, Skip and Jump" were novelty tunes suited to the time. My duets with Buddy Stewart—"That Feeling in the Moonlight," "Harriet" and "In the Middle of May"—were okay even if the last one was not released until years later.

I should have been happy, but I was tired and depressed, drawing on energy I didn't really have. Gene was right. I didn't eat regularly. But I drank. I even drank a little on the job. But I never thought of myself as looking for booze. On the other hand, I didn't look for food either. I'd never been taught you had to eat. But I should have known I was heading for trouble.

For one thing, I needed energy because I was singing a lot more than I had when I'd been with Gene originally. He was a typical leader. If he was tired or had a hangover, he'd do just enough to satisfy the customers and then let us perform our specialties. Some nights I'd be doing everything from "Drum Boogie" to "Skylark," singing almost every other song. That was tiring. Because Krupa's was a loud, driving band and to keep on top of it was an effort.

145

To keep me going, everybody was offering me drinks or a hit off a joint. That's the story of my life. Why didn't anyone think of sharing a sandwich?

I told Gene in St. Louis I didn't think I was going to make it to the Palladium. He heard me wail that song before. He just laughed and bought me a drink. I'd quit often and threatened even oftener. He thought it was just a mood. I sensed something different, but it didn't hit until after the Palladium opening.

For a couple of nights I felt, well, fuzzy. I wasn't up to par. Then one night I really started shaking. Not the hangover shakes, but an inner trembling, like a human earthquake. I couldn't keep my thoughts together. So how was I going to sing?

I felt dizzy and frightened that the walls were closing in on me. I went over to Gene and told him I really had to go home.

He advised me to have a drink.

I told him that wouldn't help, and when he didn't seem to take me seriously I told him a third time.

"Stay until after the broadcast and then leave," he said.

The Broadcast was the *big deal*. The Palladium was nice because you got to sit in one spot for a month or more without the endless packing and unpacking, but the money wasn't as good as at some other spots. The important thing the Palladium had to offer was the broadcast which was the best publicity you could get in the west. It meant money in the bank.

I tried to stick it out. I looked at the clock and saw that we'd go on the air in five minutes. That meant I wouldn't go until fourth; I'd have to hold out for twenty-five minutes. I couldn't make that. So I told one of the saxophonists to play my solo because I was sick, and then I cut out.

When I couldn't make the radio show, I guess Gene figured I had to be hurting pretty bad. Because whatever else I might do, I never sluffed off work. In all the years I'd been with him I'd missed only one job and that wasn't my fault. The desk clerk in St. Louis forgot to ring my room to awaken me. Otherwise, I was old dependable. But it just got too heavy trying to do the job and not taking care of myself. Like in the Walkathon, I couldn't last any longer. I fell out.

I took a cab home. Carl would need the car to get home. I had no idea as I left that I'd never go back to Krupa. By the time I got myself together the band had hired Carolyn Grey, a good singer who had placed third to my first in the 1944 *Down Beat* poll. I'd followed Carolyn on Woody Herman's band, and more recently she'd been singing at the Palladium with Johnny D'Varga's intermission group so she was familiar with my charts.

The night I left I thought I had a severe case of flu. What I had was a heavy emotional breakdown. Once I got inside our pad, I locked the door, took a blanket and pillow off the bed and shut myself in the walk-in closet that Carl and Ray Forman had built.

When Carl came home, it really turned his head around to find me in the closet with the door closed. He tried to persuade me to come out. I couldn't. I was terrified of something, everything. Carl thought I was drunk and tried to open the door. But when he pulled on it, I shrieked so loud he went to bed assuring me I'd realize that everything was okay in the morning. I knew better.

When he got up around noon, he begged me to come out, get dressed and let him take me to the hospital. I began shrieking. He waited until I quieted down and then gently said, "Anita, I love you. I'm on your side. Won't you let me call a doctor?"

I began to yell again. I wouldn't hear of having anyone, including Mom, brought to the house. Carl stayed home all day trying to help me, but there was nothing he could do to get me to cooperate. I was just out of it. My head was like a bicycle that had lost the chain. I kept pedaling, but I wasn't moving.

We developed a routine. He'd bring food, but I wouldn't open the door to take it. He had to place it near the wall. After I was sure he'd left the bedroom, I'd quickly open the door and snatch the tray inside. Then came the hard part. I'd study each dish. I was afraid to eat because I believed every dish except one was poisoned. Finally, I'd decided to take a chance on one of them. It was like a contest. I gambled on outwitting *them*, choosing the one that contained no poison.

Friends would visit the apartment. I could hear them asking about me. Carl always said I was okay. Was he protecting me? Didn't he know I was in danger? Didn't he care? Or was he buying time to get me? I trusted no one.

The closet was my territory. As long as I was there I was safe. But

I was afraid to lie on the bed or even to come out of the safe place to go to the bathroom. I'd wait until Carl left for the Palladium to go in there.

I'd brush my teeth and hair, take a quick shower, grab a towel and run back into the closet to dry myself. That went on for two weeks.

About that time Carl quit Krupa. He'd found a vacant lot that would be a good location for our long-planned club. Sometime during the third week when I was alone in the house, I began forcing myself to get out of the closet and lie on the bed. At first I could manage only five or six minutes before I'd begin breaking out in a cold sweat and would have to go scurrying back to the safe place. After a few days, I was up to ten minutes, and gradually I increased my time until I could spend an hour outside, then two and so on.

Carl was worried, but patient. He didn't try to open the door. He didn't nag at me to come out. He just kept telling me in low, sympathetic tones how much he loved me and wanted to help. He talked about our dream club, promising, "I'm hoping to give you everything you ever wanted, Anita. These will be happy times."

"Maybe I've been too happy," I said. "Because I'm not used to that."

Finally, though, I was able to come out of the closet when he was in another part of the house and eventually to share the bed with him all night long.

A few days later I left the house, got into my car and started the engine. Perspiration popped out all over me. I began trembling and raced back to the closet. Several days later I tried again. This time I was able to drive the car, like, six blocks to the store, buy something, and drive home again. I watched people closely to see whether they were looking at me peculiarly, but they didn't seem to notice anything.

I was so proud I felt like buttonholing someone and bragging what I'd accomplished. But I couldn't speak about it. I waited until Carl came home and told him.

He kissed me gently on the cheek and said how proud he was of me.

So that's how it came down. When I'd recovered enough to agree to see a doctor, he said I'd been suffering from "anxiety neurosis."

CHAPTER VII
SOMETIMES THE ROAD IS ROCKY

Although my emotional collapse lasted only six weeks early in 1946, the entire year remains, well, like a blurred dream.

While I'd been in the closet, Carl and Ray Forman had made a lot of progress on our club. It was to be located on the corner of Riverside Drive and Whitsett in North Hollywood which they thought would make a great location.

Luckily, Carl had struck up a friendship with a fellow named John Shuler, a would-be writer, who lived on our block. John had inherited a lot of bread from his family and was fascinated with the idea of investing in a supper club.

So John came up with the backing. Carl, who was like an amateur architect, dreamed up the plans. And Ray was to supervise the construction.

Eventually, Carl was going to run the club, Ray would take care of the bar, John would share in the profits, and I'd always have a place to do my song stylings. Since I hadn't been recording, we also started our own music publishing firm and planned to found our own label. With that kind of a base I'd never have to accept a gig or sing another song that didn't appeal to me. We'd live happily ever after, fulfilling our own destinies. Ho, ho, hah!

Suddenly in late February, the city lowered the boom. Restrictions were passed on nonessential construction. This left us with a cement foundation, the shell of a building and a lot of copper plumbing. The inspectors claimed the copper had been illegally obtained by a subcontractor. Maybe so. Who knew you needed a permit to buy copper? Not me. Certainly not John. Not Ray. Not Carl. But you've all heard the cliché that ignorance of the law is no defense. It's true. A photographer for the Department of Buildings came out and took pictures of the structure from top to bottom. You'd have thought we were setting up a bomb factory.

Carl and Ray hurried downtown to try to find The Man and put in a fix. No way. It seemed that in addition to a lack of necessary permits, the building sat on ground the city was condemning for a water conduit. Obviously that is why it had been available so reasonably. Given the facts, we decided there was no point in fighting city hall. The government proposed a settlement. The guys accepted the offer and since John Shuler had put up the cash, he received the money. I think after his dealings with the city—that's when Carl began getting a little cynical.

While he was working on the club and I'd been staying home recovering from my nervous breakdown, I'd made one last attempt to learn to cook, do laundry, clean the house. I managed some of it, but deep down inside I realized I didn't want to make it in that world. I was happier opening cans and picking fresh blueberries from the backyard than cooking. Singing was my mission and without it I couldn't imagine going on living.

For a while after the city sluffed off the club, Carl and I sat around wondering what to do. John faded from the scene. Ray Forman cut out and went to work at the track where he decided he'd stay until he retired.

Carl now began concentrating his full efforts in my behalf, and it looked as if he wasn't going to do too badly. I hadn't had a record date in over a year, and he arranged for me to cut ten sides for Bob Thiele's Signature records. What's more he got my points across to Thiele so that Alvie Weisfield's group created a rowdy barroom atmosphere for that tale of the tenderloin, "Ace in the Hole," and suitable accompaniment for "Sometimes I'm Happy."

Carl also found that the Swanee Club on North LaBrea in Hollywood, where Nat King Cole had been working for $85 weekly before hitting it big, was up for grabs. Carl snagged it for me. There, I was reunited with Max Miller's Trio for the first time since my debut at the Off-Beat Club in Chicago. Carl kept books and was the host.

I thought, Hey, man, this is going to be cool. But Carl and I had such a tempestuous personal relationship, we should never have tried working together. About the same time I got hip he was involved with Marilyn Maxwell and then Jacqueline Fontaine—or maybe it was the other way around.

The only part that came as a shock and that I resented was that these were affairs. As far as I knew, before that he'd confined his extramarital love life to one-night stands. I didn't like sharing him, but I'd been around enough so I wasn't hung up on a guy's absolute fidelity. But real involvements—they hurt me.

Instead of complaining, I started goofing up more and more. With my past, I couldn't come on like Pollyanna. But Max Miller had always said he only drank when he worked, and now I joined him. Not that we didn't do good work. We did. In fact, we had such a swinging group that after hours, all the hippest cats in town started dropping by to sit in with us.

One night I was pretty well juiced when ex-child star Jackie Cooper, who played drums, happened by. He was cute—curly blond hair, blue eyes, a turned-up nose. In other words, my type. He'd also been drinking, and before long the two of us had somehow or other retired to the bar where we decided we couldn't live without each other.

I solemnly promised to divorce Carl the next day. My new love wasn't in condition to remember whether or not he had a wife at the moment. But if he did, he said, he'd divorce her, whoever she was, and we'd elope.

With that settled, we drove to my home on Goodland Avenue so I could tell Carl, who naturally wasn't home. For some reason, I mentioned being the world's greatest dancer, a claim my new love disputed. He knew *he* was the world's greatest dancer. We got into a competition, falling around, knocking over furniture, which convinced me we needed more drinks to steady us.

I went to the kitchen for ice and when I got back the ex-kid star was missing. I looked all over, decided he must have left. When I went into the bedroom, I stumbled over his pants. Apparently, the effort to remove them and his tie proved all he was up to. I gulped down my drink and flopped on the bed beside him. Whatever we'd had in mind would have to wait. He was snoring loudly.

I don't know how long we were there, but suddenly the sound of a car door slammed into my skull, wakening me. Through an alcoholic haze I shook my bedmate, as pain shot through my sinuses. He mumbled and rolled over toward me.

Corny as it sounds, I said, "Quick! My husband!"

My guest leaped out of bed, groaned, hesitated, and looked down to discover his pants were missing. He located them and, with great effort, scooped them off the floor. Hearing Carl's key in the door, he tucked them under his arm and made an undignified exit through the window, taking the screen with him.

I burrowed my head under the pillow and waited for Carl to start yelling or beating me. I don't know what he'd been up to, but he crawled into the recently vacated side of the bed and promptly began snoring. Either he didn't notice or he didn't want me asking questions about where he'd been, because the incident was never mentioned.

Even so, the light in our marriage had dimmed. We kept trying, but the marriage worked only about fifty percent of the time.

Why?

I couldn't live in Carl's world and he seemed to be adopting the worst parts of mine. But we kept trying.

I stayed home the day disaster hit. We'd given up the Swanee and Carl had arranged a "Limited Engagement"—how limited none of us could foresee—at the Bocage. I'd opened three nights before, March 18, 1947, backed by Barney Kessel's Trio, and sharing the bill with Sir Lancelot, a calypso singer. It had been a glamorous premiere, made more so by Ava Gardner and Frank Sinatra in the midst of their hectic romance at ringside, while downstairs in the bar was Errol Flynn, applauding loudly.

The Bocage at 5927 Sunset Boulevard was a posh small club with good acoustics, an excellent sound system and poor lighting. We did capacity business on the nineteenth and twentieth and had heavy reservations for the twenty-first. The management had booked me on a percentage basis and it looked as if I'd earn some real bread.

Carl went to the club to try to get better lighting and check a few other details on the afternoon of the twenty-first. When he returned home around 5:00 P.M., he brought two fellows with him. This didn't surprise me because it was always party time at Goodland Avenue, often when we weren't even home. Sometimes the entertainment overflowed the house. One night Dizzy Gillespie, a straight cat who never used grass or any other drugs, played a spirited bebop solo from the upper branches of a tree in our yard. The house sat on a huge lot which gave us plenty of privacy and kept down the neighbors' complaints.*

When Carl approached the door with the two guys behind him, I noticed grim lines around his mouth, but he introduced the men politely, saying, "Anita, I'd like you to meet Al Melendres and Oscar Polcuch. They want to talk to you."

Taking my cue from him, I played very gracious hostess. "How do you do," I said, thinking they might be money men. "Come in!" Dumb! "What do you do?"

Carl cut in. "They're here to shake down the house." And with that he burst into tears.

Melendres and Polcuch had gambled on scaring him and had succeeded. If Carl had given me the high sign, I'd never have let them inside the door without a search warrant. By the time they got one we could have seen to it the house was clean.

But Carl was a very sheltered person, still quite naive. He came from a close-knit family—mother, father, sister. All he could think of was that they would find out he'd been smoking pot. That was no big deal to me. My family was the people I worked with. Lots of them smoked it too. But in the world Carl came from, in those days anyone who smoked grass was a "dope fiend" and would soon be shooting heroin.

Even while he was bemoaning his mother finding out, Carl let the fuzz wander around the house alone. One of them found a small brown bag of pot in the bottom drawer of our dresser. That was it! We both knew judges often handed out stiff sentences even for small amounts of grass.

No one can know what humiliation is until he's been handcuffed, shoved into a police car and hustled down to jail. In our case, it was

---

*Today there are two other houses built on the land that provided such welcome isolation for our little knotty pine cottage.

Lincoln Heights. There we were fingerprinted. They took mug shots of us. And we had to turn in our valuables plus anything we might use to "do bodily harm" to ourselves.

It was a dumb, nightmarish period. If only I'd been lucky enough to have been under contract to a movie studio or a big agency, I'd have placed a call to the head of publicity and he'd have known who to pay off. Around that time the only big movie star who landed in the headlines for using grass was Bob Mitchum, but he certainly wasn't the only one to start smoking it. There were lots of others whose drug use mysteriously never made police records.

Carl was tossed into the men's and I into the women's drunk tanks. I didn't like it, but I wasn't going to let anybody know it bothered me. And I didn't have to worry it would hurt me professionally.

Carl got all shook up when they separated us. Being a very straight, very legitimate character, he wasn't ready for this.

What I mean is that I wasn't hip to all the ins and outs of the law, but I was street-smart. Carl wasn't. Also, I was a stronger character.

We contacted a lawyer named Ray Smith, but before he got there Fred Stern of the McConkey Music Corporation in Kansas City sent around Earl Everett who had defended one of Benny Goodman's bass players and succeeded in getting the case dismissed. Finally it ended with Smith representing Carl and Everett handling me. But even with this representation, in those days our "possession" arrest was the stuff newspaper headlines were made of:

ANITA O'DAY, MATE HELD ON DOPE CHARGE
ANITA O'DAY DENIES DOPE CHARGE
NAB ANITA O'DAY FOR WEED

The last story went on to say:

What appears to be an all-out campaign by local authorities to tag a big name in the music business with a marijuana charge hit a peak with the arrest of Anita O'Day, winner of numerous national magazine polls.

I'd noticed after the Krupa bust, reporters often got their facts wrong. The various stories on my own case taught me not to believe what I read about sensational arrests. If all Will Rogers knew was what he read in the papers, he didn't know much. Some accounts said police had picked up both Carl and me at the Bocage; others, only Carl. He was sometimes identified as an "auto mechanic"— where that came from I'll never know. One account had me saying the grass had been left at the house the previous September by "a guy named Dave."

It shook me up after we'd been sprung to have Carl's lawyer suggest plea bargaining with me taking a rap in return for making the charge a misdemeanor. "They want the publicity value in your name," he explained. "Otherwise you'll both go to jail."

I couldn't believe it. Neither could my lawyer.

"You won't get more than a month or two," Carl's lawyer said.

"No way," I told him bitterly.

Carl was noncommittal.

He and I were released on $1,000 bail each. That night I reopened at the Bocage. The room was filled—standing room only. We seemed set for a run, but bad luck plagued us. The second night after our arrest, an unrelated labor dispute caused the staff to strike. The joint folded.

The fact that Carl and I had separate lawyers added to our troubles by feeding rumors we were splitting. The truth is we were having our problems before the arrest, but hadn't decided what we were going to do even though we recognized the possibility we were bad for one another. Then after a big fight in which he blamed me for the mess and I reminded him who'd brought the fuzz to the house and whose lawyer was asking whom to take the fall, we both said a lot of things we were later sorry for.

Shortly after, I instituted proceedings for divorce. Asked about my action by the press, I tried to belittle its importance, telling reporters: "It's just one of those things. Sometimes marriage just doesn't work out. Our other troubles have nothing to do with it."

With all the general confusion and shuffling of lawyers, things looked black. In fact, they were so bad for Carl that he went to work driving a bus while waiting for his trial to come up.

Jazz was in rough shape, too, but in the late spring of 1947 the McConkey Music Corporation got me a booking at the Rounders in Hollywood after my old Walkathon buddy Frankie Laine moved on to the Morocco. My unadvertised appearance hyped business until July when the McConkey people booked me into Jump Town in Chicago.

On August 11 we were brought before Superior Judge Harold B. Landreth, who heard the case without a jury. Carl and I pleaded not guilty and were convicted. Judge Landreth handed down ninety-day sentences to each of us for possession of a controlled substance in violation of the Health and Safety Code.

After serving a couple of days, each of us appealed and was released on $5,000 bail.

Carl went back to driving a bus and I hopped a plane for Chicago. From there a private aircraft, arranged for by the club's owners, took me to Milwaukee in time for a reunion with the Max Miller Sextet on my opening night at the Continental Theater Lounge.

Interviewed at the Milwaukee airport, I put up a brave front. Reporter Buck Herzog made me sound more like a Damon Runyan type trying to talk like a Vassar girl than a hip jazz singer, quoting me, "It's much ado about nothing. If I weren't in show business and if the incident had happened elsewhere but Hollywood where even judges like publicity, it would have been forgotten." His story had me predicting I'd be vindicated in September when my appeal came up. But I didn't really believe it.

Response at this Midwest spot flabbergasted me. When we approached the club and I saw the people lined up down the block and around the corner, I asked, "What the hell are those people waiting for?"

"You."

"My God, I didn't realize I had that kind of draw."

"You're out on bail," the manager said. "Dopers aren't that common around here."

I was tempted to tell him about some of the entertainers he'd had in the past, but I held my tongue. He turned out to be right. Most of the people were coming to hear "The Jezebel of Jazz," a slogan Carl got a girl friend of his to copyright for me.

A few fans said, "Gee, Anita, we're sorry," or "Tough break!" but the big mob wanted to hear how a jailbird sang.

The crowd was a little boisterous when I danced to the mike for my first number opening night. I sang the way I'd been singing, and when they seemed restive, I began wailing. I'd show them. I'd done it before. I'd do it again. And by the time I finished my first set, the scene was wild, lovely. I made it a rule not to do encores in those days. No pretense of leaving, allowing the applause to coax me back for a bow, milking the applause and finally capitulating to the demand for more from this hip chick. But that night, I made an exception. They might have come into the club to see a freak attraction, but before they left they knew they'd heard something unique.

After a sold-out engagement in Milwaukee, I flew to New York to find myself booked into the Troubador, a joint which was already two-thirds over the edge of bankruptcy. We limped through the week, then the club collapsed.

While in Manhattan, I recorded four sides for Signature with Will Bradley's orchestra. Cole Porter's "What Is This Thing Called Love?" was one of those songs that appealed to everyone from a musical square like columnist Walter Winchell (yes, I know he called me the Queen of Jazz Singers) to the farthest-out jazz cat. We cut it in a wild tempo, used a beguine beat and I even scatted some of it. The second side, "I Told Ya I Love Ya, Now Get Out," was a pseudo-tough torch song, a type having a vogue then, that I recorded before Stan Kenton and June Christy had a big seller with it. Probably the best reason for listening to "It's Different When It Happens to You" is that it shows how long after I'd stopped imitating Lady Day's mannerisms bits of them were still incorporated in my style. The fourth side was "Hi Ho Trailus Boot Whip." Over the years, a lot of my fans and people I've worked with have asked exactly what "hi ho trailus" means. Funny thing, I don't know either.

I first heard it after Roy Eldridge recorded an instrumental of it that excited me. The song itself struck me as a kicky blues pattern. Writers Buster Harding, Jack Palmer, and Buck Ram hadn't quite got down what I wanted. I had to tell myself something. Like after the beginning, it got going pretty fast. To me, it's a horse race. I'm on the horse and I'm giving him the boot and I'm giving him the whip! "Hi ho trailus boot whip/Boot whip trailus boot boot." The music was just a jazz pattern. With the tempo and the words I painted a picture of a race. All my songs paint pictures.

Since I'm talking about songs, people often ask me how I choose them. It's this simple: I like to sing songs I can *feel*. Maybe I've lived the story. But I can't sing every song I like. There are some I just can't master. I love "Yellow Days" but I can't learn it. I try and it's whsssst. "Sweet Georgia Brown" and "Honeysuckle Rose" are easy songs to master. "My Ship" and "I Can't Get Started With You" were harder. It took me two years to learn "Lush Life," and then I really had to push to work it out. They say doing this kind of singing is a gift, but you have to work at it. "Tea for Two" took me eight years to get right, but then I had four choruses you'd never heard before. And you'll never hear again. Not that you'd want to.

I even wrote a couple of songs over the years. The first was "Special Delivery" which I recorded noncommercially with Kenton in 1944. With "Rock 'n' Roll Blues" I must really have been on a power trip. I wrote the music—blues, anyone can write blues—and what passed for lyrics. ("You're gonna rock/You're gonna roll" with a few variations and additional phrases made up the lyric.) I sang it to the accompaniment of "Anita O'Day and Her Orchestra" for Clef/Mercury on January 22, 1952. Ralph Burns made the arrangement and conducted.*

About this time everyone seemed to be getting into the rhythm-and-blues field. Bill Haley did something similar, but the timing of his release was a lot better than mine.

After I returned to California late in 1947, I cut the final four sides for Signature: "How High the Moon," "Malaguena" with Ralph Burns, plus "I Ain't Gettin' Any Younger" and "Key Largo" with Benny Carter's Orchestra. I especially liked the boptinged "Malaguena" and for depth of feeling "Key Largo." "I Ain't Gettin' Any Younger" was a novelty blues and "How High the Moon" one of my several versions of a song every jazz singer has had a go at. Problems with jazz as a money-maker combined with personal difficulties ended my association with Signature and any recording

*The orchestra included: Roy Eldridge, trumpet; Bill Harris, trombone; Budd Johnson, tenor sax; Cecil Payne, baritone sax; Ralph Burns, piano; Al McKibbon, bass; Don Lamond, drums. "Rock 'n' Roll Waltz" which was written by Allen and Ware was conducted by Buddy Bregman for Verve January 5, 1956, after I'd resisted and bitched about it for months.

(except for later release of transcriptions of radio broadcasts from the Royal Roost) for the next couple of years.

On our next appearance in court, Carl and I lost our appeals. No big deal; Billie Holiday had drawn a year and a day for real hard stuff. I didn't even feel any panic when I heard the cell gate slam. You have to remember where I was coming from. In the places I'd been working, it wasn't unusual for somebody to have a record. I wasn't intimidated by rough characters. Nor did my arrival cause any excitement among the prisoners. I was just a name jazz singer who got caught with a little grass. The big noise in our cell block was some broad who'd stabbed an old lady to death.

I took to the routine as easily as I had to Walkathons. They fed us breakfast at 5:00 A.M., lunch at 11:00 and supper at 5:00 P.M. Not bad, I thought. Somebody's finally seeing to it I get nourishing food regularly. Those were the only times anyone saw to it I ate properly. I also spent a lot of time exercising and sleeping. I looked on serving my sentence as a kind of vacation. When I'd slept myself out and didn't feel like working out, I'd lie there thinking about songs. I wasn't worried about my career. A couple of prisoners who were fans told me I'd probably earn more bread when I got out just because I'd been in. So I emerged thinking it was no big deal. Rehabilitated? Hardly. Rested? Definitely.

A lot of people got vicarious kicks from my serving time. I picked up on that and began exaggerating things I'd done to excite them as the hippest of the hip.

Luckily, since I no longer had a recording contract when I got out of jail, the sides I'd cut for Signature kept giving me national exposure. So I was salable to jazz clubs all over the country.

I think it was after I got out of jail and was working my first engagement at the Rag Doll in Chicago that I walked into the club one night and the bartender said, "There's a lush singing at the end of the bar who claims he's your father." I looked at him and suddenly realized it *was* Dad. He hadn't been around for a very long time, but I recognized him. He was a little more together than when he came to see me at the Chicago Theater. He still boozed so now I had an occasional drinking buddy. After that reunion, he came around intermittently for several years. Once I was appearing at a spot that had a long bar. I came to work and heard somebody belting out a song. I asked the bartender, "What goes?" He shrugged and said, "It's some old guy who says he's your father." It was. He was down at the end of the bar singing "Sweet As the Rose In June, Dear."

A singer and a lover—that was Dad. I went to his seventh, his eighth, and his tenth weddings. After he married his tenth wife, Vivian, he told me, "I finally got lucky. This is the one I should have married originally."

Skipping ahead, after he retired he and Vi moved to a little town in Wisconsin, but we kept in touch and I even visited them. His hair had turned white. He'd lost his teeth and wouldn't wear false ones. Without a foundation, his face collapsed into a caricature. But sometime in the 1950s, while I was appearing at a top Chicago jazz club, he wanted to visit me. Vi said she'd accompany him on the condition that he wore his choppers. He resisted, but finally agreed. The result was amazing. Those teeth put his face together again.

Getting to know Dad on this free-and-easy basis made up for a lot of things I'd missed as a child. Luckily, because I wasn't singing at the Chez Paree and Dad wasn't into jazz, I was no big deal to him. He treated me like any father would treat a struggling daughter, gave me advice on how to become popular like Kate Smith had been a few years before. And if I happened to get booked into a little bigger or fancier club, he'd feel proud that I was coming up in the world. For a brief period, he and Vi let me feel like somebody's child.

Then a few years later I was appearing in Denver. One afternoon Vi called me to tell me that Dad had been walking alongside the highway, facing traffic, as he should have been, and some little old man tried to pass the vehicle in front of him. Somehow he lost control of his car, swerved off the highway, hit Dad and killed him.

I went into a state of shock. My first impulse was to charter a plane and fly to his side, but none could be found. I thought it over and realized I couldn't help Dad. I couldn't even see him once more and Vi realized how much I loved him. With most people, you've got something they want or they've got something you want so you have to learn to deal. I didn't have to play the dealing game with Dad and I wanted to remember him for what he was—maybe the only person in my whole life who was nice to me without any reason.

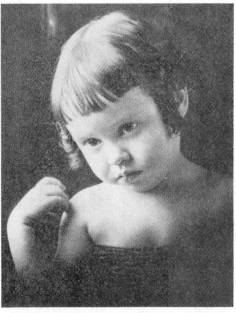

Mom loved playing the martyr; Pop, the personality kid. Co-workers at a Kansas City box factory, they hastily moved to Chicago after marrying. I was their secret reason.

Excess baggage was the way Mom made me feel about myself—even though a photographer featured this portrait of me in his window for a solid year. (*Bivins Brothers.*)

Every summer I was sent from Chicago to Kansas City to visit grandma and grandpa Colton, who gave me toys, pretty clothes, and provided basic religious training.

Remember the dime-store photo machines? Three poses for a quarter. Mom and I splurged on a set one afternoon. One was so good we had it enlarged and hand-tinted.

At **15**, I was roaming the Midwest as a Walkathon contestant. After this partner was murdered, our photo hit the front pages—even though he'd quit two weeks before. (*Cresswell*)

I'd begun to bloom enough to get a job kicking chorus in a tavern near Mom's apartment in Chicago's notorious Uptown District by the time I was **17** years old.

The original Off-Beat Club was the musicians' hangout where it all started for me, at 222 N. State Street. I worked with a different group almost every week for months. (*Seymour Rudolph.*)

Alligator (a cat who appreciates music but doesn't play an instrument) Carl Hoff ducked into the Off Beat Club to get out of the rain and into my life. Here we are posing for "funny fotos" at Riverview Amusement Park.

Trilby Hailey (a.k.a. Betty Rogers) and me, just before we got jobs as big-band singers. She was the vocalist with Russ Morgan's Orchestra and I replaced Irene Daye with Gene Krupa's big band.

Gene Krupa (right), Roy Eldridge, and I really got it all together during 1941-42, turning out Gene's first big hit, "Let Me Off Uptown." You know it's a publicity shot because not even Roy can play with three fingers up.

As Krupa's canary, I felt I was really living, man! Here I am wailing away at Frank Dailey's Meadowbrook in New Jersey just before our big opening at Hotel Pennsylvania in the Big Apple. (*George Dinnick*)

Carl traveled with me on the Krupa tour while waiting to be drafted for World War II. I'd cut "Let Me Off Uptown" and we were planning "Thanks For The Boogie Ride" for Gene, Roy, and me.

For hotel dates, I got gussied up in glamorous gowns, but when we hit the road on a series of one-nighters, I wore a band jacket, skirt and shirt. This set a style for girl singers—and started rumors about my sexual orientation.

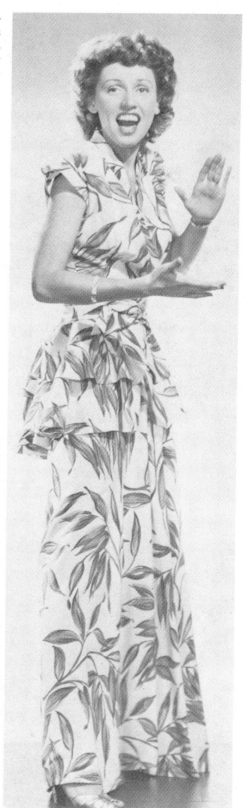

At Hollywood's famed Palladium in late
1942, both Carl and I were in uniform. His
was Air Corps; mine, band. Shortly after, I
took a leave of absence to marry him. Three
days after we wed, Gene was busted for possession of pot and the band broke up.

After a tour as a single, I joined Stan Kenton's band in **1944**. Even though swing and
progressive jazz were a hard mix, we turned
out his first million-seller, "And Her Tears
Flowed Like Wine." (*Universal Pictures
Co., Inc*)

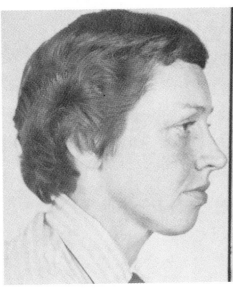
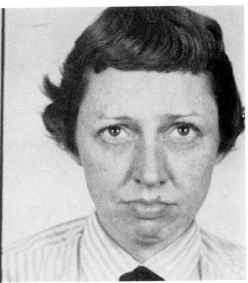

This is a mug shot—with only the numbers missing. Arrested for the fourth time in Kansas City, I was as angry as I look. On a previous occasion I was framed and served time. This time I was guilty and managed to get off without a trial. (*Courtesy Kansas City Police Department*)

Going the glamour route—long white gloves, champagne-blonde hair, etc.—was my way of countering my reputation as a user. I may have looked straight to casual observers, but three quarters of the time I was higher than a kite. (*Maurice Seymour*)

Gene and I had one of our many reunions at
Basin Street East in New York. Because of
our grass busts, we had to grease palms to
obtain a cabaret work permit to appear in
the city. (*Spilka*)

At the Hi Note in Chicago, I fell in love
with trumpeter Denny Roche. Our relationship wouldn't raise an eyebrow today, but at
the time was scandalous. I was an "older
woman," 29, and Denny was "just a kid,"
22.

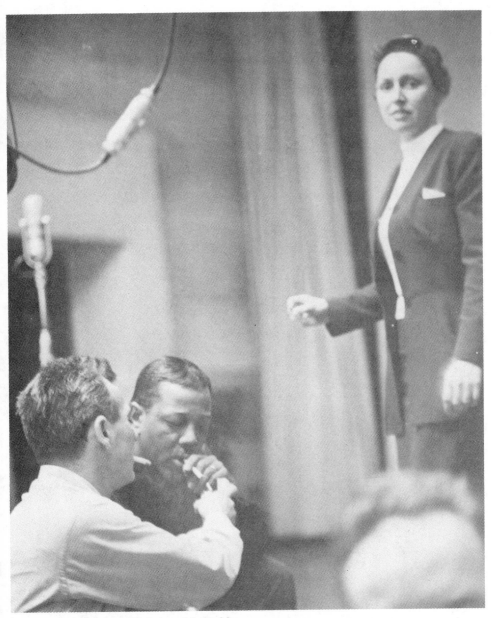

Following the success of *Anita* with Buddy
Breggman on Norman Granz's Verve label,
Gene, Roy and I reunited to do some of the
numbers associated with us from the old
days. (*Herman Leonard*)

My great drummer and true friend John Poole helped me over the rough spots for more than a quarter of a century. Our musical collaboration produced a deeper intimacy than any sexual relationship I've ever had. Here we are at Tivoli Gardens in Copenhagen during one of our foreign tours.

Jazz on a Summer's Day, the documentary Bert Stern filmed at the 1958 Newport Jazz Festival, has brought me international recognition. Filmed without my knowledge of what was going on, it has done more to spread the word about me than any other gig I've ever played.

That's me at the piano with Helen O'Connell in a publicity shot with Bob Crosby, Jack Leonard, and—in the middle—you know who.

Minnie Gugenheim decided that the classical cats who made up her audiences at Lewisholm Stadium needed a little taste of jazz, so she brought in Lionel Hampton, Louis Armstrong and me. How did the longhairs respond? They rose to their feet and cheered.

Randall's Island Jazz Festival placed me on the bill with my idol Billie Holiday. Sadly, she always ignored me, so I never had an opportunity to tell her how much I owed and admired her.

Movie acting has never been my bag, but I did enjoy making *The Outfit* with Robert Duvall and Karen Black. Earlier I'd made *The Gene Krupa Story* with Sal Mineo and *Zig Zag* with George Kennedy. (*MGM*)

photo credit: James J. Kriegsmann

This is the first photo taken when I resumed my career in 1969. Luckily, the ravages of a 14-year heroin habit didn't show.

Harry Reasoner and CBS-TV's *60 Minutes* crew spent twenty-odd hours filming me at Marty's in New York, Lulu's in Boston, and everywhere including my kitchen in Los Angeles.

Martha Raye, who influenced my style more than any other singer, made a surprise appearance at my 50th anniversary celebration in Hollywood.

Photo credit: Zarko Kalmic

Father-daughter had nothing to do with it. We enjoyed one another as people.

After we got out of jail, even though I'd dropped divorce proceedings, Carl and I agreed the smart move was for him to do his thing and me, mine. Our peaks-and-pits relationship wasn't doing either of us any good.

When he managed me, it was his job to see that I got what was right for me artistically. On the job, I'm a perfectionist. Not easy to please? Well, you could say that if you like understatement. I was never one of those "that's-it" types. I'm always striving. And when the artist and the manager go home together they take those problems with them. Also, Carl still had a roving eye . . .

The upshot was that we decided he'd continue driving a bus until he could get back into golf and I'd pursue my career. I spent most of 1947 and 1948 gigging around. I guess when you're younger everything is a kick. I know I was happy tootling off to play small jazz joints wherever they might be. But I was especially thrilled to be booked into the Royal Roost in New York for three weeks. To work there was a heavy thing. First of all, it preceded Birdland as the home of bebop which meant I was keeping abreast of developments. Also, I was the only white on the bill which meant I'd earned acceptance in a field artistically dominated by blacks.

The opening week's bill included Count Basie's band, Tadd Dameron's bop outfit and me. I worked as a big band singer with Basie and a bebopper with Dameron. Man, I was really where the action was.

Opening night got off to an unsteady start. A delayed plane and bad planning resulted in my having to open cold with the Count. But being both a superb musician and the ultimate gentleman, he made that week a memorable one. I'll admit I was a little in awe of Basie, which stimulated me to work at top form even though I was straitjacketed by a small spot that held me in a single stationary position. No matter how much I complained the manager wouldn't change it, so I lived with it, adapted, and the accompaniment was so great it all worked out.

The next two weeks I was supposed to work with my friend Dizzy Gillespie. I really looked forward to that gig because Dizzy and his band were among the leaders in bop, a direction in which I was moving. Dizzy is a nice, very straight, hard-working guy in spite of his clowning on the bandstand. He's also very upfront about what he feels and when he and his band showed up for the first rehearsal, he told me very nicely that there was no way I could sing with his outfit.

"I sang with Basie," I told him.

"But not with me," he said. "I do the singing on my band."

I'd been so thrilled with my engagement the first week at the Roost, I'd taken to calling Carl to report. By this time, he'd swallowed his pride and had gone out to the Wilshire Country Club where he literally began as a caddy. But Carl basically was a very together cat. So when the food concession in the caddy shack had come up for grabs, Carl and another guy had snagged it.

Now for his sake and mine, he should have stayed there. Because it was obvious to everybody but him and me that our relationship wasn't going to work out. And even we knew it part of the time.

But during one of our calls when I told him that Dizzy didn't want me to sing with him and things were a little rocky around the club, that was all he needed to hear. He was on the next plane.

He arrived all revved up about helping me. Both of us felt we were really together again—on cloud nine, as we used to say. Plans, plans, plans. We schemed and we planned. Nothing was going to stop us from being to jazz what Katharine Cornell and Guthrie McClintic were to the theater.

As it turned out, Carl couldn't do any more with Dizzy than I could. But it worked out okay. The management spotted me between Diz and Tadd Dameron. Tadd stepped aside and Lou Stein took his place in the Dameron group to provide accompaniment for my set.

Looking back, it seems ironic that I, who had a reputation as a "dope fiend," should have known so little about hard drugs. As I hung around listening to Dizzy's group, I'd see "Fats" Navarro or Charlie Parker apparently asleep on the job and I honestly thought they ought to get more rest, believe it or not!

But then when it came time for one of them to play, the music was so vibrant, so vivacious, so charged that I couldn't believe it. Of course, they were nodding. Later I got to know all about that too well, but in the fall of 1948 I was still naive.

Here I was on the fringe of the bebop junkie world in which I'd spend a decade that would cut those years right out of the center of my career and I didn't know the difference between nodding and sleeping. I'd never sniffed coke, snorted, or shot heroin. If anyone had told me that within five years I'd be hooked, I'd have told whoever it was he'd flipped his wig.

CHAPTER VIII
AND YOU'RE JUST ANOTHER DAME

—From a poem by Anita O'Day

Carl and I decided to make Chicago our home base. During the end of 1948 I was gigging around joints in Chicago. It wasn't Royal Roost time, but that never bothered me as long as the musicians were talented and I had a chance to experiment in developing my style. The way I looked at it I was still an apprentice. A doctor goes to school, works in a hospital, spends years preparing himself before he hangs out his shingle. Why shouldn't a singer do the same?

Carl didn't agree. He concentrated on setting a big deal, getting the money, building my name. Next to his roving eye, that's what caused most of our problems. He called my blowups temperament. I called them integrity.

Of course, that's not the whole story. Sometimes I've thought that there are two Anitas living in one body—the Good Anita and the Bad Anita. The Healthy Anita and the Sick Anita.

The Good Anita is ambitious, creative and cooperative. She's always on time and gives her performance her best shot. She's a contender and if she doesn't always win, she's in there trying.

The Bad Anita is a don't-give-a-damn dame. She's short on tact. She drinks too much, and when she's on the bottle she's capable of alienating the people who are trying to help her. The Bad Anita has to be kept in check because in a short time she can torpedo the things the Good Anita has spent years building up.

During late 1948 and in 1949, since neither was totally in control, I wasn't going either forward or backward. Unless, of course, you believe that if you aren't going forward, you're going backward.

Artistically I knew I was making some fantastic strides, but that's only half of the game. I probably couldn't have trimmed my musical instincts in the interest of popularity even if I'd wanted to, because there was a lot of confusion about jazz artists. The trade press—*Billboard, Variety, Down Beat, Metronome,* whatever—complained that many pop singers and instrumentalists who could sing or handle an instrument competently were coming on billed as jazz artists without understanding the original jazz structure.

Billie Holiday, Mildred Bailey and Mary Ann McCall were active. So were Alberta Hunter, Thelma Carpenter, Helen Humes, Chris Connor and June Christy. But bebop and cool jazz opposed traditional Dixieland. Jazz was in confusion.

Some jazz singers, realizing there was lots more bread in pop singing, chose that route. Nat King Cole told interviewers he preferred to sing jazz, but he was going the pop route because that's where the big money lay. Kay Starr altered her sound so completely a reporter inquired whether she had had a throat operation. Kay candidly told him she'd just changed to something more commercial. "You can't make enough money as a jazz singer," she announced.

Don't get me wrong, I'm not putting anyone down. There are a lot of pop singers I've admired—soloists backed by a band. Helen Forrest and Helen O'Connell are two. Helen Forrest was a good lead singer, a very together lady, who was one of the best. Helen O'Connell was a natural of her kind. She still looks sensational and sings well. Most of her songs are ballads. I'd imagine she learns the melody and stays with it, which is okay as long as it doesn't bore her.

Some—Georgia Gibbs, Jo Stafford, Dinah Shore, Patti Page and Rosemary Clooney—have worked a variety of ways. Peggy Lee is a good example of this. She began as a band singer, married a guitar player and got into songwriting. She had individuality, magnetism and beauty. She changed with the times and stayed on top for many years. But she didn't improvise. Her piano player for many years told me she always did a song the same way night after night. If the musicians varied the backing, she faltered. Fine for her, but if I'd done that I might as well have gone into musical comedy.

Back in those days, I was just beginning to get excited about using my voice as an instrument in the band. Being a pop singer or band vocalist didn't interest me. I even wrote an article for *Down Beat* suggesting arrangements be made which brought in the voice as a part of the orchestra instead of using the orchestra to back a vocal solo. That's what small groups did and do. I needed a place to experiment.

Sometimes a good thing can come out of a bad one. That's what happened to Carl and me. The bad situation was that as Chicago grew as a convention center, a lot of clip joints sprang up to cater to the carousing conventioneers who were on the town and looking for action. At first it was B-drinking, gambling and prostitution. Then the owners and girls got impatient about separating the marks from their money. Some of the girls began working the badger game. When that brought beefs with the police, Mickey Finns began getting slipped into the suckers' drinks. They were rolled and left in alleys far away from the spot where they'd been fleeced. Then for reasons unclear, several small-town good-time Charlies disappeared without a trace. Neither they nor their bodies ever turned up.

An uproar developed. The police and liquor board stepped in. The clip joints began losing their licenses. When one of those involved in the conventioneer disappearances, located at Clark and Illinois streets, came up for grabs, Marty Dennenberg, a cab-driver friend of Max Miller's, had a chance to take it over. He needed a gimmick and didn't have any ideas. He complained about his predicament to Max Miller. Max told him about me and added, "Her husband is a hip guy with a lot of good ideas." He sold us to Marty so that we went into partnership.

We decided to call the place the Hi Note and run it as a jazz joint with me as a headliner and Max's Trio providing the backing. We opened in March of 1949 and made an immediate hit. It looked as if Carl had stumbled on the home-away-from-home for me that we'd been dreaming of before we got busted in California.

In April Carl came up with the great idea of reuniting Jimmy McPartland, Max and me a decade after our big success at the Off

Beat in 1939. *Down Beat* gave us important play with a big story headlined:

ANITA, MAX AND JIMMY REUNITED AFTER A DECADE AT THE HI NOTE.

The men, they said, looked older, but I'd just "replaced my schoolgirl look with sophistication."

A lot of talent passed through the Hi Note. Our first intermission pianist and singer was a girl named Jeri Southern, whose warm, intimate style went over big with our customers. When a recording company signed her and she moved on to bigger and better things, I suggested a replacement. In my opinion this chick was a wonderful jazz singer, and through the years legions of Carmen McRae fans have agreed with me.

Whenever someone compliments me by saying that no matter how many times I sing a song, it always seems as if I'm re-creating it, I think of Carmen. She does that.

She really works over a song with her modern, free-sketch jazz technique. If the tempo is fast, Carmen and the rest of us don't phrase the same as when the tempo is more deliberate. Say we're singing a jump tune, but the mood strikes us to slow it way down. When we do we paint a different picture. Ella Fitzgerald and a lot of others sing the melody straight through once on most songs. I don't. I like to start and finish a song the way it's written but in between there are all kinds of choices to be made. And the choices we make determine the picture we paint. Each of us does what she can because nobody can do everything.

Today Carmen is a wonderful singer. This chick has a lot of voice, a lot of chops, she can sing a lot of things. But, in my opinion, she can't sing a fast tune and really get on time. Take another great, Sarah Vaughan. Sarah's got great chops, a big neck, good sound, but on a fast tune she runs behind the beat. That's why Ella is, more or less, first. In later days, she's into something other than improvising, but whatever her approach she can sing a ballad, an uptune, a novelty, almost anything. But nobody has it all. Like me, Ella doesn't have a real good voice.

Jimmy McPartland on trumpet, his wife Marion on piano, Mousey Alexander on drums and a series of players on bass came in at the Hi Note as the band. They closed and Max Miller came back. An addition to the group was the most beautiful young trumpet player I'd ever seen in my life. Flashing teeth, smiling eyes, a full head of curly hair and a bulky but tightly muscled frame. I took one look at him and there went Anita.

I was twenty-nine, married. He was twenty-two, still going to college five days and blowing good trumpet six nights a week. His name was Denny Roche. And it soon became obvious he dug me as much as I did him. Our falling in love changed a lot of things.

Until then, even though I'd once filed for divorce, I kept sending up little signals for Carl to come back. I knew he was a player, but I secretly thought I'd reform him. Reform? Nobody reforms when they're having as much fun as he was while getting no static from me.

When Carl got hip to Denny's and my relationship, I don't think he took it too seriously. Maybe he even thought it was funny. After all, Denny was only twenty-two, a kid.

I don't remember exactly what I thought then, but I can look back and say I think Carl and I loved one another, but I'm not sure either of us was in those days capable of fidelity. I'm not even sure that it was that important to either of us.

I think Denny's and my relationship really began to bug Carl when he realized that Denny wasn't just a distraction, a plaything; that I loved Denny as much as I did him. That's when it began to hurt. He didn't tell me. He didn't have to. I knew what he was going through. Because for him, Denny equaled what Marilyn Maxwell or Jacqueline Fontaine had represented to me. Neither Denny nor those chicks belonged to the all-cats-are-gray-at-night category. I think what hurt Carl most was that Denny and I enjoyed the intimacy of working together in music, something he couldn't give me or even share in.

Maybe I wanted to give him the shaft, hurt him the way he'd hurt me earlier. At first I'm sure Carl thought Denny was just a pawn I was using, because he couldn't dig the relationship. How could I be serious about a twenty-two-year-old boy? Was I going to tell him this kid could fulfill needs he couldn't?

Remember, this was 1950. Today the story of the older woman

and the young guy doesn't raise an eyebrow. Fortyish actresses and society women flaunt affairs with young studs barely out of their teens. But in 1950 having a young lover was a shocking way of expressing my rebelliousness.

Carl didn't make a big thing of it. He didn't beat me or even beg me to give up Denny. Secretly, when he got fed up with the turmoil and the tumult, he contacted his brother-in-law who was the pro at the Merrill Hills Country Club in Waukesha, Wisconsin. Carl had started him in golf at the Biltmore in Barrington and now his brother-in-law agreed to hire Carl as his assistant at Merrill Hills.

Carl told me the whole scene was getting impossible, and he wanted to get out of my world and back where he would be through having his life dependent on my whims and idiosyncrasies.

What could I say? I could understand his position. If I'd been in his place, I'd have done the same thing myself. Only a whole lot sooner.

After Carl cut out, things at the Hi Note began to fall apart. I took a brief leave in September for an engagement at the famed Apollo Theater. The Apollo was to Harlem what the Palace had been to Broadway before radio, talking pictures and the Great Depression killed big-time vaudeville.

I was the only white on the bill for the week of September 21, 1950. The others were The Ravens, Calvin Boze's twelve-piece band, comic hoofers Hap and Happy, roller-skating dancer Harold King and me, billed as "The Jezebel of Jazz."

My three numbers, all performed in bebop style, went over great with 99.9 percent of the audience, which is all a jazz singer can ask when performing for the race that originated the art.

Stimulated by the experience, I returned to the Hi Note to work an open-end engagement with Max Miller. When Carl came to Chicago from Waukesha and discovered that Denny was still with the group, he turned around and went back home. By then cold weather had hit and golf was out of season. So Carl and a couple of other dudes began publishing a jazz newspaper in Milwaukee. He also got friendly with a cat by the name of Nick Gentile, who owned the Stage Door in Milwaukee. Gentile hired Carl to broadcast from the club, patterning his disc jockey show after Symphony Sid.

Near the end of the year, the management wanted to bring a New York name into the Hi Note for the holidays. That was cool with Max Miller and me because Carl had offered us a booking at Gentile's Stage Door.

I had a week off before the Milwaukee gig, so it gave me a chance to drop in to see the Hi Note's holiday headliner, Miles Davis, who happened to be a particular favorite of mine. I'd only been able to dig him on records but I looked forward to seeing and hearing him in person.

It wasn't show time yet when I arrived at the Hi Note so I sat on a bar stool and ordered a drink. While I was enjoying it, I was playing around with a tune called "Cent and a Half." After a bit, this good-looking black man got off one of the stools and came over to ask: "Where'd you get that tune?"

"Oh, I don't know," I said, "It's in the air. Kind of a favorite of mine."

"I wrote it," he said, matter-of-factly.

"Oh, groovy. I'm Anita O'Day."

Of course, he was Miles Davis. There at the Hi Note we formed a mutual admiration society. Almost every night that week until I left for the Milwaukee engagement, I dropped in to listen to Miles and those cats of his blow. Listening to him, I added a new idol to my collection.

During 1951 I hopscotched around the country playing spots where Carl, Redd Evans and others booked me. I wasn't signed with any one manager. I just took the choice offers each could come up with. I'd probably have done better to have been with Carl, but that meant giving up Denny since he wouldn't book Max Miller anywhere I was playing.

And I wasn't about to do that. Denny's first trip away from home base was with Max's quartet and introduced him to a different kind of life. He found the excitement of traveling from city to city, plus a few beers every night, was all the stimulation he needed. But his natural high was contagious.

I could even cope with an out-of-tune piano or a bad sound system with Denny around. I carried a supply of baby spots and pink gelatins along and with him to help we'd install them. If audiences were receptive, I'd leave them for the next performer after we'd move on. My contribution: improving working conditions.

I don't remember who it was that booked me to co-headline with film star John Boles at the Seville Theater in Montreal. John Boles! I thought he'd died years ago. No, really, I was a fan of his. He had a nice, corny little act. He still looked handsome. He sang these romantic "I-Kiss-Your-Hand, Madame" songs and distributed red roses to a dozen ecstatic ladies. My mother would have loved it.

My dressing room was right next to his. We introduced ourselves and that was that except for saying good morning and good night. The men's and ladies' latrines were at the end of the hall, and he'd usually go to the men's in nothing but his shorts. But I didn't think anything of that. I didn't associate movie stars with real sex. Fantasy sex, yes. Real sex, no. To my way of thinking, they confined their romances to their equals. They were gentlemen, who wouldn't stoop to a quickie. Oh, maybe the cowboy stars from Republic or Monogram Studios would, but not a distinguished man of John Boles' stature. And for the first couple of days he behaved just as I'd expected.

Then on the third day I took my final bow at the second performance and the stage manager asked, "Where's your roommate?"

"Who?"

"Mr. Boles. He's on in fifteen minutes."

I knew where he hung out so I jumped into something and ran around the corner to this cocktail lounge. "You're on in ten minutes," I told him.

He thanked me, but sat there finishing his drink. So I ran all the way back thinking I'd fill in if he didn't show. He arrived just in time to walk on stage in his street clothes and I went out front to watch. He'd never been more charming.

When I came upstairs to my dressing room, he called to me: "Oh Anita! Come in. I want to thank you for coming after me."

He had already stripped to his shorts, but the door was open so I stepped in. He offered me a drink and invited me to sit down. I perched on the long makeup table. We laughed and agreed how easily time could get away from you when you went into a bar and lifted a couple. It was a dangerous practice when you had a show to do.

I'd almost finished my drink and was about to slip off the table and leave when Mr. Boles said something about my having very pretty legs. "In fact," he said, "you're a very pretty girl."

And with that, he made his move. Now I wasn't Snow White, but I didn't have a chance even if I had been. He stood up and suddenly he was all over me. He seemed to have more hands than an octopus. He pinned me against the dressing table, took me in his arms and really began kissing me. I was startled and helpless. He was skilled as a magician in getting his shorts and my skirt and panties off. His foot kicked the dressing room door shut. And in spite of the speed and my attempted struggle, he managed the impossible—a gentle rape.

That's the only way to describe it. Maybe unconsciously I wanted him to rape me. I don't think so, but *maybe*. I will say that if you're going to have to be raped, it's better that it be by a handsome, gentle, smiling movie star with good manners than some psycho who leaps out of the bushes and jumps you.

Mr. Boles couldn't have been more debonaire as he kissed, passed compliments—puff—puff—and made small talk—puff—puff—as if we were having tea at the Plaza.

When it was over and I got out of there I didn't know what I felt. Anger? Not really. Fear? No. Elation? Certainly not. Degradation? Quite honestly, no. Had *he* acted out one of *my* fantasies? Definitely not. Now if it had only been Gene Raymond—no, no, only kidding, folks.

Afterward, Mr. Boles didn't seem a bit embarrassed or try to avoid me or offer an apology. He was as friendly as ever and he never tried anything like that again. If it hadn't been for certain consequences I might have thought I'd imagined it.

Later I wondered whether it had been his way of thanking me for keeping him from missing his performance. If so, a bouquet of flowers, a box of candy or a bottle of cognac would have been more appreciated.

About a month or so later, I began getting that old familiar feeling. I hadn't been pregnant fourteen times for nothing. I told Carl not to set any more gigs after the Casablanca Club in Canton, Ohio. Physically I felt terrible, but I thought I could make it through that job before getting taken care of.

I did my shows on Friday, April 13, even though I noticed that my abdomen was definitely swollen. As soon as I finished I went to my hotel room. The night that followed was horrendous. I dropped in and out of consciousness and had horrible nightmares. As soon as I could see the sunlight through the drawn shades, I tried to sit up, but dropped back, dizzy and nauseated.

My stomach had ballooned up overnight. My head throbbed. My eyes felt sore. I was feverish and having chills. I let myself slide gently out of bed and tried to inch toward the telephone. I stopped, lay there with my teeth chattering, inched closer and broke into a cold sweat. I was worried about catching pneumonia. I wondered whether I was dying. The room spun around.

Finally, with great effort, I was able to move again. I got to the phone, removed the receiver, and after what seemed hours, I reached the hotel switchboard and gasped that I needed a doctor immediately. "Also—someone—with—a passkey," I mumbled. "I—can't—make it—to—the door—to let him—in."

After a long time I heard a key turn in the lock and a voice instruct the bellboy to wait outside. The doctor entered and carried me back to the bed. He tried to question me as he began his examination. When he touched my swollen belly, he said something about internal bleeding and picked up the receiver to request an ambulance.

I wanted to know what was wrong, but he said he was just the house doctor and didn't want to make a guess. He wanted to get me to the hospital and let a gynecologist take over.

I can't begin to describe what happened between the time they got me onto the stretcher at the hotel and into the emergency room of the hospital. Anything you imagine won't be an exaggeration. The last thing I remember is telling someone in the ambulance to call Carl Hoff collect.

You may have read the story he gave out to the wire services at the time, but naturally I don't expect anyone to remember:

ANITA O'DAY STRICKEN ILL

Anita O'Day, 28, one of the top girl vocalists in the land, was in fairly good condition at Aultman Hospital in Canton, Ohio, Saturday after an emergency appendectomy.

Miss O'Day, who was appearing at the Casablanca Night Club in

Reedurban, formerly sang with Stan Kenton's and Gene Krupa's orchestras. Her appendix burst early Saturday morning, her manager said.

Miss O'Day has appeared in several movie shorts, on television programs and is a Capitol recording star. Probably her most famous platter is "Let Me Off Uptown" of which one and a half million copies were sold.

That's what Carl told the reporters and that's what newspapers printed. Here is a copy of a report that Carl and I received from two physicians:

JOSEPH J. LEVEN, M.A., M.D.
General Surgery
928 Market Street
Canton, Ohio

4/15/51

Anita Hoff
Dr. Leven
  Ectopic Pregnancy

GROSS: Specimen consists of a tube and attached ovary. The tube measures 8.0 × 0.6 cm. At the proximal end of the wall is dilated, hemorrhagic and appears to be ruptured. Remainder of tube is grossly normal. Ovary measures 4.0 × 2.0 × 1.0 cm. Surface is gray and wrinkled. Cut section reveals one large corpus luteum with central hemorrhage.

MICROSCOPIC: Mucosa and wall of Fallopian tube contain a large amount of recently extravasated red blood cells showing no evidence of organization. Numerous chorionic villi and decidual cells are found in the lumen, and chorionic villi are found invading the wall. Sections of the ovary reveal one active corpus luteum.

DIAGNOSIS: TUBAL ECTOPIC PREGNANCY WITH RUPTURE

Dr. Henderson

Chances for such a pregnancy are about a million to one, according to Dr. Henderson, which made me something of a rarity.

Carl was wonderful to me. He took over as soon as I was well enough to travel back to Waukesha where I moved into his apartment. We kept trying to convince ourselves, against all logic, that we could make the marriage work. Long after we should have given up, we kept trying, but our relationship was an on-again, off-again thing. Before Denny, I could blame Carl and his chicks. Now it wasn't so simple. The result was that none of us knew where we stood.

My relationship with Carl improved so much during the last half of 1951 that in 1952 we decided he'd be my exclusive manager again. This meant finding a new back-up group. Shortly after, Carl came home all steamed up one day. "How would you like to work with Roy Kral?" he asked.

"And have Jackie Cain snatch me bald? Who wouldn't like working with Roy? But he and Jackie are a team."

It turned out Jackie was pregnant and Roy was available. Carl reactivated our association with Freddie Williams of Associated Booking, Joe Glaser's Chicago office, and they began setting up gigs. We opened in Milwaukee and after that engagement moved to the Blue Note in Chicago on May 16, an engagement that was heralded by a very nice promotional piece the Glaser people got Stanley Kenton to write about me:

> Anita O'Day is the most uninhibited singer I've ever known. She sings without fear and that's what makes her so dynamic.
> Working with Anita I learned that when she hears a sound rolling around in her head, she's never obsessed with worrying, "Will it go?" If she likes that sound she gets out and makes it . . . ," he began and he ended, "There walks a gal who owns a patent on showmanship.

Truthfully, I think Stanley appreciated me more after I'd gone and vice versa.

Working with Roy Kral proved a blessing because here was a cat who lived for music in the same way I did. We worked out every afternoon, if that's the word for it. Because if it was work, it was the best kind, the kind I would wish all the people on this earth could look forward to when they get up each morning.

The results were evident too. Working (or playing) in the afternoon was reflected in my performances at night, and the results didn't escape a critic from the *Chicago Sun-Times* whose name, in my passion for neatness and symmetry, I clipped off the story:

> Anita O'Day is demonstrating at the Blue Note why she is one of the little handful of great stylists among jazz singers. She can give any song her unmistakable imprint.
>
> It's no small accomplishment to breathe a new personality into such a ballad as "Lover Come Back To Me" which for years has borne the stamp of Mildred Bailey. But Anita does it.
>
> What's more, she's constantly remaking her repertoire. Her current version of "How High the Moon" is something completely different from the way she used to sing it.
>
> This girl is so modern she's almost ahead of herself. Her minor keys and offbeat phrasings have a weird other-worldliness akin to the atmosphere of certain Salvador Dali paintings.

When they start writing that kind of stuff about you in your own hometown, you know you're really cutting it. Further proof emerged during July in Chicago when I made a second session for Norman Granz' Clef label. In January I'd cut "Rock 'n' Roll Blues," "Love for Sale," "Lover Come Back to Me," and "Lullaby of the Leaves" with Ralph Burns' Orchestra in New York. In Chicago, with Roy Kral's Combo I cut "No Soap No Hope Blues," "Speak Low," "The Lady Is a Tramp" and "Strawberry Moon." The last two, which were issued on Mercury, impressed many reviewers as the most artistically successful sides I'd done for Mercury. Man, I was living!

After Chicago, Roy stayed in the Midwest while Carl and I cut out for a working vacation in Hawaii in mid-1952. We stayed at the Moana Hotel in Waikiki Beach where I could spend a lot of time in the sun. I filled an engagement at the Brown Derby beginning July 21 and Eddie Sartain, who was doing a great job promoting American jazz artists in Japan, offered me a tour. I decided not to take it because Carl was busted on the twenty-fourth when he went to the police station to pick up a valise he'd reported stolen a couple of days earlier. After the fuzz recovered the luggage, they checked out the contents and found five joints that I'd stashed away. So when he arrived to reclaim it, the narcs nabbed him.

An experienced street player would have known there was no

way they could make the charge stick. That bag had passed through both the thief's and the police's hands. Anyone could have planted the evidence.

Instead of going to Japan, we came back to the United States where I played the Blackhawk with Dave Brubeck for a couple of weeks in August, and we did what may have been the first live-TV remote from a nightclub.

Carl got all excited about the possibilities of bringing jazz to mass audiences via TV after seeing the result. So he made a deal for the same kind of a setup from the 331 Club in Los Angeles. NBC-TV bought a package, including Stan Getz, Chet Baker, Gerry Mulligan, Tiny Kahn and me. Carl looked on it as the opportunity of our lives, having this Sunday afternoon gig telecast coast to coast. I don't remember all the details, but I do remember a very disturbed Carl demanding how the hell he got involved with such a bunch of junkies as he and Gerry Mulligan scuffled around trying to locate everybody thirty minutes before the telecast.

After that experience, he said, "This is the end. If you cats want your lives to go down the drain, that's okay with me. But I'm not going down the tube with you."

He went to the apartment we had on Wilshire Boulevard, took his clothes and the money he had in his pocket and said, "See you later. This is the end."

Of course with the publicity the TV show had given me, I had no trouble moving over to the Tiffany, sharing the bill with Stan Getz. Now that was a job I'd have paid them to let me do. Because Stan rates as one of my all-time favorites. He was about seventeen when he joined the Kenton band. I remember him from that era when he mostly blew eighth notes because that's all he knew. But he was always working at that saxophone and he progressed. Later on, he progressed so far that he was out there all alone for a long time before anyone caught up. Then he progressed some more until he got too far out for me. Whatever the melody was, I couldn't find it. And I'm a professional. What did ordinary listeners get? Still, listening to Stan work over that tenor sax was a pure joy most of the time.

By this time, I looked upon myself as a really hip chick. I believed I could get away with anything—and was doing it. I could outdrink most of the boys. If I got drunk, I didn't show it. Point of honor. I flirted with the idea of shooting heroin once just for kicks, but the night I was going to try it my old friend Gerry Mulligan happened into the room and threatened to bash some skulls if anybody showed me how to fix. Then he got me out of there.

In every way I was getting more careless. I seemed to be looking for trouble. I tried to get Carl back and have Denny around too. I thought I'd learned how to keep both happy. If, as I've sometimes thought, there's a Good Anita and a Bad Anita fighting for dominance, in late '52 and early '53 Bad Anita, who wants to shock, mock and put everybody and everything down, was definitely in control. Carl had walked out, and I'd asked Denny to join me on my next gig at the Club Alabam, located on Central Avenue next to the famed Dunbar Hotel, which provided the best accommodations available to blacks visiting Los Angeles. The Alabam was a club where such greats as Ella Fitzgerald, Count Basie, "Bojangles" Robinson, Ethel Waters and many other black headliners played. Herb Jeffries, who made such a hit singing "Flamingo," was for a long time master of ceremonies. Opening night, October 15, 1952, was everything I could ask for. But Denny thought I was too juiced to risk letting me drive. He and pianist Shell Robin insisted on taking me to the Wilshire Apartments. As soon as I was in the car, I broke out a joint and lit up. Neither of the guys smoked, but I really enjoyed myself until Shell ran the boulevard stop at Jefferson and Hill.

A second later, Denny was rolling down the window, telling me to ditch the joint because a police car was about to pull us to the curb. I tossed the roach out the window just about the time the flasher and siren started. Shell slowed and pulled over into a rolling stop.

Patrolman K.C. Noland and William Zimmerman later claimed they saw me throw the roach out the window as they approached the car. Wrong. I flipped it out before Shell even slowed down. But they did manage to find it—or at least find one—whether it was mine or not.

"All three of them just kept sitting there acting like they had ants in their pants," Zimmerman told a *Mirror* reporter.

They rousted us from the car, shook us down, went over the car and came up empty-handed. Still they took us to University Station for more questioning, then transferred us to the city jail. They had nothing on Denny so they let him go, and Shell got off with a traffic ticket.

I was tossed into the drunk tank with eight whores, a drunk with DTs and the pleasant one, a pickpocket. Denny promised to see about bail and get me a lawyer. But by the time I got out I had to toss out my new gown. I had body vermin and had to shave myself and use blue ointment. Disgusting? Right. But true.

Somewhere along the way I encountered reporters from the *Mirror* who seemed to be having a good time covering my latest troubles, and I was high enough to think I could tough it out with them instead of remaining silent.

When they asked for my side of the story, I asked what story. They reminded me I was there on a narcotics rap and I brazened it out with, "Man, I don't even know what you're talking about."

They wanted to know where the arrest had occurred.

"Why don't you ask me something I can answer?"

What time had I been picked up?

"Man, I don't even know what time it is now." Then I went back to my cell.

Next day there I was on the front pages of the *Los Angeles Mirror* and the *Daily News*, a sultry-looking brunette chick with long, dangling crystal earrings, painted-on eyebrows to replace the real ones I'd sacrificed to the worship of Jean Harlow many years ago, a crystal choker and an off-the-shoulder dress that revealed acres of bare neck and shoulders and cleavage reminiscent of the Grand Canyon. NAB SINGER ANITA O'DAY was my identification. The smaller caption read:

> Bailed out for $500 singer Anita O'Day faces a hearing Monday on a marijuana charge. Police arrested her and two companions Tuesday morning, found smoking reefer in the street. Story pg 12.

The *Mirror* was more mysterious, lifting a quote from the story on the inside of the paper about my not knowing what the reporters were talking about. When I read that write-up, I regretted not sticking to the standard "no comment." Trying to play everything lightly, I gave the reporters an opportunity to turn me into one hard-boiled cookie.

After my initial hearing, the case was advanced five times before coming to trial. While awaiting my date in court, I fulfilled my engagement at the Club Alabam. It was there that I sniffed heroin for the first time. When I say this people think I mean cocaine. I don't. People who regularly sniff heroin have what's called a stomach habit.

I didn't have any experience with it at all until I came into the dressing room of this cat they called Harry "The Hipster." He had all this stuff around and invited me to try it. I don't recall even asking what it was. But once I'd used it I felt great and I thought Wow! Now I don't have to drink.

Of course, sniffing is really a dumb way to go. It's a terrible waste because you have to use about ten times as much of this expensive stuff as if you'd injected it. Also, by sniffing it you burn out the lining of your nose, lungs and stomach.

I sniffed only one other time before my trial which began on February 3, 1953, in Superior Judge Charles W. Fricke's Court. This time I had a jury.

During the testimony, the cops made a couple of mistakes. My lawyer led them to testify the police lab had found no traces of "flowering tops and leaves of Indian Hemp (*Cannabis Sativa*)" in the car or on the clothes of Shell, Denny or me. Then my lawyer, Fred Steinmetz, led Patrolman Zimmerman to describe my throwing the object onto the street where Zimmerman recovered it.

Steinmetz wanted to know how the police could be certain the roach they found came from Shell's car. Wasn't it possible whoever tossed the thing from Shell's car had discarded a Kool?

Answer: The reefer was the only butt to be found at the intersection of Jefferson and Hill at about 3:00 A.M., October 15.

That established, Steinmetz called several witnesses who testified that on two separate Friday nights they'd gone to the intersection at 3:00 A.M. for spot checks. On both occasions, each witness reported seeing scores of cigarette stubs within one hundred feet of the spot where Shell's car had been pulled over by the police.

After all the evidence was in on February 4, the jury hardly left the box before they filed back with their verdict. Not guilty.

I made a point of personally thanking each juror. It reinforced my rebellious feelings and reassured me I could handle myself in any situation. Looking back, I wonder whether getting off easy may not have been one of the unluckiest breaks of my life.

CHAPTER IX
BUSTED

For a chick who'd recently been busted and cleared on a "posses-sion of a controlled substance" charge, Long Beach wasn't the greatest place to be appearing. A lot of things were going on down there. It was rumored the relative of a newspaperman had got hooked on drugs, spawning a full-fledged witch-hunt in news-papers and on radio stations. Suggestions were made to "curb the menace," ranging from a mandatory death sentence for dealers to increased sentences for users, and confiscation of any auto em-ployed to transport drugs.

Obviously such a campaign has to produce some kind of visible results. Capture of a major dealer or a sizable haul of narcotics would have been acceptable. But since neither was available, some other sacrifice had to be found. Guess who got fingered? Jazz (the word had a dirty connotation in a lot of people's minds) singer, ex-vocalist with Gene Krupa (wasn't he busted for grass?), two previous arrests, one conviction—add them all together and what have you? Headlines!

I'd opened at the Samoa, a jazz club run by the Ashley family, located at Fourth and Orange, in the midst of the drive. When I heard news of the drug hunt on the radio and somebody pointed out the newspaper series, I switched from pot to booze. I was the most recognizable name in town and wasn't interested in offering myself as the sacrificial lamb. All I had to worry about was drunk driving, and I took care of that by calling Denny and asking him to come down to chauffeur me around since Carl and I were in "splitsville" as Walter Winchell used to say in his column.

I really felt good about the way I'd handled myself when the manager decided to hold me over for a second week. Denny and I planned to drive back to Los Angeles after the Friday night gig so he could pick up some fresh laundry and then return in time for the Saturday show.

Crowds were big, with some fans dropping in a couple of times during the first week. The management were good people. Everyone in the club, that is, with the exception of the piano player who kept bugging me to score for him. He'd been around long enough to understand that anyone who had been on the jazz scene the way I had was bound to know a connection.

At first, I treated his suggestions as jokes, but when he kept pestering I began to get suspicious. A lot of users kept out of jail in those days by finking on coworkers. And with this guy, I sensed a setup. You only had to look at him to know he was a junkie, and since the narcs had never bothered him, the odds were that he was a snitch.

On Saturday night of my first week, this guy was in obvious need of a fix. His nose was running, he had the sweats. He was one sick cat. So I made a point of keeping out of his way until Denny drove up, and I got into the car and we zoomed off to Los Angeles.

Returning to Long Beach, heavy traffic caused a long delay on the highway, and we lost more time when Denny stopped to register us at a nice hotel we'd spotted at 2900 East Pacific Highway. We'd decided to move there for my second week, and while I waited in the car Denny went in to register us as Mr. and Mrs. Denny Roche.

We arrived at the Samoa just in time for me to hop out of the car, rush into my dressing room, slap on my makeup, and get changed for the first set. In the hallway, I passed the piano player who, judging from his together appearance, had made a connection. I hurried by with just a "Hi!"

When I came out, I was surprised to see him still standing where he'd been when I arrived. "Hey man, we're due on the stand," I said, as I was passing him. Suddenly, he pushed something into my hand and mumbled, "Hold this until after the last set." Before I could reply, he was on his way to the piano.

I felt the little packet in my hand and looked at the pulled-together individual that had replaced the sniffling, sweating wreck I'd left two nights before, and I pretty much knew what I was holding.

Remembering the furor in the papers, the one thing I wasn't going to do was keep the packet on me. Since he was already at the piano, I couldn't hand it to him in front of the crowd anymore than I could hold it while singing. I considered dropping it on the floor and finally decided on a quick trip to the ladies' latrine to get rid of it.

When I got in there, I slipped the packet onto a ledge, pretended to wash my hands and left. Nobody else was in there, and I felt sure no one could see through the small window. It had been painted black and was held by chains at an angle to prevent anyone looking in.

I left and hurried toward the stand just as the emcee announced me. There was a full house and the customers gave me a big welcome. We went into an up tune, "Fine and Dandy," as an opener. It got over to good response. Then the lighting dimmed to a pin spot on my face. As I closed my eyes and went into the verse of "I Cover the Waterfront," I could feel the audience respond, and I knew we had a hip crowd. I looked forward to a really mellow night.

I was just getting into the chorus when I sensed, more than actually heard or saw, someone on the stage. Probably some drunk taking a short cut to the latrine. Why didn't they have the bouncer get him out of there?

All at once, I felt someone grab my arm. Before I could react, the lights went up. I looked around and saw half a dozen cops. Two of them marched me off the stage, ignoring my questions about what they thought they were doing.

As they pushed me toward the ladies' room, I saw that Denny was being rousted from the bar. They tried to get me to point out where I'd put the packet or at least admit I'd taken it in there. Failing, they gave up and marched me toward my dressing room.

One cop questioned Denny in the hall and another took me into my dressing room to prevent us from hearing what the other said. A couple of others proceeded to take my dressing room apart looking for drugs. They emptied my makeup box, rummaged in my purse, dismantled my lipstick, searched my clothes, and gave the room a thorough going-over. They came up empty.

I wasn't unduly alarmed though the one officer announced they'd found the packet in the ladies' room. After all, all kinds of people were in and out all night. I thought they'd take me down to the station, try to scare me, and finally let me go after reaping headlines. The worst would be an arrest and dismissal for lack of evidence.

As we were about to leave, one officer picked up a big ring, cheap costume jewelry, and said, "This looks expensive. Put it on. If somebody steals it, don't accuse us." He slipped it on my finger.

Then they took Denny and me to the station for grilling. Both of us denied owning the packet the police officer had found. Somewhere during this time, a guy with a big cigar came by and quietly told me, "For twenty-five hundred dollars, you won't have to go for arraignment." I laughed and he left. I'd never cleared the kind of money people thought I had. After I'd hired muscians and paid living expenses there wasn't a lot left. If I could have come up with that twenty-five hundred, everything might have been forgotten. As it was, after a lot of hassling, Denny was freed for lack of evidence. But they decided to hold me on suspicion of violating Section 11500 of the Health and Safety Code. This was on March 14, 1953.

At this point, I want to clear up a story I've told and believed for a quarter of a century. I've always said that in 1952 Carl had scheduled a recording session and we needed a fourth song. The way I remembered it, a guy in some joint heard me telling the bartender about this. This cat said he wrote songs. We went over to his apartment and he played some for me. I picked one and asked him how much he wanted. He said five dollars. The song was "Vaya con Dios."

My record came out on Mercury. A fellow from Capitol who was associated with Les Paul and Mary Ford heard it. While the three of them were on a promotion tour in Duluth or Detroit, he called a local disc jockey who played it for them. Les and Mary flipped, and I got a $10,000 check for the song—which I gave to my husband because we were splitting up, and I felt he'd neglected his career to manage mine.

Newspaper reporters, disc jockeys, and TV interviewers always dug that story. I don't know why unless it's because of most people's preoccupation with money.

My collaborator liked the story too. But he began checking and learned from ASCAP that the song was written by three successful professionals, Buddy Pepper, Inez James and Larry Russell. He asked me how I'd acquired any rights, since it wasn't special material. I told him I didn't know, but to call Mike Gould, who had been at Capitol and would clear up everything.

Mike, who has always been friendly to me, denied I'd ever received a check. He agreed I'd been the first to record the song and had been scheduled to go on Peter Potter's *Juke Box Jury*, a TV show, on which judges voted new releases "a hit or a miss." But he said that the night before my appearance, I'd been arrested in Long Beach on a heroin charge and Potter said he couldn't have "a dope fiend" on his show. Gould asked, "Would it help if she brought on a hypodermic needle to play the record?"

Gould also said that my ex-husband had not dropped dead on a golf course as I'd heard, but was living in Sacramento. My collaborator called Carl, who said that *he* had got the song from Larry Russell and had produced the recording session. He was also definite that he had published the song and sold it to Capitol.

I felt terrible when I heard this. I hadn't meant to lie. I still believed the story. But given Mike's and Carl's denials I decided maybe part of my problem was that I was drinking heavily while awaiting trial on a charge that could draw a long sentence. I've always said that I drink to forget and apparently I succeeded. I'm also inclined to agree with Carl that over the years the story had been added to by interviewers, and I'd incorporated their embellishments and added some of my own until I believed it myself.

People do get confused. At first Inez James' representative insisted others had recorded the song before me, but finally recalled that I was the first. And Carl claimed Larry Russell had insisted he, Carl, be credited as one of the writers. He isn't. So we're all human. We all make mistakes. I apologize. Can't we be friends, Carl, Mr. Pepper, Ms. James? Mr. Gould?

was the headline April 10.

My attorney George Shibley appealed to Municipal Judge Frank Chavaral to dismiss the case for lack of evidence and the judge did say, "I agree that no one saw it [the packet] in her hand, but her hand was seen to go up and down and later this object was found." On that circumstantial evidence and a record of three arrests, I was held.

Judge Chavaral set an April 24 hearing, but on the plea that I was destitute and could fulfill a singing engagement in April, he set the date back to May 4 before Judge Sherrill Halbert.

A hint of what faced me surfaced when Deputy District Attorney Lynn "Buck" Compton applauded and made derisive noises. He met his match in Shibley, a stormy petrel, good for many cases, but too abrasive for my particular needs. Prior to my arrest, Shibley had represented a Marine from the El Toro Base, and just as my case was to go to trial, Mr. Shibley was indicted for allegedly hiring a private investigator to "secure" records of the inquiry regarding his client by a Marine court. In the indictment and news stories, this was translated into "stealing records from the El Toro Base" and it didn't help me that, guilty or innocent, he was free on $2,500 bond.

Worse still, on July 1, Shibley appeared before Judge Halbert in my behalf. He proceeded to get into such a jackpot with Halbert that my case was transferred to Superior Court Judge Fred Miller.

Before the transfer, Halbert accused Shibley of "a studied and deliberate scheme" to delay my trial, causing Shibley to cite the Judge's comments as "prejudicial misconduct." Result: Halbert tossed Shibley into jail, commenting he would not "have this Court abused in the presence of the public." Twenty minutes later—yes, twenty minutes—Shibley was brought back and Halbert laid a five-day suspended sentence on him.

Angered at this turn of events, Shibley went before Judge Miller to complain about being treated "rudely and brutally" and being prevented from explaining he was not deliberately stalling my case. "I don't know why you're telling me this," Miller said. "I'm not involved and I'm going to disqualify myself from hearing this matter."

Encouraged by Shibley, I was confident that I'd easily beat the rap. So when Mr. Ashley, who owned the club, invited me to come back to the Samoa I decided to prove I was a stand-up broad. I needed the bread and he'd been good enough to arrange bond for me. Also, I wanted to prove to the community and police that nobody was going to take away my rights to sing by intimidating me. I even needled the arresting officers by sending them invitations to be my personal guests at the opening. That hit the newspapers. Officer Robert Shaw told a reporter, "It was thoughtful of her to ask us, but I'm sure she'd cry 'frame-up' the minute we walked in." Inspector Vic Armitage said, "She's a very good singer, but unfortunately I have another engagement." And Darrell Goldsmith pretended to be offended, claiming he hadn't received a "personal invitation."

After more skirmishing, the trial finally got under way on July 8 before Judge Thomas Cunningham, who was brought in from Los Angeles to hear the case. The jury, selected after much wrangling between Shibley and Deputy District Attorney Compton, was composed of eleven women and one man.

The prosecution produced its witnesses, beginning with policewoman Ann Jolly McLaughlin, who told of finding the packet of powdery substance on the ledge and my refusal to answer questions about it. She was followed by a parade of narcs who came to the stand to bolster the contention that they'd heard a person enter the ladies' john, heard her sniff something, saw her hands close the packet, reach up and place it on the ledge. Their vantage point had been through some scratches in the black paint that covered the window.

Shibley hadn't fought to obtain a jury so weighted with women for nothing. "Some of them are going to feel a little queasy about cops spying on them in the can," he predicted, and at every opportunity he drove that point home by referring to the officers as "the window-peepers."

He hammered away at any point where the prosecution exhibited weakness. One of the cops testified he'd seen me at the club at 9:45. Shibley promptly produced the registration card of the motel where Denny and I had registered at 9:30.

He put me on the stand to deny having sniffed heroin or done anything except wash my hands. I testified I hadn't gone into the latrine until 10:20, a few minutes before the first set and more than half an hour after the cops claimed to have spied on me.

When "Buck" Compton asked, "Now, Miss O'Day, you have used narcotics in various forms for some time, haven't you?", Shibley was on his feet shouting at Compton for prejudicial misconduct. For once, Judge Cunningham ruled in our favor and told the jury to disregard inferences of the question. He told me I didn't have to answer.

Shibley also called Dr. Leslie Irwin of Long Beach, who testified that when he examined me shortly after my arrest he concluded I wasn't a heroin addict and that I had never been one.

Shibley also called Denny, who testified for me. When "Buck" Compton asked, "Just what is your relationship to Miss O'Day?", Denny, looking as guileless as Joel McCrea, turned to the jury and said, "I love her," which brought me close to tears.

Then he went on to explain in simple terms that he wanted to marry me, but that religious considerations prevented his doing so at present. The fact that I was still married to Carl naturally wasn't brought up by my side and, happily, was overlooked by Compton.

The trial dragged on with Shibley scoring points for me some days and "Buck" Compton hurting my defense on others. On July 20, most of the session was taken up quibbling over whether I had or had not applied lipstick when I entered the restroom. I was bored. I felt no jury could convict since even the police didn't claim to have seen me open the packet and sniff the heroin. Their strongest claim was that they had heard sniffing and then had seen a hand place the packet on the shelf. There were all the waitresses, a hatcheck girl, and who knows how many other females in the club that night who might have been in the restroom. Would the jury believe my hands were so unusual that they could be identified through peepholes in the glass transom? I felt sure they wouldn't.

Then the subject swerved to the ring which the police had

insisted I put on so that it wouldn't be stolen. I had testified that I hadn't worn a ring. The subject came up again while Shibley was reading the property slip cataloging my belongings when I was booked. He mentioned wristwatch and Compton was immediately on his feet challenging that reading, questioning Shibley's honesty. When Judge Cunningham allowed Compton to correct the listing to include the ring, Shibley cited both the prosecutor and the judge for misconduct.

"Your Honor," Compton said, "you're not in a position to do anything about it, but it's an imposition on all of us to have to take abuse from this Communist!"

The judge ordered Compton not to refer to Shibley as a Communist and Shibley announced, "I wish to say that it's an unmitigated lie that I'm a Communist!"

Where did these shenanigans leave me? Or Judge Cunningham? He recessed for lunch. Compton, who weighed 225 pounds, challenged Shibley, a 155-pounder, to peel off his coat and settle their differences right there.

"If you'll reduce, I'll be happy to," Shibley said. Neither made a move toward the other and off we went to lunch.

The feud continued into the afternoon when Police Matron Nina E. Gaskill told of seeing the ring on my finger and entering a description of it on the property slip.

My spirits sank lower with each confrontation, but Shibley remained confident those eleven women were going to flip their wigs at the idea of window-peeping.

On July 23, the case went to the jury with Shibley hitting equally hard on that and my contention I'd been framed.

"Buck" Compton warned the jury that if they failed to convict me they were giving the green light to all narcotics violators to yell "frame-up" and go free. Given the crusaders' climate created by the media, I wouldn't have been surprised at a swift conviction no matter how well or poorly my case had been presented.

The jury filed out and began deliberations. After a couple of hours had passed, I began to feel some ray of hope. Clearly, even in this lynch-the-dope-fiend atmosphere that gripped Long Beach at that time, the prosecution hadn't presented an open-and-shut case.

After six hours, the panel was taken to dinner, then locked up at

189

a hotel with instructions to continue deliberations the next day. They remained out until lunch break, returned, deliberated through the afternoon and into the evening.

Sometime after 9:00 P.M., they returned to the courtroom. I looked into their poker faces and when none of them seemed to want to meet my gaze, I whispered to Shibley, "We've lost."

He didn't dispute my hunch.

Foreman Erwin Janssen announced the jury had reached a verdict. The paper on which it was written was passed to the city clerk who read, "Guilty as charged."

I felt a rush of blood to my face, but I was determined not to let reporters see any response.

Shibley was on his feet immediately, demanding that the jury be polled. I felt like telling him to sit down and shut up. I'd had enough of his antics.

"Guilty," said the foreman. "Guilty," "Guilty," "Guilty" said one after another and then suddenly, "I went along with it."

My head snapped sharply toward the jurors. Which one had said that?

The courtroom exploded. My attorney was before the judge asking that Juror Betty C. Ludwig's vote be tallied as "not guilty."

Ignoring Shibley, Judge Cunningham ordered the jury back to their chambers to continue deliberations.

Shibley was on his feet moving for a mistrial on the grounds that the jurors had not been properly instructed before having the case turned over to them for deliberations.

The motion was denied, but Shibley could not be stopped. He claimed that Judge Cunningham had shown partiality throughout the trial, reprimanding him on "infinitesimal points" while allowing the deputy district attorney to behave in a "truculent, boastful, vicious, arrogant" way. He described the conduct of the court and of "Buck" Compton as "palpable and notorious."

An angry Judge Cunningham silenced Shibley, telling him he would be able to make his charges when the court reopened at 10:00 A.M. next day. Then observing that he was suffering from a "terrific headache," he called the jurors back to the courtroom at 11:30 P.M. and ordered them locked up at a hotel for the night, to return the next day for further attempts to reach a verdict.

The jurors began deliberating next morning, continued after

lunch until late in the afternoon and finally announced themselves hopelessly deadlocked eleven to one.

"Buck" Compton asked that Mrs. Ludwig be taken somewhere out of Shibley's hearing so it could be determined if she had been subjected to undue duress.

Immediately, Shibley was demanding the right to question the other eleven jurors about undue pressure from Compton.

Ignoring both, Judge Cunningham instructed me to appear in Superior Court at 9:15 A.M. on July 28 for the purpose of setting a new trial date. He continued my bail.

On the appointed morning, Shibley moved for dismissal of the case on grounds of insufficient evidence. Judge Joseph Maltby to whose court the case had been transferred denied the motion. Shibley, busy with personal problems, requested that Judge Maltby set the new trial sixty to ninety days in the future. Again Judge Maltby denied the motion, explaining that hung jury cases were retried as quickly as possible. He set the date for August 11. My bail was continued.

On the eleventh, Judge Maltby granted a motion for continuance and allowed the less flamboyant George Chula to replace Shibley. Judge Maltby made a comment that generated some excitement in Long Beach:

O'DAY CASE "EXAGGERATED,"
SECOND TRIAL STARTS FRIDAY

the headline on the story read.

"The Anita O'Day trial on heroin charges has been exaggerated, 'out of all proportion,'" Judge Joseph Maltby declared in Superior Court Tuesday. He set tomorrow as date for Miss O'Day's second trial.

"Calling the trial a simple narcotics case, Judge Maltby recognized George Chula of Santa Ana as new defense attorney. . . ."

Well, you can imagine official reaction to that kind of non-inflammatory talk. My case was called the following day before Judge Ralph K. Pierson. My new attorney challenged ten prospective jurors. Two were excused after admitting prejudice against me. A third said she had known the police chemist since he was a boy. Compton challenged only one person so the panel of six women and six men was completed. There was time only for Chula and Compton to make their opening statements before we recessed for the weekend.

When we returned on August 17, the week was fairly dull even for me with a possible six-year sentence facing me if Judge Pierson turned out to be a hanging judge. But on Friday Compton again asked whether I hadn't been wearing a ring the night of my arrest.

He'd made what we now call such a sexist thing about "feminine hands" that I blew my stack, telling him, "I have no rings—my hands aren't feminine." And at that point he whipped out a picture of me flashed by a news photographer on the night of my bust. There on my finger was the junk-jewelry ring the cops had conned me into putting on. I panicked. Compton realized that the look of terror on my face as I saw the picture was as incriminating as any admission I could have made.

Chula took over for cross-examination and asked whether the photo hadn't refreshed my memory. When I denied it, he made a motion for a conference.

I stepped off the stand and he asked what in God's name I thought I was doing denying photographic evidence. I filled him in on how the ring got there. Why, he asked, hadn't I told him? Didn't I see that the ring made the disembodied hand identifiable?

I'm tough. I couldn't have lived the life I have and come through still smiling if I wasn't. I began to laugh then. How could I hope to explain what I thought was happening. All I knew was that the piano player had planted heroin on me. I had a gut feeling it would be useless to mention that or accuse him of being a fink for the police.

But I went back to the stand and obediently recalled how, why and when I'd put on the ring. On August 25, the evidence summations were completed and the case went to the jury. They deliberated only five hours before returning the verdict.

Newspaper reports stated that I "flushed slightly" as Jury Foreman Harvey A. Omers delivered the felony rap, then sat blinking rapidly while the jurors were polled.

"She made no other display of emotion except to bite her lip when Judge Ralph K. Pierson thanked the jurors for their service," the story concluded.

My bail was continued.

I wanted only to get out of the place, but my way was blocked by a reporter. "Asked to comment on the verdict," he wrote, "Miss O'Day smiled wanly: 'I don't know what I can say about it,' she said."

I knew damn well what I wanted to say, but I also knew better than to say it. What I was thinking was that people are always claiming to be framed. The fact is that I was framed at the Samoa, but earlier I had sniffed heroin a couple of times. And because they knew or thought they knew this, those cops felt that gave them the green light to frame me. I guess from their point of view it didn't make any difference when I'd done it. But in my opinion that's not how the law is supposed to work. Worse still, if I'd had the twenty-five hundred the fat guy asked for, I probably wouldn't have had to go for arraignment. But when your head is on the block you don't make admissions or cite legalities, you just try to save your skin.

With all my other problems, wouldn't you know I'd get pregnant? I missed my period, my breasts got larger and more sensitive, and I began feeling nauseated mornings or when I was overtired. During the break between the hung jury and the beginning of the second trial, I'd been booked into the Café Gala on the Sunset Strip in Los Angeles. The Gala catered to a show business crowd so the sound system, lighting and presentation were above average. For backing I had the Jimmy Rowles Trio. Jimmy's been a musical favorite of mine for years. He's always known all the songs. He's got good chording and there's not much he's afraid to try musically. It doesn't faze him to play a novelty against a ballad or whatever.

Over the years my problems were dope and booze. Jimmy's was booze. He was a nasty drunk. He'd see me and say, "Awww, there's that O'Day"—and he meant it. Not only toward me, but also toward other people. Then quite a while after we'd worked together at the Gala he went to New York, gathered a little success, quit drinking and became a different person. I'm happy for him personally, especially since his music is as good as ever.

I was feeling bad before I went into the Gala and while I was there I got worse. When I started having morning sickness, I knew what was wrong. It made me even sicker to realize I had nobody to turn to. I couldn't call Carl out of the blue and announce I was pregnant.

Even worse, I *wouldn't* let Denny know. Hell, he might be twenty-six years old, but he was a straight-arrow kid. He loved me and I loved him too much to put him into a position where he had to choose between his religion and me. I wanted with all my heart to marry him, but his Roman Catholic faith forbade marriage to a twice-divorced woman, which is what I'd have been if I'd got rid of Carl. And to ask him to help me with an abortion? From his point of view it would have been the same as asking him to put a knife through my heart. The kindest thing was to let Denny think I was fluffing him off. So even though it broke my heart, I told him to get lost.

Luckily, I had a true friend. Joe Arden showed up at the Gala just when I needed him most. Joe had always been a weird cat. I'd first met him ten years earlier when I was appearing in Santa Monica after Carl and I were busted for possession of grass. Joe was a part-time trumpeter and a part-time bartender. He's been a boozer ever since I've known him. Despite the fact he became one of my closest buddies,* he's never smoked, sniffed or shot dope. From the moment he heard me sing his ambition has been to play bass for me. But he became a friend and I have a rule, which I broke only a couple of times, not to work with friends. I don't want personal feelings to cloud my professional judgment.

Anyway, I was living at the Halifax Apartments in Hollywood waiting for Judge Pierson to sentence or place me on probation. So Joe used to come by to play cards. I kept telling him I thought I was pregnant because I was having morning sickness.

I could talk to Joe about it because we were just buddies, not mattress dancers. The best thing about Joe is that he makes me laugh a lot. But after a while when I'd laugh, it got so painful tears

*On his wedding night, he left his wife alone, came to my apartment, joined in the poker game we had going and didn't cut out to go back to his wife until 3 A.M. Now how much greater show of devotion can you think of? To me, not his wife.

would roll down my cheeks. That's when we started looking for a medical cat who'd check me out.

Joe found a doctor who'd examine me and perform an abortion, if I needed one, for $400. So I got the money together and he drove me somewhere out in the Valley.

This was a proper doctor, not the butchers' helpers I'd gone to so often before. His office was paint-fresh. He had all the right equipment, very clean. But I didn't know the guy and I didn't want to know him. I said, "Joe, don't go away. Take me home."

The doctor suggested that Joe wait in the car. He had me slip into a hospital gown and gave me a careful examination. He told me that in his opinion, I was pregnant and explained his procedure. After I'd said to go ahead, he asked for his $400 in advance. Pushers, whores, and abortionists always demand their money before performing their services.

After I lay on the table, the doc gave me a shot of sodium pentathol. "Count ten backwards," he said.

"Ten, nine, eight, seven, six, five—"

I woke up confused. I thought the shot hadn't worked, but the doc said the operation had been performed. He helped me with my clothes and reminded me Joe was waiting in the car.

After I got home, I lay around the house a couple of days. I didn't really feel that much better, but I decided I needed to eat to get my strength. I called Joe and asked him to bring in a steak. "I'm starving and I'm too sick to go out," I explained.

"Don't worry about a thing. I'll bring the works."

He arrived loaded with a huge bag of groceries and his own big wooden salad bowl. When he unloaded the sack, he took out romaine lettuce, eggs, anchovies, cheese, whatever.

"Where's the meat?"

"Don't worry. I'm going to fix something nice for you."

I lay back in the bed and after a while he set this enormous Caesar salad in front of me. I'd never tasted one in my life. My system said, nooooooooooo! I started to cry, but he lifted a forkful to my lips. Hunger forced me to take a nibble and I loved it. I ate two huge portions and Joe said, "You've had your nourishment. Now you need entertainment. Get your mind off yourself."

He helped me into a chair, but I still didn't feel well. So I went back to bed and he fed me more Caesar salad.

Next day, he brought me a hamburger and we tried to play cards again. "I still feel pregnant," I told him.

"That's a reaction," he said impatiently. "Deal, deal."

"I really think I'm pregnant."

"Don't be silly. You just had an abortion."

"How do we know he did it? I think he ripped me off."

We played and replayed variations of that conversation. Next day I got dressed and walked to a doctor's office in the vicinity. I went in and told the nurse that it was an emergency. She seemed to recognize me because she disappeared for a minute, then opened the door and let me into one of the examining rooms.

When the doctor came in, I told him my story. "I'm still sick," I said. "I won't give you the other doctor's name, but I think he took my money and didn't do the operation."

My new doctor began his examination. He seemed puzzled. He suggested I be hospitalized right away. I leveled with him on the money situation. I told him I wasn't sure I had enough to cover everything. But I promised if I was a little short, he'd get paid as soon as I got a gig.

I wasn't in that hospital long before they had me in surgery. They used a spinal block so that I couldn't feel anything from the waist down. I couldn't see anything either because they had a sheet up between me and the doctor, who kept asking about my career to keep me occupied, I guess.

Then he said, "Well, you are pregnant all right, but not in the womb. It's a very rare thing. . . . "

"Chances of it happening are one in a million, right?"

He straightened up and looked at me as if I were a witch.

"Ectopic pregnancy? In one of my Fallopian tubes."

"But how—"

"I had one that burst," I told him. "What about that guy who took my four hundred dollars, doc?"

"He did his job. He gave you what you asked for."

"Can I still get pregnant?"

"Well—let's say the chances are one in ten million. A case has been rumored—"

"With my luck, if it can be done. . . . "

He laughed.

Years later, I talked about all those abortions with my personal physician and asked him how it was possible for me to get pregnant so often. He is a very understanding, concerned human being. And in the kindest, most tactful way, he suggested that probably I hadn't actually been pregnant that often. He suspected that beneath all my rebelliousness, don't-give-a-damn attitude, I had a strong puritanical streak that made me feel guilty. One part of me wanted to show my mother that I was just as worthless as she said. If I couldn't be good, I was going to be as bad as, or worse than, she predicted. Still another part felt guilty about not being more like her. The guilt or the dope made me tense so I'd miss my period. Terrified, I'd rush out and get another D and C. Some of the quacks gave me one whether I needed it or not. The way I understand it is that a lot of the time I just imagined I was in trouble. Getting an abortion was a way of punishing myself.

I could buy that because after I supposedly couldn't get pregnant anymore, I lost a lot of the desire for sex. Maybe because most of the danger was gone. Maybe a lot of my drive came from sneaking around and getting away with it, like a kid, even if I was thirty-three years old. Maybe that was a cause of my promiscuousness.

On September 28, I appeared in court, and my case was continued until October 23 in whatever court Judge Pierson happened to be sitting. My bail was revoked, and I was held in city jail. While you're sitting in the "dead tank" waiting to find out what is going to happen to you, how long you're going to serve, that's a really hard time. Because everybody's got a story, and you've got to listen to all of them. Luckily, word reached Carl, who contacted me. Upon learning that I wasn't seeing much of Denny, he wrote a long letter discussing us:

> Please don't punish yourself about Denny. What happened happened. The only thing wrong about it was you tried to carry on both of us at the same time.

As if he hadn't done the same thing with who knows how many chicks during our marriage!

> Are you sure that Denny is out of your heart. Unfortunately, the three of us can never be friends.

197

I, frankly, am a little skeptical, based purely on past performance about two things (1) Denny (2) Whether you can love all-out, completely, without reservation. So many times you told me you were afraid because you might get hurt. Well, it's that doubt and lack of confidence that undermines everything . . . It's that all-out feeling that I want because that's the way I feel, and I won't settle for less. I'd rather go on alone and lonesome.

That would be the day, I thought. It didn't increase my belief in his sincerity to have him arrive wearing a new suit each time he visited me without ever suggesting he leave a penny for fresh fruit, milk or a candy bar. And I was too angry and proud to ask.

Denny visited, too, and he never offered me so much as a dollar either.

On the day I was sentenced to the Women's Section of the County Jail on Terminal Island, Carl replied to a note I'd sent him:

Received your letter with mixed emotions. You say I am on your mind constantly. Well, that goes double. I have been thinking of you 24-hours-a-day . . . I have deliberately not come to see you because of last Saturday night's phone call . . .

Somebody had shown me an item about him and some chick in a gossip column, and I'd made a big thing out of it.

. . . and because a certain party [Denny] was around. It seems funny that after all these years we have to cope with a kind of thing that is nonexistent and you know that. You always have been and always will be number one in my heart and mind. How can you expect us to be happy if you are jealous over a nonexistent thing . . . In the meantime, keep your chin up and remember you are not alone in the world. I love you, and we will try to work things out.

The same day I received that letter, I appeared before Judge Pierson, who denied Chula's motion for continuance of probation and application for a new trial on grounds of newly discovered evidence. I was placed on probation for five years under these conditions: 1) I must serve six months of the probation in the County Jail with credit given for the thirty days I had already served; 2) I was forbidden use or possession of narcotics; 3) I could not leave the state of California without the consent of my probation officer; 4) I must be a law-abiding citizen; 5) I must obey all rules and regulations of the probation officer.

Upon arrival at Terminal Island, I was installed in Dorm A, which was nice territory because everybody worked. I didn't know what to expect when I arrived. I'd seen a lot of B-movies with sadistic matrons, prisoners who fashioned razor rings to cut up their enemies, thinly veiled bull dykes, and slobbering creatures who made you want not to touch anything.

I'd known some pretty rough characters over the years, and these weren't anything I didn't feel capable of handling. When one wanted to know what I was in for, I didn't go for anything as simple as dope. I wanted to serve notice that I wasn't somebody to be messed up with. "Murder," I snarled. "What's it to you?"

Then I retreated to my bunk, lay down and prayed for strength, asking God to watch over me.

Later that day, all the new girls lined up in front of a big gate that shut off little gates beyond it. Then they called out the positions we new girls had drawn.

I got the donicker detail. The idea, I've always thought, was to humiliate me. But I didn't feel bad. Somebody always has to clean toilets. They provided the equipment, and I didn't think I was above it just because I'd been a name band singer.

I pitched in and got through so quickly that I went to my bunk and lay down. When one of the guards saw me lying there with my feet up, she wanted to know why I wasn't cleaning. When I told her I'd finished, she went to inspect my work. She came back and said, "Very good. We'll find something more for you tomorrow."

Sure enough, I was put on the mop crew that went downstairs to clean this huge dining area seating 190 people. I had a mop and a big bucket full of water that I pushed around.

I still had the bandages on from the operation for the ectopic pregnancy. I could handle the dry mop easily, but the incision really pulled when I tried to lift the wet mop out of the water. I told another girl, and through the grapevine word got back to the big lieutenant. I guess she was worried I'd really hurt myself because I was sent to one of the prison docs for examination.

After looking me over, he grumbled, "You junkies are all alike, always complaining," acting as if I'd only had the abortion to get out of mop detail. He was the bad side. He had no heart, no feeling, no compassion for any of us as people, which we were, no matter how flawed we may have been.

The other side was the big lieutenant, who'd been in the army and had learned to be firm, but not cruel. After I got back from the visit to the jail doc, the guard sent me to the big lieutenant's office. She said even though I hadn't been there long, she was impressed that I hadn't complained about my assignment, and she thought I deserved something better than the mop detail. That was fine with me. She assigned me to the kitchen crew. "And I'm taking you out of the blues, putting you in gray and giving you a stripe. You'll be a trusty, Anita."

"Oh boy! Good deal!" I said. To get a job like that around all those knives, I knew she thought I had to be okay. Anyone who was suspected of being even a little psycho didn't stand a chance.

There were only ten of us in the kitchen in addition to the nice old lady who was in charge. She didn't talk to anybody unless they started sluffing off. She arrived at the same time every morning, smiled her way through the day, while seeing everybody did their jobs. Then she went home.

I wasn't in the main part. They put me in charge of salads, and I had a helper. The room we worked in had a back door so we could step outside and stand in the sunshine while we prepared the vegetables.

I was also moved to a room with only three other prisoners who were doing good time. Each of us had a real bed, not a bunk, and there was a bathtub so I could bathe every night instead of only twice a week, as when I was in Dorm A.

I could also wash and set my hair as often as it needed it. At one time I'd considered becoming a beautician so I was always well groomed, which made me feel good about myself. One day one of my roommates asked me to set her hair, and pretty soon I was doing the same for the other two.

The upshot of that was since I was a trusty and was allowed to have a pair of scissors, I became the unofficial barber in my spare time.

I'd always been an outdoor girl, so a week or so after I got transferred to the kitchen I organized an exercise class for the kids in my room. Then some prisoners who'd put on weight from the starchy diet and the girls who were coming off dope and were getting the "shucks" (ballooning up because they'd eat anything, anytime, to substitute for their fixes) wanted to join. I talked to the big lieutenant, and she granted permission for an exercise hour between 9:00 and 10:00 A.M. We started with four and ended with fifty-four participants.

I kept myself in great shape because I stayed away from the starchy dishes, even gave away my bacon, and concentrated on fresh vegetables and fruit. Because I'd never been on hard stuff, Compton said, "Hey, you're looking good. I played golf with your husband the other day." I couldn't believe his *chutzpah* in speaking to me after the way I'd been railroaded into this place, so I kept walking without acknowledging him. Then he had the guts to yell, "Looking at you, maybe we made a mistake."

His mention of Carl really depressed me. Most of the time I was as contented as anybody who'd been shut off from the outside world could be. Since I'd begun cutting hair and giving the exercise class, I felt I was making a contribution. But mention of Carl's name riled me up. I didn't hear from him or Denny while I was at Terminal Island. I didn't want to. But when my mother died shortly after I was sentenced, and I was refused permission to attend her funeral because it was out of state, I nearly became catatonic.

The person who really pulled me through was Joe Arden. He was tending bar in San Francisco, but every Saturday as soon as he got off work, he'd jump into his car and drive to Terminal Island. He'd get there just in time to spend an hour or so with me. And always before he left, he'd give me a dollar or two, whatever he could spare. When visiting hours were over, he'd hop into his car and drive four hundred miles back. He did that for five months. I told him he was crazy, I didn't expect him to make the trip every week, but it bugged him to think of me without someone to talk to. Otherwise, I guess I'd have had only a couple of visitors all the time I was there.

I was really doing easy time until one day I looked out of a little window into the dining hall and saw this chick from city jail. She waved. "Hi, remember me from the twelfth floor?"

"I thought you got out," I said.

"Yeah, well, they got me back. I gotta do six months. How about an orange?"

Now those of us who worked in the kitchen could have an orange or an apple any time we wanted as long as we asked the old lady in charge. But it was strictly taboo to give one to other prisoners.

I reminded this girl of the rules, but she said she thought I was a pal after all we'd been through, so finally after we chitchatted a while, I slipped her this dumb orange.

Off she goes, but instead of putting it in her pocket until she got to her cell, she walked along the corridor whistling, tossing the orange into the air, catching and tossing it again. Who should spot her but one of the guards, who sent her to the big lieutenant. Now the question became how she got that orange.

"I ain't tellin'," the girl said. And she wouldn't. So off she went with a guard while the big lieutenant came to the kitchen and ordered all ten of us to line up.

"Okay," she said. "I've called you here to find who passed an orange to another prisoner. Will the person who did that step forward."

Everybody looked at everybody. The lieutenant looked at everybody. I wanted to look at everybody, too, but I couldn't look at anybody. I stepped forward. "Okay. I gave her the damn orange."

The rest of the crew all seemed to draw a deep breath at the very same time. It was really an eventful moment.

The big lieutenant stepped toward me and ripped off my stripe. "Go to my office," she ordered.

I went and I waited. She came in and talked about violating her trust. When I started to speak, she snapped, "I don't want to hear why. You're going to Dorm D."

That was rough. Dorm D had all the baddies. People who refused to work were there. Some who didn't bother to go to the toilet. Psychos who couldn't conform. One girl screamed every few minutes. Nobody had personal belongings because a lot of them were violent and anything could be used as a weapon. I'd always thought I was a strong chick, but I was scared. I stayed to myself, not wanting to invite trouble. And I kept my back to the wall.

I was there three weeks before I received a note from the lieutenant asking whether I was ready to go to work.

I was. She called me to her office and said how surprised she'd been I'd stayed three weeks. I didn't tell her it was because I'd lived by myself. Because no one could associate with those animals. Luckily, I didn't—and don't—need people. I can live alone. And a cat who can live alone is one-up on the cat who cannot.

I didn't get my trusty stripe or my kitchen job back, but I was moved from Dorm D to a cell where everyone was doing one-to-six months and was on her way out. We'd all cooled it, learned to be responsible for ourselves. I realized suddenly what a luxury it was just to feel free to turn your back to someone.

They gave me a job in the sewing room, assigning me to the patch detail. There was a long table with piles of patches for us to pin on garments and then pile them up. An inspector came by every hour and counted how many each of us had completed. After three or four days, I was doing 190 patches an hour. Unheard of. The previous record was 80.

"Wait a minute" the inspector said. "What are you doing?"

"Pinning patches," I said, idiotically.

She thought I deserved to be moved up to cutting new materials. That was fine with me because all they talked about at the patch table was dope.

On the cutting detail, there were only three of us and we had more privacy. It was also in a cleaner area with lots of big windows to let in the light. All I had to do was follow the pattern and I enjoyed it. Since I had started to smoke, cutting gave me something to do with my hands. The supervisor was really pleased with me and in a week or so she said, "You're promoted to one of the new machines."

I didn't know whether I wanted that job. I had no idea how to operate a sewing machine, but the supervisor said I'd be taught. There were three machines that took care of old clothes and three that worked on new clothes. I caught on right away and liked it better than cutting. There was no pressure. In fact, girls on the machines got extra breaks to go out into the sunshine. It was really okay. I thought if my voice ever goes and I can't sing, I can go into factory work.

I didn't have to think about that though. Because suddenly, I learned that with credit for the time I'd spent in jail awaiting sentencing plus the judge's decision to forgive me a month's time for good behavior, I was eligible for parole if I'd accept a job offer. The offer came from Vido Musso, so naturally I jumped at the opportunity. Vido was a natural musician and a clown. He'd played with Benny Goodman and Harry James and had been with Kenton's Herd when I was.

The paper work took four or five days, but I was so excited about getting back to singing that I didn't sleep an hour or more for five nights. By then I was so tired I conked out and overslept for the first time—on the morning I was to get out. Does that tell you something about me?

I was released on February 25, 1954. I'd paid my "debt to society," whatever that meant. At least partly, because one of the conditions of my probation was that I couldn't see or associate with either Carl or Denny for five years. They were considered bad influences on me.

I didn't think too clearly then, but couldn't they say I'd been the bad influence on them? Carl had been a straight-arrow golf pro until he met me. Denny was just a naive, beer-drinking kid. I'd introduced them to a different world. The judge who thought he was freeing me of them also freed them of me. Eventually they would rebuild their lives long before I got back on an even keel.

CHAPTER X
GOT THE NAME, WILL PLAY THE GAME

The last time I'd worked with Vido was in 1948 shortly after he'd won *Down Beat's* poll as the best tenor sax man for 1948. He'd always cracked me up with the things he said, and when he blew such inventive solos I felt as if I'd died and gone to Kingdom Come.

I should have been comfortable joining him and his combo. I wasn't. I couldn't have been comfortable with any group. Vido's were all young guys—bassist Monte Budwig, pianist Don Trenner, trombonist Milt Bernhardt, trumpeter Maynard Ferguson and drummer John Poole. They had an open-end engagement at Club Starlite on Manchester Boulevard in Los Angeles. It was a bit off the beaten track, but not far enough for me. No place was hidden away enough to satisfy me. When I got out of jail and had to face audiences, I knew exactly how freaks in a carnival sideshow feel.

The guys' attitudes toward me didn't help either. If musicians were going to behave that way, what about civilians? I didn't realize, until John Poole told me months later, that except for Vido none of them had had too much experience and they were nervous working with me. They couldn't have cared less about my prison term.

If I'd been myself, I could have fixed everything by walking in and saying, "Relax, guys. The only thing I can get at Ciro's or the Coconut Grove is arrested again. I've worked far worse joints than this and I've dressed among the beer cases too. Just be glad you're young. I am. Because you're apt to be more inventive."

But those five months in jail had turned my head around. I wasn't the hip swinger who'd given Krupa and Kenton their first big hits. I still knew I had something to offer, but could I get it across to the people who lined up down the block to see the jailbird canary? I'd spent twenty years developing a style, but I didn't know whether I could ever again get an audience to listen to me.

What's more, it didn't lift my spirits on opening night to have a reporter squat on an empty beer case, hurling questions at me while I perched on a stool in front of a cracked mirror in the make-shift dressing room the owners had rigged up. Even worse, the reporter wasn't into music. He wanted gory details of my stay in jail. How could I tell this square that the people hadn't been all that different from those I'd known all my life. His angle, he said, was my "struggle on the comeback trail." And he glowed when I gave him such stuff as, "My life's been a roller coaster. It's been a dizzy ride up and down" or "From now on I'll be flying high and straight." I was hip to what he was after. I couldn't blame him. It would sell papers and bring out some loyal fans and a lot of freak show customers.

Opening night was a commercial gold mine and artistic disaster. My arrangements had temporarily been lost which put a lot of strain on both the musicians and me. Because they were into one thing and I was into another.

But even under these handicaps, the drummer impressed me. He'd turn the beat around in the middle of a song and then find his way back to the right place. It struck me that this horse not only could run, but he could do a dance right in the middle of the track and still come around the turn to win. I thought that was ter-rific.

When I wasn't singing, I loved watching this cat work. I guess I stared at him so much he thought I was coming on with him. I wasn't. I'd always dug good drummers whether it was my first hus-band, Tiny Kahn, Buddy Rich, Gene Krupa or this cat whose name turned out to be John Poole.

Between sets, I headed for the bar. John tried to talk to me first, but I wasn't talking to anybody except Vido, and that was only when absolutely necessary. I was silently drinking because from my point of view I had plenty to make me drink. I had this big mark on me now—*drug addict*—and it wasn't true. If I hadn't been so damned mad, I might have killed myself. As it was I chose the slow route by getting on zombies—five shots of rum in each tall glass. I got so I could down four zombies and walk away. I didn't keep tally, but John claims I was putting away two fifths of Bourbon before 4:00 P.M. They didn't call me "the zombie girl" for nothing.

The drunker I got, the more rage I could let out even if I didn't talk to any of my coworkers. Nobody would have compared me to Daddy now. I wasn't interested in a good time. I became just a tough, cantankerous drunk.

The owners had rented me a room at the Lido Motel on Figueroa. It was close by the club and I'd appear at the bar by 11:00 A.M. every morning to keep from thinking. Now that I was out of jail, it had hit me what I'd done to my career, and I was determined to blot the memories out.

Things did improve some as soon as my sextet music was located and Vido cut down a couple of big-band arrangements. We began to rehearse like mad. I'd be there listening and nodding my head. We'd run through a number. I'd do my thing. Vido would begin to work on whatever needed it, but when he'd turn to speak to me I'd have disappeared.

Looking back, those guys showed a lot of patience because they'd have to go looking for me. But after the first few times, it was obvious where to go. I'd be in back of the club, standing in the middle of the dirt parking lot, like a wild dandelion soaking up the sun.

Vido would have to come after me himself because I wouldn't obey anyone else. Back on the stand, we'd try the number again, and again after I'd finish singing I'd take off for the parking lot or the bar.

When I'd been working at the Starlite for a month or two, the club, which held four-hundred people, began not to be so jammed. So old man Mystokos, who owned it with his son, asked me to take a week's break after which they'd make a big thing of bringing me back "by popular demand."

The "big act" he booked turned out to be Fifi D'Orsay. I'd been a fan of hers in the movies when I was a kid. Naturally, I went to see her and so did a lot of other people such as George Raft, Slapsie Maxie Rosenbloom, "Prince" Mike Romanoff, Bruce Cabot, and a lot of her movie fans. There was no denying she was still a big draw, but all I could think of was: My God, she's so old. What is she doing in this tavern?

Well, looking back I realize I'm older now than she was then.

When I began working at the Starlite again, I'd loosened up a little. I began hanging out with all these characters at the bar. Pushers and users, not even musicians—they were people who wanted to get to know me because they thought I had money.

They invited me to parties where there was a lot of drugging and drinking. Of course, I was boozing. I can't swear to it, but I think I snorted heroin a few times, too.

Anyway, I was a mess. By this time I was so unhappy about what I'd done with my life, I'd become a falling-down drunk. I passed out a couple times on beer cases in what they called my dressing room. Then one day I heard the owner's son, our bartender, bragging, "Yeah, I fucked her in the back room." I knew that wasn't my style. I never completely passed out, and as drunk as I might have been, I'd have fought off that terrible, foul-mouthed animal.

I was fascinated by John Poole. Not because he was tall, slim and good-looking or was a terrific drummer, but what interested me was that he never took alcohol of any kind. I guessed he had a secret I wanted to be let in on. I decided to speak to him. He'd given up trying to talk to me. But the only dumb thing I could think of to do was offer him a drink.

"Thanks, but I don't use liquor or cigarettes," he said.

"Never?"

"It's against my religion."

He was serious. Before getting into music, he'd studied for the ministry at the Moody Bible Institute in Chicago. So I bought him a 7-Up, and he told me how he worshiped Krupa and by extension me, and how I'd deflated him that time in San Francisco during the war when I refused to sign his snare drum and had told him to bug off.

We talked about music and he came at me with the suggestion that we pick up the tempos of the jump tunes so the ballads would have more impact. Most of the squares at the Starlite didn't notice, but a few people paid attention. In the *Los Angeles Daily News*, a fellow named Bill Brown wrote: "Anita . . . [has] got a new sound and it's better than anything she's ever done in the past. The girl is hitting fantastic notes and demonstrating a control that's hard to believe. . . . She has a hushed, almost reverential delivery that scores and all in all is the most exciting voice we've heard for a long time."

I decided then and there that John was a cat who had interesting ideas. So I had two reasons for wanting to get to know him: 1) to talk music, 2) to find out what he used so he didn't have to drink. Because the Good Anita was nagging at me to stop boozing before I got cirrhosis of the liver.

One day I asked why he didn't come to the motel for dinner. It wasn't romance I had in mind. I realized I needed a friend and John was it.

He showed up with a record player, Charlie Parker's "Just Friends"—I guess he didn't have romance in mind either—plus a book for me. I thanked him, but suggested he take back the book. My eyesight wasn't up to reading.

"That's not just any book," he said. "That's the Bible, Anita." Then he told me that he'd been hanging around the club the day I was to arrive, wanting to meet me and scared to death of a repeat of our San Francisco hassle. John tends to idolize people and the fact I'd sung on all those Krupa records made my joining the group a big event for him. What really made him flip was that when I walked through the door with old man Mystokos, John saw this bright-as-sunlight angel at my side. He said he knew at once he had to give me a Bible.

That night at the motel, we played the Bird's record and talked about my days with Krupa. I begged him to give me a taste of whatever he was using, but he refused.

"You're the most 'no' person since my first husband," I kidded. "You don't drink. You don't smoke. What do you do?"

"I don't have sex outside marriage," he said.

"So? That's okay with me. I just want a friend. I have to stop drinking so much. You don't drink. Why?" I have this way of pounding away until I get an answer and I kept crowding him about how he got his kicks.

"I have a pretty good idea that you know," he said.

I did and I didn't, but I kept pushing.

Finally he said, "I don't like anything you smoke or drink. If I can't shoot it, it doesn't interest me."

When he said that, I knew I wanted to try it. I looked at him. He was very together. I thought if I go that route I won't end up in an alcoholic ward or with cirrhosis. Anyway, I've got the name, I'll play the game. At first John wasn't having any part of turning me on. He tried to talk me out of it. I begged. I got mad. I pleaded. At last he agreed that we'd fix. Not then, but after his connection delivered.

The next night we went to a room he had near the club. An old lady rented out two single rooms. She rented only to men, and we had to be stealthy as burglars slipping in because of her rule against female visitors. I always thought that was ironic because sex was the farthest thing from our minds. At first John idolized me and a guy doesn't try to make his idol. As for me, with all my abortions I'd been turned off sex. Later we became so close, it would have seemed incestuous.

Once in the room, John broke out the stuff, got the apparatus and cooked up the shit. He put it in the syringe and tied off my arm. "Believe me, Anita, I wouldn't do this. But the way you're coming on, if I don't, somebody else will. And you're likely to get a hot shot and end up in the morgue."

"Cut the sermon and get on with it," I told him. I looked at him and could see he was really torn about what he was doing. Sweat popped out on his forehead. He hesitated, then plunged the needle into a vein on the outside of my arm.

"Why there?"

"I'm hiding the mark. The first place cops look is on the inside."

What I got was one tiny, diluted drop. "That's it?" I asked. I was waiting for the glow produced by a fast shot of whiskey or something.

Meanwhile, he was giving himself all the rest because he had a pretty big habit by then. By the time he'd finished, I began to feel the glow. I was really getting a ding. Mentally I was into it, thinking now I'm shooting heroin I won't need to drink.

I knew heroin was for me because I didn't feel angry about what had happened to me in Long Beach, and I didn't feel sorry for myself anymore. When I'd come out of jail, I'd had long hair that hung down my back. One day in an orgy of anger, bitterness and self-pity I whacked it off. I did a lot of self-defeating things like that. But after John stuck that needle in my arm, I relaxed. I stopped drinking as soon as I began using heroin, and for the next eight years I hardly touched booze.

John and I were constantly together. Everyone assumed we were lovers. Carl even called me "Mrs. Poole." He was wrong. John and I were hype friends. Nobody thought of that. One night I left a Kleenex with lipstick on it in John's room. The landlady ordered him out for "having a girl in there." What could we do? Explain it was dope instead of sex?

Anyway, it was a complicated relationship. We loved one another dearly and still do. We admired one another professionally and still do. But we weren't *in love*. John has always carried a lot of guilt about jabbing that needle in my arm. That's made him very protective of me. For instance, the Mystokoses were grossing $14,000 a week and paying me $200. John got in a beef with them over it. "She's the one who brings people in," he told them. "These crowds aren't coming for your drinks or to hear the combo!" He turned to me. "How can you let them do this to you?"

I knew I needed help when it came to handling money. Because suddenly the IRS was after me. Including interest, they said I owed $41,000 for a lot of things I didn't understand, such as withholdings for musicians who had played in groups I'd hired. I didn't have a dime. Most of what I owed came from the 1940s when Carl and I were trying to make money operating clubs. I just assumed I was too d-u-m-b to understand about such things as W-2 forms and other government rules. That was Carl's department. If he tried to warn me that we were falling behind in our payments, I wouldn't listen. Anyway, he filed the forms for the guys, but I guess day-to-day expenses took whatever bread there was, so the government just never got paid.

Now, as if I didn't have enough hassles at the Starlite, the Internal Revenue Service swooped down and attached my salary. I couldn't collect a dime for a cup of coffee. So I asked John to go with me to the IRS to see whether we couldn't work something out.

John was terrific. He explained my situation to them—that I didn't have any assets, not even a car. If they insisted on withholding my entire salary, I'd have to go on welfare. Finally, it was worked out that I'd turn over three-fourths of my net salary whenever I had an engagement. Under that setup, it took me over three years to square things.

I remember the day we went for the final payment. I never had any money so naturally I didn't have a checking account. Over those years I'd either take the money to the office in an envelope and get a receipt or send them a money order. Actually, John had usually given them the money and got the receipt, but this time he said, "Here, you go up and pay it. You've worked long and hard and done without to pay up. So you deserve the joy of making the last payment."

I trotted up to the desk and told them this was the big day. They didn't smile or congratulate me. This square opened this big book, checked his figures, counted the money, looked up, and said, "You owe us one penny."

I exploded with laughter at the ridiculousness of it. I didn't have a cent.

The square got defensive and said, "Well, if I'm short, they take it out of my pocket. It all adds up."

"How well I know!" I said, calling John over to ask him to lend me a penny. John's not as businesslike as the government. To this day he's never dunned me for it.

While we were still at the Starlite, John again brought up the subject of the Mystokoses exploiting me and I asked how to change it.

"Free-lance," he said. "Let the guy who can come up with the best deal back you. Your probation officer will go for that."

I confessed to John I couldn't handle these things and suggested we team up. So in June we handed in our notices. The Mystokoses tried to talk us out of it, but he held firm. We got our final checks the day before we were to close and when we took them to the bank to be cashed, the cashier stamped them "Insufficient Funds."

John was half sick, not having any heroin and trying to get by on Dolophine pills, whatever. So he jumped into the car and we went back to the club where he showed the checks to the younger Mystokos. Mystokos tried giving him double-talk. John started yelling and picked up a bar stool which he used to knock young Mystokos down, screaming he was going to kill him.

Somebody phoned the police.

I tried to keep John from hitting Mystokos again and killing him. Mr. Mystokos came running out of the backroom, shouting for help.

The police arrived and grabbed John. The younger Mystokos got to his feet, screaming John had tried to murder him. The police asked whether he wanted to press charges of assault with a deadly weapon with intent to do bodily harm. The younger Mystokos said he did.

"Go ahead. Have them arrest me," John yelled at him as he pulled our checks out of his pocket. He turned to the police. "Look at these. We'll press charges for passing bad checks. Which charge is more serious?"

Crunnnnnch! That brought things to a halt. The old man pulled out a bankroll and peeled off enough folding money to cover our salaries. "Now get out!" he shouted. "Enough aggravation! You're fired!"

We called Vido to tell him what had come down, got permission to leave the state from our probation officers, piled our belongings into John's Plymouth, and headed toward Detroit. It was summer so we decided to go the northern route which was prettier and would take us through San Francisco. There we got waylaid by an offer from the Blackhawk for me to pick up some extra bread augmenting the Vernon Alley-Cal Tjader combo. Tjader had majored in music at San Francisco State and played both vibes and drums which left no opening for John, although Cal would let him sit in occasionally. Still, the gig did fatten our bankroll. So in his spare time, John found a druggist who sold us 2 cc bottles of Methadrine or speed.

Man, we were really flying. With that stuff, you felt as if you didn't need any sleep. You were sure you could do anything. We could hoard our Dolophine pills. The speed killed our appetites, so we saved on food bills. While I was working, John had plenty of energy to look for a connection. The trouble with speed was when you came off it, you crashed for, like, twenty-four hours.

When we set out to cross the Rocky Mountains, we had enough little packets of heroin to last us until we got to Detroit, but it was a rough go and we got into those packets pretty heavily.

We didn't want to spend money on restaurants, so we got individual cereal boxes, bananas, and Carnation canned milk. We opened the cereal, poured the milk in and ate out of the box. It wasn't good, but it was cheap, and we didn't know how much bread we were going to need to get a new supply of smack.

By the time we hit Wyoming, we'd run out of everything and were beginning to get sick. John looked around Cheyenne, a city of about forty-thousand. He tried to find some musicians who would know somebody. But wherever he turned, he came up empty-handed. Finally he returned to the car and woke me. "Listen, I got a great title for a song," he said, "We Ran Out of Shit in Cheyenne."

Sick as I was, that cracked me up. I still think it's funny. But it really didn't help solve our problem. John decided the only thing to do was to wire $50 to Carol Wills, a hype who was a plumbing contractor he'd met in jail in 1953, and have him send the stuff special delivery to Omaha. It sounded like a great idea.

We finally limped into town and John went to the Omaha post office every two hours for two days. Live entertainment wasn't too plentiful, but John finally met a couple of musicians who had heard of us. A lot of good that did. We were too hot to monkey with because of my Long Beach bust and publicity.

John phoned Wills to ask where the dope was.

"Man, the narcs were there when I came out of Western Union." It seemed they'd been watching all of us while John and I were at the Starlite. There was no way Wills could send anything—not even our fifty bucks.

We flopped back into the car and John drove straight through to Chicago. I passed out and don't remember a thing until we got to my hometown. Then we bought a paper to see what jazz clubs were going.

The Bee Hive on the South Side had a couple of known users advertised.

John didn't want me along in case he got busted making the buy, so he checked me into a fairly nice hotel across the street and went to the Bee Hive. He said when he walked in a world-famous sax player spied him, took a deep breath and pointed toward the men's room. John got the message and went in. A guy immediately got up from the bar and followed him. The door was hardly closed when the pusher asked: "How much do you want?"

John had $17. This cat told him he had a $15 bag and John bought it. The whole transaction was so obvious. If there'd been a narc in the club, he'd have nabbed both of them. But you get careless when you're strung out.

We fixed, got on our feet, freshened up and went over to the Bee Hive to catch the last set. That's how fast heroin can straighten out the chemical imbalance in your body that causes all the trouble. Before leaving Chicago, John arranged with the night clerk at another hotel to special delivery more heroin to Detroit. When we arrived, it was waiting on the dresser of the room reserved for John. That wasn't the smartest thing to do because sending dope through the mail is a Federal rap. But we were into playing cops and robbers in those days.

Our engagement was at the Flame Show Bar for a week, and between the big shows the house band took over. During their set one night, I slipped over to the Crystal Lounge where the legendary Charlie Parker was blowing. I didn't really know him. But in 1950 when I'd been at the Show Boat in Philadelphia with Buddy De Franco backing me, during a number one night I heard this thrilling alto sax solo propelling me. I was too shook to look around but when I finally did no one new was there. Afterward, I asked Buddy who sat in to play the solo. He said, "Oh, that was Bird."

"It sure was," I said, "and he flew out as quick as he flew in."

The first night I visited the Crystal Lounge, Bird told the audience, although he only knew me professionally, "I'd like to acknowledge the presence of my good friend Anita O'Day, but I'm not going to ask her to sing because she's under contract to another establishment in this city."

I didn't sing, but I kept thinking about it all day long and regretted the lost opportunity. So the next night I went back and sang some numbers with Bird and his group. Charlie offered to introduce John and me to some of his *friends* at closing time. Then we'd all be able to buy plenty of stuff. He and John got in the front seat and I was in the back. He had us stop at a place where he picked up three roasted chickens which he ate while we talked.

He'd been to the doctor that day for a checkup. I asked how he'd done. He laughed and said the doctor had told him he had four months to live.

I was alarmed.

"Aw," he said, laughing some more, "those guys are quacks. I don't pay no attention to what they say."

I felt the same way. Looking at him, it didn't seem possible. He was young. We were about the same age, thirty-four, and I had a lot to accomplish before I checked out.

I idolized Charlie Parker because I would say he was one of the great jazz geniuses of all time. He changed the whole face of music. What I mean is that when Louis Armstrong became popular, all trumpet players had to change their styles. Not the rest of the band. But when Charlie Parker became popular with his be-bop tunes, everybody had to change his style—the drummer, the piano player, the singer, whoever.

In the car he paid me the highest compliment. He said, "You come from the same branch of the tree as I do when it comes to time." That means my time is in the fourth dimension.

He wanted us to do an album together. We called Norman Granz, who said okay. So it was planned we would do one with strings. But that was not to be. A month later Charlie attempted suicide. He was in and out of hospitals for the rest of 1954 and he died March 12, 1955, eight months after he told us what the doctor in Detroit had predicted.

We closed at the Flame on Saturday and I opened at the Orchid Lounge in Kansas City on August 16, 1954.

Now that we were so deep into drugs, we secretly made it a practice to stay at different hotels. I checked in at the Andrew Jackson and John at a nameless dive on East 12th Street. "If they ever come after us, I'll take the heat," he said, and a couple of times he did.

The Orchid Lounge at 1519 East 12th was another black club where Charlie Parker, Miles Davis and a lot of jazz stars played. I was happy to be accepted there. But on opening night after I'd begged off to a real ovation, this red-necked sheriff who was right out of a B-movie stopped me and snarled, "We don't like white girls workin' nigger joints in this town. You know that, don'cha?"

I smiled. "What do I know? I'm from Los Angeles."

That was a bad scene, but when owner Buddy O'Neil came around after closing time and told me I'd set an attendance record that night I cheered up. And we continued to do it almost every night that week. The Long Beach scandal had hurt me in radio and helped in clubs. It brought in people and they liked what they heard.

As soon as we opened, John began trying for a connection. Tuesday night this guy Jimmy—a lot of people had no last names in the dope scene—showed up. He claimed he was a fan but he obviously wasn't into music. After a bit he said he could get some great stuff and suggested he and his hype girl friend get together with John and me.

He'd lay it on us free because my singing really sent him. We agreed.

Next day he and this chick came to the room where everybody thought John and I were staying. The girl was an addict, but there was something phony about the way the guy cooked his dope. He used a lot of water while an addict tries for a minimum amount. I wondered what John thought, but nothing happened and I decided maybe I was just paranoid.

The minute they were out the door John started going over the room checking for anything they might have planted. "I got a hunch he's a stoolie for the Feds," John said. At that time, the government couldn't bring its informants into court because it would have disclosed their identities.

We agreed not to have anything more to do with Jimmy. We'd try to get by on Dolophine pills and Cosynal cough syrup if we couldn't make another connection. It would be good for our health to clean up a little anyway.

On Wednesday night after the last set, John was covering his drums when this old janitor came along sweeping up. As he passed the part of the bandstand where John was, he mumbled, "Gonna be a big bust! Watch it!"

John and I went to his room after the janitor's warning. We were both a little sick, but I tried to read a paperback called, *Hooked: Narcotics, America's Peril*, telling John we didn't want to become case histories in a book like this.

We managed to get to work the next night and during the evening Jimmy showed up. He said he had a packet for me if I'd meet him at the bar across from the East 12 Street room. Even though we knew we shouldn't, all I could think about was getting that stuff into my arm and I agreed. When Jimmy showed up he apologized for being empty-handed, but said he'd have it when this joint opened next morning.

So early Saturday morning, I got up, went over and ordered a beer. Pretty soon Jimmy hit the bar. I was waiting in a booth. He got a drink and sat with me. We talked. He slipped a packet under the table and I passed him some money. He finished his drink and got up. I got up, too. He was a gentleman and let me go first—a gentleman who would kill you for forty cents!

He walked behind me and said, "When we hit the street, you go one way. I'll go to the corner and cross." Then just before he cut out he muttered, "Doan whadayado goatayerroom."

I asked him what he said, but he was gone. What did he mean? I looked around. Everything looked normal—just a Saturday morning's deserted street. So I went to the hotel and told John what had happened.

John went to the window. There was no action outside. Nothing took place in the first five minutes so we decided it was cool.

I made a little space on the table and opened the packet. It was a nice little pile. John was running around getting the paraphernalia. So I snitched a little taste, folded it in another paper and stuck it under the windowsill. I was learning to squirrel away a little for when we were sick and couldn't score because John had a big habit by now.

Someone knocked on the door. I thought it must be the cat coming to tell me something. I opened the door. That was a goof on my part—not asking John. Because here were these two guys with drawn guns. They were both big. The city narc was ordinary big, but the other one who turned out to be the Treasury Guy was super-big, weighed about 270 pounds, all muscle. He had his gun in his right hand. The local narc held his gun in his left hand. They were so nervous, not knowing whether they were going to have to use them, their guns were clacking together. I looked at those guns, walked over, put a hand over each muzzle, and said, "Please gentlemen! Those may be loaded."

If I do say so, it blew their whole act. They were stunned to have anybody make a funny about guns, but I knew the shit was on the table and they had to be distracted. Stalled.

We'd been right about Jimmy and his girlfriend. The narcs had a search warrant. Jimmy's "Jane Doe" swore she had seen us inject heroin into our veins two days before. I knew it was her when they removed my wristwatch to look for needle marks underneath it.

Suddenly it struck me that the guy must have had a change of heart at the last moment. What he'd mumbled was, "Whatever you do, don't go to your room."

To keep them away from the table, John pulled out a hypodermic needle still wrapped in cellophane and held it out. He handed it to the Treasury Guy who said, "There's no law against them in Kansas City."

John knew it, but he also knew he'd get ten years if they found the shit because he'd been busted for heroin in Long Beach before I met him. He began to warm up for what he called his "madman act." If the narcs discovered the shit, he knew my career was down the drain and he was convinced he'd never survive ten years in prison where humiliation, rape, murder and everything else went on. It would be all over.

"Take off your shoes," the city narc ordered.

We did. He examined them and came up empty-handed.

"It's not in the room," John said. "It's down the hall in the john." That was logical because a lot of hypes hid the stuff there. The Treasury Guy stayed with me and the local narc marched John to the latrine where, naturally, they didn't find anything. They continued pressuring us. John said, "Those guns have me all upset, but I think I took most of the stuff. The rest is under the bed."

I began to dig what he was up to. It was all a ruse to confuse the fuzz. The Treasury Guy had a low boiling point. He took his gun by the barrel as if he intended to hit John with the handle.

John was really going to it now, talking one thing one minute and another the next, chattering away, making no sense. The man stepped toward him and as he did John urinated on the guy's lower pants leg and shoe.

The Treasury Guy yelled, "Why you dirty—"

"I'm sorry," John whimpered. "I can't stand violence. Just let me get a cigarette and I'll give you the stuff."

The Treasury Guy was trying to wipe off his pants and shoe. John was at the table, asking where his cigarettes were. He was shielding the shit by placing his body between it and the cops. If he'd been a trumpeter instead of a drummer we'd both have gone to jail. But John's left hand went one way, his right the other, his body was in action, his head bobbed and his feet moved as he pretended to look for cigarettes.

When it was all over, he told me how he maneuvered his body between the heroin and the cops as he flipped the stuff on the linoleum floor. I didn't see it. Neither did the cops. How could we? He mopped up the heroin with the bottom of his wet sock as he walked over to ask, "Cigarette?"

I took one. So did he. He was cool now. In fact, I couldn't figure out why he was so relaxed. He offered the cops cigarettes. I knew he'd succeeded in getting rid of the shit but I couldn't figure out how he could have.

The cops sensed it too. "We've fooled around long enough," the Treasury Guy said. "We're going to find it and we're going to bust your asses. She's on probation. She goes back to jail for five years. This is your second offense, you'll get ten."

Well, all they found was one codeine tablet in John's shaving kit and the empty bottle. Prescription. Not what the warrant described.

"Give up," John told them. "She doesn't even live here."

"Nah, I live down the street at the Andrew Jackson," I said. "I'm only visiting."

"That's an immediate release," John said.

They ordered us to put on our shoes, took us down to the desk, flashed their IDs and found I *wasn't* registered. Out came the handcuffs and we were marched through the streets to the Andrew Jackson Hotel.

At the desk, the cops ignored the fact they had no search warrant. They flashed their IDs, found out from the frightened desk clerk I was on the registry and ordered that terrified kid to take us to my room. The clerk took us.

They really went over that room. The local narc apparently wasn't into deodorants. He unscrewed the top of my Mum, dipped in his pinky, and touched it to his tongue.

Half an hour later, they decided the dope was back in John's room. Still handcuffed, we were marched through the streets filled with pre-luncheon shoppers. I felt degraded which was exactly what they wanted, but I refused to let them know that. If John could pull off his crazyman act, I could play the hard-boiled dame.

Why would they do it? Their search warrant for the East 12 Street address spelled out the heroin and the glacine envelope, the size of the one postage stamps are kept in. Subsequently, it was alleged that—get the *alleged*? I learned about libel during my troubles—their determination to recover the heroin was based on the fact that it belonged to the government. Its strength was estimated at about 84 percent as opposed to the 10 percent purity of stuff bought on the streets in Kansas City—pure enough to kill anyone who used it.

For the next four hours, they searched John's room. They ripped off baseboards, tore off molding around the windows, tore up the linoleum where it was loose, opened the mattress, dismantled the bed—left the room a shambles.

What finally came down was that John was charged with illegal possession of codeine and I was held for investigation in connection with narcotics violations. I guess what they hoped was that my California probation would be revoked and I'd have to serve four years in prison.

They told a *Kansas City Star* reporter I'd been tailed since my arrival the previous Sunday and my room had been frequented by known drug addicts. Untrue. I had hardly used my room at the Andrew Jackson myself. They also said I'd been purchasing heroin since my arrival. Half true. I'd bought a packet from Jimmy the Fink which had probably been supplied by them. They claimed to have found several hypodermic needles, syringes and some burned spoons plus the codeine bottle and some capsules in John's room.

Exaggerated, there was only one codeine tablet and (I'm guessing) not all that many needles, syringes or burned spoons as they hoped readers would believe.

We were held without bail which meant spending part of Saturday and all of Sunday, before our cases came up before Judge Joe W. McQueen on Monday.

Those fifty-odd hours were as near hell as I ever hope to experience. I was first thrown into an overcrowded cell with three drunks, two broken-down whores and a psycho. The screams, vomiting and menacing atmosphere frightened me more than my months in prison.

When the shift changed, I asked the new guard whether there wasn't another cell. She immediately transferred me to one with only one other occupant. I congratulated myself on my good luck and lay down to get some rest. An hour later, I was awakened by strange animallike sounds and opened my eyes to see my elderly cellmate on the floor frothing at the mouth. I screamed for help and when the guard came she said the woman was *only* having an epileptic fit. I was so terrified I asked to be returned to the overcrowded cell that I'd thought a few hours before was as close to hell as I ever wanted to get.

After word of my arrest broke in newspapers, Uncle Vance showed up. I hadn't wanted to embarrass him with his new second wife so I'd claimed I had no relatives. But Uncle Vance loved me and through his first wife Gladys, now an attorney herself, had obtained a high-priced lawyer, John C. Pohlman, who got me released by filing a writ pointing out I'd been held beyond the statutory limit of twenty hours. He also succeeded in quashing the Federal government's request that I be held on bond. Mr. Pohlman brought it to the judge's attention that no charges had been filed against me by the Federal government or the State of Missouri and that my California probation officer had wired there was no intention to press violation of probation charges against me. So I was released. John appeared for his preliminary hearing on possession of codeine on Monday afternoon and was given a Friday arraignment.

I knew I couldn't help John on my own so I went to my old friend Tootie Clarken. Tootie ran the Mayfair. He loved jazz and the people who played it.

At his club, he sold ice cubes and mixes. Each party brought its own bottle. The club was located outside the city limits and to give you an idea of what kind of a guy Tootie was—when the boundary line of Kansas City was expanded to include his club, he had the building dismantled brick by brick and reassembled on Highway 40 outside the city's jurisdiction.

I got Tootie to go bail for John so we could fill a gig at the Mayfair. When we opened, the scandal brought in huge crowds and everything was cool.

A couple of days later we went into the Kansas City post office to the General Delivery window to pick up any mail we might have. As it was handed to us, two plainclothesmen walked up and ordered us to open the letters.

John demanded their court order, reminding them they were city cops and this was Federal property. They didn't have one, but to avoid trouble we opened the envelopes containing work offers, fan letters and notes from friends. There was nothing illegal. When the police saw they'd come up empty-handed, they took John and handed me over to a female officer who took me into a room, made me disrobe and bend over for a thorough search of my body cavities. Finding nothing on either of us, they ordered us out of the post office, warning, "We don't want to see you in here again."

Now John and I weren't innocents, but some musicians who were got the treatment. Norman Granz threatened to sue the U.S. Customs for their harassment of Ella Fitzgerald. And as I understand it, Ella is such a straight chick she never touches anything stronger than beer.

Of course, we weren't angels. One night Tootie and John got into a real hassle. John's got a superloud voice and Tootie couldn't understand somebody who could yell as loud and talk as fast as he could. So the next thing I knew the cops marched in, grabbed John off the stage and hauled him to jail. Tootie had revoked the bail bond.

That turned out to be a lucky break. The prison doctor took one look at John and asked when he'd begun turning yellow. John had a serious case of hepatitis. I had a talk with Tootie, who liked me very much, and persuaded him to go John's bail so he could be admitted to the Veterans' Hospital.

To an operator like Tootie, that's not as unusual as it sounds. He'd dealt with jazz musicians for years and was used to their peculiarities. For example, when Charlie Parker made his debut at Tootie's, his sax was held together with rubber bands and glue. Bird got wonderful sounds out of it, but he wasn't always there. Once when he arrived late, Tootie chewed him out and the Bird flew. Later Tootie hunted him down, apologized and bought him an expensive new sax. Charlie tearfully thanked him and promised never to be late again. He took off with the sax and didn't show up for a couple of days. Tootie went looking for him again. He eventually located Charlie, but the new sax had been hocked for dope. So Tootie redeemed it and Charlie returned to work. In that perspective, a little shouting match with John wasn't going to keep Tootie from going bail.

For a couple of weeks I visited John every day and worked at the Mayfair at night. Then I got an offer from the Streamliner in Chicago at more bread which would help pay Mr. Pohlman, who was going to defend John. I gave notice. When I told John, he advised telling Tootie I'd be hanging around until the middle of the week because Tootie's family was close to the sheriff's department and some reason might be found to detain me.

So I fooled Tootie and after the last set on closing night, I got into the already packed car, gulped a couple of bennies and took off for the Streamliner.

When John got well enough to appear, Mr. Pohlman got him off by pointing out the search warrant was for heroin and they were prosecuting John for possession of a prescription drug.

John immediately called to give me details on his arrival. I met him at the railroad station and took him to the Streamliner where the boss, a fan of mine, got him a set of drums (John's had joined many of our other belongings in a pawnshop) and we went to work. After our first set, the busboy asked, "What're you doing with just piano and drums when I play bass?"

John took off his jacket for hot solos anyway. So he lent the busboy his jacket for a tryout. And the kid was so good we kept him on.

John's long stay in the hospital and my awkwardness in handling a needle without him meant we were both pretty clean. If our addiction had been only physical instead of psychological, we probably could have stayed that way. But we didn't *want* to give up dope. So we started asking the kid if he knew where we could score. That changed his attitude toward us and when we closed, he split.

Integration wasn't a big issue in most spots I played, but the Comedy Club in Baltimore was an exception. White clubs and black clubs nestled side by side in the same block, but there was plenty of prejudice. John and I were working a club catering to blacks and no whites were allowed in. And black entertainers could work white clubs, but their black brothers couldn't get in to see them. Coming from the world of jazz where talent had always been the great equalizer, I became even angrier and I was pretty angry to begin with.

Here I was thirty-five years old, the ex-*wunderkind*, drifting like a ship without a rudder. Luckily, John, who'd never got over feeling guilty about putting that first needle in my arm, was like a tugboat giving me direction. We headed for the West Coast, playing here and there for expenses and gas, eating mostly hot dogs and hamburgers.

At one point I got to feeling sorry for myself because I couldn't afford having my hair done, so I whacked it off short as a boy's. I had no clothes. I wore shirt and slacks. Could I blame anyone for looking at me and jumping to the conclusion I was a dyke?

It didn't have to be that way. There are white-collar hypes who hold regular jobs, own homes and live nicely. They don't go out looking for dope. Their dealer delivers it.

We were spending ten to twelve hours a day looking for it and playing games. I couldn't guess how much we spent on cosmetics I'd never wear and sundries John would never use just so we could add, "Oh yes, and hypodermic needles for my vitamin shots."

It was hilarious. Who did we think we were fooling?

The year 1953 looked like a total wipeout except for a $200 record date for Norman Granz' Norgran in August and a couple of weeks club work here and there.

To give you an idea of how bad our situation was, when John called his Aunt Lois in Long Beach, she really wanted us to visit, but made us come in the back door so the neighbors wouldn't know we were there.

For a while John played a strip joint while I lay around a farmhouse we'd got cheap in Midway City. I was too sick to work. By October, things were so bad we gave up the farmhouse. I moved into a trailer and John slept over a garage.

The only faint hope lay in Maynard Sloate's taking over as my manager and Joe Glaser, who was representing Billie Holiday and Krupa, wanting to sign me again. He assured us he could keep me busy at $750 a week, with me paying the musicians out of that.

I signed. I didn't expect to turn out any gold records or have my own television show or star in movies. Nobody was ever going to turn me into a package like they had Dinah Shore. But then, who the heck would want to be Dinah? I just wanted to be able to sing my songs and have enough money to keep my habit supplied. And when I looked around and saw some of the older hypes who were still working, I realized that this wasn't an impossible dream. In fact, there was no reason I couldn't do better than that.

In that frame of mind I went to the track one day and saw this horse Grey Towers listed at fifty to one. I remembered playing him when he was seven. I wondered what the hell he was doing running. He had to be eleven years old. And horses, like entertainers, become passé young.

Then I thought that he came from a good stable and had had good care. I decided if he gave it his best shot, with his past experience—something younger horses didn't have—he might just get where he wanted to go.

So I put $2 on him and he paid $99.

If he could do it, why couldn't I?

CHAPTER XI
WHAT A DIFFERENCE A HIT MAKES

I hadn't thought of the promise Jesus made to me in Springfield for a long time. John read his Bible, but I seldom opened the one he'd laid on me in Long Beach. I guess deep down I didn't believe anymore after I got out of jail that I was going to entertain the world. But as Fats Waller used to say, "One never knows, do one?"

I've mentioned Norman Granz before. I'd known him since the days when I was singing at Billy Berg's on Vine Street and he was hanging around the club. Norman took $300—which was all he had, I guess—and invested it in a jazz album. He made a profit and founded his record company. I'd been recording for him on Norgran and Clef since January 1952.

In those days, if you were a hype most major record companies wouldn't have anything to do with you. But Norman built his labels on junkies. In the bebop era it was hard to have a jazz label if you didn't deal with hypes. Norman had Charlie Parker, Billie Holiday, Lester Young, and most of the known users including me.

One thing I can say for him, he's honest. He charged for recording time, but not for record promotion. He could be charming or heartless depending on which would get him farther. He was shrewd about waiting until the people he had under contract were strung out to begin negotiating. Then he was in top form and you were in the worst possible shape. Guess who took every hand. Feeling as I did, John and I went to Norman's office to try to get a release from my Norgran-Clef contract.

What I didn't know was that he had already put the wheels in motion to form the new Verve label on which he intended to record pop material. We also didn't know that he'd been playing tennis every day with Buddy Bregman. Buddy was a dark-haired, personable, twenty-four-year-old playboy, Hollywood's arranger-of-the-moment who was riding a big hit with Gogi Grant's "Suddenly There's a Valley."

Buddy was also the nephew of Jule Styne and Maury Stein and he talked a nice game whether it was arranging, recording or tennis. Norman got intrigued and told him about Verve. Would Buddy like to do an album for him?

Buddy looked over the list. "Hey," he said, "Anita and I both went to Senn Jr. High." Norman didn't see anything to get excited about in that. Then Buddy added, "Okay, I'll take a chance on O'Day."

Those seven words put me back in the business because I hadn't recorded with a full band for eight years. Everything, like, fell into place from the beginning. Ours was to be the first album on the new label—Verve 2000. All the tunes Buddy chose (and Norman okayed) were good. Not two tunes out of twelve, not six out of twelve, but twelve out of twelve were groovy songs that ordinary people as well as jazz buffs liked.

Buddy and I got along, too. He used to come over to my little cottage at Eighty-Sixth and Hoover and we'd work out, say, the second chord of the bridge or a couple of bars here and a couple of bars there.

Working on the *Anita* album in December 1955—and on *Pick Yourself Up* at the end of 1956—was excellent shop work and without my big band recordings and workouts with small groups on other records, I don't think I'd have been up to it, because these were Class A studio musicians who ate well and slept in the same bed every night, cats who could really get the music going.

The album was recorded in December 1955 at the old Capitol building on Melrose where Sinatra and a lot of other singers did marvelous sessions. It had originally been built as a theater but Capitol took it over for recording because of its great acoustics.

The sound engineer was also tops—Doris Day's man on everything she did—records, movies, whatever. Luckily, he dug my singing, and in a way he made the *Anita* album possible because he made sure he kept my voice on top. With singers such as Billie Holiday and me, that was hard to do, because we had what they call false peaks. Today, when everything is on separate tracks, it doesn't make so much difference, but in 1955, the engineers had to get the right mix on the take—there was no remixing.

The musicians that Buddy hired were all tops and some were chosen to augment one tune and some another. The string section created moods for "I Can't Get Started with You" and "I Fall in Love Too Easily" without getting sticky and overpowering. With the help of Corky Hale on the harp and Paul Smith on the piano and celeste, I rescued one of my favorite ballads, "A Nightingale Sang in Berkeley Square," from post-World War II oblivion.

I don't know what Cole Porter would have said about some cat updating the second chorus of "You're the Top," but I do know how Andy Razaf, who with Fats Waller wrote "Honeysuckle Rose," felt about my rendition of it. He wrote to tell me it was *his* favorite recording of the number. He was especially high on my phrasing, elongating the first syllable of "Honnnnnnnn—eee." And *I* really dug Joe Mondragon's bass accompaniment.

My friend Barney Kessel was there with a memorable guitar solo on George and Ira Gershwin's "Who Cares?" and another on Harold Arlen and Ted Koehler's "As Long As I Live."

If anyone asked me to name one musician among the greats who contributed most to the success of the album, I'd choose Paul Smith, who played piano and celeste. He played eighth notes which filled a lot of time and kept anybody from feeling a song was too slow. If the song had an upbeat, he played "comp" style which was like quarter, eighth, whatever had the feeling. It's just a technicality, but the reason all those tunes made it was because Smith proved to be such a great fill man.

If you happened to read Norman Granz' series about his career in *Down Beat*, you may be wondering why he didn't mention me and why I haven't mentioned his contribution to my career. He claimed he came to every recording session. He did. He also claimed he supervised the session. Maybe we have different definitions of "supervised." Not that he interfered, but it did bug me to glance into the sound booth and see him sitting there with a newspaper in front of his face, apparently oblivious to what was coming down. After all, I was trying to please him, but he acted as if he were completely bored—and maybe he was.

Nevertheless, I'm grateful to him for giving me the joy of working at the top of my ability with the best possible musicians, arrangements and songs. I was flying high. Is it any wonder that instead of the usual moody, sentimental reading of "I'll See You in My Dreams," I gave it an uptempo happy lilt?

When Norman heard the album, he got behind it with trade ads and other promotion. He also got hungry for a big-selling pop single and the first week of February 1956 he had Buddy and me cut "Rock 'n' Roll Waltz" with Bobby Troup's "I'm with You" on the flip side. I mention it because it was my only attempt at a hot single. We also recorded four more tunes on February 23, one of which, "The Getaway and the Chase," could have been a hit but got buried.

As news about Anita spread, everybody started welcoming me back. I felt like a kid again, back in the days when I'd walked along Broadway after making "Let Me Off Uptown" and everybody was saying, "Hi, Anita," "Hi, Anita."

I got on a psychological high at the response. The Los Angeles disc jockeys promoted Anita as the album of the week. Variety, until then not one of my big boosters, was converted. Cash Box put my picture on the cover and Metronome welcomed me back in an editorial. In the New York Daily News, Bob Sylvester described me as "perhaps the most high-styled jazz singer in action today."

On April 28, The New Yorker, whose influence spreads far beyond its readership by swaying opinions of writers on publications with larger circulations, ran the following review:

> Anita O'Day, the jazz singer, lines out a dozen songs with impressive virtuosity on a new Verve record entitled "Anita." Her voice, which she uses like an instrument (like a saxophone, I'd say, considering the saxophone's mellifluous, somewhat breathy quality) and pushes along in modern-jazz phrasings that are striking in

230

themselves, yet seldom at the expense of the lyrics, is set off to good advantage by shifting musical backgrounds arranged and conducted by Buddy Bregman. The basic accompaniment consists of Paul Smith, piano; Barney Kessel, guitar; Joe Mandragon, bass; and Alvin Stoller, drums. This quartet is joined now and again by four trombones, which are added for emphasis, and on other occasions by a string section.

Miss O'Day's style is fascinating in at least half the numbers, and in all of them she displays abilities that set her far ahead of most of the competition. Incidentally, the competition is increasing—in quantity, if not in quality—for, to judge by the stuff that has been turning up on my phonograph, the record companies have been indenturing inexperienced young women in carload lots, thrusting them into the company of jazz bands or string orchestras, making them sing their little lungs out. As you can imagine, the results have not been too happy. It's different with Miss O'Day, though; she has been developing her skills for fifteen years or so, and besides, her musical instincts are as sure as those of any jazz singer I can think of. The recital reaches its peak with three choruses of "Honeysuckle Rose," which she constructs with ease and humor. Here is a jazz vocal that is just about perfect. As a matter of fact, the whole performance of this piece is superior. In the first chorus, she is accompanied by the bass only; in the second, the piano and drums are added; and in the third, the guitar and the trombone join in, so that there is a feeling of mounting excitement.

Other highlights of the set are a deft treatment of "I Can't Get Started" and a rather haunting delivery of an innocent work, "A Nightingale Sang in Berkeley Square," which I supposed was buried, along with "The White Cliffs of Dover" and the like, in the musical rubble of the Second World War. I was particularly struck by an amusing second chorus of "You're the Top," and by her sensitive rendering of lyrics in general. All the pieces I have mentioned happen to be on the first side of the record. Curiously, there is a slight letdown—almost imperceptible, but vaguely troubling—on the second side, which was recorded a couple of weeks after the first.

I used to worry over those last two sentences. But then I reread them recently, and I think I discovered the reason for them. How can a self-respecting critic uphold his reputation as discriminating, unless he's somewhat critical?

Remember "What a Difference a Day Makes?" I'd like to alter that to "What a Difference a Hit Makes." Between the release of *Anita* in 1956 and the end of my contract in 1963, I was sailing in more ways than one. Offers came flying from all directions for appearances at clubs, jazz festivals, overseas tours, films, and television.

Professionally there were a lot of highs. A clever public relations man could have made a case for me riding the crest of the wave without a care in the world. First take my recordings:

> The music world is agog at the startling reemergence of Anita O'Day as one of the premiere jazz singers at work today. A true original, Miss O'Day once more is demonstrating that she is the peer of such all-time greats as Billie Holiday, Mildred Bailey, and Ella Fitzgerald.
>
> Following the success of her *Anita* album, Miss O'Day consolidated her position as a recording artist with *Pick Yourself Up*, produced and arranged by Buddy Bregman. It is a tribute to the esteem in which musical stars hold Miss O'Day that Stan Getz, Andre Previn, Buddy Di Meoa and others volunteered to work unbilled and for scale on this album. A month later, the star recorded *Anita Sings the Most*, accompanied by the unbilled Oscar Peterson combo with John Poole on brushes for equally satisfying results.
>
> Between 1957 and 1963 she issued a cornucopia of memorable recordings including *Anita Sings the Winners, Anita O'Day Swings Cole Porter* with Billy May, *Anita O'Day and Billy May Swing Rodgers and Hart, Cool Heat, Incomparable Anita, Waiter, Make Mine Blues, All the Sad Young Men, Time For Two* with Cal Tjader, *Anita O'Day and the Three Sounds* and *Travelin' Light*. Impeccable triumphs all.

That would have been the hype.

In reality, aside from the $50 per song I got recording each tune, I received a single $100,000 advance against royalties which were never large enough to wipe out the cost of recording sessions and the advance. *Pick Yourself Up* and *Anita Sings the Most* please me artistically because the preparation was careful and the musicians Class A. If the sessions were hurried, it was in my interest not to run up overtime wiping out possible royalties.

On *Anita Sings the Winners*, I had two arrangers, Russ Garcia and Marty Paich. Garcia was excellent for the tributes to Gene Krupa, Benny Goodman, Stan Kenton, Artie Shaw, Gerry Mulligan, Coleman Hawkins, and Jimmie Lunceford. Marty Paich handled the hits associated with Duke Ellington, Oscar Peterson, Dizzy Gillespie, Miles Davis, Stan Getz, and Woody Herman. His arrangements with their elevenths and thirteenths wiped me out. I came in ninth in my own race. On "Four Brothers," the band drove me out so completely that the arrangement had to be partly rewritten during the recording session while time and money slipped away.

Billy May's two albums? I sketched the tunes on tape and Billy embellished them for arrangements. Good deal, except that his music was too loud for me and the engineer put us all on one track so remixing was impossible. My problem was that I was always being buried by the band. The needle would be bouncing around the dial making the engineer think my voice was on top of the music, because of my false peaks.

Once when I complained the strings were too loud on Rodgers and Hart, Billy bristled: "Get your own fucking orchestra." Inside I flared, but outside I smiled: "Too late, Billy. I've already had my own band." Humor got us through.

Bill Holman, who did *Incomparable Anita*, is a great big-band writer. But his arrangements aren't ideal for a dumb little jazz stylist. Holman, for instance, got his kicks by ending one song up a third. Good musically, but the down-home swing people I played to would never buy it.

Then there was Garcia's "Waiter, Make Mine Blues" and Cal Tjader's Latin-tinged approach. Cal was a sweet, beautiful cat and it was a relaxed, easy session. I had a ball. *Anita O'Day and the Three Sounds* came off well, too. I sang every other tune. Their piano player Gene Harris was great and it was one swinging session.

I've saved the best for last. It wasn't a record I looked forward to doing. It was a tribute to Billie Holiday and who wants to invite comparison to Lady Day? The arrangers were Barney Kessel, who is a sweetheart, and Johnny Mandel, who's extremely professional. Johnny knew just how to write for me. He kept his arrangements simple, leaving space for me to sound big on top. And in the studio, he muted the trumpets, muted the trombones, not believing in a lot of vibration. One of the magazines said I took Lady's tunes and made them my own. I knew it wasn't true, but it was nice to hear.

The weirdest session came after Norman had sold out to MGM records. *All the Sad Young Men* was arranged and conducted by Gary McFarland. John and I were waiting for tickets to go to New York to do the session when one day, the mailman delivered a letter and a package. The letter said that in the package I'd find the finished product plus my parts. John played the tapes from dawn till midnight while I studied the charts. One place it said "ad lib." That was it—nothing about notes against chord and time, just ad lib. I didn't think I could pull it off, but we listened and listened. On the appointed day, I went to the Sunset Studio, stood on a box in front of a stand that held the charts, and sang into a microphone to the music that came out of boxes on the wall. Would you believe it turned out well? The listener couldn't tell the difference. And I didn't meet Gary McFarland until four or five years later.

The reviews generally were enthusiastic. But it soon became obvious Ella was Norman's main girl. She wasn't going to get most of the good stuff, she was going to get it all. I was an afterthought, a tax write-off.

Even second best wasn't bad. Norman was unique in pairing jazz artists. An exciting idea. But was it chance to put me with all these arrangers first, listen to the results and then pair the goodies with Ella? Did he? Or did I imagine it?

I don't think there's any question Norman respected Ella for more than her talent. She is a straight cat who doesn't drink hard liquor, drug or make waves. That made her one of the few easy people to handle around Verve. This was the time of bebop and hard stuff. Norman knew John and I were in it up to our eyeballs. He didn't care. In my opinion, he had a very businesslike attitude: He decided he might as well take advantage of the junkies because somebody else would if he didn't.

I didn't see it that way and when I asked for my release from my contract, which I'd been told I could have anytime I wanted it, he refused on grounds the company had treated me very well. John reacted by yelling at Norman, and I became very grand. The upshot was Norman advanced us $300 against the next recording session, then told us, "Now get out! You're just a couple of junkies.

234

You're still under contract to me, and I'll be putting out your albums when you're six feet under."

Because of my recording successes, offers came bouncing in from all directions. Man, I was so hot I played back-to-back, week-long gigs at rival clubs located on the opposite sides of Pittsburgh.

A date I'll never forget was the Colony Club in Dallas. I followed Candy Bar, the stripper who was once sentenced to twenty years for possession of grass. During this time, I got to know a chubby, nondescript guy who managed the club and seemed very tight with the Dallas police force. If all the cops hanging around at the Colony hadn't made me nervous about a heroin bust, I probably wouldn't even remember the club or the guy's name. It was Jack Ruby. I'm not a political animal. I don't know whether President Kennedy was killed by Oswald or whether there was a conspiracy. But one thing I do know is that Jack Ruby was very tight with members of the Dallas police force.

I really wanted to get back to playing New York, but my Long Beach heroin conviction made me think it would be a tough go. Known narcotics addicts found it almost impossible to get a cabaret work permit, but, as I discovered, there are ways and there are ways. The management of Basin Street East wanted to costar Gene Krupa's combo, Chico Hamilton's Quintet and me for a ten-day stand. And suddenly a lawyer appeared who said that for $1,000 he could grease some palms and I'd get my work permit. Naturally, I lost money on the gig, but I looked on it as a bet on my future.

I should have been happy, but it bugged me that I couldn't play Manhattan without paying someone under the table when New York was where the action was. Deals were set there. Reputations were established. I *had* to get a cabaret work permit.

The license business had begun around the time when repeal of prohibition caused a lot of ex-bootleggers to turn their speakeasies into nightclubs. So the cabaret license was set up to keep the mobsters out. A lot of good that did. The mob hired some presumably honest cat to front the joint for them and laundered their money through the club.

Then in 1937 a French actress, whose best credits were that

235

she'd shot the French ambassador to Italy and had an affair with Mussolini, arrived to star in a cabaret show. To protect "the good name" of the night club business, the police commissioner succeeded in getting a law passed that placed all establishments offering entertainment and serving liquor under his jurisdiction. After 1937, every performer from Sophie Tucker to Frank Sinatra—neither of whom, it turned out, bothered to comply—had to get a work permit.

This meant going downtown and filling out a life history, which provided space for arrests, but not for disposition of the charges. The examiners went out of their way to humiliate you by making you strip so they could look for marks. You were photographed, fingerprinted, and questioned. For the permit, a performer paid $2 which went into the Police Pension Fund. The permit was good for two years for entertainers with clean noses. For those with a record, a permit had to be obtained for each engagement.

Several assaults on that law had gone nowhere, but at the beginning of 1958, two musicians with narcotics arrests and an orchestra leader who claimed his rights to engage the best-qualified musicians available were being denied hired attorney Maxwell T. Cohen to challenge the police department's denial of 5,000 permits a year.

Police Commissioner Kenney swore he wouldn't budge, but John and I heard that entertainers with records who could prove they were now straight could get licenses. So we rented a pad on Grove Street in Greenwich Village and began cleaning up. We weaned ourselves away from heroin by using Cosynal cough syrup that contained codeine phosphate or some other narcotics, but were sold from the open shelves in drugstores. We drank bottles of the stuff to keep from getting sick while we cut down and finally stopped fixing. After three or four weeks, we were convinced that we were clean. We talked to Max Gordon at the Village Vanguard and he offered us a two-week gig if we could get permits.

We inquired. The first word was a flat refusal. Then Max and his club manager Lou Gonopolar did a nice thing for us. The law allowed a performer to work forty-eight hours while awaiting an answer on his application for a permit. Lou and Max booked me for Friday and Saturday. I was off Sunday and Monday. I worked Tuesday and Wednesday, was off Thursday and worked Friday and Saturday.

Meanwhile, John and I appealed to Joe Glaser to help us. After screaming at everybody to no effect, Joe sent his lawyer to 56 Worth Street with John and me. We kept pushing even when we got the runaround and were finally fingerprinted and went through whatever rigamarole was required. We swore we were no longer using heroin, cocaine, or pot. After some further chitchat, the decision was handed down that if we submitted to and passed something called a "Nailline Test" permits would be granted.

We agreed and went to a doctor's office near New York University Hospital. I don't remember his name or address. But for some reason, I remember a picture on his wall of Patty Duke, then a child actress.

As I understand it, Nailline was used by hospitals as an antidote to inadvertent overdoses of morphine and its derivatives. But if administered in a certain dosage to anyone who had used heroin in the preceding seventy-two hours, the Nailline produces such a severe reaction that you felt sick enough to die. Nor did officials do anything to reassure you.

"Are you sure you're not using anything?" the doctor asked. "We don't want to take chances. If you're still on drugs this will kill you. You can still change your mind. Others have."

I was determined. I thrust my shoulder forward. I'd signed the papers swearing that I no longer used heroin and absolved the city from liability for administering the Nailline.

Finally, the doctor ushered me into the room where the test was to be conducted. There, prominently displayed was a respirator. I wondered whether it was there for use or display. Looking at the doctor's face, I decided it wasn't for shock value.

I was wet with nervous perspiration when he plunged the needle in my vein. I knew what I was sweating about. I'd heard that long-time addicts collected heroin in the marrow of their bones and wondered whether there was enough remaining in mine to produce a reaction.

I waited. Nothing happened. I didn't go into shock. The pupils of my eyes didn't change. I was clean.

237

Then the procedure was repeated on John. He came through as well as I had. We didn't have to submit to urine or blood tests. We were in! We could work in New York again.

Talk about irony, that Nailline made us feel so rotten we were weaving down the street, feeling as if we had the world's worst hangovers. We began looking for a fix. Thinking back, I guess that indicates our addiction wasn't physical, but psychological. Heroin was the mother that soothed us when we felt ill or hurt emotionally.

I guess it wouldn't have made any difference where we were to work, but I really felt glad it was the Village Vanguard, which is the oldest and most famous continuously operating jazz club in the world. Max Gordon and Herbert Jacoby originally opened it. (Later Jacoby concentrated on the Blue Angel and Max on the Vanguard.) So I'm going to use the Vanguard to represent all the jazz clubs around the country. If you saw me in Chicago, San Francisco, Milwaukee, Salt Lake City, wherever, during the Verve years I was on about the same trip. A lot of times I was higher than a kite. It didn't interfere with my singing as long as I got a good fix. With a good one, I could go on for hours. It wasn't the kind of high people get from cocaine or speed. Heroin just brings the body back to what has become normal. It was when my body got chemically out of balance that the trouble started and my work was affected.

The Vanguard is a groovy place. It's small and there are enough buffs around so that it's always crowded no matter who works there. And man, it has housed some wild scenes. All during the 1950s and '60s, which were the heyday of bebop, almost everyone who worked at the Vanguard could have been arrested and hauled off the job at any time.

Luckily, Lou Gonopolar looked after the details and kept things running smoothly. He also kept a close eye on the cash register to see profits didn't disappear. Just as important, Lou had a good relationship with the cops so that when they came in they never "found" anything in anyone's dressing room.

Lou was a prince. He took care of us all. And that wasn't easy. Both performers and customers could be difficult. One night when a loud-mouthed customer annoyed Dinah Washington, she told him to shut his fucking mouth while she was singing. The customer jumped up and slapped Dinah. She hit back and a brawl might have developed if Lou hadn't stopped it.

Dinah was a wild, flamboyant character with a star's huge entourage. One night she showed up with eight or ten fur coats which she hung in her dressing room. She sold some wholesale and gave more to friends. She said somebody had given them to her. I wanted one very badly, but I didn't want to risk receiving hot goods so I sadly passed up the bargain.

Once I came to work with wet feet, high as a kite. Lou took a look at my sopping feet, went out and bought me galoshes.

Since we closed earlier than Birdland, he'd often take me there where I'd sit in for the last set. He knew I didn't like going alone because I was afraid someone would give me something and I'd wake up with my valuables gone. He was a great guy. Very protective.

I don't know how he could have been unaware of a little room— more of a closet—located directly behind the stage. It was too small to lie down in, but we'd jam our backs against the door, cook up some dope and fix before we went on. It just wasn't mentioned.

I played the Vanguard every six to seven months for years after getting my cabaret card. I could always find a connection and as long as John and I had the stuff we were okay. That's the thing about heroin, it's not a week-to-week or day-to-day thing. It's hour-to-hour. You can be really strung out, get a fix, restore the chemical balance and you're fine.

John was always my nervous watchdog. I guess it's because he felt that he was the culprit who started me. He was so protective during most of my junkie years, he always insisted on putting the needle in my arm. He wouldn't teach me to use one. That way he could control my habit. He gauged very carefully. He knew in 1958 in New York "street-pure" heroin was about thirty percent. In most towns, it was eight percent or 10. He was very selfish with me. He'd give me two or three drops. Only if the stuff had been cut way down would he give me more.

Around '58, I took an apartment uptown on Riverside Drive and was working steadily. During my May gig at the Vanguard, late one afternoon, John, Philly Joe Jones, the jazz drummer, and I decided to fix. John had carefully measured the smack and had almost cooked it when a breeze came through the window and blew out the flame. He handed the spoon to the drummer and went to close the window. The drummer, who had a much bigger habit than ours, dumped more heroin into the spoon and cooked it. By the time John got back, the drummer had the needle in my arm.

I heard John say, "What're you doing, man?" Because he was always very careful not only of me, but also of himself.

"Trust me, brother, trust me," the drummer said.

BAM! That's the last thing I heard. I hit the floor. John says he panicked and his first impulse was to throw the drummer out the twentieth-floor window, but he looked at me and I was turning blue. He told the drummer I was dying.

"Quick. A big spoon of table salt," the drummer told him, pulling a vial of cocaine from his pocket.

He cooked up all that he could get into the syringe and shot it into my veins. Heroin is a downer. Cocaine is an upper. What the salt did I don't know, but I came around. I couldn't function, but my heart was beating. John grabbed me under the arms and dragged me to the bathroom where he and the drummer put me into the icy shower and held me there.

They turned off the shower and gave me mouth-to-mouth resuscitation to keep me breathing. Then they got me on my feet and back into the icy shower I went again.

By now I was conscious, but out of it. John said my eyes were staring, wild. Water oozed out of my scalp, my face, my body as if I were still under the shower.

They wiped me dry and the perspiration still poured out. They walked me, dragged me like a dead weight when my legs gave out. They rubbed me, pummeled me, pushed and pulled me. Some of the time I knew I was in New York, some of it I thought I was back in Muskegon in one of the endurance grinds.

An hour passed. Two. It was time to go to the Vanguard. Needless to say, I missed the first show, but they kept working with me. Suddenly, I mumbled, "Aw, gotta go to work."

John got me out of the wet clothes and into dry ones. He and the drummer half-walked, half-dragged me into the elevator and out to the street to a cab. They worked on me on the way to the Vanguard.

Somehow they got me on stage and I did a full show on automatic control. My hair was still plastered to my scalp, but I made a little joke about it. "Sorry, folks. I forgot to put on my shower cap."

I wish I could say I did my best set ever. I can't. But I got through it without anybody demanding his money back. Max Gordon is a sweetheart. When we came off the stand, he said to John, "She missed the first show. I'll have to deduct that."

"Yeah," John said.

"That's the first time Anita's missed a show," Max said.

"She was sick."

Max gave him a knowing look.

"It won't happen again," John promised. Then, "By the way, Max, we need a fifty-dollar advance."

"First you don't show up, then you want a loan," Max grumbled as he was digging into his pocket. "No more funny business," he said, shoving the money into John's hand.

During this period Max Gordon gave Sunday afternoon concerts with a section limited to non-alcoholic beverages reserved for teenagers at the Vanguard. There were lots of kids who came in every week to listen to jazz stars. I wish I could tell you one girl stood out in that crowd. I can't. But ten years later when I was appearing in Las Vegas, I didn't have any trouble recognizing this woman wearing a scarf and dark glasses, who joked, "Teacher, I've come for my singing lesson." It was Barbra Streisand. She had been one of the Sunday afternoon regulars.

Jumping ahead, in 1979, Max Gordon, in his late eighties, called to ask me to play the Vanguard again. I got excited and sentimental and wanted to do it for old times' sake. Then my managers sat me down, put the figures before me and pointed out that I couldn't make expenses. So I reluctantly had to pass. But I remember Max and Lou and the Vanguard fondly. I don't think I ever worked for nicer men.

Recording and club work led to jazz festivals and a European tour. I played Stratford, Connecticut, with Dave Brubeck; the Hollywood Bowl with Count Basie, Joe Williams and the Oscar Peterson Trio; Lewisohn Stadium with Louis Armstrong and Lionel Hampton; Randall's Island, New York, with Billie Holiday;

the Beaulieu Festival and a provincial tour of England; the New-port Jazz Festival in Rhode Island in 1956, 1958, 1969, and 1979; plus the New York Newport Jazz Festival in 1973.

At Lewisohn Stadium, Minnie Guggenheim introduced her sub-scription audiences, who had signed up for classical programs, to jazz. Mrs. Guggenheim called Joe Glaser for Satchmo. Joe felt I needed the exposure. So he said, "You take Anita O'Day, you got Louis Armstrong." Mrs. Guggenheim accepted me a little reluc-tantly and I stopped the show.

For my debut in Great Britain, I hobnobbed with Lord and Lady Montague, had dinner at Beaulieu Castle, and sang "Tea for Two" on the lawn of the Palace House. The orchestra, by the way, was led by John Dankworth, Cleo Laine's mentor.

Randall's Island provided my second opportunity to meet my idol Billie Holiday. The first time had been when the desk clerk of a Southside hotel in Chicago arranged for us to pool our money to make a buy. That meeting, I wasn't only in awe of her singing, I was in awe of her habit. She didn't cook up on a spoon. Man, she used a small tunafish can and shot 10cc into her feet. (Later, I understand she ran out of veins all over her body. So she used those on each side of her vagina. One sure thing, no narc was going to bust her for fresh tracks.)

The second time we met, she and I sat side by side, sharing a long mirror in the ladies' dressing room. I longed to tell her how much I admired and owed her, but she acted as if I weren't there. I'm sorry to say she had no use for me at all. Because to me Lady Day is the one true genius among jazz singers. She was unique. Only somebody who'd gone through the things she did and had survived could sing from the soul the way she did. It would have been nice to have been able to call her my friend.

Of the four appearances in Newport, 1958 was the watershed appearance. In '56, we were under-rehearsed. In '69, it was singing in the rain. In '79, it was just nice to be back, but 1958 I remember with a lot of heart.

Today there are jazz festivals all over the place, and half the performers aren't really jazz musicians. In those days, Newport was probably the only great one. When you appeared there, you were among your peers. Louis Armstrong, Dizzy Gillespie, Max

Roach, Miles Davis, Gerry Mulligan, Teddy Wilson, all hung around the park, making it an up thing.

I was scheduled for 5 o'clock in the afternoon and I asked myself what to wear. "It's teatime," I told the Italian lady who ran a dress shop in Greenwich Village. She brought out this black dress, trimmed with white. We both knew it was right, but I asked what I could wear on my head. She went into the backroom and came out with a black cartwheel, trimmed with white feathers. Both went with my see-through, plastic pumps and for a fun touch I added short white gloves.

Unbeknownst to me, Bert Stern, a famous advertising and fashion photographer, was there with a camera crew shooting a full-length documentary. It had rained, and if you watch closely you can see me scrape the mud off my shoe as I start up the first step toward the stand. Bert Block of Associated Booking asked John to get me to sign a release to allow them to film my set. John signed it and never brought the subject up.

So to me this was just a swinging gig, not a turning point in my career. Performing in the afternoon was a bonus, because I could see the audience. I spotted Chris Connor out there. That was good, because I can make my performance the way I want it to be when I know some of the audience digs what I'm doing and I can relate to them.

I was high as a kite, but I was really functioning when we swung into the first of the nine numbers. (Incidentally, it was John Poole on drums, not Max Roach as is usually assumed.) *Metronome* called me "the festival's outstanding act." *Esquire* said I was *the* hit. All I knew was that I began working to a rather apathetic audience, but they responded quickly and by the end of the nine-tune set I really had them. In those days we'd just begun doing "Tea for Two" as a fast tune, and it was as fresh to us as to the audience. There was a big reaction, a lot of applause at the end of the set. In a club I'd have given more, but at a festival you take your bow and get out of the way so they can bring on things for the next group.

It seems to me there's no better example of not knowing when Lady Luck is going to touch you on the shoulder than this Newport gig. Bert Stern was shooting my whole set, but that didn't mean they'd use any of it. Also, they were using sixteen tracks and it took them almost a year to edit and coordinate the sound and the images. I didn't have much faith in the commercial appeal of a documentary called *Jazz on a Summer's Day*. In fact, I could have bought a full share for $200 and passed it up.

Then suddenly, I began hearing from everybody about the picture, and especially about my two spots, "Sweet Georgia Brown" and "Tea for Two." *Newsweek* ran a lovely photo of me along with a rave review. *The New York Times* reported—and I quote—"Anita O'Day, making mincemeat of 'Sweet Georgia Brown' and 'Tea for Two' is as vivid and insinuating as is Mahalia Jackson booming 'The Lord's Prayer.' "

The moviegoing public who had only heard my records or read about my problems got a good look at me, and for the first time they had an image to go with the sound. I've thought about it a lot and I've concluded that the fact I looked so together after all the horrendous things they'd read about me going through caught their imaginations. If there is a legend, as writers keep insisting, I think it began with *Jazz on a Summer's Day*. I know the film made me a star singer in Japan and paved the way for international tours. The film and Voice of America broadcasts created a demand for my services abroad.

In 1959 Benny Goodman, the cat who, back in Chicago, hadn't wanted to hire a girl who never sang the melody, decided I might do for his tour of Germany and Sweden. He called my manager, Maynard Sloate, and said, "Don't hit me too hard, but I want to take Anita to Europe with me." So Maynard talked it over with me. I admired Benny as an artist, but I wasn't sure I liked the man. Finally, Maynard worked it out for John to go along to replace Benny's drummer during my numbers.

We again weaned ourselves from heroin with Cosynal—and took a suitcase full of cough syrup to Europe with us. I was still a little nervous about possible trouble at customs, so I called Lou Gonopolar to ask him and his wife to drive us to the plane. But everything was cool.

I was thrilled to be a part of Benny's world. As a musician he's been out there a long time and he deserves a lot of respect; after all, he popularized the swing band. As a human being, he's something else again. I began singing five numbers which went over well. Too well. That's when I began experiencing some of the much-talked-about Benny Goodman competitiveness. Benny doesn't want anyone or anything to stand out above him and his orchestra. If it does, he doesn't just compete, he undercuts the competition. He'll pick his teeth during your number, sit behind you and pick his nose or scratch his private parts—do anything to distract the audience's attention.

We'd only made two or three appearances when I began getting hip to him. One night he said, "You don't have to sing tonight. Just stay at the hotel."

I went looking for John to tell him what Benny had said. It was true that I was half sick because we were running low on heroin, but that wasn't going to stop me. I still regarded singing as my sacred calling.

John and I decided we'd show up as usual because we were being paid by the performance, and if I wasn't at the theater Benny could claim I'd been sick and unable to work.

As performance time neared, I flipped out and began raging around my dressing room. I kept telling John that I didn't understand this man. "I'll hit him in the fucking mouth!" I said. "Either he lets me sing or I'm going home."

John calmed me down and suggested we have a talk with Benny. So we went to his dressing room. He was my boss, so no matter what kind of bastard I felt him to be, I called him "Mr. Goodman." I said to him, "Mr. Goodman, either I sing tonight or I want out. And since you obviously don't want me on the bill, may I have our plane tickets back to New York?"

Apparently some of his guys had heard me threaten to hit him in the mouth, because he made a big thing about not understanding my wanting to leave.

"Simple. I'm being paid to sing and I'm not being allowed to. Singing's what I do. And if I'm not going to do it, I want to go home."

One way or another he decided to let me do two songs until he could get the performance routined. His excuse was that the show was running long. So that was it. No matter how loud the applause after my numbers, he'd come out and kill it.

One night in Stockholm I sang my two songs, and if I do say so myself, there was a tremendous ovation. As I was taking my bow, I spotted Stan Getz, who was living in Stockholm, standing in the wings. As Benny started coming on stage, I ran over and got Stan. I brought him out and announced, "Ladies and gentlemen, Mr. Stan Getz. It's his birthday."

Even Benny couldn't kill the audience's response. Stan got a horn and we went into "Four Brothers" which he was famous for making on the Woody Herman recording. Well, the walls just caved in. There was pandemonium. But do you know what Benny did during the number? He stood there twirling his clarinet the way Ted Lewis used to do. Anything to keep the spotlight on himself.

Finally John got friendly with the road manager. He explained that I needed to arrive earlier in cities we were playing because I had to go to the beauty shop to have my hair done. He also said he thought Benny and I would get along better if we didn't see so much of one another. One way or another, he persuaded the road manager to let us have our tickets so we could take the first train or plane to the next stop.

The truth was that in Paris a couple of musicians had put us in touch with an Algerian—complete with long robe, turban, and a curved sword—who sold us a full envelope of heroin for $1,500. So we'd get to town early, check into a hotel, fix, and be in great shape by the time the group came straggling in two or three hours before the concert.

It's sad that things had to work out the way they did because Benny had the potential for a memorable group among the people he'd hired. There was Red Norvo on vibes, Bill Harris on trombone, Flip Phillips on saxophone, Russ Freeman on piano, plus Jerry Dodgion on saxophone. Jack Sheldon on trumpet, Red Wooten on bass, John Markham on drums, and Jimmy Wyble on guitar. Benny's envy didn't keep us from being a success, but it did prevent us being unforgettable.

As the end of the tour approached, I wrote Lou Gonopolar to be at customs with a couple of thousand in cash just in case there was any trouble. Good, dependable Lou was there, but luckily we didn't have any need for him.

Next day, we were desperately looking for a New York connection without much success. So we wised up. After that when we left the country for a tour, we'd check our things with the doorman in the storage room. In one bag, we'd always hide enough shit so that when we returned to New York we could go right to the apartment, retrieve our bags, and fix.

Only once was there a problem when we arrived at 2:00 A.M. The desk clerk insisted that only the doorman who reported for work at 8:00 A.M. had a key to the storage room. We weren't about to wait that long. John slapped a ten-dollar bill on the counter and asked whether there wasn't some way we could get our bags. Seeing the ten-spot, the clerk's memory suddenly improved. He located a key. We got our luggage and went to the room to shoot up so the day was saved.

By now you're probably asking why if I had all this success I didn't have any money. First of all, a lot of what I earned went into my arm. But more importantly, in the United States my biggest successes came before the days when a rock star could have one hit recording or album and parlay it into a mansion and a Rolls-Royce. Pop singers who worked the commercial vein had made a lot of money in the late 1930s and '40s, but not many people in jazz did it.

The thing we jazz artists did that most pop people failed to do was build a loyal following that never deserted us. In my case the work I did for Verve stood me in good stead. At the end of my contract with that company in the United States, Japanese promoters took over the rights to the albums. That move opened up opportunities for me that I'd never dreamed of. In January 1964 I began the New Year embarking on a venture that was to have a deep effect on my professional life.

CHAPTER XII
HARD TIMES

My private life during the years just described was a nightmare. Finding a new connection on the road meant meeting a musician who was a user and having him guide John and me to a dealer. It took most of our free time because there was seldom enough money to make a big buy. And even if we bought a huge amount, all the users would hear about it through the grapevine and come scratching around the door asking for a little taste. The other side was getting burned with an imitation—powdered sugar and instant coffee which gave you diarrhea instead of a high. Or else you'd never see the connection or your money again.

I'd kept an apartment in Playa del Rey, California, since 1954, but a lot of my time was spent in hotels in strange cities. John was generally my drummer, but other members of the group changed constantly.

In April 1958, when Verve was going to record the live album at Mr. Kelly's in Chicago, we talked it over and decided to fly in Joe M——, a talented, Italian pianist from Boston, for the date. He'd impressed me during my twentieth-anniversary gig at Storyville a few months earlier. On this recording session I was more stimulated by Joe's work than I had been the first time we played together. The upshot was that he stayed on working the dates Joe

Glaser had me booked for and, eventually, he and John and I all ended up living at Playa del Rey in my apartment. It was share and share alike.

As far as my love life was concerned I'd played it pretty cool since the judge forbade me to see Denny. Also, after I got into heroin, I really didn't care that much about anything but music and dope. But Joe got a nice boy-girl thing going with me. I believe he was the only guy I ever dug that John approved of. John felt Joe was a big, strong guy who had my interest at heart. It used to drive me crazy the way John would butt in. He felt he had a right. He looked on me as a sister. I'd get interested in somebody and he'd chase the guy, saying he wasn't good enough for me. Even though there was nothing physical between us, John wasn't going to let me have a life of my own.

I really wasn't in love with Joe the way I had been with Don Carter and Carl Hoff, but I was really tight with him. I'd been tight with a lot of people and it made me happy, but *in* love with someone is way, way over there.

For quite a while neither John nor I got hip that Joe was a hype. He dressed in shirts and sweaters that gave him bulk and he was smart enough to handle his money, live nicely and still get his kicks. Unlike the dumb hypes like me, he didn't go out on the streets playing cops and robbers.

But when I saw him without his dark glasses his eyes were pinpointed, and without his bulky clothes his body was a little wasted. Gradually I found out a few other things. His story was brought out in the open when John and I didn't have a connection and Joe touted us onto paregoric.

What made that cool was you didn't have to spend eight or ten hours hunting the stuff. All you had to do was walk into a drugstore and buy it. It took fifteen minutes and you were set. Ten ounces was all you needed to boil down. Whatever was left was the goodie. It was a combination of alcohol, opium and camphor. You took it and thought you were Dracula.

After we got to California, we had a problem. Neither paregoric nor any of the nonprescription cough syrups that gave you a high were sold on open shelves. We didn't have a doctor to write a prescription so we were back looking for a connection. John started making the run from the ocean down Manchester Boulevard to

Watts a couple, three times a day. It was awful. We didn't have much money so we were selling and pawning everything in the apartment between gigs.

Unbeknownst to John and me, Joe kept bugging our local druggist, trying to talk him out of the goodies Joe liked. And the sicker he got, the more he bugged the druggist to help him. If John scored, Joe would use heroin, but what he really craved were those other chemicals.

One day John went into the store for a legitimate purpose and the druggist took him aside for a private talk. "You people have this fellow from back east staying with you," he said. "I wish you'd get it across to him that I'm going to have to call the police if he comes in here again begging me to give him medicine without a prescription."

John assured the druggist he'd take care of the problem, that he was eager to cooperate. The druggist couldn't have known how eager, because we had needles and other paraphernalia all over the place.

Without mentioning the situation to me, John went over to a friend's house and discussed Joe's flipping out. He and this other cat decided the only solution was to send Joe back to Boston. The friend lent John the price of the plane ticket. Then John made another trip over the hill to our dealer. This cat put John in touch with an ex-con who guaranteed getting Joe on the plane for $100. John didn't have the bread but the ex-con was a jazz buff who agreed to do it as a favor and let us pay whenever we could.

At 1:00 A.M. the following morning, Joe and I were sound asleep when John came into the bedroom and tapped Joe on the shoulder, whispering, "Hey man, get up! I'm getting some really good stuff. But we have to meet the guy at the corner."

Joe got up and into his trousers and shirt. When he sat on the side of the bed to put on his shoes, it disturbed me. "Where are you going?"

"To score," Joe mumbled. "I'll be right back."

So I turned over and went to sleep.

That was the last time I saw him for almost a year. John told me later that when he and Joe got into the waiting car, the ex-con in the back seat put a gun to Joe's head and said, "Don't panic, Joey. You're just goin' back to Boston."

There was no argument. Joe was given his ticket and escorted to the "red eye" special. A week later, I received a card: "Would you please send my laundry. Love, Joe."

I sent his clothes, and when we ran into him in New York he was very good-natured about it. He just laughed and said to John, "You know, you didn't need a gun. All you had to do was ask me to go."

We've all been friends ever since. He worked with Lenny Bruce a lot until Lenny OD'd. After that, Joe got off the stuff and settled in Palm Springs where he sings and plays the piano for the amusement of some of the biggest names in show business.

John's and my exit from Playa del Rey wasn't any more voluntary than Joe's. One night when we were desperate for a fix, we drove to Watts to wait for Hampton Hawes to get home from a gig. We'd given him money to make a buy for us.

Hawes' wife was a schoolteacher so we couldn't go inside his house and disturb her. But when it got near time for him to return we parked near his home. We knew it was dumb, but when you're sick with need of the stuff you'll take chances. We were clean. We hadn't picked up anything yet, but we had needle marks, and in those days you could get ninety days to six months in jail just for tracks.

About 3:30 A.M., a car came out of the alley with no lights on. It was the police. Man, they zipped across in front of us, were out of the car and had us covered before we even realized what was happening. They pulled us out of our car, took John on one side of the street and kept me on the other. The question was what were two whites doing in a black neighborhood at 3:30 A.M.

That was easy. John and I had agreed to say that we'd been driving for several hours on our way to Playa del Rey, got tired and pulled off the freeway to rest.

The cop asked for my driver's license. Luckily, it was made out with my real name, Anita Belle Colton.

Had I ever been arrested?

John and I had never discussed what to say. So I took a wild chance and yelled across the street where the other cop had John, "Hey John, he wants to know if I've ever been arrested."

The cop wanted to know what the hell I thought I was doing.

John, the quick thinker, yelled back, "You'd be embarrassed too, officer, if you had syphilis."

That answer turned everybody's head around. The young cop

took me over to John and the other policeman, who said nobody went to jail for syphilis.

"You don't understand," John told him and went on to manufacture a story about how we'd gone for a physical checkup several months before and had a big positive on our Wassermann tests. We were certain we didn't have syphilis so we didn't go down to clear up the matter. Then some police officers came to the house, arrested us, took us down to the County Health Department and held us in jail while they made new tests and discovered their mistake.

"Okay," the cop said. "But get out of this neighborhood and back where you belong."

As we drove off, I asked John what that story was all about. He said he'd had a mistake on a Wassermann once and it was the only thing he could come up with that was wild enough to keep them from examining us for tracks. "Now we've got to clear out of the house," he concluded, "before they discover Colton equals O'Day and come looking for us."

We raced home, threw some things into the car and took off for Palm Springs where we checked into a cheap motel with our last $12 in cash. Hampton Hawes had our money and we couldn't go near him.

We began getting sicker. John went out, pawned some of our things and managed to get us some Dolophine. Then a few days later, he drove back to the house in Playa del Rey to pick up whatever belongings we had left. He rented an old garage at LaBrea and Melrose and stored our stuff there. Later, when we got back to town we still didn't have any money, so we stayed with friends. When we could get a gig or borrow, we'd buy some junk and sneak over to the garage to fix. I thought we'd gone about as low as we could go. Little did I know!

It's hard to work, but it's harder to be on the bum. Luckily, Joe Glaser was always there to line up something or give us an advance. He knew we'd never burn him. But by this time the Good Anita began telling me that the Bad Anita was going to sink us both. John also agreed that we had to clean up and get out of town. He asked around and that's how we happened to land in Pacoima where I bought a house.

With an advance from Joe Glaser, I not only put down a payment on the house but also made one on a new Chrysler. I was determined to become one of those cautious nine-to-five types instead of a street player. I'd decided I wanted to become domestic, grow our own vegetables, do some canning, the whole schmeer. It was just a fantasy though, because after a couple of months we both got so unhappy up there that we rented a place on Hollywood Boulevard and went back to town.

One morning John said he was going out. He'd be back in a couple of hours. I didn't pay much attention. I was half nodding. Later that afternoon, Joe Arden dropped by. He asked where John was. I'd been so far out of it I hadn't even wondered.

Joe and I played cards. When it came time for the news, we turned on TV and heard George Putnam announce there's been a *big* drug bust in Pocioma. I thought that was funny. There wasn't any action there that I knew of. Then on TV we saw them herding these people into a paddy wagon and suddenly I said to Joe, "There's John!"

At just about the same time, Putnam was telling everybody in his audience that one of those arrested was the husband of jazz singer Anita O'Day. He'd been clocked doing 120 miles an hour on the freeway in my new Chrysler. Joe wanted to call the station and protest Putnam's making John my husband, but goofed up as I was I knew we'd better cool it.

That announcement was like the end of Pacoima. I never again saw my Chrysler New Yorker which had only three-hundred miles on the odometer. After John stepped out of the car with his hands in the air and was carted off to jail, the government confiscated my car as a vehicle used to transport drugs.

I used the house as security for John's bail bond. To cut expenses, John and I had let some neighbors move in and make our mortgage payments as rent. We were too strung out to have them turn over the bread to us. We trusted them to send it directly to the bank. They took care of the first mortgage but forgot or didn't understand the second. Goodbye house! I didn't really care. I could never have been happy there.

Luckily, John's case came up before that. He and the public defender had a preliminary hearing in the judge's chambers. The public defender was a smart cat who had done a terrific job gathering letters vouching for John's moral character and musical achievements. He also presented a favorable probation report.

The judge wasn't listening. He looked John in the eye and said, "You're guilty and you're going to get two to five in San Quentin just like everybody else in a second offense."

That scared John because he was convinced he'd never survive prison. He looks tough and has a loud voice, but actually he's a pussycat. So I called Joe Glaser, explained the situation and Joe wired me $5,000 in exchange for an extension of my contract. A loan. He recommended a "juice attorney," who was paid the $5,000 to take over the defense. When it came time for the trial, The Juice asked for a postponement to allow him time to familiarize himself with the case and make certain motions. That was his gimmick. One way or another, he kept getting postponements, moving the case from one judge to another for a year and a half. At that point, he secured permission for us to leave the country for a gig and while we were gone, he got John placed on five years' probation.

I later gave The Juice another $2,500. I think I got it for singing "Memories of You"—a song I'd never sung with the Krupa band—in Columbia Pictures' *The Gene Krupa Story*. The film was shot on the Columbia lot, and while I was working, at least half the employees found a reason to come over to the set to see how a real live junkie performed.

Between 1961 and 1966, there is very little I can tell you for sure. Every day was a full day. All these things happened, but they were personal things and I didn't keep a diary. I certainly wasn't thinking about writing a book so I can't sort out the order in which they occurred, but they did happen in this time frame.

I moved frequently. Sometimes I lived alone, sometimes with friends. John got married, so for a while I lived in a big room behind his and his wife's apartment. It had been an office or workroom.

I didn't worry about money. I liked the gypsy life. My attitude was, if I needed money when I got older I'd make it then. You don't think much about money when you're younger. Not as much anyway. You're more interested in what you're achieving artistically and looking ahead. Not that I was in control of my destiny as part of a letter from Joe Glaser makes clear:

> . . . . I started to write this earlier, but neglected to finish my thought, but I must call it to your attention. There are certain people in Chicago who are making it a practice to look up past records of people and the minute they come to Chicago they go out of their way to place them in an embarrassing position, as in the case of Lenny Bruce, and I am writing this letter to you to put myself on record to let you know about it, and I trust I am not hurting your feelings and that everything is in order with you and John as I don't want either of you to go to Chicago to play the engagement, if everything is not all right. I am sure you understand what I mean, and if you and John want to discuss this with me you have all the numbers. Nobody answers either one of those phones but me.

We didn't play Chicago, but when I did work elsewhere, the reviews were all I could ask for. In 1961, in spite of the life I was leading, Variety found me "as trim and perky as ever . . . a delight to look at and listen to . . . a song stylist of the first order." 1962? In the New York Telegram and Sun, Leonard Harris warned: "You can never tell what she'll do on stage, but you can rely on some swinging singing." In 1963, Leonard Feather, who has written about me as often as anyone, came out with: "I'm not merely being gallant in observing she looks and sounds even better at present than in the era of her first major impact on the scene."

In January 1964 I began something that was to be a salvation: I made my first tour of Japan with Bob Corwin at the piano. Variety caught me at both afternoon and evening performances at the Tokyo Video Hall and complimented me on not shortchanging either audience. The reviewer called me "first rate," congratulated me on "taking plenty of chances" and said I "merited rediscovery by the major jazz rooms." That's enough to give you an idea that whatever the disarray of my personal life, I didn't let my offstage activities interfere with my missionary work on stage.

Still, there was no denying my private life was a shambles. Naturally, that statement brings to mind Bruce Phillips. I met him through a bass player who was living with Bruce's mother. I'd been exposed to some weird scenes in my time, but this bunch were too wild for me. The whole family was mixed up because mama was el dinko and all four children were inkle dinkles.

Bruce Phillips was fooling around with heroin. One sister was on acid, the other a speed freak. Bruce's brother was relatively straight, but all four were dealers—heroin, cocaine, acid, speed, pot, whatever. You name it. The general atmosphere of the home was set in my mind when Bruce opened his mother's refrigerator and there was a fruit jar labeled ACID.

Bruce was like a big, playful St. Bernard on first meeting. I made the mistake of talking to him as you would to any ordinary human being. That seemed to be a novelty to him because he was immediately smitten with me.

In the beginning, he was just my connection, as far as I was concerned. Then he started hanging around clubs where I was playing. I didn't mind. He gave me a few laughs and I thought this big guy with the St. Bernard eyes was cute.

When he wasn't on anything, Bruce had a sweet, affectionate nature. I mistakenly thought nobody had ever taken an interest in him before. He got such childlike pleasure from the simplest things; even a trip to the supermarket seemed like an adventure to him. But he was so obviously out of control that something terrible was going to happen to him. I tried to point that out. Maybe that seems like a funny relationship to you—a junkie trying to get her pusher to straighten up and fly right—but it was serious as far as I was concerned.

What I didn't realize was that other people had tried more than once. And when Bruce's mood swung, watch out! I should have known better. The Good Book says never to sign for anyone else's debts, ever. You do and that person doesn't become your friend, but you both end in the sewer.

Even though we saw one another at least once a day, Bruce began sending me letters discussing his feelings for me. He printed them in a big, childlike fashion on loose-leaf notebook paper. At either the beginning or the end there was always a heart in which he linked our names, or some variation of them, "forever."

I still have a few of them. The first seemed touching and I felt I was getting to him about responsibility, which might help him to straighten himself out. The spelling and punctuation are his. This first one read:

My Dearest Anita,

Just a few lines to tell you that, I love you!! very much. I have been thinking about the word respect, and it is something that I have never known, and never been taught. You mention the word quiet often, and not only mention it (but you use and practice the meaning very well.) I will try to use respect towards you, and treat you right, and beautiful. Like the beautiful person that you are!!! You gave me a warm feeling in my hart, a feeling that is so warm I could never begin to describe it. You also give me a drive to go foreward and the fact that we are going foreward and trying to make progress, it's the best thing that has ever happened to me in my life, I am a very happy man, and you give me that happiness.

Love, and Forever Yours

Dawn

In a way, that first letter stirred maternal feelings in me. He seemed so lost, but he was trying. And I tried to help him find respect for himself. But my concern only led him into the fantasy that I was *in love* with him. A later letter, though brief, dwelt on that same theme:

My Dearest Anita,

I am trying very hard to do my part as a man. I wish and pray that I could learn to do it half as well, as you do your part as a woman.

A few days later talk of respect was replaced by ardent declarations of his love and a kind of kinky fantasy about our relationship that frightened me. He wrote:

Anita My Darling,

You are the most loving person, that I have ever been with in my whole life, you really turn me on, Baby. Tonight you came to me and you were very warm, and beautiful and sexie. I had a pill in me that wouldn't allow me to make it sexually, and I really feel bad about it, I have had it on my mind all evening. When I am on a natural, I crave love more than anything in the world, and I can do my part as a man when I hold you in my arms, and *love* you it isn't only for me, but for you. Because you are the important one, and I love you more than anything.

Forever Yours

Dawn

P.S. I love you more each day.

Luv

Luv   Luv
                       Brue
                         +

                      Anita

                    FOREVER

Shortly after, the going began getting rough. He'd show up at my apartment at any hour of the day or night, pound on the door and create a disturbance. I decided he was not only a danger to himself but also to me. If someone complained and called the police he was going to get us both busted. He was too erratic even to use as a connection.

I moved and warned my bass player not to give Bruce my new number or address. It wasn't two days before Bruce had both. I might as well have saved myself the move. When I saw the bass player, I chewed him out. He wanted to know wha. I was getting all excited about. Bruce seemed okay to him.

"Bruce is one troubled cat," I told him. "Really self-destructive. And I don't want him taking me along when he goes."

The bass player laughed and accused me of getting paranoid.

Desperate, I called Joe Arden for help. The best offer he could make was to let me share his pad. It was a way of buying time. I wrote John asking him to come back from Hawaii for a gig in Detroit and, more importantly to me, to help me shake the kid.

John arrived in Los Angeles, got one look at "the kid," a six-foot hunk of muscle with a flash-point temper, and John decided we had a problem on our hands.

To be honest, John and I didn't go about it in the smartest way possible. Instead of fixing with just enough stuff to get our bodies back in chemical balance, we really got stoned. Just to give you an idea of how stoned, one evening I fixed some corned-beef hash for John and me and opened a can of dog food for Penny, my French poodle. Halfway through dinner, John asked why our food tasted so funny. You guessed it! I'd given Penny the hash and we were eating dog food.

One way or another we managed to get to Detroit, and when we arrived at the club Bruce was on hand to meet us. By now he was wildly jealous, imagining there was something going on between John and me.

Half an hour later, while John was out front testing the lights and the sound system, I was alone in my dressing room. Suddenly Bruce appeared in the door. "You think I'm a dummy," he said.

"Bruce, I don't—"

"You talk respect. Then you treat me like a dummy."

"I still mean what I told you about respect. And this—"

"You bring him here. He only wants to make a living off you."

"Bruce, there's nothing more between John and me than between you and me."

"He wants to use you. I'll fix that," he said and came toward me with a switchblade in his hand. "I'll cut your vocal chords. Then nobody but me will want you."

I could barely speak. "Bruce—listen . . . carefully . . . please!"

He stopped.

"Bruce, if you cut out my vocal chords, I won't be me. Singing is everything to me. Do a final job on me, but don't make it impossible for me to sing."

"You'll still be you."

"I won't. I won't be able to sing and make you proud. Think about that."

Those may not have been our exact words, but that was the gist of it. Bruce looked puzzled, but calmer.

"I won't be able to talk to anybody, Bruce—even you. You don't want to make it so you can't hear me call your name or sing—ever again. You can't—" I don't know exactly what I said, but gradually, sulkily, Bruce's young kid's rage subsided. He began feeling uneasy, guilty. He closed the knife and slipped it into his pocket. I suggested we go to the bar and have something. And talk. He agreed.

I talked to him until it was time for me to go on. I tried to sell him on the idea that if he really wanted to please me he'd go back to LA. *He* wouldn't buy that, but *I* bought time.

When I got on the stand, I managed to let John know what

Bruce was up to. John gave the manager the high sign to get the bouncer over there. When we finished, John and the bouncer and I passed Bruce. He started to get up. I waved him down, saying, "Got work to do."

The bouncer and another big lug drove John and me to the police station where I explained everything about Bruce except that he was an addict and my connection. They listened and asked questions. We were in a catch-22 situation. They wanted to know whether he had actually harmed me. I had to admit he hadn't, but pointed out that when he did it would be too late. He was threatening to fix me so I couldn't speak, let alone sing. They refused to interfere. Nobody had seen him with the knife or heard him threaten me. Their best suggestion was to have the manager eighty-six Bruce from the club.

I tried to explain to the captain that this wasn't a run-of-the-mill character. This was a certified psycho. I got nowhere.

The bouncer and the other big guy took us back to the club. We decided to let Bruce stay there so we'd know where he was. I even waved to him as I went on for the second set and said good night when the bouncer and his friend drove John and me to John's hotel and escorted us to his room.

Before they left, John went out in the hall to talk with them, and when he came back he was noticeably calmer. Half an hour later the phone rang. John picked it up and told whoever was on the other end to come up. Shortly, there was a knock on the door and a voice inquired: "Poole?"

"Who's there?"

The voice gave two names and John opened the door. He'd arranged for the bouncer to send over two gunzels. When they took off their coats, each wore a .45 in a holster.

"My God, what are you planning?" I asked, I could see poor Bruce sprawled on the floor with a bullet in his head. Neither John nor the gunzels answered, but John was giving instructions to find Bruce, take him out in the country, shoot him in the legs and leave him there.

I began to cry. "I can't have that on my conscience," I told John. "No matter what he does, don't do that!" I wasn't getting anywhere. So I tried another tack. "My God, think what the publicity will do to my career!"

That got John. He turned to the gunzels and told them to find Bruce, show him their weapons and tell him if he bothered me anymore what they'd do to him. Also, they were to take the switchblade away from him.

There was a knock on the door.

"Who is it?" John asked.

"I want to see Anita."

The gunzels signaled John to admit Bruce. When he saw me crying, he wanted to know who'd upset me. Tell him. He'd take care of them.

John turned to the gunzels. He told them to show Bruce their guns and then demanded the switchblade which Bruce handed over. "If you bother Anita anymore, you're going to hear from them," he snarled. "They'll be watching. If you go near her, they're going to take you to a deserted spot and shoot up your legs. Understand?"

I begged Bruce to get out of town.

He looked at the guns, obviously shaken. "Anita? Will you kiss me goodbye?"

I gave him a peck on the cheek. "Now for God's sake, leave town."

The gunzels said they'd see he didn't cause me any more trouble. I wasn't to worry. That was the last we saw of him in Detroit. We decided he'd taken the bus to Los Angeles.

Ten days later, on opening night at the Showboat Lounge in Washington, D.C., Bruce was sitting at a front table. When I spied him, I felt as if my throat was going to close and I'd never get through my opening number. Somehow I made it through the set. After I finished, I ran to my dressing room, locked the door and sent John to deal with the club owner. My message was that I couldn't perform with a closed throat and the sight of Bruce closed it.

This owner had wonderful connections with the police. Very quickly, two plainclothesmen quietly asked Bruce to step outside. I don't know what was said, but it came down to my giving Bruce $81—or maybe $82 or $83—plus another $20 for incidentals, whatever. The plainclothesmen saw Bruce board the bus. But to play it safe, I made John sleep in my room at my hotel. I also insisted on keeping the light on all night. I was certain Bruce was going to sneak back and cut out my vocal chords so that he could "look after" me.

The next night at the club I got five or six postcards from stops along the way. (Mail service was excellent in those days.) The messages were all practically the same: I love you. I miss you. Why do you want to send me away? How can you do this to someone who respects and loves you?

Poor Bruce. His brain was about the size of my little finger. Temporarily, I was rid of him. But he showed up in 1966 when I appeared at the Flamingo in Las Vegas. In 1967, Bruce landed in the joint for dealing and was transferred to the California Rehabilitation Center. Afraid of him, I attempted to get a restraining order, but was reassured by his parole officer: "He [Bruce Phillips] will be released when the institution and staff and the Narcotic Addict Evaluation Authority agree that he is both ready in terms of public protection and personal rehabilitation. In other words, we may expect that when Mr. Phillips will have undergone such changes as may lead to less delinquent behavior. Nevertheless, I understand your concern for your safety and independence."

A couple of months later, I received a letter from another correctional counselor telling me he had discussed the matter with Bruce, ". . . and he is aware of your feelings regarding him. He seems to be looking at the situation realistically and expresses no desire to see you again. He is aware of the fact that any contact with you could lead to his return to this institution."

Heroin makes strange friends.

Dee was a connection around the same time Bruce was. She was built like a Mack truck and had a funny voice, neither really masculine nor feminine. She was on the shady side of forty when John got to know her and she began to supply us with some very good stuff.

I'd met her around 1949 when I was playing an open-end engagement which Carl and I had had with Marty Denenberg at the Hi Note. Dee began dropping in to catch at least one set every night. Right away, she began sending over drinks, asking me to join her.

"What's her story?" I asked one of the bartenders who knew her. He told me she'd married young and had a child. Pronto, she'd realized she was in love with a neighbor's wife. She didn't do anything about that, but she couldn't deny her feelings. She knew she was gay. So she got an office job and cut out.

I've told you that for practical reasons I'd begun wearing band jackets and skirts instead of frilly gowns when I was touring with big bands. I was the only girl, so I drank as much as any of the other cats and played better poker than most of them. Those facts were played up in the news and a lot of gay girls—and plenty of other people too—got the mistaken idea I marched to the beat of a different drummer, as the gays say.

No way. Whatever a person wants to do is okay with me as long as it doesn't harm anyone else. But, personally, just the idea of going to bed with a chick has always turned me off. If the most gorgeous woman in the world went on the make for me, she'd have less chance of getting me into the sack than Frankenstein's monster would.

I'd asked the bartender to get this message over to Dee in a nice way and add that my husband was part-owner of the club. But instead of cutting out, she started coming into the club oftener. Generally, she was solo. Other times, she'd show up with a big, expensive-looking bimbo decorating her arm like a trophy. On those nights she'd give me the freeze. I guess I was supposed to be jealous. Either way was just fine as far as I was concerned, because Dee had enough class never to make any passes at me.

This situation at the Hi Note went on for some time. Then one night while I was singing "What Is This Thing Called Love?", Dee, who was pretty loaded, got up and went to the ladies' latrine. During my third chorus, a gunshot rang out. A few seconds later, Dee stumbled out of the john and fell to the floor. Customers, employees, everybody in the joint including me rushed over to see whether she'd killed herself. She hadn't. She seemed to be unconscious, but it turned out she'd only shot herself in the hand. As they were carrying her to the ambulance, she opened one eye, looked at me accusingly and said, "Well, Anita, now maybe you'll pay some attention to me."

Most people probably would have run at the sight of her after that. Cautious people, not me. Sure, she carried a gun and was a little mixed-up. But I figured if a bit of conversation with me meant that much, the least I could do was to have a drink with her between sets the next time she came in. That turned out to be the following night, since the bullet hadn't gone through her hand but had only grazed the skin slightly.

After a few nights we gradually became singer-fan–type friends. In other words, I saw her only at the club. Then in Los Angeles, in the 1960s, she turned up at one of my openings. How she happened to come to California I really don't know. People like Dee always walk in a veil of mystery. Anyway, for a long time she showed up at every club I played.

After John met her and found out what a great connection she was, we took her into our circle of friends. And she took us into hers. I'm pretty sure that seeing me around with Dee's pals, who were pretty sturdy-looking little "fellows" led a lot of people to jump to the conclusion they'd been right about me all along.

The truth is that most lesbians, once they understand that you don't play their game, aren't out to recruit you. But they are very loyal people, generally speaking, who are there to help when you are in trouble. Looking back, I feel John and I kind of exploited Dee, but she didn't seem to mind. As far as anyone could tell she was just glad to call us friends.

During the summer of 1963, I began to realize that jazz clubs weren't what they once had been. In an interview in Variety while making a tour of Japan in early 1964, I spoke up about the lack of opportunity for middle-income acts. "You either have to play little-bitty clubs for five hundred dollars or at least be a three-thousand dollar-a-week act," I said. "That means you can play all the time if you're an unknown or a Peggy Lee."

I'd never been materialistic. If I had something somebody admired, I'd make that person a present of it. It was almost as if I didn't want material things to interfere with my art. I had a chorus of "Body and Soul" that I carried in my head, and as long as I had that I thought I was rich. I didn't think much about the $300,000 or $400,000 that I'd shot into my arm. I felt as long as I had my voice I could always make money. That's not the way to handle yourself, of course, because as I found out it's a monetary world.

At the time I gave the Variety interview, rock was winning. Jazz was running out of the money. All across the United States, jazz clubs were folding. In the future I had a three-week booking at the

Losers in Los Angeles. *Period.* There was nothing else on the horizon except another tour of Japan.

One night I was talking to—not *with*, because he seldom said anything—this cat named Arthur. He'd been a fan of mine and sometimes took me out. I could see he was deeply depressed so I was up and outgoing and vivacious whenever I was around him. But one day I'd had it up to here with everything. I was grousing about life. I said I'd like to get out of Hollywood. Very unexpectedly, he said, "Come be my guest. I'm at the beach."

He didn't have to ask me twice. I packed a couple of suitcases and left my other belongings with friends. That evening he came to pick me up. We drove and drove and drove until finally I said, "Well, where do you live?"

When we got there, it was an apartment a couple of doors down from the fire station in Malibu.

"Man, you didn't say you had a pad on the beach at Malibu!"

"I only rent," he apologized.

I don't know any words to describe the eleven or twelve months we spent together. It wasn't a relationship. I was strung out and he was emotionally numb. His wife had left him, which didn't seem to bother him much, but she had taken their son and that really banged him out. When he'd start to think about it, he couldn't talk. He'd just write notes.

I was a good influence because I could distract him. He was good for me because he wasn't into drugs. He didn't even drink except when we'd go into a bar to hear some jazz group.

Arthur worked as an aerospace technician in Redondo Beach. At first I didn't work at all. I was just lying around on the beach. A lot of important people lived nearby in the Malibu colony and on the fringes. One day I got to talking to this interesting, intelligent woman. I told Arthur what a good day I'd had. "Boy," I said, "would I like to have a mind like hers." The nice thing about him was that when I pointed her out later he didn't laugh because I hadn't recognized Jane Fonda.

Except for a couple of dollars that John would send from Hawaii occasionally and a few times when Arthur gave me money to pick up food, I didn't have a penny to spend. So I opened a little service like I'd had going in prison: cutting, washing and setting hair. It gave me a little pin money and when the lady left she was happier

and I felt good, too. As the song goes, "Make someone happy . . . ."

I didn't have a car so I hitchhiked a lot. If you've got no wheels,
it's about the only way to get around out there. Once this car
stopped and picked me up. The guy looked familiar, but I couldn't
place him. As we were riding along talking about this and that, he
asked what I did. I said I'd been a singer, sort of.

"In the movies?"

"Naw, big bands. Krupa, Kenton, Woody Herman."

"Oh? I used to be in films, but I'm retired. Do you drink?"

"If someone buys."

"Well, let's stop and have one."

We stopped and went into this nothing place. The bartender
obviously knew the guy, called him Jimmy. I looked at him. Jimmy? It couldn't be Cagney or Stewart. Finally, I said, "Your face is
familiar, but I can't come up with a name."

"Jimmy Dunn," the bartender said. "*A Tree Grows in Brooklyn.*
Won for an Oscar. Best supporting actor."

"Meet my press agent," Jimmy laughed. He told the bartender
I'd sung with Gene, Stanley and Woody.

"Hey, we're getting a celebrity clientele. This calls for a drink,"
the bartender said, setting them up.

All I could think of was how unpredictable life was. Who'd have
thought I'd meet James Dunn hitchhiking? Or that he'd invite me
for a drink? And the only one of the three of us who could get a
steady job was the bartender!

As we left, Jimmy asked where he could drop me off. I told him
near Synanon, which was just getting big and which I was thinking
of looking into. He dropped me there and that was the last I ever
saw of him.

I could never get the nerve to go inside to talk to anyone at
Synanon either. As things turned out, maybe it was just as well.
But I used to meet Dee at the top of the hill overlooking the building whenever I could scrape together enough money to make a
buy. We'd make our transaction, look down and discuss how there
were people in there really trying to break their habits. I said, "I'm
going to break mine, but not their way."

"You're like Snow White," Dee said. "You believe wishing will
make it so."

I didn't argue, but I knew better. John had always doled out as few drops of cooked heroin to me as possible and took care of putting the needle in my veins. I was having a hard time managing by myself. I wanted to quit, but this time it was harder to do than when John and I cleaned up before. There was no cough syrup on open shelves to wean myself on anymore. I'll admit I began to get scared. I had a habit I couldn't support and no way to make a decent amount of bread anymore. When I turned on the radio I didn't even hear my kind of music. It was all Elvis, Jerry Lee Lewis, Little Richard and Bill Haley or Pat Boone, Perry Como, Frankie Avalon and, of course, the Beatles. I don't think I felt sorry for myself. I know I didn't complain. But my sunny disposition began to curdle and I grew bitter.

Even though Arthur and I didn't talk much, we helped one another by being there. Finally, he decided to take his wife to court over custody and visitation rights. The upshot of it was that the judge ruled he could have The Kid spend a weekend with him once a month.

The Kid was obviously being strictly brought up and he made me uneasy even though he couldn't have been more than five or six. But do you know what he said when Arthur introduced us?

"How do you do? I'm so happy to know you." As I mumbled something, he turned to his dad and said, "Thank you, Father, for introducing me to your girl friend who sings." Then he turned back to me. "I hope you'll sing for me while I'm here."

That Kid could talk enough for both Arthur and himself.

He visited us once a month after that. About the third or fourth time, I told Arthur that I got the impression he was testing me to see if I could accept the boy. I explained that I could accept his child *if* I could accept any, but I'd made sure I'd never have one because my own childhood had been a mess and I didn't want to compound the mistakes that had been made with me.

I couldn't cheer Arthur up after that conversation. I'd unintentionally wounded him. He wasn't unkind. He just stopped talking altogether. If he had something he wanted to know he wrote me a note. That kind of behavior doesn't exactly make you feel welcome.

So around October 1964 I decided to accept a gig at the Downbeat in New York. The money was useful, but it was more than that. I hadn't realized how much I missed singing. What made the gig such a kick was that the house sextet was good and even though this was a club, the management had a really incredible sound system. They not only employed a sound man, but a lighting man as well. Working there I realized I couldn't go on giving shampoos and sets at the beach the rest of my life. The problem was that I was so far down I didn't know how to find my way back.

When time came for me to return to the West Coast I was really low. To make matters worse, the airline lost my baggage. My attitude was, well, if it's lost, it's lost. There's nothing I can do about it. Since Arthur had stopped talking to me, I didn't expect any help from him. But he surprised me. He filed a claim without mentioning it, and one morning in the mail I had a check for $240 in settlement.

In 1964 you could still do a lot with that kind of money. For instance, there was a nifty old Ford for sale at one of the gas stations down the highway. I took the check over and asked the owner of the car how much he wanted for it. The price was $150. We talked and he finally let me have it for $140, which meant I could pocket an even hundred bucks.

I drove it back to Arthur's where I put all the possessions I had with me into the car. I was going to write a thank-you note, but then I thought how in his way Arthur was a kind man who had tried to help. So I decided I just couldn't cut out and let him find the note.

I drove down to the plant in Redondo Beach and waited for him to get his lunch break. When he saw me, he just nodded. He didn't ask why I was there or invite me to sit down. He just looked at me.

"Arthur, I came by to thank you for everything and say goodbye."

He just sat there.

I wanted to come up with a big speech that would let him know that he'd helped me and I hoped I'd helped him before we drifted apart. But everything I could think of sounded corny. I began getting very nervous. All I said was "Goodbye and good luck."

Then I hurried out to my car and drove off. I've never seen

Arthur since, but I've heard he found a pleasant, no-problems, fat chick and they have a child. I hope it's a boy. If it is, Arthur is wildly happy and everything worked out for the best for everybody.

While I was living with Arthur my health began to break. The long use of heroin had upset my digestive and intestinal processes. Constipation and heroin go together. I was plagued by headaches and lower abdominal distress caused by a packed colon. So every five to seven days, I'd buy a pint of Citrus of Magnesia. That night I'd drink the whole bottle and the next morning I'd be able to go to the bathroom again.

I also developed arthritic attacks while in Malibu. Calcium deposits were beginning to form causing my right arm to lock, and my knees kept going out. Lack of proper diet over the years had brought on these ailments, I'm sure. I used to kid John about first turning me on in the morning and then giving me a vitamin pill. I should have taken more vitamins. Because now I began feeling I was falling apart.

There were three doctors nearby, but the one everyone recommended was twenty-three-year-old David Boska. Dr. Boska sounded a little young to me, but the woman next door was surprised I hadn't heard of him. He'd treated President John F. Kennedy when the President had visited his brother-in-law Peter Lawford. That did it. I was still a kid, at least emotionally. I thought if the President trusts him, he's good enough for me.

I went to Dr. Boska for treatment of the complaints I've mentioned, but he was so sympathetic and reassuring that I found myself blurting out my life story. He was too young to have heard of me as a singer. But he responded to my problems of living with Arthur, and he didn't seem shocked when I confided to him I was a junkie. He quietly asked whether I sincerely was trying to get off drugs.

I lied and told him I was. Now, my grandmother on Dad's side had given me good religious training so I never stole or prostituted myself. To this day I believe that when you're strung out or high, just as when you're hypnotized, you won't do anything you wouldn't do when you're straight. But you do *have* to become a liar to keep out of jail.

As I understood what the doctor told me, there were at the time certain things that could be prescribed to reduce pain. There was empirin-codeine, but I'd fooled around with that and knew that I needed so much to relieve pain I tended to get addicted. Percodan made me sick to my stomach. There was also Dolophine*, which took away the pain, but didn't set you buzzing around in an unsafe condition to drive a car. Dolophine is basically the same as Methadone, only a little more convenient since it's a tiny pill that you can carry around with you. Then if you need a fix, you take a half—they're strong—and it takes care of the desire for a fix without giving you a high. If I'd followed what he said, I'd probably have got off dope. I'm sorry to have to admit that sometimes I betrayed the doctor by trading the prescription pills for heroin.

Time passed. There were just enough gigs and friends to keep me from becoming a bag lady. I hadn't had a recording contract for a couple of years. Maynard Sloate had given up on me. I was dependent on picking up, when I could, a weekend gig in some dive that catered to jazz buffs. And there always seemed to be some hungry, young reporter who turned up to write about quote the greatest white jazz singer unquote, who was reduced to working sleazy clubs that might be out of business before she cashed her salary check or the interview appeared.

What those guys said didn't bother me. I could handle the headlines such as LOOT, SCHMOOT AND THE MISSIONARY FOR A LOST CAUSE. Guess who! Or, FORMER STAR SQUINTS IN BRIGHT LIGHTS. By now I knew this was a monetary world. Those writers had to earn a buck to survive the same as I did.

When John finished in Hawaii and moved back to Los Angeles with his wife, he saw the precarious position I'd fallen into and began encouraging me to try to clean up. He had kicked his habit while he was in the Islands and now he was urging me to do the same. My intentions were as good as my will was weak. I wanted to get off drugs and get on with my career, but the temptations were too great. I'd get in pretty good physical shape, but I kept falling back into my old habit. The need was in my mind.

The Pooles hadn't been in Hollywood long when he got an offer

---

*Dolophine was named in honor of Adolf Hitler, who had had it developed during World War II when Hermann Goering's supply of heroin was cut off.

to go back to Hawaii in the early part of 1968. Since I was living in a little out-of-the-way room, they suggested that I move into their apartment to sit out the rest of their current month and the month's deposit that they would forfeit. I leaped at the opportunity.

We agreed that he'd introduce me to the landlady as Miss Colton. She was friendly and quite agreeable to the plan until shortly after the Pooles left. Suddenly her attitude changed. She became cold. Distant. I knew by instinct that the cops had paid her a visit and given her my history. Later, through the grapevine between the States and Hawaii, John learned the fuzz were just waiting for me to get a little careless. In fact, he called the apartment every day between noon and 1:00 P.M. to remind me to take no chances and to ask if everything was cool.

For a week or so, I could truthfully answer yes. Then I made the mistake of trading my prescription Dolophine for some smack which I soon shot up. That left me stranded. I couldn't go back to the doctor for more tablets and I didn't have the bread to buy street drugs. I met Dee and told her I was going to try going cold turkey. She gave me a wise, old-junkie look and said, "Good luck, kid. But if it gets too bad, you know where I am."

Dee was not only a connection, she was a friend, so I was relieved to go back to the apartment knowing that if things got too horrendous I could get something from her on credit. I thanked God I hadn't walked away from her when she shot herself in the hand in Chicago.

I decided that I'd just stay in the apartment, not even leaving for food until I'd worked through my physical symptoms. It was the only sensible thing to do since I knew the police were poised to grab me. And I kept telling myself all I had to do was prove I was stronger than my need for chemicals.

The second day I lay there slithering in pain, my body recoiling from the softness of the bed, demanding the punishment of the hard wooden floor. The slightest movement of air seemed to burn my skin. Cold felt hot. Nothing comforted me. Nothing could comfort me except the chemical that was causing all my problems. I thought of calling Dr. Boska and confessing what I'd done, but I was ashamed of my weakness and dishonesty. Because I had to admit to myself that deep down I really didn't want to quit.

271

Time didn't seem to pass. Lying there on the floor of that cheap little garage apartment, I was physically and emotionally wrung out. Sweat popped out of every pore. My nose was running. My arms felt as if they weighed three hundred pounds. I was having terrible trouble with my stomach and bowels. The thought of eating made me feel as if my tongue was swollen so that it completely filled my mouth.

Every joint in my body ached, even those in my fingers and toes. I felt as if I was down with the severest case of flu you can imagine. Every pore in my skin stung. A fix would provide peace and elation. Normality. Otherwise, I'd soon be.getting chills and shakes. Then I'd begin throwing up.

When I opened my eyes, the California sunshine that had lured me to the West Coast tore at my eye muscles. Why did I lie there enduring this torture when a few drops of heroin would make me feel brand-new?

I'd survived the Walkathons, the Uptown taverns, the big-band scene with eighty-plus one-nighters on a bus, but now I was forty-six years old. I wasn't some teenager who'd popped a few pills, dropped a little acid and sniffed cocaine a few times. I wasn't facing some mild withdrawal symptoms and a little mental depression. Granted, that's unpleasant. But when you try coming off a fourteen-year heroin habit, you're facing something as close to hell on earth as you'll find.

The temperature was hot, but no matter how many blankets I tucked around me I was freezing. Then suddenly everything changed and I began sweating again. If I took a teaspoon of water, it set me retching. I kept dreading being wracked by the dry heaves that I knew were ahead of me.

I'd injected into the veins on the back of my arms for fourteen years. Some of those veins collapsed. I knew my arms would always ache, but if I was going to get myself out, it meant retraining my mind. If I kicked, I was going to have to re-teach myself to eat, drink, think, sing. I'd sung songs when I was high and then had to relearn them when I was straight. I'd have to start all over again.

The trouble with drugging is that at first it's all laughs. Then suddenly it's as if you've stepped into quicksand. You have to have it just to keep normal, and suddenly you're in so deeply you don't know how you're going to get out. In the beginning, if you're street-smart, you're sure that you can handle any problem. I never knew a junkie who didn't initially feel that way.

I turned over on the floor and propped up my head. I made myself open my eyes and focused them to see what time it was. In another hour Dee, my angel of mercy, would be in the office. In another few hours, I'd begin getting very sick. I might go into convulsions. The realization destroyed my vow to stay clean. Where I was at just then, I was so desperate I didn't care if the cops were watching. I refused to think about dying or getting busted. Nothing was important except that warm flush that spreads from the center of your being when the chemical hits and makes you able to function again.

In jail I'd seen cats with terrible habits—habits on a whole different dimension and plane from mine. Faced with cold turkey, they chose suicide. I wasn't into that. Not me. I still wanted to sing, to help people get out of themselves. I wanted to live and make a contribution to the world. No matter how wasted I got, that thought was always with me.

But on the morning of March 4, 1966, I decided Joe Glaser was right when he'd said, "Anita, you have a million dollars' worth of talent and no class." Because I wanted dope more than I wanted to get back on my feet.

Once I'd accepted that, I dressed and went to the AGVA office where I found Dee. I went into the latrine where they found me on the floor with the needle still in my arm. And, well, you know the rest of the story.

CHAPTER XIII
I'M STILL HERE

At the airport in Hawaii, when I told John of my financial condition, he drove to a couple of pawnshops where he left some of his drums to get enough bread to cover my first month's rent and give me a little walking-around money.

He got me installed in an efficiency apartment and spent as much time with me as possible, which wasn't a lot because he hadn't told his wife I was there. I was so sick I could hardly walk, but I was determined to get well. Every day I pulled myself together to get to the ocean which was about a block from the apartment.

There, I'd lie on the hot beach until I got the sweats and then go into the cold water. After I'd cooled down, I'd come out and lie in the sun again. If I developed chills, John or some other cat would cover me with warm sand.

I'd got a supply of Dolophine pills before leaving, but I tried to use them as sparingly as possible to give my body a chance to eliminate the chemicals and stabilize itself. In the depths of my misery, John began showing up with a Bible from which he'd read to me.

I don't know how long it takes for the system to free itself of the chemicals that have been shot into it. I do know that frequently in those days I'd awaken in the middle of the night having dreamed that I'd been shooting up. My body would actually feel as if I'd had a fix. Occasionally even now, twelve years later, it still happens.

My plan was to substitute food and sunshine, heat and cold, plus as little Dolophine as possible, for the heroin my body and mind craved. As I did, little by little, I could feel that I was getting better.

I also got a little help I hadn't counted on. During all those years I'd been zonked out, I'd never fallen completely away from God, but I hadn't given Him all that much thought either. At first when John had read to me from the Bible, I'd been in such bad shape physically I hadn't received much comfort from it. But as I improved physically, I began listening to the beauty of the words. Not so much the meaning as the sound. Slowly, I also recognized that some of those things related to my life and the wrong paths I'd taken. I didn't have a dramatic rebirth, but I did find myself responding more positively.

As time went by, sometimes at dawn when I'd awaken frightened and lonely, I'd pick up the Book and read at random. Almost always there was some passage or phrase that seemed to leap out and comfort me. In the simplest way I learned the truth that I never needed to be alone. Whenever I wanted to take advantage, I had a friend waiting there to lend support, someone to forgive me when I found it hard to forgive myself.

Others rallied to my support. During the first month in Hawaii, I got to know a gentleman named Alfred Harned. Alfred was an old-time guitar player, who now worked for the musician's union. He claimed, and I see no reason to doubt, that he went to high school with Glenn Miller in Iowa. According to him, they had the band that had developed the distinctive Miller sound before Miller became a pro. The way Alfred told it, a couple of members of the band failed to show up for rehearsal one night. So Alfred came up with the idea of placing the members of the band in such a way that the two guys weren't missed. In this way, Miller stumbled onto the sound that he made synonymous with big-band music.

Maybe the story is true. Maybe it's like my "Vaya con Dios" tale. Anyway, Alfred eventually retired to Hawaii where he got a job at the musicians' union. And he made a very nice gesture by inviting me to take over his bedroom while he would sleep on the couch. I gratefully accepted.

Alfred's duties as property man called for him to be at work at 4:30 A.M., and every morning before he left the apartment, he'd tap lightly on the bedooom door to ask if I was all right. Not that he was trying to get in, you understand. He just wanted to make sure that I wasn't having any physical problems.

That went on for months. I had no money. He fed me and I kept telling myself I was getting better, stronger. Finally I did begin to feel pretty good.

Alfred was an elderly gentleman, but he obviously was very fond of me. I'd always been able to sketch tunes by singing my head arrangements into a tape recorder, but to distract myself while I was getting off drugs, I studied with him, learning how to make written sketches. He was my school.

Alfred's great ambition was to write a song I'd record. He wrote several that didn't quite come off. Then one night he invited me to dine at Michelle's, a place on the ocean by Diamond Head. It had pink tablecloths, pink candles, the works—a very romantic atmosphere. The pink candles, the green ocean, the good wine and our friendship inspired Alfred. He wrote a song for me called "Candlelight and Wine."

I liked it and promised to record it someday. Several years later I was doing a live album in Japan and included it. Unfortunately, the piano player was not from my school. When I played the record for Alfred, I apologized, saying, "You know, I never did get started with this."

"Yes," Alfred agreed. "The piano man gave you the wrong entrance."

I looked at the arrangement, and the pianist had hit the wrong chord. After finishing recording the album *Live at the Sometime Club*, John and I had given the company all the information on each number. But upon receiving advance copies, I felt terrible. Instead of crediting Alfred as author following "Candlelight and Wine," it said, "Writer, Unknown." All I could do was apologize and promise to see he got credit when I issued the album in the United States on my own Emily label.

* * *

My life in Hawaii was a series of contrasts. I was too sick to work anything but a few undemanding gigs occasionally to help pay expenses. But through Alfred I visited fine restaurants. And because I was a jazz stylist, Alfred with the musician's union and John a drummer, Joe Castro (Doris Duke's great friend) often invited us to Shangri-La on Blackpoint. That was where Doris and Joe lived. The main house was named after Doris' favorite motion picture. It was a copy of the Taj Mahal which sat in the midst of a twelve-acre complex. Behind it was a pool and what were called "pool cottages" but, man, there were four bedrooms, four bathrooms and little swings out front. She had twelve black Irish wolfhounds—one of which was named Anita after me.

Those pool houses were where Joe Castro spent a lot of time, and he often asked us to stop by to drink Polish vodka and listen to him play the imported Beethoven piano. If you didn't want vodka, there was hundred-year-old brandy.

We'd all jump in the pool, and often Doris would come down to join us. One day she gave a gathering for Joe's friends. She got up in the morning and made Mexican food—everything from the bottom up. She might be the richest woman in the world, but on that day she did it all herself. So for me one day it was luxury and the next day poverty.

By July 1968, five months after I'd OD'd, I was well enough to undertake a six-week tour of the Far East. My friend Joe Arden, who was living two miles outside Bangkok with a Thailand broad, arranged it. He played bass in a group that accompanied acts booked into that area by one agency.

On July 5, I checked into the Siam Inter-Continental where I was to open at the hotel's Leopard Room for six nights. After the opening, the manager came back to tell me that this was the best show they'd ever had and that the house attendance record had been broken. That meant I could draw some advance loot and indulge in a little shopping. When I went out next day to pick up some things, I found I'd been without money for so long that a kind of spending paralysis had set in—but I forced myself to get over it.

After hearing me sing at the opening, the booking agent got excited and set me for a late-evening gig at the American Officers' Club for the last three nights. I really dug Bangkok. It was full of surprises. At one club I saw a photo of Maurice Rocco, the stand-up pianist. Twenty-nine years before when I was working at the Off-Beat in Chicago, between sets I sometimes meandered over to a joint called Elmer's to dig Maurice's showmanship. I went into this club. Maurice and I shook hands, had a drink and talked about life and time going on and on and on.

The second week, I left for my tour which included the Manila Hilton and the Hotel Indonesia in Jakarta where I was the second—Tony Scott had preceded me—jazz act ever to play there. At the Indonesia, a full week's lodging, food, scrumptious service, whatever, cost me a grand total of $37.64.

The whole tour was a ball. To make it perfect, the drummer in the house band at the American Service Club in Bangkok fell in love with me. While I was away from the city, he phoned me every day. He was twenty-four, Filipino and Spanish on his father's side, and Chinese on his mother's. He was young enough and short enough to be my son, but he was charming, intelligent and a complete gentleman. He called me "Number One Lady." I had no intention of getting romantically involved, but his pursuit made me feel more attractive and desirable than I had for a long time. (Later he studied in Europe and finally the University of California, Berkeley.)

You know what? I sensed during my tour that the Far East was where the action was—or would be. Writing John Poole, I told him all the things that had been happening and asked:

> . . . Remember when we had ambition? And fully believed that the future could fulfill our dreams? Some people are still hopeful.
> Luv,

By the time I got back to Honolulu I'd decided that I was ready to resume my career. John placed a few calls and set me for six weeks at the Half Note on the corner of Hudson and Spring Streets in Greenwich Village beginning in February.

I flew into Kennedy to find all of Long Island had been turned into the Great White Way. Only one runway at the airport was open. To get to Manhattan was another scene. Even to get from the street to the entrance of the building at Eighty-third and Lexington created as much suspense as Liza crossing the ice in *Uncle Tom's Cabin*.

Charles Cochran, who plays the piano and sings in chic little clubs on the upper East Side, generously had invited me to use his guest room for a week. We got along so well I ended up staying nine months. To show you what kind of a cat Charlie is, he asked me the second morning if I'd slept well. Half-kidding, I said I had, once I'd adjusted my body to the sag in the mattress. He left the apartment shortly and two days later I was surprised by the arrival of a brand new bed.

Charlie is really a doll to all the down-and-out entertainers, especially singers. His family has money. He's never been on drugs, but he's very sympathetic to people who have messed up their lives with them. The last week in May, he came in and said, "By the way, Anita, you're going to have a couple of new roommates." Naturally, I offered to move, but Charlie wouldn't hear of it. He gave up his bedroom and checked into a hotel.

My new roommates turned out to be Judy Garland and her husband Mickey Deems. There wasn't much chance for me to get to know Judy well. I was a girl who'd been on pot, booze, pills, heroin—you name it—but I had periods when I was functioning offstage.

Judy just never seemed to have an hour when she wasn't taking something. That doesn't mean there weren't laughs. She had a wild, self-mocking sense of humor that was wonderful. Even so, I worried about her being so thin—seventy-four or eighty-four pounds—and I never saw her eating. My heart went out to her. I didn't have much money, but sometimes I'd run out and buy her a chocolate malted or a tunafish sandwich. Most of the time I'd get back and she'd have had a vodka or a pill and gone to sleep.

I knew what she was going through. I was still occasionally tempted. Before going to Hawaii, I'd been taking anything available. But now when some cat who knew my history would urge me to have a little taste, if I felt the stirrings of the old urge, I'd take a Dolophine. And I'm happy to say that when I met Judy I'd weaned myself down to where I could go for days without a pill, but I still kept a prescription supply just in case.

One night I came home and found my pill bottle empty. My pills had all disappeared and I was very unhappy. I knew which way to look, but I didn't want to start a brouhaha. So I told Charlie about it. He checked her room while she was asleep and found the few that she hadn't already swallowed. That little betrayal cooled it between Judy and me for a while, but eventually we got friendly again.

From the day she and Mickey arrived, Judy had wanted to come down to the Half Note to hear me, but she was always too zonked out. A couple of times the date was set, but she just couldn't make it. One night as I was getting ready for work, she announced that this was the night. She and Mickey and Charlie were going to drop by. She went into her bath and started putting on her makeup. After fifteen minutes or so—our doors were always open—I said, "How are you doing?"

"Great."

"You almost ready?"

"Check."

Ten minutes later I went into her room and she was in front of the mirror with one little line across her eyelid. She had no idea of time—which is what happens to you.

But she and the guys actually showed up at the Half Note. During one set, I introduced Mickey Deems, who took a comic bow. "Now I'd like to introduce you to another of my roommates—Charlie Cochran," I said. "Come on up, Charlie."

He came on stage and we did a novelty, with him singing "Cruel One" and me doing "Mean to Me."

Then I said, "Now I'd like to introduce you to my other roommate."

Judy stood up. Naturally the place went wild. Judy ducked under the bar and unsteadily climbed the steps to the platform which was inside the horseshoe bar. We sang "April Showers" together.

Then I stepped back. Judy kicked off her shoes in that famous way of hers, walked over to the edge of the platform, and sat down, dangling her legs over the edge. The light man took his cue. Only a pin spot lit her face as she went into "Over the Rainbow." It was the last song she ever sang in America.

On June 19 Judy and Mickey Deems took off for England. That was Thursday. Charlie left for California on a two-week vacation the following Saturday.

After Judy left, I mentioned several times to Charlie that seeing her around the apartment those last few days made me think of those sleepwalking girls in the zombie treadmills. She gave the impression of being one of the walking dead. So I wasn't too surprised by a call I got from Charlie on the twenty-second, saying Judy had died.

Charlie had called her and Mickey to find how their trip had been. Mickey had gone to call Judy to the phone and after being gone long enough to crawl out a window along the ledge to see her slumped over dead on the toilet, he had come back to stammer out the terrible news.

It wasn't unexpected, but it shook me up. It also reminded me to go right on telling hypes who were always offering me "a little taste" that I wanted to pass. Half the people I'd once been friendly with were dead. The others I didn't see. Judy's death reinforced my determination to keep away from all that street stuff.

The original six-week engagement at the Half Note provided me with an ace in the hole. Of course, working conditions were deplorable, but then that's why the job was available. I was there on and off between February 1969 and August 1970.

And speaking of jobs, this one was a lulu. Sometimes I was there as the star attraction. Sometimes I was the house singer, and near the end of our association I worked only Fridays, Saturdays and Sundays. The club became my home away from home.

Originally I'd been booked with Zoot Sims. But salaries were low and Zoot fell out when he got a better-paying gig in Chicago. So Roy Eldridge was held over and we worked happily together. Our temperamental clashes of the Krupa days were forgotten. Given our schedule there was no time for temperament. Tuesday through Thursday we did sets at 10:00, 11:00 and 12:00; Friday and Sunday, 10:30 and 12:30 P.M. and 1:30 A.M.; and on Saturday at 11:00 P.M., 1:00 and 3:00 A.M.

Everything was subject to change. Musically I had to wing it and sometimes I'd just call the key, beat out the time and take off. It was an atmosphere where the jazz buffs got more excited over adventurous failures than safe successes.

Ordinarily a popular singer looks at the music, sees the lyrics and melody. She learns them and that's the way she sings it ever after. Not me. For me the primary thing is the chord structure which can be developed in various ways through the use of off-notes and chromatics.

The main thing though is that being a jazz stylist I never do the song the same way. I avoided classical music for years. Why? Because I didn't believe it was worthwhile doing something which had already been done.

The Half Note provided an atmosphere where jazz followers really got off on the risks we took. Not that I was influenced by audience reaction. I don't go out to *make* listeners like me. They can decide that for themselves. I'm just a working girl. I do what I do. I know what I'm doing and where I've been. They know what they're doing and where they've been. Hopefully, we meet.

Drummers came and went swiftly. Contractually, I was obligated to provide a piano player. Don't ask me why. The bread wasn't so hot anyway. That first six weeks, I grossed $425 a week minus $150 for Alan Marlowe's salary as a pianist. That left me $275 before taxes. Since Alan and I split expenses on a rented Volkswagen to get back and forth to work that didn't leave me much walking-around money. In fact, without Charlie Cochran's hospitality, I couldn't have made it.

As the six weeks neared an end, the club wanted to pick up my option. I passed, promising to come back real soon. With nothing better on the horizon, I reopened the second week in April. Roy Eldridge stayed on for a week; then he left and Zoot Sims joined.

This time I'd talked the club into paying for all musicians and they brought in Ross Tompkins, a fantastic jazz pianist who worked a lot on NBC-TV's *Tonight* show.

As long as the music was going, I was happy enough. Otherwise, it was lonely. Monday, my day off, was often lost because Charlie and I would start tipping a few and overindulge. There were a couple of cats around the club who wanted to be my partner, but they were young and I was too old to play the game anymore unless I was sincere. The winter and spring cold depressed me and I did a lot of muttering about "hating this lousy Chicago-type weather" and wanting to "get back to the land of sunshine." Happily, John had reintroduced me to the Bible while I was kicking my habit, and when I got too down I'd close my door and just begin reading anywhere. Almost invariably it helped buoy my spirits.

My financial problems became pressing after the dentist persuaded me to have a new set of caps to prevent losing my teeth. I resisted, thinking, There goes my career. But I finally agreed to have the work done. Then, when he finished, the caps seemed a little large, but the dentist said they'd "settle" and I was happy that at least they were *all the same color.*

I was signed for the Newport Jazz Festival for July 3 at $1,000 for the night, negotiated a movie role for the fall and made plans with Charlie to visit John and Elaine Poole in Hawaii.

With the arrival of warm weather and the jazz festival plus the financial windfall from the movie, my spirits lifted. There was another reason, too, as I explained to John in a letter:

My new life, as you call it, is not a repeat of my earlier ones. No, this one is not a "Bruce," thank you.

Had a date last Sunday evening—the doorbell rang. It was the Lt. from Hawaii who had a crush on me, the one whose father is head of the FBI in Idaho or Oregon. He had a few hours in town on his way to Phoenix.

After a phone call to my "new interest," the Lt. and I had a drink and dinner—he split. I kept my date. Walla!

On June 29 I wrote John again:

Tonite is my closing nite at the Half Note at least thru the month of July. Mike has asked me back in August. Time will tell.

Maynard (Sloate) has reserved a room for me across from the Tropicana in Las Vegas. $40 per week. Check in July 10th if all goes well.

The letter was interrupted and later I continued:

Got a deal at the Half Note for August 12–17th. Some $s. Also the B & B Agency came through—one week, Boston at Pall's Mall—so I have 13 consecutive days. Wow!

Then nothing unless a little weekend at the Half Note. (My ace in the hole.)

Of couse, you are aware of my Sept-Oct deal with MGM pictures—not recordings.

Myself? I'm straight. I sleep, eat and hope for happy happenings in the future. God bless!

Luv,

I wrote another longie on August 3 which I'll excerpt from, omitting inquiries about the Pooles and the receipt of a letter from Bruce:

Las Vegas? After buying my two gowns, one pair of shoes, paying for Penny's [my poodle] operation, the LA trip, etc., etc., etc., I wound up with $150 out of $750. No one wins on the road. It was a fling.

New York holds little for me except—The Vanguard and the Half Note—but a girl must work.

I'm not very happy. New York is lonely for me. Charlie is here, but he parties all night. I sleep. . .

A brand new start would be welcome. Incidentally, hold onto the piano. Keep it for the time being, kindly. . . .

Should I speak to Mrs. Church about England? Or can you not leave your love?

I really do understand about holding-hands relationships. Makes life seem *almost* real. Ha!

Roy's quite a guy—fast, wheeler-dealer type. Reminds me of Carl. He's not been around. . . . which is welcome as far as I'm concerned. . . .

That's what I thought. I met a young guy at the Half Note one evening. I'd just left the stage and come into the bar on my way to the dressing room.

"You sing very well, Miss O'Day."

I'm very sound conscious and that voice went *boing* right to my soul. It was beautiful. I turned around and here was this tall, attractive black man. He bought me a drink. We started talking and we seemed to like one another. He was a free-lance television newsman and radio announcer. "Some days I sell one featurette and make three-hundred dollars. When I'm lucky I sell two and make six-hundred dollars. Other days, nothing."

He started coming into the club every night. At first we just hung out together. There was no romance. After all, as I told myself often, he was twenty-nine and I was fifty. But he kept pressing and I kept trying to play it cool. Because I felt I had just one more go-round. I wasn't entitled to any more.

Not that I had that many choices. There was Alfred in Hawaii, sweet and lovable and, as he said, too old for me. There was the timid, forty-nine-year-old patron with the bold knee at the Half Note. There were the two younger guys. All except Alfred were strangers to my world. So I decided to take a chance on the long shot—this twenty-nine-year-old.

I was off drugs. People told me I didn't look my age. I was emotionally young and he seemed older than his calendar age. I wasn't prejudiced. He could have been white, yellow or purple instead of black. Color was no problem to me and he didn't even seem aware of it.

We were proud of one another. He wore $150 shoes, had nice clothes and an easy way of talking with people. But none of these things were what counted. I needed someone to be my friend, someone for me to confide in and someone to comfort me. He did that.

I think he was proud of my being on the bill at the Newport Jazz Festival and appearing with George Kennedy in MGM's *Zigzag*. I wasn't just a song stylist in the bar near his apartment.

He was happy and I was happy. I'd practically stopped the pills, and in mid-October I went for a solid week without taking a drink. "What a change of disposition," I wrote John about myself. I told him that on the previous Saturday my man had taken me to see and hear Bill Evans at the Top of the Gate. He'd introduced me to the owner, Art D'Lugoff. I'd inquired about work, but he said he was solidly booked until after the first of the year. I decided I had to get better organized if I wanted to move up. I was beginning to worry that I'd outstayed my welcome at Charlie's, but he was too much of a gentleman to say anything about it to me.

Then two things happened. In September 1969 Bruce Phillips sent me a letter in care of Joe Glaser's office. I asked the secretary to return it marked "Address Unknown." Shortly after, Charlie's phone rang. I picked up and Bruce was on the other end of the line. He said he'd gotten out of prison but was going back to pushing dope. He wanted to send me some as a present. I told him I was finished with that scene and didn't even want to hear about it. He said he'd call another time and hung up.

I was so petrified I called my man, who urged me to move to the Village with him. Next day we carried my belongings up four flights to his pad on LeRoy Street. It was a small but sunny place. He already had a hi-fi, but to celebrate my arrival he went out and bought a color television set. During the day while he was out chasing down stories, I spent my time cleaning and fixing the place.

We were surrounded by old folks and hippies, but we were within easy walking distance of my gig and it looked good for a couple of months.

We both seemed genuinely content. Everything about the relationship seemed to be going so well I decided to have John ship my musical arrangements and my little Wurlitzer piano by air freight C.O.D.

John had never met my man, but knowing my record of choosing the wrong guy he wrote inquiring about his youth and said he hoped I hadn't got myself another "errand boy."

Touched at his concern and a little sad that with him in Hawaii and me in New York, our long professional collaboration seemed to be ending, I fortified myself with a couple of scotches (I stayed on the wagon a week only) and wrote a little apprehensively and very sentimentally about times past and future:

> Hearing from you, knowing someone cares about what I'm doing and how revives my faith in people *one more time.* New York, especially in winter, puts me back to how I began my travels (mostly to avoid city living—booze for companionship—and cold), lo and behold, searching for????????????
>
> I find myself still searching for ?????????? Only a little older, still no monies, no warm friends nearby or whatever else people who appear happy do have.
>
> The Half Note job begins December 12th thru the holidays—and then who knows? All the good jobs are taken, booked in advance, mostly to people with *tact,* taste, talent—people who seem to be liked by people. Always my worst subject.

* * *

I finally faced the fact that life is *hard*. I recognized that I couldn't continue running away from my problems. I realized that I was too old and too tired to do more than make the most of what I had.

What I had was some kind of gig which partially satisfied my need to perform. A very strong need. But I desperately wanted better conditions. I think that's why Peggy Lee's "Is That All There Is?" hit me so hard.

I played it over and over on the hi-fi Christmas day. My man was out covering the prison release of Willie Sutton. In midafternoon he called to say he'd made reservations for Christmas dinner at the Penguin on Ninth Street.

It's very difficult for me ever to admit feelings of pain or regret. When he arrived home, I put on such a happy face there was no way he could have guessed I'd had anything but the happiest of days. And later as we dined at the Penguin, enjoying our Christmas turkey and holiday brandy, I convinced myself that this was one of the nicest Christmases I remembered.

Over the years I've sometimes wondered what it would take to make me happy. Three days before my January closing at the Half Note, I got an offer to play midtown at the Down Beat Club. So after a couple of weeks rest, I'd again be drawing a paycheck. Still, writing John I complained:

> I surely do abhor Sundays in New York. It's cold. It's snowing. That's (1) That's 2 (3) I'm overeating. (4) Over drinking. Why do I do these things to myself? *And still bored.* Looks like doomed unless a miracle happens.

The Down Beat engagement was swinging with capacity business which lifted my spirits. For once I had my own private dressing room instead of having to change among the beer cases. And the management allowed us to order steaks and other goodies at half price.

In between sets, I worked paid parties, benefits, did radio and TV promotions and snagged a Ford commercial for radio. Suddenly everything seemed to be going my way. I began squirreling away a little money.

My man and I got along well. He had a lot on the ball and was making enough to invest in part ownership of a restaurant and, sharing my enthusiasm for racing, he bought a race horse.

I felt so good about my life that I went on a health kick, writing John, "Do it! It's the only way to fly." As I dropped a few pounds, I let my hair grow into a pageboy and had it dyed champagne blond.

Bookings picked up in spots around the country. When Charles Bourgeois offered me a year-end date with one of four packages George Wein was putting together to tour England and Germany in November, I held out for my Newport salary and got it.

It seemed to me I was doing everything right, but either I have the world's worst luck or I'm dumb. I thought my man would be thrilled at the way my career was picking up. He wasn't. I couldn't believe it was just bad luck that I'd chosen another competitor instead of a teammate. There must be something that made me make such a choice. Because he turned out to be a great Me, Me, Me man with a super-macho attitude. So when I became busy looking after my career, we began clashing because I didn't have time to cater to his whims and wishes.

He accused me of being married to music. "I don't think that's fair," I told him. "Yes, music is clean, honest and rewarding. I've never denied that. You know I've always got a lot of fun out of it—as you have from your job."

Comparing my gig to his made him flip. I couldn't believe it.

"Why you broken-down, ex-junkie bum! You compare your singing in a Greenwich Village toilet for a hundred people to being on TV?"

"No!" I interrupted. "I don't count numbers any more than money."

"Good thing."

"You can't buy what I do. You can pay me and I do it. But I don't do it better if the money's big and I don't do it better if it's at Carnegie Hall instead of the Half Note. I do my best wherever I am. And when the spirit moves me I get inspired—whatever the circumstances."

I couldn't believe he didn't understand more than that about me. When it finally sank in, I packed my things and moved into a little residential hotel nearby. I could still walk to work and they agreed I could keep my dog, Penny, in the room for a dollar a day extra.

Suddenly I felt hard times were back. I was alone again. And you've never been as alone as when you're fifty years old, your type of music is temporarily out of style and you find that the relationship in which you cared deeply about someone didn't really exist. The one thing I had to cling to that made me hold my head high was that, depressed as I was, I didn't go looking for a fix. At last I could face these hard facts without using a chemical escape.

But I wasn't completely well. Two days after I moved out he was on the phone apologizing, denying he meant what he'd said, pleading with me to come back. I kept refusing for over a week. Finally I agreed to have a drink with him at the club. Then I let him take me to dinner. And after weeks of thinking it over, I decided to give our relationship another chance.

It was a mistake. I hadn't been back at the apartment more than a few days before he was at the Half Note every night, all over the place bugging everyone about the presentation, the musicians, the salary I was getting.

Sure, some of the things he suggested would have helped, but I overlooked them because I was working with top jazz artists and I was working when there weren't that many clubs using my kind of music.

When the manager told me to tell him to cool it or not come around, I lost my cool. Not because I disagreed with him, but because of the way he told me. Goofy me, with my usual lack of tact, didn't discuss it. I just gave him a brisk, "I quit." No other dialogue. Just burned my bridges behind me.

Since I had no gigs in sight I was deeply depressed and my man was very sweet. He suggested we fly to Puerto Rico for a week in the sun. In light of his peculiar behavior around the club, I was surprised and delighted. I loved the beach and he knew a little French hotel in the old part of San Juan that was clean, cheap, located adjacent to the beach and within walking distance of town. It was a wonderful relaxed week.

So it was a bad scene to come back to New York to discover a neat hole in the door where the lock had been. Not only the lock, but everything else in the apartment was gone—including my arrangements, tapes, the little Wurlitzer piano and even my bed.

I wanted to call the police. I swore and stomped and did things I hadn't done in years. But my man seemed strangely calm, cool and collected. I told him so. He flipped. He told me to let him take care of it. All I knew was that I was tired of fighting. Without another word, I picked up my little bag and Penny and sadly walked away. I went back and checked into the same hotel where I'd been before.

Finally, in November, I was able to get away from New York as part of the group assembled by Wein to play such cities as Oslo, Copenhagen, Belgrade, Barcelona and Berlin. There was Buddy Rich's Big Band, Dave Brubeck's Quintet, Earl "Fatha" Hines' Sextet, Gerry Mulligan's Quintet and me with a French trio. At the Berlin Jazz Festival, I recorded the *Live in Berlin* album with them as backing. They couldn't speak English, but they sure could make those instruments communicate.

Afterward I flew directly to Hawaii to visit the Pooles. I toured the Islands with John and a ukelele player who was into jazz, believe it or not. The last of May, John and I opened at Ronnie Scott's in London where *The Times* headed its review SUPER-SOPHISTICATED LADY, and the Manchester *Guardian* summed up its notice with "moments of pure magic." Get the idea? I don't want to brag, but I was a *hit*.

When we closed, John flew to Ohio to pick up Elaine and drive her to New York. I called my sometime man and when I dropped into his pad I was shocked to see my little Wurlitzer piano. When I inquired where it had come from, he was noncommittal. When I demanded to know, he got angry. I quit asking.

Upon John and Elaine's arrival in the city, I told them about it. By now I suspected he also had my arrangements and videotapes. They suggested taking him out for coffee without me to try to find out what he knew about where my music had gone. After chitchatting for a while, the Pooles became as convinced as I was that he knew where the arrangements were. They asked point-blank and he ignored their questions.

When they got back to the hotel, Elaine went through the Yellow Pages looking for storage places in Greenwich Village. The second one she called admitted having my music. She and I went over. Without a receipt, the attendant was powerless to release my property. But Elaine described my sometime man so accurately, the fellow in charge admitted her description fit the guy who had rented the space.

I called him and told him what we'd found. I begged. I pleaded. I threatened. No response. Finally I hired a lawyer. The case was filed in Manhattan Supreme Court on August 10, 1971, but unfortunately my lawyer died before we reached trial and I finally dropped the suit.

I'd gone into the relationship so idealistically, it broke my heart to have it end this way. Worse still, without arrangements I was confined to improvising with small groups which limited available gigs. Fortunately, I'd never got around to having Al Lyons send the material stored at his place, including the Tiny Kahn sextet book, so I still had a few arrangements left.

Jumping ahead, after one of my mid-1970s appearances at Reno Sweeney's, my onetime man came in a couple of times. Then during a 1979 engagement at Marty's, he came to a table and sat with me between sets. I was cool but polite.

After we'd finished the last set of the night, he came bounding into my dressing room, hugged me, held my hand and asked, "How you doing?"

"Just fine," I said, disentangling myself. I'd assumed it was obvious to him that whatever we'd had I'd outgrown. Because I put a lot of time in on him and all I got from it was heartbreak. When we split I put man-woman relationships behind me. Living alone with a tiny two-and-a-half-pound Yorkshire Terrier named Emily (Penny had died) isn't the worst thing that can happen to anyone.

When my new manager Alan Eichler, John and I reached the street, John hailed a cab. Neither he nor Alan knew exactly what my move would be.

When I said, " 'Bye" to my onetime man broad smiles spread across their strained faces. We got into the cab and drove off leaving a lonely, stunned-looking figure standing on the corner gazing after us.

My seesaw life continued throughout the first six years of the 1970s. John and Elaine had a big five-bedroom house in Hesperia,

California. There John put together two albums released by the Anita O'Day Record Company. Customers could get them by mail order only, but their real purpose was to serve notice I was still out there and functioning. We sent promo copies to any disc jockey who dug jazz.

Meanwhile, I went to stay with John and Elaine. I had my own room, my own shelf in the refrigerator. I tried not to use the kitchen when Elaine was preparing meals or to take up too much of John's time. I relearned to drive and finally had myself fitted with eyeglasses which made it possible for me to spend a lot of time reading.

Still, it wasn't easy on Elaine having me around. She knew there was nothing physical between John and me. But the intimacy John and I had created working together over the years caused stress between Elaine and me. Then, one night I got drunk and put a note on Elaine's washing machine. "Please don't run this before noon. A. O'Day."

That did it. The next day Elaine delivered her ultimatum and I moved to Palm Springs. By this time *Once Upon a Summertime*, my initial recording for Anita O'Day Records, was ready for release. Eventually reviews began trickling in. The critics praised the freshness of my approach and seemed delighted that after all I'd gone through my sound and ability to improvise had survived. *Playboy's* man said I still ranked with Billie, Ella and Sarah.

Booking offers came from all over the country. The nearest and easiest was from Donte's in the San Fernando Valley. So I moved from Palm Springs to a cheap hotel in North Hollywood and began playing Donte's a couple of nights a week, selling my records between sets.

A couple of significant things happened there. One night Bruce Phillips walked in. Another night Leonard Feather showed up to hear me.

First, Bruce. He was deep into drugs, unkempt and his obsession with me had seemingly passed. I looked at him and thought someone has to help. But I'd matured enough to know it couldn't be me, because I needed all my energy to perform and earn a living.

His mother? She still didn't seem to realize anything was amiss. So I just tried not to think about him.

Then one night his mother came into Donte's and said with real cool that Bruce had OD'd.

I felt a rush of pity. "Did they find him in time?"

They hadn't. Like so many others I'd known from the old days, Bruce was dead.

The night Leonard came in, he suggested doing a Sunday piece on me for the *Los Angeles Times*. As a critic, Leonard belongs in a class with Nat Hentoff, John S. Wilson and a few others. In this profile, he penetrated my hip-flip facade, said I looked closer to thirty-five than fifty-three, that I was about to work the Little Club in Beverly Hills, that I was making a movie called *The Outfit* with Robert Duvall and Karen Black at MGM and that in July of 1973 I'd appear in New York as part of the Newport Jazz Festival. Yet all anyone recalls from the story was his opening paragraph that I was living in a $3-a-day hotel room without a telephone. It was no big deal. There was nobody I really wanted to call and, in my time, I'd slept in worse places.

But the news that Krupa's and Kenton's former vocalist had hit hard times really brought the vultures out. Some hack named Tom Kirkpatrick lifted Feather's firsthand reporting, slurred Feather's eyesight for saying I looked closer to thirty-five than fifty-three and, in the words of Melinda Abern in the *Village Voice*, "he [Kirkpatrick] had her [me] one skid past skid row" just as I was about to open at Radio City Music Hall in New York.

The truth is my career had begun a steady climb and by 1975 when I returned to Japan for my first tour since 1969, it was first class all the way. The bookings were arranged for intimate clubs in which forty to fifty jazz aficionados paid the equivalent of $100 a person for dinner and a set of ten or twelve tunes. Then they left and another forty enthusiasts followed. Response was so big and business so good that the promoters gave me a hi-fi as a bonus the first year and a Toyota the next. Young people in Japan are very much into American jazz. They're also very Westernized. It's nothing for me to walk down the street and hear some English-speaking Japanese kid call out, "Hi, O'Day."

Out of the 1975 and '76 and subsequent Japanese tours came my present recording company, Emily Records, named after my Yorkie, using her paw print as the logo. Larry and Carol Smith, John and I are partners. John and I provide artistic control and the Smiths look after the business end from their North Haven, Connecticut base. Originally strictly a mail-order company, Emily has grown until it is now distributed nationally through several small distributors and also in the Schwann catalog. In addition to tapes made and released originally in Japan, I recorded *Live at the City* in San Francisco during 1979. Although the backing is still limited to a quartet, I look forward to enlarging to a sextet soon and will gradually embellish until I can someday hire Johnny Mandel to write arrangements.

Beginning with those Japanese tours, everything in my life seemed to begin to come together. It was about time. Holy cremoly, I was fifty-five years old and I had, like, two cents. I realized I couldn't hack the gypsy life anymore. I had to admit I was no longer a kid.

But God takes care of fools and sinners. In late 1976, I got to know Alan Eichler, who was the press agent at Reno Sweeney's and Hopper's. He also dabbled in management and soon was paving the way for my bookings and seeing to my publicity. A strange, brilliant cat. Everyone else in that field has always wanted most of the money without doing any of the work. Alan worked as hard as anyone I've ever known in his field and when I bugged him about what I owed him he'd say, "Nothing," or "Oh, just help out with my telephone bill." Through him I moved on to Les Mouches and to regular stints at Marty's ("The Garden Spot of Jazz") at Third Avenue and Seventy-third Street in New York. Marty Ross ran a happy club which became my home away from home where I played six times in little more than a year.

At about the time I was closing at Hopper's in 1977, I got a note from a writer. I'd been threatening to do my autobiography for years, but plans always collapsed. Closing night, this writer sent back photos of me during my Walkathon days wrapped around a copy of one of his books. He'd been a follower of mine since the time when practically the only song I did was "The Lady in Red."

Through him I met and signed with a warm, caring literary agent named Gloria Safier, who not only sold this book, but lent me money against the advance when the publisher was slow in issuing the check.

Then in 1978 Alan Eichler booked me into Studio One's Backlot where I attracted attention from all the major Los Angeles publications.

How did I do? In the *Los Angeles Times*, Leonard Feather began his review:

> Genuine, unabashed jazz singers, few in number these days, are distinguished by their ability to use the voice as if it were an instrument; by the extent to which they are rhythm-motivated; by the choice of their material and their accompanists. Using any of these yardsticks, Anita O'Day must be rated as the definitive, unceasingly creative artist in this shrinking field.

He ended his notice:

> Between the opening "Wave" and her closing reprise of the same theme, O'Day offered an hour-long seminar in the art of jazz singing. Her students, who should include any vocalists with aspirations beyond the cliches of contemporary pop music, are advised to show up for classes any evening through Sunday.

It's one thing to get a rave notice from the *L.A. Times'* jazz critic, but for a boozer and ex-junkie to get written up in the *Christian Science Monitor* is something else again.

> There's a jazz giant in town [the review began]. Anita O'Day is much more than a singer, although that would be enough . . . she is also a director of her three-piece group. The interplay and exchange of musical ideas between her (and her musicians) is an experience for both the eyes and ears . . .
> Miss O'Day's voice is simply amazing, pure and never strained, full, but never belted. Her phrasing is unlike that of any other singer and further enhances each song. And she is also very funny. She is one of those serious musicians who refuses to take herself seriously.

Intrigued by the reviews, Gene Norman came into the club to catch both sets one night. Then he contacted Feather to suggest he produce an album on Gene's Crescendo label with me. Leonard and pianist Lou Levy did arrangements for the group that included my rhythm section (Levy, bassist Harvey Newmark and John) plus

Brazilian guitarist Laurindo Almeida for samba rhythms and guitarist Joe Diorio for others, plus reed man Ernie Watts, Brazilian percussionist Paulindo da Costa. The result was my first formally structured album in many years. Happily, Jim Donovan, who began as a fan and became a supportive friend during the bleak days, drew on his expertise as an advertising copywriter to come up with the title *Mello'day*.

Alan Eichler again set me at Marty's for what was to develop into a series of frequent appearances. That rarity, a perceptive syndicated columnist, Liz Smith spread the word that I was back in top form. Another syndicated writer, Rex Reed, coaxed a lot more of my life story out of me than I intended to tell for a major profile that appeared in over one hundred newspapers.

After the Smith and Reed breaks, inquiries came pouring in. Publicity seemed to feed upon itself. While I was working at Lulu's in Boston, I did a show, caught a plane to New York, taped two segments for Dick Cavett's PBS interview show (in one half hour I taught Dick the rudiments of jazz singing), rushed to the airport and caught a plane back to Boston in time for the first set at Lulu's the next night.

Inquiries about rights to my life came in from several movie producers and directors.

Then I shared Tom Snyder's *Tomorrow* with Joan Fontaine. I was a little nervous about Tom because he has a reputation for being a tough interviewer, but he was a pussycat with me.

It was one nervous cat who did Johnny Carson's *Tonight*. The Russian Olympic games were coming up and a coach showed up unexpectedly to discuss whether or not the United States ought to boycott a sporting event for political reasons. First, the Carson people told me that I'd definitely be bumped. Then they said I'd probably be bumped but that I'd better go to makeup and get into costume in case there was time for me. Then they decided that they could use only one of the two songs I'd prepared. Naturally, I was far from my best.

Shortly after the *Tonight* debacle, a distinguished-looking gentleman came into Marty's one evening and sat through two sets. Afterward, he approached me and introduced himself as Harry Reasoner. The name meant nothing to me.

"I'm on television," he said. "I'd like to cover your activities in

New York, wherever you play next, and at home in Los Angeles for *60 Minutes.*"

Dummy me asked, "Is that a local show?"

Luckily, Harry seemed to have a sense of humor. But when I told John and Alan what I'd said, they groaned and predicted I'd killed the spot. Not at all. A couple of nights later Harry showed up with some coworkers to catch my work again, and they asked us to attend a meeting. When we got together to talk seriously, I stopped all discussion to inquire, "By the way, how much does this pay?"

Everybody laughed as though I'd made a joke—except John. He said that was called pocketbook journalism and was frowned on.

So I went along with it. "But don't I at least get a free lunch?"

Harry smiled and said he'd spring for that. Finally in January of 1980, *60 Minutes* began filming some twenty-odd hours of me at Marty's, at Lulu's and at home in Los Angeles. My collaborator moaned a lot and worried I'd give away the whole story. But whenever Harry turned the subject to my bout with drugs, I'd give him a two-count, smile, shrug and dismiss it. I did that so well even my collaborator was pleased when the show aired on June 22, 1980.

The first segment of the nation's number-one television program was devoted to my up-and-down life, offering examples of my style and predicting that I seemed to be headed for triumphs that would eclipse earlier achievements.

After all I'd been through, *Who's Who* included me in its latest edition and, irony of ironies, the California Legislature passed a resolution "commending" me as a "distinguished American and Californian whose artistry and sophistication as a jazz vocalist" had made me "a goodwill ambassador for the United States and the state of California" with my "many successful tours throughout the world."

As Harry Reasoner had noted, jazz, like me, had had its ups and downs, but in 1980 and 1981 we were both on the upswing. And the big paychecks have begun to materialize. That couldn't have pleased me more, because when I'm up there with my rhythm section, improvising as the fourth musician in the combo—that's the time when I'm happiest.

EPILOGUE

All my life I've wanted to be where the action is. My ambition? Be street smart. Brazen it out. Never look back. As a kid, I'd called myself the Jezebel of Jazz—gloried in shocking people. Years later, in working on this book, I'd allowed myself to be persuaded to let everything hang out. But after the manuscript went off to the publisher, I began to think about the rough roads I'd traveled. How smart had I been to lay it all out for anybody to read?

I soon found out. The editors began leaking the most sensational parts to the press. Liz Smith tipped her readers my story was "red hot," Radie Harris said the book was "sizzling" and The New York *Post's* gossipy Page Six headlined—Anita's Story: Drugs and Rape". Rex Reed set down "The Dark Nights of Anita O'Day." I could see what would be coming down when TV interviewers got hold of me on the book promotion tour.

After the initial publicity, crowds began to jam clubs where I appeared. But when I stepped into the spotlight I sensed these weren't the cats who'd followed my career for years. This was a different breed of cat. They didn't come to dig my singing. They were there to stare at the woman who'd done all the things they never dared to do. Things, let me say, I wished I'd never done. And so I began to come apart a little. I lost the ability to assume the sunny demeanor that I'd always used when it was to my advantage. I experienced a new emotion for me—embarrassment. No. Shame. Ultimately, I suffered a mini breakdown. Not as bad as when Carl and I were living in the San Fernando Valley and I'd spent my days and nights huddled in the closet, but bad. I locked myself in my new trailer home, refused to air my dirty linen on TV and cancelled the entire promotional tour, including the prestigious TODAY show. I also turned down all singing engagements and wouldn't see or talk to anyone—not even John. I wanted to be where the action wasn't.

What did I care that The New York *Times* said the book was "in the the tradition of the best jazz biographies, written in a hip style and filled with vivid images of Gene Krupa, Stan Kenton, Roy Eldridge and Billie Holiday"? Or that the Los Angeles *Times* called it "a valuable, revealing, read-at-a-gulp account of a premier American artist and the punishing winds that shaped her life and career"? I hated the book and what it had done to me—even when The New York *Times* chose it as one of the "Notable Books of the Year."

I hid myself in the California desert and rode my bicycle and lay in the sun and played with my small canine friend, Emily. Gradually I began to feel better. I began to think that maybe the washing of all my dirty linen in public had served to cleanse me and make me feel freer. I moved to Las Vegas and went back to work, taking a couple of gigs with the big bands of Buddy Rich and Woody Herman. I also played the Dunes Hotel in Vegas and expanded to the Fairmont Hotel chain in New Orleans, Dallas, Denver and San Francisco. After all those years of playing every jazz joint in North Beach and dressing among beer cases, I have to admit it was like a dream come true appearing in the Venetian Room at the Fairmont and having my own suite complete with a well-stocked refrigerator. But I wasn't selling out. I was still doing my own thing.

Somebody—probably Alan Eichler—realized that I was approaching my fiftieth year in show business. So during one of my many engagements at the Vine Street Bar and Grill in Hollywood, a celebration of the event was organized. What a night! My idol Martha Raye, Clint Eastwood, Dudley Moore, Jo Stafford, Bea Wain, Johnnie Ray and many more turned out. Mayor Tom Bradley issued a formal proclamation declaring it "Anita O'Day Day" in Los Angeles—which wasn't too shabby considering I'd once spent time in the city jail.

That night turned out to be such a kick for everyone involved, it was decided we should do a full-dress Carnegie Hall concert to mark my half century as a professional singer. The only problem was that Carnegie was booked solid into the next year. So I just had my fiftieth anniversary concert during my fifty-first year in the business. And what a gig that turned out to be!

The program was divided into two parts. In the first half I worked with Hank Jones on piano, Jay Leonhart on bass, John Poole on drums and Richie Cole on alto sax. That small group gave me the freedom to improvise—as I'd been doing mostly for the past thirty years. (It's also in my view really the essence of jazz.)

The second segment I worked with a sixteen-piece orchestra put together for the occasion by Jay Leonhart. Since I'd done so much more work with just a rhythm section, I spent several weeks rehearsing the new big-band charts. Some were recreations from the original "Anita" album and I hadn't done them since 1955.

But whether with the big group or the small, the concert was a blast from the moment I danced on stage in my glamorous new Bob Mackie outfit—quite a change from the band jackets I used to wear—and launched into my opening number. It was a hip audience and I took chances that that kind of crowd digs.

The first part was artistically satisfying but the second segment was something else. Most of those cats out front had heard me with small groups before, but they hadn't caught me with a big aggregation for over thirty years—if at all. So they not only dug what they heard, they—and I—were transported back to our youth. It was an emotional bath. Especially when Roy Eldridge walked out on stage and joined me for our first million seller, "Let Me Off Uptown."

Interspersed with the music and reminiscences were congratulatory letters and telegrams from President Reagan, Ella Fitzgerald, Frank Sinatra, Governor Cuomo and Mayor Koch. At the end, with the audience on their feet screaming for more, more, more, I couldn't help thinking that if you stay in the business long enough, you get it all.

Things keep changing. After 35 years, John and I decided to go in different directions. I still feel most comfortable when I'm up there improvising—whether in the living room of a friend or the Venetian Room of the Fairmont. What goes around comes around.

Life continues to be a series of gigs, which is just the way I want it to be. It's a whole different world when the music stops.

APPENDIX

RADIOLOGICAL CONSULTATION REPORT
PA AND LATERAL FILMS OF THE CHEST   dated
3-4-66 shows the diaphragmatic leaves to be smooth and
the costrophrenic angles clear. The heart is not enlarged in
its transverse diameter. The aortic and tracheal silhouettes
are normal. Both hilar areas are normal. The lung fields are
clear of recent parenchymal infiltrates. There is no evidence for pneumothorax. There is no osseous abnormality
seen.
IMPRESSION: Negative chest.
H.D. Segall, M.D.
3-8-66

THE PSYCHIATRIC REPORT
5.P.M.   47   Wo brought to E R in comatose condition
5 hours previously and requiring resuscitation procedures.
At the time of examination she relates for the past two
weeks suffering from flu-like symptoms, since breaking off
with a boy friend, drinking heavily unknown quantities of
whiskey, wine and beer daily, eating and sleeping poor,
moving from place to place until on the day of admission

finding herself without money or lodging   Went to place of employment of a friend   Entered the restroom where she suddenly became unconscious without warning. She was subsequently discovered in an unconscious condition and brought to the UCLA E R

There is no previous history of psychiatric hospitalization or epilepsy. She admits to former abuse of narcotics but denies recent narcotic usage and admits only to 5 mg. Valium and a "Resoxin" capsule on the day prior to admission.

Mental Status

Middle-aged, casually dressed, Caucasian female with slurred speech, lint without loosing [sic] of associations or delusions or hallucinations. She relates well to the examiner, is well oriented, but appears mildly sedated after 5 mg IV Nalline. She admits to "I drink because I'm depressed" but denies suicidal intentions or attempt. Affect appears mildly depressed. There is no evidence of recent or remote memory loss   Intellectual functioning appears within average range. Judgment is unimpaired.

Impression:

Other than mild depression and minimal blunting of sensorium possibly due to alcohol or sedatives there is no evidence of severe psychiatric illness sufficient to fully explain the patient's sudden loss of consciousness, which she firmly denies being self-inflicted.

Recommended:

Thorough medical and neurological evaluation for etiology of syncopal episode. If then no pathology is elicited, should the patient desire psychiatric help for emotional problems, evaluation in the MPT induction service is available.

M. Young

Discography
Compiled by Robert A. Sixsmith and Alan Eichler

INTRODUCTION

This discography is divided into two sections. Section A covers Miss O'Day's work in a chronological progression. The numbered selections designate material intended for phonograph record release, whether on 78-, 45- or 33⅓-format, either studio recordings or "live" concert/nightclub material. The only exception to the above is the inclusion of rehearsal and "live" material utilized in Miss O'Day's two albums on the Anita O'Day label, the forerunner of the Emily label.

Broadcast material has been listed (though unnumbered) where reference copies (acetate discs or tapes) are known to exist. The broadcast material from the 1941–45 period has been preserved on 16-inch transcription discs made by the Armed Forces Radio Service (A.F.R.S.) for circulation to the troops.

Section B covers Miss O'Day's long-play album releases including reissues of recordings made with the bands of Gene Krupa and Stan Kenton on 78s. In an effort to be as comprehensive as possible, the editors have included unauthorized (bootleg) albums as well as LPs from the owners of the material, i.e. Columbia Records.

In the Verve period of Section A when two prefixes appear, i.e. MGV/MGVS or V/V6, the first designates monaural release while the second indicates stereophonic release.

The following label abbreviations appear in Section A:

OK	=	OKeh
CN	=	Conqueror
CO	=	Columbia
Sig	=	Signature
Cor, CRL	=	Coral
AOD	=	Anita O'Day
GLS	=	Glendale
MB	=	MPS
PA, PAP	=	Trio
TD	=	Trio
LDC	=	Lobster
GNPS	=	GNP/Crescendo
ER	=	Emily
MGV	=	Verve
V	=	Verve
N	=	Norgran
HSR	=	Hindsight
BBM	=	Bob Thiele Music
TJ	=	Tono
MJ	=	Polydor
WHCD	=	Hendring

IN APPRECIATION

The editors extend special thanks to Miss O'Day and to Mr. John Poole for their encouragement and assistance in the preparation of this discography.

REFERENCES CONSULTED

Chris Albertson formerly of Polydor Records.
BG on the Record: A Bio-Discography of Benny Goodman by

D. Russell Conor and Warren W. Hicks. New Rochelle, NY: Arlington House, 1969.

The Complete Encyclopedia of Popular Music and Jazz 1900–1950 by Roger D. Kinkle. New Rochelle, NY: Arlington House, 1974.

Gene Krupa and His Orchestra by George I. Hall and Stephen A. Kramer. Laurel, Md.: Jazz Discographies Unlimited, 1975.

Jazz Records 1897–1942 by Brian Rust. New Rochelle, NY: Arlington House, 1978.

Jazz Records 1942–1962 by Jorgen Grunnet Jepsen. Copenhagen: Karl Emil Knudsen, 1963.

Verve Tape Library Catalogue by Chris Whent. New York: Verve/Polydor, Inc., 1979.

Peter Welding of Capitol Records.

SECTION A

CHRONOLOGICAL LISTINGS

Part One—VOCALIST WITH GENE KRUPA's BAND

STUDIO MATERIAL	MATRIX	RECORDED	OKEH COLUMBIA CONQUEROR	LP REISSUE
1. "Alreet" with Ensemble	CO 29921-1	New York 3/12/41	OK 6118	BS-7117 AJAX-138
2. "Georgia on My Mind"	CO 29922-1	3/12/41	OK 6118 CN 9616	LN-3136 EG-7122 20AP-1439 EE-22027 KG-32663 AJAX-146
3. "Fool Am I"	CO 29924-1	3/12/41	OK 6154 CN 9655	HL-7148 AJAX-146
4. "Let's Get Away from It All" with Ensemble	CO 29974-1	New York 3/19/41	OK 6130	AJAX-146
5. "Just a Little Bit South of North Carolina"	CO 29976-1	3/19/41	OK 6130 CN 9654	KH-32663 AJAX-146
6. "Slow Down"	CO 29977-1	3/19/41	OK 6154 CN 9787	CL-753 BS-7117 KG-32663 AJAX-146

STUDIO MATERIAL	MATRIX	RECORDED	OKEH COLUMBIA CONQUEROR	LP REISSUE
7. "Drum Boogie" with Ensemble	419	New York 3/41	Lang-Worth Transcriptions 636	MES-7012 VC-5015
8. "Alreet" with Ensemble	419	3/41	636	MES-7012
9. "Fool Am I"	419	3/41	636	MES-7012
10. "I Take to You"	CO 30239-1	New York 4/11/41	OK 6187 CN 9784	HL-7148 20AP-1439 AJAX-146
11. "Green Eyes" with Howard DuLany	CO 30442-1	New York 5/8/41	OK 6222 CO 38212	CL-6066 EE-22027 KG-32663 AJAX-154 P6-14954
	CO 30442-2	5/8/41	unissued	C238033
12. "Let Me Off Uptown" with Roy Eldridge	CO 30443-1	5/8/41	OK 6210 CO 37532 CN 9957 V-Disc 197-B	CL-6010 CL-753 20AP-1439 HL-7252 HL-7277 D 405 C2L-29 KG-32663 P4-1374 LP-2008 JC-36743 AJAX-154 AJAX-502
	CO 30443-2	5/8/41	unissued	C238033
13. "Kick It" with Ensemble	CO 30604-1	New York 6/5/41	OK 6278	EE-22027 AJAX-154 20AP-1439 AJAZZ-502
14. "Amour" with Howard DuLany	C-3965-2A	Chicago 8/18/41	OK 6400	AJAX-161 AJAZZ-502
15. "Stop! The Red Light's On" with Ensemble	C-3967-1	8/18/41	OK 6411 CO 50071	EE-22027 20AP-1439 KG-32663 AJAX-161 AJAZZ-502
16. "Watch the Birdie"	C-3977-1	Chicago 8/20/41	OK 6400	BS-7117 AJAX-161

STUDIO MATERIAL	MATRIX	RECORDED	OKEH COLUMBIA CONQUEROR	LP REISSUE
17. "The Walls Keep Talking" with Roy Eldridge	C-3979-1	8/20/41	OK 6438	EE-22027 20AP-1439 KG-32663 AJAX-161
18. "Two in Love" with Johnny Desmond	H-527-1	Hollywood 10/3/41	OK 6447	AJAX-161
18a. "How Do!"	H-545-1	Hollywood 10/14/41	prev. unissued	P 14379
19. "Skylark"	H-546-1	10/14/41	unissued	—
20. "Coppin' a Plea"	H-547-1	10/14/41	OK 6498	AJAX-161
21. "Bolero at the Savoy"	H-548-1	10/14/41	prev. unissued	P 14379
22. "Skylark"	31800-1	New York 11/25/41	OK 6607	CL-641 20AP-1439 KG-32663 AJAX-161 C2L-29
23. "Bolero at the Savoy"	31801-2	11/25/41	CO 36726	CL 2515 C2L-29 P6-14954 KG-32663 20AP-1439 AJAX-167
24. "Thanks for the Boogie Ride" with Roy Eldridge	31802-2	11/25/41	OK 6506	BS-7107 20AP-1439 KG-32663 AJAX-167 SM-4085
25. "Pass the Bounce"	32063-1	New York 12/29/41	OK 6619	EE-22027 20AP-1439 AJAX-167
26. "Side by Side"	32310-1	New York 1/23/42	CO 36726	AJAX-167 P6-14538
27. "Harlem on Parade"	32312-1 32312-3	1/23/42 1/23/42	OK 6607 unissued	AJAX-167 C238033
28. "Fightin' Doug MacArthur"	32495-1	New York 2/26/42	OK 6635	AJAX-167

STUDIO MATERIAL	MATRIX	RECORDED	OKEH COLUMBIA CONQUEROR	LP REISSUE
29. "That's What You Think" with Ensemble	32496-1	2/26/42	CO 36621 CO 37533	CL-6017 20AP-1439 CL-753 G2L-29 HL-7252 KG-32663 AJAZ-203 C3-10046
30. "Barrelhouse Bessie from Basin Street"	C-4210	Chicago 4/2/42	prev. unissued	AJAZ-203 AJAZZ-502
31. "Deliver Me to Tennessee"	C-4212-1	4/2/42	CO 36591	AJAZ-203 20AP-1439
32. "Massachusetts"	CO 33001-1	New York 7/13/42	OK 6695	CL-6066 CL-753 20AZP-1439 C2L-29 KG-32663 AJAZ-203
	CO 33001-2	7/13/42	unissued	C2 38033
33. "Murder, He Says"	CO 33002-1	New York 7/13/42	OK 6695	CL-753 KG-32663 AJAZ-203
	CO 33002-4	7/13/42	unissued	C238033
34. "Opus #1"	CO 35110-1	New York 8/21/45	CO 37224 CO 50052 V-Disc 555	CL-6066 20AP-1439 C2L-29 KG-32663 JC-36580 AJAZ-211 AJAZ-502
35. "(Did You Ever Get) That Feeling in the Moonlight" with Buddy Stewart	CO 35111-1	8/21/45	CO 36862	KG-32663 AJAZ-211
36. "Boogie Blues"	CO 35113-1	8/21/45	CO 36986 CO 37530	CL-6017 CL-753 D 403 C2L-29 20AP-1439 HL-7252 KG-32663 AJAZ-211

STUDIO MATERIAL	MATRIX	RECORDED	OKEH COLUMBIA CONQUEROR	LP REISSUE
37. "Jose Gonzales"	VP 1515-D	New York 8/45	V-Disc 543-B	LP-2008 GOJ-1006 VC-5015 VC-5015
38. "Oh! Hot Dawg (Boogie Blues)"	VP 1515-D	8/45	V-Disc 543-B	LP-2008 GOJ-1006 VC-5015 VC-5015
39. "Chickery Chick" with Ensemble	CO 35239-1	New York 9/26/45	CO 36877	KG-32663 D 403 AJAZ-211 AJAZZ-502
40. "In the Middle of May" with Buddy Stewart	CO 35240-1	9/26/45	prev. unissued	KG-32663
41. "Tea for Two"	CO 35335-1	New York 10/23/45	CO 38345	KG-32663 AJAZ-219
42. "Harriet" with Buddy Stewart and Ensemble	CO35336-1A	10/23/45	CO 36890	KG-32663 AJAZ-219
43. "Hop, Skip and Jump"	CO 35342-1	New York 10/24/45	CO 36931	AJAZ-219 20AP-1439

BROADCAST MATERIAL	BROADCAST	REFERENCE	LP ISSUE
"Kick It"	6/7/41	NBC Radio	10-110
"Let Me Off Uptown" with Roy Eldridge	6/7/41	NBC Radio	—
"Let Me Off Uptown" with Roy Eldridge	9/11/41	NBC Radio	—
"Let Me Off Uptown" with Roy Eldridge	9/17/41	NBC Radio	—
"Hut Sut Song"	9/21/41	NBC Radio	—
"Stop! The Red Light's On" with Ensemble	9/21/41	NBC Radio	—
"Armour" with Johnny Desmond	9/21/41	NBC Radio	—
"Stop! The Red Light's On" with Ensemble	9/22/41	NBC Radio	—
"The Walls Keep Talking" with Roy Eldridge	9/22/41	NBC Radio	—

BROADCAST MATERIAL	BROADCAST	REFERENCE	LP ISSUE
"The Walls Keep Talking" with Roy Eldridge	9/23/41	NBC Radio	—
"Armour"	10/1/41	NBC Radio	10-110
"Drum Boogie"	10/1/41	NBC Radio	10-110
"Armour"	10/3/41	NBC Radio	—
"Stop! The Red Light's On" with Ensemble	10/3/41	NBC Radio	—
"Cow-Cow Boogie"	11/13/42	CBS Radio	10-110 AJAZZ-502
"Drum Boogie"	9/1/42	Command Performance 33	AJAZZ-502
"Private Jimmy Johnson"	12/25/42	Spotlight Bands	44-144
"Drummin' Man"	12/25/42	Spotlight Bands	10-110
"I'd Do It All Over Again"	8/15/45	MBS Radio	GOJ-1028 AJAZZ-502
"Opus #1"	8/17/45	Spotlight Bands	—
"Bolero at the Savoy"	8/45	One Night Stand	—
"Chickery Chick" with Ensemble	11/19/45	Spotlight Bands	—
"(Did You Ever Get) That Feeling in the Moonlight" with B. Stewart	11/27/45	CBS Radio	—
"Chickery Chick" with Ensemble	11/27/45	CBS Radio	—
"My Guy's Come Back"	12/6/45	CBS Radio	—
"Chickery Chick" with Ensemble	12/6/45	CBS Radio	—
"Hop, Skip and Jump"	12/12/45	CBS Radio	—
"My Guy's Come Back"	12/12/45	CBS Radio	—
"Tea for Two"	1/1/46	One Night Stand 860	GK-1468
"Chickery Chick" with Ensemble	1/1/46	One Night Stand 860	GK-1468
"Otto Make That Riff Staccato"	1/1/46	One Night Stand 860	GK-1468
"Bolero at the Savoy"	1/18/46	CBS Radio	—
"(Did You Ever Get) That Feeling in the Moonlight" with Buddy Stewart	1/18/46	CBS Radio	—
"Let Me Off Uptown" with Roy Eldridge	1942	Soundie (film)	KD-7
"Thanks for the Boogie Ride" with Roy Eldridge	1942	Soundie (film)	—

Part Two—VOCALIST WITH STAN KENTON's BAND

STUDIO MATERIAL	MATRIX	RECORDED	TRANSCRIPTION	LP ISSUE
		1944	MacGregor	
				SB-213
44. "Ride On"	—			SWH-26
45. "Build It Up, Paint It Nice and Tear It Down"	—			SB-213 SWH-26
46. "You Betcha!"	—			SB-213 SWH-26
47. "In a Little Spanish Town"	—			HSR-136 AJAZZ-502
48. "Blues"	—			HSR-147
49. "Special Delivery"	—			SWH-26
50. "Tabby the Cat"	—			HSR-147
51. "And Her Tears Flowed Like Wine"	—			SWH-26
52. "I'm Going Mad for a Pad"	—			—
53. "My Guy's Come Back"	—			—
54. "I Lost My Sugar in Salt Lake City"	—			HSR-136
55. "The Lady in Red"	—			HSR-136

	MATRIX	RECORDED	CAPITOL	LP REISSUE
56. "I'm Going Mad for a Pad"	248	Los Angeles 5/20/44	prev. unissued	WDX-569 ECJ-50075
57. "And Her Tears Flowed Like Wine" with Ensemble	249	5/20/44	166 V-Disc 309A	— VC-5015
	249	5/20/44 (alternate take)	15196	HT-358 DT-2327 RD-4-139 ST-1050 STB-12016 056-85 612 ECJ-50075 AJAZZ-502
58. "Gotta Be Gettin' "	321	New York 9/26/44	178	ST-1062 AJAZZ-502 ECJ-50075
59. "Are You Livin' Old Man"	525	New York 12/15/44	187	ST-1029 ECJ-50075

			CAPITOL	LP REISSUE
60. "I Want a Grown Up Man"	547	Los Angeles 1/16/45	prev. unissued	ST-1028
61. "Travelin' Man" with The Kentones	548	1/16/45	48012	ST-1029
62. "Them There Eyes"	550	Los Angeles 1/18/45	prev. unissued	TBO-1970
63. "Memories of You"		1/18/45	prev. unissued	SLB-6952
64. "How Come"	552	1/18/45	unissued	—
65. "I Can't Believe That You're in Love with Me"	553	1/18/45	unissued	—

Editor's Note: It is known that after Anita left the Stan Kenton band to work as a "solo," she did some recording at Capitol Records with the Nat King Cole Trio. The details of the recording sessions are unknown and the material remains in the Capitol vaults unreleased.

BROADCAST MATERIAL	BROADCAST	REFERENCE	LP ISSUE
"And Her Tears Flowed Like Wine"	4/15/44	V-Disc 309A	VC-5015 TLP-108
"Gotta Be Gettin' "	11/30/44	One Night Stand 447	—
"Wish You Were Here Waiting for Me"	11/30/44	One Night Stand 447	—
"Tabby the Cat"	11/28/44	One Night Stand 474	—
"Gotta Be Gettin' "	11/28/44	One Night Stand 474	—
Film Short: *Artistry in Rhythm*			
"Tabby the Cat"	12/44	Hollywood	LP-3003
"I'm Going Mad for a Pad"	12/44	Hollywood	LP-3003

Part Three—GUEST SINGER WITH DUKE ELLINGTON & BENNY GOODMAN

BROADCAST MATERIAL	BROADCAST	REFERENCE	LP ISSUE
With Duke Ellington "Wish You Were Here Waiting for Me"	Los Angeles 1/17/45	Esquire Second Annual	SB-219

BROADCAST MATERIAL	BROADCAST	REFERENCE	LP ISSUE
"I Can't Believe That You're in Love with Me" With Benny Goodman	1/17/45	All-American Jazz Concert	LP-1003
"The Christmas Song"	12/23/46	Meadowbrook Gardens, Hollywood	SB-156

Part Four—SOLO (1947–1960)

STUDIO MATERIAL	MATRIX	RECORDED	'78' RELEASES	LP REISSUE
accompanied by Alvy West & the Little Band		Los Angeles 2/47		
66. "Ace in the Hole"	SRC376		Sig 15127	LP-8 CRL-56073 BBM1-0595
67. "Sometimes I'm Happy"			Sig 15127	LP-8 CRL-56073 BBM1-0595
accompanied by Will Bradley & his Orchestra		New York 9/47		
68. "What Is This Thing Called Love?"	SRC564		Sig 15162 Adv 2008 Cor 60803	LP-8 CRL-56073 BBM1-0595
69. "Hi Ho Trailus Boot Whip"	SRC565		Sig 15162 Adv 2008 Cor 60697	LP-8 CRL-56073 BBM1-0595
70. "I Told Ya I Love Ya, Now Get Out"	SRC566		Sig 15181	LP-8 BBM1-0595
71. "It's Different When It Happens to You"	SRC567		Sig 15217	BBM1-0595

315

accompanied by Ralph Burns &
his Orchestra

72. "How High the Moon"	SRC657	Los Angeles Late/47	Sig 15185 Adv 2117	LP-8 CRL-56073 BBM1-0595

accompanied by Benny Carter &
his Orchestra

73. "I Ain't Gettin' Any Younger"	SRC658	Late/47	Sig 15217 Cor 60803	LP-8 CRL-56073 BBM1-0595

accompanied by Ralph Burns &
his Orchestra

74. "Malaguena"	SRC659	Late/47	Sig 15181 Adv 2997	LP-8 CRL-56073 BBM1-0595

accompanied by Benny Carter &
his Orchestra

75. "Key Largo"	SRC660	Late/47	Sig 15185 Cor 60697	CRL-56073 BBM1-0595

accompanied by Abbey Brown &   Los Angeles   TJ-6003
his Cool Cats   9/11/49

76. "Jamaica Mon"	105		Gem 8	
77. "Don't Kick It Around"	107		—	
78. "So Much of Nothing to Do"	108		Gem 8	
79. "Poor Simple Simon"	109		—	

accompanied by Paul Jordan &   Chicago   TJ-6003
his Orchestra   1/5/50

80. "Blues for Bojangles"	DLG-50154		London 616	
81. "Your Eyes Are Bigger Than Your Heart"	DLG-50194		London 616	
82. "Them There Eyes"	unknown		unissued	—
83. "Nice Dreaming"	unknown		unissued	—

316

STUDIO MATERIAL	MATRIX	RECORDED	'78' RELEASES	LP REISSUE
accompanied by Ben Homer & his Orchestra		New York 10/26/50		TJ-6003
84. "Tennessee Waltz"	DLG-50580		London 867	
85. "Yea Boo"	DLG-50581		London 867	
86. "Something I Dreamed Last Night"	DLG-50582		London 879	
87. "If I Could Steal You from Somebody Else"	DLG-50583		London 879	
accompanied by Jack Pleis & his Orchestra		New York 12/27/50		TJ-6003
88. "You Took Advantage of Me"	DLG-50689		London 964	
89. "Once There Lived a Fool"	DLG-60690		London 958	
90. "I Apologize"	DLG-50691		London 964	
91. "Black Moonlight"	DLG-50692		unissued	
92. "Lovesick Blues"	DLG-50692		London 958	

BROADCAST MATERIAL	BROADCAST	REFERENCE	LP ISSUE
FROM THE ROYAL ROOST, New York City			
"What Is This Thing Called Love?"	10/2/48	—	AL-702 TDFN-10230
"How High the Moon"	10/2/48	—	TDFN-10230
"September in the Rain"	10/9/48	—	AL-702 TDFN-10230
"How High the Moon"	10/9/48	—	AL-702 TDFN-10230
"Malaguena"	1948	—	AL-702
Medley: " 'S Wonderful" "They Can't Take That Away from Me"	1948	—	TDFN-1500
	1948	—	TDFN-1500
"Malaguena"		—	
"Sweet Georgia Brown"		—	
"Stella by Starlight"		—	

FROM *STARS OF JAZZ* TELECAST, Hollywood

CAL-3021

"You're the Top"	11/12/56	—	
"The Man I Love"	11/12/56	—	
"Love Me or Leave Me"	7/1/57	—	
"My Funny Valentine"	7/1/57	—	
"A Cent and a Half"	7/1/57	—	

FROM 1959 EUROPEAN TOUR
BENNY GOODMAN AND HIS ORCHESTRA

"B-Flat Blues"	10/15/59	Freiburg	—
"Honeysuckle Rose"	10/15/59	Freiburg	—
"Gotta Be This or That" with Benny	10/15/59	Freiburg	—
"Honeysuckle Rose"	10/18/59	Stockholm	—
"Come Rain or Come Shine"	10/18/59	Stockholm	—
"Let Me Off Uptown" with Jack Sheldon	10/18/59	Stockholm	—
"You Turned the Tables on Me"	10/18/59	Stockholm	—
"Tea for Two"	10/18/59	Stockholm	—
Medley: "Oh! Hot Dawg (Boogie Blues)" "Let Me Off Uptown" with Jack Sheldon	10/22/59	Berlin	SWH-37
"But Not for Me"	10/22/59	Berlin	—
"You Turned the Tables on Me"	10/22/59	Berlin	—
"Gotta Be This or That" with Benny	10/22/59	Berlin	SWH7
"Four Brothers" with Jack Sheldon			SWH-37
"But Not for Me"	10/28/59	Basel	—
"Four Brothers"	10/28/59	Basel	—
"You Turned the Tables on Me"	10/28/59	Basel	—

FROM *THE SWINGIN' YEARS* TELECAST, Hollywood

"Drum Boogie" with Gene Krupa Orchestra	2/9/60		SG-8001 SH-2087

318

	MATRIX	RECORDED	'78'/'45' ISSUE	LP ISSUE
accompanied by Ralph Burns' Orchestra		New York 1/22/52		N MGN-1049 V MGV-2049
93. "Lover Come Back to Me"	671-2		Clef 8967 EPC-134 MGC-130	
94. "Lullaby of the Leaves"	672-3		Clef 8989 EPC-134 MGC-130	
95. "Rock and Roll Blues"	673-1		Clef 8967 EPC-134 MGC-130	
96. "Love for Sale"	674-2		Clef 8989 EPC-134 MGC-130	
accompanied by Roy Kral Combo		Chicago 7/52		N MGN-1049 V MGV-2049
97. "No Soap, No Hope Blues"	814-4		Clef 89012 EPC-168 MGC-130	
98. "Speak Low"	815-13		Clef 89074	
99. "The Lady Is a Tramp"	816-8		Clef 89012 EDC-168 MGC-130	
100. "Strawberry Moon"	817-2		Clef 89074 EDC-168 MGC-130	
accompanied by Larry Russell's Orchestra		Chicago 12/52		N MGN-1049 V MGV-2049
101. "Pagan Love Song"	1096-5		Clef 89032 EPC-152	
102. "Ain't This a Wonderful Day"	1097-6		Clef 89047 EPC-152	
103. "Somebody's Crying"	1098-2		Clef 89032	
104. "Vaya Con Dios"	1099-2		Clef 89047 EPC-152	

accompanied by Anita O'Day's Quartet: Arnold Ross, piano; Barney
Kessel, guitar; Monte Budwig, bass; Jackie Mills, drums

		Los Angeles 4/54	EPN-79	N MGN-30 N MGN-1057 V MGV-2050
105.	"The Gypsy in My Soul"	1570-3		
106.	"Just One of Those Things"	1571-10		
107.	"The Man I Love"	1572-3		
108.	"Frankie and Johnny"	1573-1		

accompanied by Anita O'Day's Trio: Bud Lavin, piano; Monte Budwig,
bass; John Poole, drums

		Los Angeles 6/28/54	EPN-80	N MGN-30 N MGN-1057 V MGV-2050
109.	"Anita's Blues"	1850-3		
110.	"I Cover the Waterfront"	1851-5		
111.	"I Didn't Know What Time It Was"	1852-3		
112.	"Let's Fall in Love"	1853-3		

accompanied by Anita O'Day's Quartet: Jimmy Rowles, piano; Tal
Farlow, guitar; Leroy Vinnegar, bass; Larry Bunker, drums

		Los Angeles 8/11/55		N MGN-30 N MGN-1057 V MGV-2050
113.	"You're Getting to Be a Habit with Me"	2419-1	—	
114.	"From This Moment On"	2420-7	—	
115.	"You Don't Know What Love Is"	2421-1	—	
116.	Medley: "There Will Never Be Another You" "Just Friends"	2422-2	—	

	MATRIX	RECORDED	'45' ISSUE	LP ISSUE
accompanied by Buddy Bregman's Orchestra		Los Angeles		MGV-2000 V-8483
117. "Beautiful Love"	2555-6	12/6/55	—	
118. "As Long As I Live"	2556-6	12/6/55	—	
119. "Who Cares?"	2557-7	12/6/55	—	
120. "Fine and Dandy"	2558-4	12/6/55	—	
121. "I Fall in Love Too Easily"	2559-10	12/7/55	—	
122. "I Can't Get Started"	2560-4	12/7/55	—	
123. "A Nightingale Sang in Berkeley Square"	2561-4	12/7/55	—	
124. "Time After Time"	2562-9	12/7/55	—	
125. "You're the Top"	2563-7	12/8/55	10014	
126. "No Moon at All"	2564-10	12/8/55	—	
127. "Honeysuckle Rose"	2565-1	12/8/55	10001	
128. "I'll See You in My Dreams"	2566-8	12/8/55	—	
129. "I'm with You"	2704-17	1/5/56	10000	—
130. "The Rock and Roll Waltz"	2705-6	1/5/56	10000	—
		New York		
131. "The Getaway and the Chase"	20100-8	2/23/56	10001	MGV-2036
132. "Your Picture's Hanging on the Wall"	20101-16	2/23/56	unissued	unissued
133. "We Laughed at Love"	20102-7	2/23/56	10014	—
134. "I'm Not Lonely"	20103-7	2/23/56	unissued	unissued
with Gene Krupa and his Orchestra		New York 2/12/56		
135. "Boogie Blues"	2760-2		10008 EP5000	MGV-2008 VSP-4
136. "Opus #1"	2761-7		EP5000	MGV-2008
137. "That's What You Think"	2762-2		EP5001	MGV-2008 VSP-4
138. "Let Me Off Uptown" with Roy Eldridge	2764-6		10008 EP5001	MGV-2008 VSP-4
139. "Drummin' Man"	2765-2		EP5002	MGV-2008
140. "Slow Down"	2766-6		EP5002	MGV-2008

	MATRIX	RECORDED	'45' ISSUE	LP ISSUE
accompanied by Anita O'Day's Combo		Los Angeles 12/18/56		
141. "Don't Be That Way"	20468-7		EPV5038	MGV-2043
142. "Let's Face the Music and Dance"	20469-8 20469-10		EPV5038 unissued	— MGV-2043
143. "I Used to Be Color Blind"	20470-6		EPV5036	MGV-2043
144. "Pick Yourself Up"	20471-5		EPV5037	MGV-2043
accompanied by Buddy Bregman's Orchestra		Los Angeles 12/19/56		
145. "There's a Lull in My Life"	20479-9		EPV5038	MGV-2043
146. "Man with a Horn"	20480-3		EPV5037	MGV-2043
147. "Ivy"	20481-6		unissued	unissued
148. "Stars Fell on Alabama"	20482-4 20482-8		— EPV5036	MGV-2043 —
149. "Let's Begin"	20483-8		EPV5037	MGV-2043
150. "Sweet Georgia Brown"	20484-4		EPV5036	MGV-2043
151. "I Never Had a Chance"	20485-2		EPV5037	MGV-2043
152. "Stompin' at the Savoy"	20486-9		EPV5036	MGV-2043
153. "I Won't Dance"	20487-15		EPV5038	MGV-2043

	MATRIX	RECORDED	LP ISSUE

accompanied by Anita O'Day's Rhythm Section: Oscar Peterson, piano; Herb Ellis, guitar; Ray Brown, bass; John Poole, drums

		Chicago 1/31/57	MGV-8259
154. Medley: " 'S Wonderful" "They Can't Take That Away from Me"	20684-6		
155. "Love Me or Leave Me"	20685-9		
156. "Old Devil Moon"	20686-4		
157. "Tenderly"	20687-9		
158. "We'll Be Together Again"	20688-10		
159. "Stella by Starlight"	20689-14		
160. "Them There Eyes"	20690-4		
161. "Taking a Chance on Love"	20691-4		
162. "I've Got the World on a String"	20692-6		

	MATRIX	RECORDED	LP ISSUE
163. "You Turned the Tables on Me"	20693-1		
164. "Bewitched, Bothered and Bewildered"	20694-3		
accompanied by Russ Garcia's Orchestra		Los Angeles 4/2/58	MGV-8283 MGVS-68283 V/V6-8485
165. "Morning Glory"	22182-9		
166. "My Funny Valentine"	22183-3		
167. "Sing, Sing, Sing"	22184-8		
168. "Body and Soul"	22185-1		
169. "The Peanut Vendor"	22186-4		
170. "Frenesi"	22187-2		
accompanied by Marty Paich's Orchestra		Los Angeles 4/3/58	MGV-8283 MGVS-68283 V/V6-8485
171. "Take the A Train"	22194-6		
172. "Tenderly"	22195-8		
173. "Four Brothers"	22196-5		
174. "Early Autumn"	22197-7		
175. "Interlude"	22198-4		
176. "Four Brothers"	22199-6		
accompanied by the Anita O'Day Trio: Joe Masters, piano; Larry Woods, bass; John Poole, drums		Mister Kelly's Chicago 4/27/58	MGV-2113 MGVS-62113
177. "But Not for Me"	22226		
178. "I Have a Reason for Living"	22227		
179. "My Love for You"	22228		
180. "The Varsity Drag"	22229		
181. "It Never Entered My Mind"	22230		
182. "Tea for Two"	22231		
183. "Every Time I'm with You"	22232		
184. "The Song Is You"	22233		
185. "Have You Met Miss Jones?"	22234		
186. "The Wildest Gal in Town"	22235		
187. "Star Eyes"	22236		
188. "Loneliness Is a Well"	22237		
with Billy May and his Orchestra		Los Angeles	MGV-2118 MGVS-62118
189. "Just One of Those Things"	22786-2	4/2/59	
190. "Love for Sale"	22787-4	4/2/59	

	MATRIX	RECORDED	LP ISSUE
191. "All of You"	22788-4	4/2/59	
192. "Easy to Love"	22789-7	4/2/59	
193. "You'd Be So Nice to Come Home To"	22790-2	4/2/59	
194. "I Get a Kick Out of You"	22798-6	4/9/59	
195. "I Love You"	22799-4	4/9/59	
196. "I've Got You Under My Skin"	22800-2	4/9/59	
197. "Get Out of Town +"	22801-2	4/9/59	
198. "What Is This Thing Called Love?"	22802-2	4/9/59	
199. "Night and Day +"	22803-9	4/9/59	
200. "It's De-lovely"	22804-4	4/9/59	

+ also issued on 45 #10119

accompanied by Jimmy Giuffre's Orchestra		Los Angeles	MGV-8312 MGVS-68312
201. "Come Rain or Come Shine"	26301-5	4/6/59	
202. "You're a Clown"	26302-3	4/6/59	
203. "Easy Come, Easy Go"	26303-1	4/6/59	
204. "A Lover Is Blue"	26304-13	4/6/59	
205. "Mack the Knife"	26305-12	4/7/59	
206. "Gone with the Wind"	26306-4	4/7/59	
207. "Hershey Bar"	26307-4	4/7/59	
208. "My Heart Belongs to Daddy"	26308-2	4/7/59	
209. "Orphan Annie"	26309-2	4/8/59	
210. "The Way You Look Tonight"	26310-6	4/8/59	
211. "It Had to Be You"	26311-5	4/8/59	
212. "Hooray for Hollywood"	26312-12	4/8/59	

with Gene Krupa and his Orchestra		Los Angeles	
213. "Memories of You"	26235	12/59	V/V6-15010 AJAZZ-502

with Billy May and his Orchestra		Los Angeles	MGV-2141 MGVS-62141
214. "Falling in Love"	23243-4	6/6/60	
215. "Johnny One Note"	23244-12	6/6/60	
216. "Lover"	23245-5	6/6/60	
217. "Have You Met Miss Jones?"	23246-3	6/6/60	

218. "Little Girl Blue"	23247-4	6/7/60	
219. "Spring Is Here"	23248-5	6/7/60	
220. "It Never Entered My Mind"	23249-5	6/7/60	
221. "Bewitched"	23250-6	6/7/60	
222. "I've Got Five Dollars"	23251-5	6/8/60	
223. "To Keep My Love Alive"	23252-5	6/8/60	
224. "Ten Cents a Dance"	23253-2	6/8/60	
225. "I Could Write a Book"	23254-3	6/8/60	
accompanied by Bill Holman's Orchestra		Los Angeles	V/V6-8572
226. "It Could Happen to You"	23307-8	8/16/60	
227. "Blue Champagne"	23308-12	8/16/60	
228. "Avalon"	23309-10	8/16/60	
229. "Old Devil Moon"	23310-7	8/17/60	
230. "The Party's Over"	23311-6	8/17/60	
231. "Why Shouldn't I"	23312-3	8/17/60	
232. "Easy Livin' "	23313-7	8/17/60	
233. "Can't We Be Friends"	23314-3	8/23/60	
234. "Slaughter on 10th Avenue"	23315-4	8/23/60	
235. "If I Love Again"	23316-7	8/23/60	
236. "Speak Low"	23317-5	8/23/60	
237. "Indian Summer"	23318-7	8/23/60	
accompanied by Russ Garcia's Orchestra		Los Angeles	MGV-2145 MGVS-62145
238. "Yesterdays"	23290-4	8/60	
239. "Mad About the Boy"	23291-5	8/60	
240. "That Old Feeling"	23292-4	8/60	
241. "Waiter, Make Mine Blues"	23293-6	8/60	
242. "When Sunny Gets Blue"	23344-4	10/4/60	
243. "Angel Eyes"	23345-6	10/4/60	
244. "Whatever Happened to You"	23346-4	10/4/60	
245. "A Blues Serenade"	23347-4	10/4/60	
246. "The Thrill Is Gone"	23348-9	10/7/60	
247. "Detour Ahead"	23349-7	10/7/60	
248. "Goodbye"	23350-4	10/7/60	
249. "Stella by Starlight"	23351	10/7/60	
accompanied by Johnny Mandel's Orchestra		Los Angeles 1/18/61	V/V6-2157
250. "Trav'lin' Light"	23441-5		
251. "Don't Explain"	23442-3		
252. "I Hear Music"	23443-7		
253. "Crazy He Calls Me"	23444-2		
254. "Lover Come Back to Me"	23445-3		
255. "If the Moon Turns Green"	23446-4		

	MATRIX	RECORDED	LP ISSUE
accompanied by Barney Kessel's Sextext		1/19/61	V/V6-2157
256. "Remember"	23447-6		
257. "What a Little Moonlight Can Do"	23448-7		
258. "The Moon Looks Down"	23449-6		
259. "Some Other Spring"	23450-8		
260. "Miss Brown to You"	23451-9		
261. "God Bless the Child"	23452-14		
accompanied by Gary McFarland's Orchestra		New York	
262. "One More Mile"	61VK283	9/20/61	rejected
263. "Boogie Blues"	61VK284	9/20/61	"
264. "The Ballad of the Sad Young Men"	61VK285	9/20/61	"
265. "You Came a Long Way from St. Louis"	61VK458	9/20/61	"
266. "Senor Blues"	61VK459	9/20/61	"
267. "Up State"	61VK401	9/21/61	"
268. "Boogie Blues"	61VK481	10/16/61	V/V6-8442
269. "The Ballad of the Sad Young Men"	61VK482	10/16/61	V/V6-8442
270. "Up State"	61VK483	10/16/61	V/V6-8442
271. "You Came a Long Way from St. Louis"	61VK484	10/16/61	V/V6-8442
272. "Senor Blues"	61VK485	10/16/61	V/V6-8442
273. "One More Mile"	61VK486	10/16/61	V/V6-8442
274. "A Woman Alone with the Blues"	61VK487	10/16/61	V/V6-8442
275. "I Want to Sing a Song"	61VK488	10/16/61	V/V6-8442
276. "Night Bird"	61VK489	10/16/61	V/V6-8442
277. "Do Nothin' Till You Hear from Me"	61VK490	10/16/61	V/V6-8442
with Cal Tjader and his Combo		Los Angeles	V/V6-8472
278. "Peel Me a Grape"	62VK388	2/26/62	
279. "The Party's Over"	62VK390	2/26/62	
280. "Spring Will Be a Little Late This Year"	62VK393	2/26/62	
281. "Thanks for the Memory"	62VK383	2/27/62	
282. "It Shouldn't Happen to a Dream"	62VK384	2/27/62	
283. "Just in Time"	62VK385	2/27/62	
284. "Under a Blanket of Blue"	62VK386	2/27/62	
285. "That's Your Red Wagon"	62VK387	2/27/62	
286. "An Occasional Man"	62VK389	2/27/62	
287. "I Believe in You"	62VK391	2/28/62	
288. "Mr. Sandman"	62VK392	2/28/62	

289. "I'm Not Supposed to Be   62VK394   2/28/62
     Blue Blues"

with The Three Sounds: Gene Harris, piano; Bill Dowdy, drums; Andrew
Simpkins, bass

		New York	V/V6-8514
290. "All Too Soon"	62VK682	10/12/62	
291. "(Fly Me to the Moon) In	62VK685	10/12/62	
Other Words"			
292. "You and the Night and the	62VK683	10/14/62	
Music"			
293. "When the World Was	62VK686	10/14/62	
Young"			
294. "Whisper Not"	62VK688	10/14/62	
295. "My Ship"	62VK687	10/15/62	

with Bob Corwin, piano; Toshiyuki Miyama   Tokyo   23MJ-3470
& All-Star Orchestra   12/30/63
296. "Drum Boogie"
297. "Trav'lin' Light"
298. "Honeysuckle Rose"
299. "Avalon"
300. "Bewitched"
301. "You'd Be So Nice to Come
     Home To"
302. "Night and Day"
303. "Let's Fall in Love"
304. "Sweet Georgia Brown"
305. "Tea for Two"
306. "Stella by Starlight"
307. "Love for Sale"
308. "Get Out of Town"
309. "That Old Feeling"
310. "Four Brothers"

Part Six—THE LATE 1960s, 1970s, 1980s

	RECORDED	LP ISSUE

accompanied by her rhythm section   "Live"   AOD-1
                                  Stockholm/Hawaii/Detroit
                                           Late/60s
311. "Sunny"
312. "So Nice (Summer Samba)"

313. "My Funny Valentine"
314. "Watch What Happens"
315. "Walk on By"
316. "Bluesette"
317. "Here's That Rainy Day"
318. "Fly Me to the Moon"
319. "Quiet Nights of Quiet Stars"
320. "Green Dolphin Street"
321. "Street of Dreams"
322. "Lush Life"

accompanied by her rhythm section	"Live" Hollywood/Stockholm/ Hawaii/Detroit Late/60s	AOD-2

323. "Sweet Georgia Brown"
324. "Let's Fall in Love"
325. "Honeysuckle Rose"
326. "Yesterdays"
327. "Boogie Blues"
328. "Tea for Two"
329. "Once upon a Summertime"
330. "The Girl from Ipanema"
331. "Is You Is or Is You Ain't
      My Baby?"
332. "Soon It's Gonna Rain"
333. "Anita's Blues"
334. "A Nightingale Sang in
      Berkeley Square"
335. " 'S Wonderful"   GLS-6000
336. "They Can't Take That Away   GLS-6000
      from Me"
337. "Night and Day"   GLS-6000

accompanied by Billy May's Orchestra	Los Angeles Spring 1970	

338. "Boogie Blues"   STL-351
339. "And Her Tears Flowed Like   STL-352
      Wine"

accompanied by trio, augmented by strings	Miami 1973	unissued

340. "Cookie Jar"
341. "Once upon a Happy Time"
342. "Rock n' Roll Rag"
343. "How Could I Go On"

344. "Fat Man"
345. "Goodbye Old Dream"
346. "I Take It All Back"
347. "All the Time"
348. "No Machine Can Take Your
     Place with Me"
349. "Tender Loving Words"
350. "That's Love"
351. "When It's Time to Tell"
352. "What's Wrong Clyde"

accompanied by orchestra	Hollywood 1974	
353. "Dr. Pepper" (commercial jingle)		DP-1974

accompanied by George Arvanitas, piano; Jacky Samson, bass; Charles Saudrais, drums	"Live" Berlin Summer 1970	MB-20750

354. "Let's Fall in Love"
355. "Your Wings"
356. "Soon It's Gonna Rain"
357. "Honeysuckle Rose"
358. "I Can't Get Started"
359. Medley: "Yesterday"
     "Yesterdays"
360. "On a Clear Day"
361. "Street of Dreams"
362. "Sunny"

accompanied by Ronnell Bright, piano; George Morrow, bass; John Poole, drums; Don Raffell, reeds	Los Angeles 4/25/75	PA-7105

363. "A Song for You"
364. "Undecided"
365. "What Are You Doing the
     Rest of Your Life?"
366. "Exactly Like You"
367. "When Sunny Gets Blue"
368. "I Get a Kick Out of You"
369. "It Had to Be You"
370. "Opus #1"
371. "Gone with the Wind"

accompanied by Merrill Hoover,
piano; George Morrow, bass; John
Poole, drums

"Live"
Tokyo
6/19/75   PA-7140
ER-9579

372. "Wave"
373. "You'd Be So Nice to Come
     Home To"
374. "Honeysuckle Rose"
375. "A Song for You"
376. "Exactly Like You"
377. Medley: " 'S Wonderful"
     "They Can't Take That Away
     from Me"
378. "I Get a Kick Out of You"
379. "I Can't Get Started"
380. "Anita's Blues"
381. "Sweet Georgia Brown"
382. "Tea for Two"
383. "Wave"
384. "Is You Is or Is You Ain't
     My Baby?"
385. "I Cried for You"

384. TD-26
ER-13081
385. TD-26
ER-13081

accompanied by Merrill Hoover,
piano; George Morrow, bass; John
Poole, drums

Tokyo
6/30/75   PA-7126
ER-11279

386. "Satin Doll"
387. "Mean to Me"
388. "Why Shouldn't I"
389. "Body and Soul"
390. "My Ship"
391. "Our Love Is Here to Stay"
392. "After You've Gone"
393. "A Nightingale Sang in
     Berkeley Square"
394. "The Man I Love"
395. "Penthouse Serenade"
396. "Come Rain or Come Shine"
397. "The Days of Wine and
     Roses"

	RECORDED	LP ISSUE
accompanied by Norman Simmons, piano; Bob Maize, bass; John Poole, drums	"Live" Tokyo 10/22/76	PAP-9059 ER-11579

398. "As Time Goes By"
399. "Stardust"
400. "I Didn't Know What Time
    It Was"
401. "The Very Thought of You"
402. "Anita's Blues '76"
403. "I Could Write a Book"
404. "Sophisticated Lady"
405. "I Hear Music"
406. "I Cover the Waterfront"
407. "The Way You Look
    Tonight"

accompanied by Dave Frishberg, piano	Hollywood 1975	unissued

408. "On the Sunny Side of the
    Street"
409. "Old Folks"
410. "Beyond the Blue Horizon"
411. "Breaking Up Is Hard to Do"
412. "Saloon"
413. "The Sunshine of My Life"
414. "It Doesn't Mean a Thing"
415. "Fools Rush In"
416. "I'm Just a Lucky So and So"
417. "Hand-me-down Love"

accompanied by Dwight Dickerson, piano; John Poole, drums; Harvey Newmark, bass	"Live" Tokyo 6/13/78	LDC-1012 ER-13081

418. "You'd Be So Nice to Come
    Home To"
419. "When Sunny Gets Blue"
420. "Angel Eyes"
421. "Honeysuckle Rose"
422. "Send in the Clowns"
423. "Black Coffee"
424. "There Will Never Be
    Another You"
425. "Bewitched"

accompanied by Dwight Dickerson, piano; John Poole, drums; Harvey Newmark, bass	"Live" Tokyo 6/15/78	PAP-9127

426. "On a Clear Day (You Can See Forever)"
427. "Candlelight and Wine"
428. "It Don't Mean a Thing"
429. "This Is All I Ask"
430. "Lover Come Back to Me"
431. "Skylark"
432. "Like Someone in Love"
433. "I'm Getting Sentimental Over You"
434. "Night and Day"

accompanied by Lou Levy, piano; Harvey Newmark, bass; John Poole, drums; Laurindo Almeida, Joe Diorio, guitars; Ernie Watts, reeds; Paulinko Da Costa, percussion	Los Angeles 1/31–2/1/79	GNPS-2126

435. "Old Devil Moon"
436. "Lost in the Stars"
437. "Meditation"
438. "You're My Everything"
439. "You Could Have Had Me Baby"
440. "Them There Eyes"
441. "On the Trail"
442. "You Can't Go Home Again"
443. "When the World Was Young"
444. "So Nice (Summer Samba)"
445. "Yellow Days"
446. "Limehouse Blues"

accompanied by Norman Simmons, piano; Rob Fisher, bass; Greg Smith, baritone & flute; John Poole, drums	"Live" San Francisco 9/29–30/79	ER-102479

447. "Blue Skies"
448. "What Are You Doing the Rest of Your Life?"

449. "In a Mellow Tone"
450. "Hershey Bar"
451. "P-Town"
452. "P-Town"
453. "Emily"
454. "Little Orphan Annie"
455. "Close Your Eyes"
456. "Shakin' the Blues Away"
457. "Four Brothers"

accompanied by Norman Simmons, piano; Rob Fisher, bass; Greg Smith, baritone & flute; John Poole, drums	"Live" San Francisco 9/29–30/79	ER-42181

458. "Wave"
459. "I'm Getting Sentimental Over You"
460. Medley: "Falling in Love with Love" "Love for Sale"
461. "A Nightingale Sang in Berkeley Square"
462. "On Green Dolphin Street"
463. "My Funny Valentine"
464. Medley: "Tea for Two" "Wave"

accompanied by Don Abney, piano	Tokyo 12/21/81	LDC-1033

465. "Misty"
466. "The Night Has a Thousand Eyes"
467. "Am I Blue"
468. "Afternoon in Paris"
469. "My Heart Belongs to Daddy"
470. "You Go to My Head"
471. "A Sleepin' Bee"
472. "Bluesette"
473. "I'm Old Fashioned"
474. "Speak Low"

accompanied by Harold Danko, piano; John Poole, drums; Rick Laird, bass; Roger Neumann, soprano & tenor sax & flute	San Paulo 8/21–22/84	93-84-0454

475. "Wave"
476. "It Had to Be You"
477. "A Sleepin' Bee"
478. "Time After Time"
479. "Stompin' at the Savoy"
480. "The Man with a Horn"
481. "Body and Soul"
482. "Lush Life"
483. "The Song Is You"
484. "Wave"

accompanied by Joe Castro, piano;	Los Angeles	
G. Smith, bass	10/84	X-101C

485. "One More Christmas"
486. "White Christmas"
487. "Christmas Song"
488. "Let It Snow, Let It Snow,
Let It Snow"
489. "I'll Be Home for Christmas"
490. "Jingle Bells"

accompanied by Hank Jones,	"Live"	
piano; Jay Leonhart, bass; John	Carnegie Hall	
Poole, drums; Richie Cole, alto	New York	
saxophone plus 13-piece orchestra	5/24/85	ER-92685

491. "Opus #1"
492. "Honeysuckle Rose"
493. "Sweet Georgia Brown"
494. "Four Brothers"
495. "P-Town"
496. Medley: " 'S Wonderful"
"They Can't Take That Away
from Me"
497. "I Can't Get Started"
498. "And Her Tears Flowed Like
Wine"
499. "Let Me Off Uptown"—duet
with Roy Eldridge
500. "Boogie Blues"
501. "I Get a Kick Out of You"
502. "I'll See You in My Dreams"

accompanied by Hank Jones, piano; Jay Leonhart, bass; John Poole, drums; Richie Cole, alto saxophone	"Live" Carnegie Hall New York 5/24/85 0685

503. "Wave"
504. "You'd Be So Nice to Come Home To"
505. "I Cried for You"
506. "Falling in Love with Love"
507. "A Nightingale Sang in Berkeley Square"
508. "Love for Sale"
509. "Lover Where Can You Be?"
510. "My Funny Valentine"
511. "It Don't Mean a Thing"
512. "Lush Life"
513. "Tea for Two"

accompanied by Merrill Hoover, piano; Tommy Whittle, saxophone & flute; Lenny Bush, bass; John Poole, drums	"Live" London 3/86 WHCD005

514. "Wave"
515. "You'd Be So Nice to Come Home To"
516. "On Green Dolphin Street"
517. "I Can't Get Started"
518. "It Don't Mean a Thing"
519. "Street of Dreams"
520. " 'S Wonderful"
521. "They Can't Take That Away from Me"
522. "Is You Is or Is You Ain't My Baby?"
523. "My Funny Valentine"
524. "I Cried for You"
525. "Four Brothers"
526. "Wave"

SECTION B

Album Listings

THE COLLECTED RECORDINGS
Part One—VOCALIST WITH GENE KRUPA'S BAND

	RECORDED	ORIGINAL '78' RELEASE
DRUMMIN' MAN—Gene Krupa		
Columbia 10" LP CL-2515 (mono) (1953)		
"Bolero at the Savoy"	11/25/41	Columbia 36726
GENE KRUPA DANCE PARTY		
Columbia 10" LP CL-6066 (mono) (1950)		
"Green Eyes" with Howard	5/8/41	OKeh 6222
DuLany		
"Massachusetts"	7/13/42	OKeh 6187
"Opus #1"	8/21/45	Columbia 37224
THE GIRL FRIENDS—various artists		
Columbia Harmony HL-7148 (mono) (1958)		
"Fool Am I"	1/17/41	OKeh 6154
"I Take to You"	4/11/41	OKeh 6187
GENE KRUPA'S SIDEKICKS		
Columbia CL-641 (mono) (1955)		
"Skylark"	11/25/41	OKeh 6607
Reissue: GENE KRUPA'S SIDEKICKS		
Columbia Special Products CSP JCL-641 (mono) (1977)		
THE GENE KRUPA STORY IN MUSIC		
Columbia Harmony HL-7252 (mono) (1960)		
"Let Me Off Uptown" with	5/8/41	OKeh 6210
Roy Eldridge		
"That's What You Think"	2/26/42	Columbia 36621
"Boogie Blues"	8/21/45	Columbia 36986

GENE KRUPA AND HIS ORCHESTRA
Columbia CL-753 (mono) (1956)

"Murder, He Says"	7/13/42	OKeh 6685
"Massachusetts"	7/13/42	OKeh 6685
"Let Me Off Uptown" with Roy Eldridge	5/8/41	OKeh 6210
"Slow Down"	3/19/41	OKeh 6154
"Boogie Blues"	8/21/45	Columbia 36986
"That's What You Think"	2/26/42	Columbia 36621

Reissue: GENE KRUPA AND HIS ORCHESTRA
  Columbia Special Products JCL-753 (mono) (1977)

THAT DRUMMER'S BAND—GENE KRUPA
Epic EE-22027 (mono) (1963)

"Georgia on My Mind"	3/12/41	Conqueror 9616
"Kick It"	6/5/41	OKeh 6278
"Stop! The Red Light's On"	8/18/41	OKeh 6411
"Green Eyes" with Howard DuLany	5/8/41	OKeh 6222
"The Walls Keep Talking" with Roy Eldridge	8/20/41	OKeh 6438
"Pass the Bounce"	12/29/41	OKeh 6619

GENE KRUPA, HIS ORCHESTRA AND ANITA O'DAY
Columbia KG-32663 (simulated stereo) (1974)

"Georgia on My Mind"	3/12/41	Conqueror 9616
"Just a Little Bit South of North Carolina"	3/19/41	OKeh 6130
"Slow Down"	3/19/41	OKeh 6154
"Green Eyes" with Howard DuLany	5/8/41	OKeh 6222
"Let Me Off Uptown" with Roy Eldridge	5/8/41	OKeh 6210
"Stop! The Red Light's On"	8/18/41	OKeh 6411
"The Walls Keep Talking" with Roy Eldridge	8/28/41	OKeh 6438
"Skylark"	11/25/41	OKeh 6607
"Bolero at the Savoy"	11/25/41	Columbia 36726
"That's What You Think"	2/26/42	Columbia 36621
"Massachusetts"	7/13/42	OKeh 6685
"Murder, He Says"	7/13/42	OKeh 6685
"Opus #1"	8/21/45	Columbia 37224
"That Feeling in the Moonlight" with Buddy Stewart	8/21/45	Columbia 36862
"Boogie Blues"	8/21/45	Columbia 36986
"Chickery Chick"	9/26/45	Columbia 36877
"In the Middle of May"	9/26/45	unissued
"Tea for Two"	10/23/45	Columbia 38345

	RECORDED	ORIGINAL '78' RELEASE
"Harriet" with Buddy Stewart and Ensemble	10/23/45	Columbia 36890

WIRE BRUSH STOMP 1938–1941
Bandstand Records 7117 (mono) (1974)

"Alreet"	3/12/41	OKeh 6118
"Slow Down"	3/19/41	OKeh 6154
"Watch the Birdie"	8/28/41	OKeh 6400

THE RADIO DISCS OF GENE KRUPA
Joyce LP-2008 (mono) (1976)

"Let Me Off Uptown" with Roy Eldridge	5/41	V-Disc 197
"Jose Gonzales"	8/45	V-Disc 543
"Oh! Hot Dawg (Boogie Blues)"	8/45	V-Disc 543

GIANTS—GENE KRUPA—ACE DRUMMER MAN
Giants of Jazz GOJ-1006 (mono) (1977)

"Jose Gonzales"	8/45	V-Disc 543
"Boogie Blues"	8/45	V-Disc 543

GENE KRUPA—AIR CHECKS 1938–42
Fanfare 10–110 (mono) (1977)

"Kick It"	6/7/41	—
"Cow-Cow Boogie"	11/13/42	—
"Amour"	10/1/41	—
"Drum Boogie"	10/1/41	—
"Drummin' Man"	12/25/42	—

A LEGEND—GENE KRUPA AND RAY MCKINLEY
Blue Heaven BH6-608 (mono) (1978)

"Alreet"	3/41	Lang-Worth Transcription

GENE KRUPA/ZIGGY ELMAN
Monmouth-Evergreen MES-7012 (simulated stereo) (1976)

Lang-Worth Transcriptions

"Alreet"	3/41	
"A Fool Am I"	3/41	
"Drum Boogie"	3/41	

DRUMMIN' MAN—GENE KRUPA
Columbia C2L-29 (mono) (1963)

"Let Me Off Uptown" with Roy Eldridge	5/8/41	OKeh 6210
"Skylark"	11/25/41	OKeh 6607
"Bolero at the Savoy"	11/25/41	Columbia 36726
"That's What You Think"	2/26/41	Columbia 36621
"Massachusetts"	7/13/42	OKeh 6685

THE GREAT LADIES ON V-DISC—VOL. 2
Japanese DAN VC-5051 (mono) (1979)

"Jose Gonzales"	8/45	V-Disc 543-B
"Oh! Hot Dawg (Boogie Blues)"	8/45	V-Disc 543-B

BIG BANDS REVISITED
Columbia Special Products P75-5122 (simulated stereo) (1975)

	RECORDED	ORIGINAL '78' RELEASE
"Let Me Off Uptown" with Roy Eldridge	5/8/41	OKeh 6210
"Skylark"	11/25/41	OKeh 6607

KRUPA SWINGS
Columbia Encore P-14379 (mono) (1980)

"How Do!"	10/14/41	prev. unissued
"Bolero at the Savoy"	10/14/41	prev. unissued

GREAT VOCALISTS OF THE BIG BAND ERA
Columbia Special Products P6-14538 (simulated stereo) (1978)

"Side by Side"	1/23/42	Columbia 36726

BIG BAND BASH
Columbia Special Products P6-14954 (simulated stereo) (1979)

"Green Eyes" with Howard DuLany	5/8/41	OKeh 6222 Columbia 38212
"Bolero at the Savoy"	11/25/41	Columbia 36726

BODY AND SOUL
Columbia Special Products C3-10046 (simulated stereo) (1965)

"That's What You Think"	2/26/42	Columbia 36621 Columbia 37533

THE BEST OF THE BIG BANDS
Columbia Musical Treasures D-403 (mono) (1968)

"Chickery Chick" with Ensemble	9/26/45	Columbia 36877
"Boogie Blues"	8/21/45	Columbia 36986

THE BEST OF THE BIG BAND SINGERS
Columbia Musical Treasures D-405 (mono) (1968)

"Let Me Off Uptown" with Roy Eldridge	5/8/41	OKeh 6210

THE BLACK BANDS AND GREAT BLACK VOCALISTS
Columbia Special Products P4-13744 (electronic stereo) (1976)

"Let Me Off Uptown" with Roy Eldridge	5/8/41	OKeh 6210

LET'S DANCE
Columbia JC-36580 (mono) (1980)

"Opus #1"	8/21/45	Columbia 37224

DANCE THE NIGHT AWAY
Columbia JC-36742 (mono) (1980)

"Boogie Blues"	8/21/45	Columbia 36986

COME DANCE WITH ME
Columbia JC-36743 (mono) (1980)

"Let Me Off Uptown" with Roy Eldridge	5/8/41	OKeh 6210

GENE KRUPA IN DISCO ORDER—VOLUME 11
Ajax 138 (mono) (1978)

"Alreet"	3/12/41	OKeh 6118

GENE KRUPA IN DISCO ORDER—VOLUME 12
Ajax 146 (mono) (1978)

"Georgia on My Mind"	3/12/41	Conqueror 9616

	RECORDED	ORIGINAL '78' RELEASE
"Fool Am I"	3/12/41	Conqueror 6154
"Let's Get Away from It All"	3/19/41	OKeh 6130
"Just a Little Bit South of North Carolina"	3/19/41	OKeh 6130
"Slow Down"	3/19/41	OKeh 6154
"I Take to You"	4/11/41	OKeh 6187

GENE KRUPA IN DISCO ORDER—VOLUME 13
Ajax 154 (mono) (1978)

"Green Eyes" with Howard DuLany	5/8/41	OKeh 6222
"Let Me Off Uptown" with Roy Eldridge	5/8/41	OKeh 6210
"Kick It" with Band	6/5/41	OKeh 6278

GENE KRUPA IN DISCO ORDER—VOLUME 14
Ajax 161 (mono) (1978)

"Armour" with Howard DuLany	8/18/41	OKeh 6400
"Stop! The Red Light's On"	8/18/41	OKeh 6411
"Watch the Birdie"	8/28/41	OKeh 6400
"The Walls Keep Talking" with Roy Eldridge	8/28/41	OKeh 6438
"Two in Love" with Johnny Desmond	10/3/41	OKeh 6447
"Coppin' a Plea"	10/14/41	OKeh 6498
"Skylark"	11/25/41	OKeh 6607

GENE KRUPA IN DISCO ORDER—VOLUME 15
Ajax 167 (mono) (1978)

"Bolero at the Savoy"	11/25/41	Columbia 36726
"Pass the Bounce"	12/29/41	OKeh 6619
"Side by Side"	1/23/42	Columbia 36726
"Harlem on Parade"	1/23/42	OKeh 6607
"Fightin' Doug MacArthur"	2/26/42	OKeh 6635

SWINGING FLICKS—VOLUME ONE
Kaydee KD-7 (mono) (1979)

"Let Me Off Uptown" with Roy Eldridge	1942	Soundie

GENE KRUPA IN DISCO ORDER—VOLUME 16
Ajax 203 (mono) (1979)

"That's What You Think" with Ensemble	2/26/42	Columbia 36621
"Barrelhouse Bessie from Basin Street" with Roy Eldridge	4/2/42	prev. unissued
"Deliver Me to Tennessee"	4/2/42	Columbia 36591
"Massachusetts"	7/13/42	OKeh 6695
"Murder, He Says"	7/13/42	OKeh 6695

GENE KRUPA IN DISCO ORDER—VOLUME 17
Ajax 211 (mono) (1979)

"Opus #1"	8/21/45	Columbia 37224

"(Did You Ever Get) That Feeling in the Moonlight" with Buddy Stewart	8/21/45	Columbia 36862
"Boogie Blues"	8/21/45	Columbia 36986
"Chickery Chick"	8/26/45	Columbia 36877

GENE KRUPA IN DISCO ORDER—VOLUME 18
Ajax 219 (mono) (1979)

"Tea for Two"	10/23/45	Columbia 38345
"Harriet" with Buddy Stewart	10/23/45	Columbia 36890
"Hop, Skip and Jump"	10/24/45	Columbia 36931

ANITA O'DAY SINGS WITH GENE KRUPA
Japanese CBS SONY 20AP 1439 (mono) (1980)

"Georgia on My Mind"	3/12/41	OKeh 6118
"I Take to You"	5/8/41	OKeh 6187
"Let Me Off Uptown" with Roy Eldridge	5/8/41	OKeh 6210
"Kick It" with Ensemble	6/5/41	OKeh 6278
"Stop! The Red Light's On" with Ensemble	8/18/41	OKeh 6411
"The Walls Keep Talking" with Roy Eldridge	8/20/41	OKeh 6438
"Skylark"	11/25/41	OKeh 6607
"Bolero at the Savoy"	11/25/41	Columbia 36726
"Thanks for the Boogie Ride" with Roy Eldridge	11/25/41	OKeh 6506
"Pass the Bounce"	12/29/41	OKeh 6619
"That's What You Think" with Ensemble	2/26/42	Columbia 36621
"Deliver Me to Tennessee"	4/2/42	Columbia 36591
"Massachusetts"	7/13/42	OKeh 6695
"Opus #1"	8/21/45	Columbia 37224
"Boogie Blues"	8/21/45	Columbia 36986
"Hop, Skip and Jump"	10/24/45	Columbia 36931

BIG BANDS' GREATEST VOCALISTS—ANITA O'DAY
Ajazz 502 (mono) (1984)

"Chickery Chick" with Ensemble	1945	CO 36877
"Kick It" with Ensemble	1941	OK 6278
"Let Me Off Uptown" with Roy Eldridge	1941	OK 6210
"Cow-Cow Boogie"	1942	Broadcast
"Opus #1"	1945	CO 37224
"I'd Do It All Over Again"	1945	Broadcast
"Memories of You"	1959	—
"Barrelhouse Bessie from Basin Street"	1942	prev. unissued
"Amour" with Howard DuLany	1941	OK 6400
"Drum Boogie" with Ensemble	1942	Lang-Worth Transcription

	RECORDED	ORIGINAL '78' RELEASE
"Stop! The Red Light's On" with Ensemble	1941	OK 6411
THE EXCITING GENE KRUPA		
Giants of Jazz GOJ-1028 (mono) (1982)		
"I'd Do It All Over Again"	1945	Broadcast
GENE KRUPA 1942–43		
Fanfare 44-144 (mono) (1982)		
"Private Jimmy Johnson"	1942	Broadcast
THE GREAT VOCALISTS MEET BOOGIE WOOGIE VOLUME 5		
Italian Joker SM-4085 (mono) (1984)		
"Thanks for the Boogie Ride" with Roy Eldridge	1941	OK 6506
ROY ELDRIDGE—THE EARLY YEARS		prev. unissued takes
Columbia C2-38033 (mono) (1982)		
"Green Eyes" with Howard DuLany	1941	
"Let Me Off Uptown" with Roy Eldridge	1941	
"Harlem on Parade"	1942	
"Massachusetts"	1942	
"Murder, He Says"	1942	
THE GREAT LADIES ON V-DISC VOLUME 2		
Japanese DAN VC-5015 (mono) (1981)		
"Drum Boogie"	1941	V-Disc 279A
"Jose Gonzalez"	1945	543B
"Oh! Hot Dawg (Boogie Blues)"	1945	543B

Part Two—VOCALIST WITH STAN KENTON'S BAND

	RECORDED	ORIGINAL '78' RELEASE
THE FABULOUS ALUMNI OF STAN KENTON		
Creative World ST-1028 (simulated stereo) (1975)		
"I Want a Grown Up Man"	1/45	prev. unissued
THE LIGHTER SIDE		
Creative World ST-1050 (simulated stereo) (1975)		
"And Her Tears Flowed Like Wine"	5/44	Capitol 166
SOME WOMEN I'VE KNOWN		
Creative World ST-1029 (simulated stereo) (1975)		
"Are You Livin' Old Man?"	12/44	Capitol 187
"Travelin' Man"	1/45	Capitol 48012

STAN KENTON'S ARTISTRY IN RHYTHM
Sunbeam SB-213 (mono) (1975)   1944   MacGregor
                                                                 Transcriptions
   "Build It Up, Paint It Nice and
   Tear It Down Again"
   "Ride On"
   "You Betcha!"
FILM TRACKS OF STAN KENTON
Joyce LP-3003 (mono) (1976)   12/44   Hollywood Film
                                                                    Short
   "Tabby the Cat"
   "I'm Going Mad for a Pad"
BY REQUEST SERIES—VOLUME THREE
Creative World ST-1062 (simulated stereo)
   "Gotta Be Gettin' "   9/44   Capitol 178
STAN KENTON AND HIS ORCHESTRA 1943–44 VOL. III
Hindsight HSR-136 (mono) (1979)   MacGregor
                                                                 Transcriptions
   "In a Little Spanish Town"   1944
   "I Lost My Sugar in Salt Lake City"
   "The Lady in Red"
CLASSICS—STAN KENTON
Capitol H-358 (10") T-358 (12") (mono) (1952) (1956)
   "And Her Tears Flowed Like Wine"   5/44   Capitol 15196
KENTON ERA
Capitol WDX-569 (mono) (1955) (4-record set)
   "I'm Going Mad for a Pad"   5/44   prev. unissued
STAN KENTON'S GREATEST HITS
Capitol DT-2327 (simulated stereo) (1965)
   "And Her Tears Flowed Like Wine"   5/44   Capitol 15196
JUKEBOX SATURDAY NIGHT
Reader's Digest RD-4-139 (simulated stereo) (1975)
   "And Her Tears Flowed Like Wine"   5/44   Capitol 15196
THE GREAT GIRL SINGERS
Capitol Special Markets SLB-6952 (simulated stereo) (1974) (2-record set)
   "Memories of You"   1/45   prev. unissued
THE GREAT LADIES ON V-DISC—VOL. 2
Japanese DAN VC-5015 (mono) (1979)
   "And Her Tears Flowed Like Wine"   4/15/44   V-Disc 309-A
BING CROSBY 1945—COMMAND PERFORMANCE USA MUSIC
HALL
Tulip TLP-108 (mono) (1974)
   "And Her Tears Flowed Like Wine"   4/15/44   Broadcast
STAN KENTON AND HIS ORCHESTRA
1944–45 VOL. 4   MacGregor
Hindsight HSR-147 (mono) (1979)   1944   Transcriptions
   "Blues"
   "Tabby the Cat"

343

THE COMPREHENSIVE KENTON
Capitol STB-12016 (mono) (1979) (2-record set)
"And Her Tears Flowed Like Wine"	5/44	Capitol 15196

TOP TWENTY HITS USA 1944–45
German EMI Electrola 056-85 612 (mono) (1978)
"And Her Tears Flowed Like Wine"	5/44	Capitol 15196

ESQUIRE'S WORLD OF JAZZ
Capitol TBO-1970 (mono) (1963)
"Them There Eyes"	1/18/45	prev. unissued

THE GREAT LADIES ON V-DISC VOL. 2
Japanese DAN VC-5015 (mono) (1981)
"And Her Tears Flowed Like Wine"	4/15/44	V-Disc 309A

NINETEEN FORTY-FOUR
Swing House SWH-26 (mono) (1981)
	1944	MacGregor Transcriptions

"Ride On"
"Build It Up, Paint It Nice and
Tear It Down"
"And Her Tears Flowed Like Wine"
"You Betcha!"
"Special Delivery"

BIG BANDS' GREATEST VOCALISTS—ANITA O'DAY
Ajazz 502 (mono) (1982)
"And Her Tears Flowed Like Wine"	5/44	Capitol 15196
"In a Little Spanish Town"	1944	MacGregor Transcription
"Gotta Be Gettin' "	9/26/44	Capitol 178

STAN KENTON—THE GIRLS
Japanese EMI/Capitol ECJ-50075 (mono) (1981)
"I'm Going Mad for a Pad"	5/20/44	prev. unissued
"And Her Tears Flowed Like Wine"	5/44	Capitol 15196
"Gotta Be Gettin' "	9/26/44	Capitol 178
"Are You Livin' Old Man"	12/15/44	Capitol 187

Part Three—GUEST SINGER WITH DUKE ELLINGTON & BENNY GOODMAN

BROADCAST MATERIAL	RECORDED

ESQUIRE SECOND ANNUAL ALL-AMERICAN JAZZ CONCERT
Sunbeam SB-219 (mono) (1976)
"Wish You Were Here Waiting for Me"	1/17/45

AN EVENING WITH THE DUKE	
Giants of Jazz GOJ Lp-1003 (mono) (1977)	
"I Can't Believe That You're in Love with Me"	1/17/45
BENNY GOODMAN BROADCASTS FROM HOLLYWOOD	
1946–47	
Sunbeam SB-156 (mono) (1978)	
"The Christmas Song"	12/23/46
JAM BENNY GOODMAN AND THE ALL-STARS	
English Swing House SWH-37 (mono) (1982)	
"Four Brothers"	1959
Medley: "Oh! Hot Dawg (Boogie Blues)"	
"Let Me Off Uptown" with Jack Sheldon	1959
ROLL 'EM BENNY GOODMAN AND THE ALL-STARS	
English Swing House SWH-7 (mono) (1979)	
"Gotta Be This or That" with Benny	1959

Part Four—REUNION WITH GENE KRUPA

	RECORDED
GENE KRUPA—DRUMMER MAN	
Verve MGV-2008 (mono) (1956)	2/56
"Opus #1"	
"Boogie Blues"	
"Let Me Off Uptown" with Roy Eldridge	
"That's What You Think"	
"Drummin' Man"	
"Slow Down"	
THE GENE KRUPA STORY	12/59
Verve V-15010 (mono) (1960)/ V6-15010 (stereo) (1960)	
"Memories of You"	
THE ESSENTIAL GENE KRUPA	
Verve V-8571 (mono) (1963)/ V6-8571 (stereo) (1963)	2/56
"Let Me Off Uptown" with Roy Eldridge	
GENE KRUPA AND HIS ORCHESTRA	
Verve VSP-4 (mono)/ VSPS-4 (stereo) (1966)	2/56
"Boogie Blues"	
"That's What You Think"	
"Let Me Off Uptown" with Roy Eldridge	
THE BIG BAND SOUND OF GENE KRUPA	
English Verve 2317 078 (mono) (1977)	2/56
"Let Me Off Uptown" with Roy Eldridge	
"Opus #1"	

"Boogie Blues"
"Drummin' Man"
"Slow Down"
"That's What You Think"
THE SOUNDS OF SWING (telecast)
Sounds Great SG-8001 (1981)   1960
"Drum Boogie"—with Gene Krupa Orchestra
THE SWINGIN' YEARS (telecast)
Sandy Hook SH 2087 (mono) (1984)   1960
"Drum Boogie"—with Gene Krupa Orchestra

Part Five—SOLO (1947–1979)

	RECORDED	ORIGINAL '78' RELEASE

SINGIN' AND SWINGIN' WITH
ANITA O'DAY
Coral 10" LP CRL-56073 (mono) (1952)

"Key Largo"	Late/47	Sig 15185
"Hi Ho Trailus Boot Whip"	9/47	Sig 15162
"I Ain't Gettin' Any Younger"	Late/47	Sig 15217
"Malaguena"	Late/47	Sig 15181
"How High the Moon"	Late/47	Sig 15185
"Sometimes I'm Happy"	2/47	Sig 15127
"Ace in the Hole"	2/47	Sig 15127
"What Is This Thing Called Love?"	9/47	Sig 15162

HI HO TRAILUS BOOT WHIP
Bob Thiele Music BBM1-0595 (mono) (1974)

"Hi Ho Trailus Boot Whip"	9/47	Sig 15162
"What Is This Thing Called Love?"	9/47	Sig 15162
"Malaguena"	Late/47	Sig 15181
"I Told Ya I Love Ya, Now Get Out"	9/47	Sig 15181
"Sometimes I'm Happy"	2/47	Sig 15127
"Ace in the Hole"	2/47	Sig 15127
"How High the Moon"	Late/47	Sig 15185
"It's Different When It Happens to You"	9/47	Sig 15217
"I Ain't Gettin' Any Younger"	Late/47	Sig 15217
"Key Largo"	Late/47	Sig 15185

Reissues: HI HO TRAILUS BOOT WHIP
        Doctor Jazz FW 39418 (mono) (1984)
        SINGIN' AND SWINGIN'
        Japanese Doctor Jazz K25P6331 (mono) (1985)

346

"What Is This Thing Called Love?"[1,2]	10/2/48
"How High the Moon"[2]	10/2/48
"September in the Rain"[1,2]	10/9/48
"How High the Moon"[1,2]	10/9/48
"Malaguena"[1]	unknown
Medley: " 'S Wonderful"[3] "They Can't Take That Away from Me"	unknown
"Malaguena"[1]	unknown
"Sweet Georgia Brown"[3]	unknown
"Stella by Starlight"[3]	unknown

[1]COUNT BASIE—ANITA O'DAY Alto AL-702 (mono) (1972)
[2]FAT'S GANG! Talcrip TDFN-10230 (mono) (1975)
[3]TADD DAMERON Ult-Tadd TDFN-1500 (mono) (1977)

RECORDED

ANITA O'DAY 1949–50   1949–50
Tono TJ-6003 (mono) (1984)   Los Angeles/
Chicago/
New York

"Jamaica Mon"	"Lovesick Blues."
"Don't Kick It Around"	"Yea Boo"
"So Much of Nothing to Do"	"Tennessee Waltz"
"Poor Simple Simon"	"If I Could Steal You From
"Blues for Bojangles"	Somebody Tonight"
"Your Eyes Are Bigger than Your Heart"	"Black Moonlight
	"Once There Lived A Fool"
"Something I Dreamed Last Night"	"I Apologize"
	"You Took Advantage of Me"

347

SONGS BY ANITA O'DAY   1954
Norgran MGN-30 (mono) (1954) (10" LP)   Los Angeles
  "I Cover the Waterfront"   "The Gypsy in My Soul"
  "I Didn't Know What Time It   "Frankie and Johnny"
    Was"   "Just One of Those Things"
  "Let's Fall in Love"   "The Man I Love"
  "Anita's Blues"
Reissues: AN EVENING WITH ANITA O'DAY Norgran MGN-1057
  (1955)
  AN EVENING WITH ANITA O'DAY Verve MGV-2050 (1957)

ANITA O'DAY SINGS JAZZ   1952
Norgran MGN-1049 (mono) (1952)   New York/Chicago
  "Rock 'N Roll Blues"   "Pagan Love Song"
  "Love for Sale"   "Ain't This a Wonderful Day"
  "Lullaby of the Leaves"   "Somebody's Crying"
  "Lover Come Back to Me"   "Vaya Con Dios"
  "No Soap, No Hope Blues"   "The Lady Is a Tramp"
  "Speak Low"   "Strawberry Moon"
Reissues: THE LADY IS A TRAMP Verve MGV-2049 (mono) (1957)
  THE LADY IS A TRAMP Japanese Verve MV-2553 (mono)
  (1977)

AN EVENING WITH ANITA O'DAY   1954-55
Norgran MGN-1057 (mono) (1955)   Los Angeles
  "Just One of Those Things"   "You Don't Know What Love Is"
  "Gypsy in my Soul"   Medley: "There'll Never Be Another
  "The Man I Love"   You" "Just Friends"
  "Frankie and Johnny"   "I Don't Know What Time It Was"
  "Anita's Blues"   "Let's Fall in Love"
  "I Cover the Waterfront"   "You're Getting to Be a Habit with
  "From This Moment On"   Me"
Reissues: AN EVENING WITH ANITA O'DAY
  Verve MGV-2050 (mono) (1957)
  Japanese Verve MV-2526 (mono) (1977)

HERE COME THE GIRLS—various artists   1955-56
Verve MGV-2036 (mono) (1956)   Los Angeles/New York
  "You're the Top"   "Honeysuckle Rose"
  "The Getaway and the Chase"
Reissue: HERE COME THE GIRLS Verve MV-2697 (mono) (1980)

ANITA   12/55
Orchestra—Buddy Bregman   Los Angeles
Verve MGV-2000 (mono) (1956)
  "You're the Top"   "As Long As I Live"
  "Honeysuckle Rose"   "No Moon at All"

"A Nightingale Sang in Berkeley   "Time After Time"
Square"   "I'll See You in My Dreams"
"Who Cares?"   "I Fall in Love Too Easily"
"I Can't Get Started"   "Beautiful Love"
"Fine and Dandy"
Reissues: THIS IS ANITA Verve V-8483 (mono) (1963)
      THIS IS ANITA Japanese Verve MV-2560 (mono) (1977)

PICK YOURSELF UP   12/56
Orchestra—Buddy Bregman   Los Angeles
Verve MGV-2043 (mono) (1956)
   "Don't Be That Way"   "Sweet Georgia Brown"
   "Let's Face the Music and   "I Won't Dance"
   Dance"   "Man with a Horn"
   "I Never Had a Chance"   "I Used to Be Color Blind"
   "Stompin' at the Savoy"   "There's a Lull in My Life"
   "Pick Yourself Up"   "Let's Begin"
   "Stars Fell on Alabama"
Reissue: PICK YOURSELF UP Japanese Verve MV-2611 (1978)

ANITA SINGS THE MOST* with   1/57
Rhythm Section (Oscar Peterson Quartet unbilled)   Chicago
Verve MGV-8259 (mono) (1957)
   " 'S Wonderful"   "Stella by Starlight"
   "They Can't Take That Away   "Taking a Chance on Love"
   from Me"   "Them There Eyes"
   "Tenderly"   "I've Got the World on a String"
   "Old Devil Moon"   "You Turned the Tables on Me"
   "Love Me or Leave Me"   "Bewitched, Bothered and
   "We'll Be Together Again   Bewildered"
Reissue: ANITA SINGS THE MOST Japanese Verve MV-2501 (mono)
   (1977)
*also released on American Recording Society ARS-G-426 under title ANITA
SINGS FOR OSCAR

ANITA O'DAY AT MISTER KELLY'S   4/58
Verve MGV-2113 (mono)/MGVS-62113 (stereo) (1958)   Chicago
with Rhythm Section
   "But Not for Me"   "Every Time I'm with You"
   "I Have a Reason for Living"   "Have You Met Miss Jones?"
   "My Love for You"   "The Wildest Gal in Town"
   "Varsity Drag"   "Star Eyes"
   "It Never Entered My Mind"   "Loneliness Is a Well"
   "Tea for Two"   "The Song Is You"
Reissue: ANITA O'DAY AT MISTER KELLY'S Japanese Verve MV-2550
   (stereo) (1977)

ANITA O'DAY SWINGS COLE PORTER WITH BILLY MAY   4/59
Verve MGV-2118 (mono)/MGVS-62118 (stereo) (1959)   Los Angeles
"Just One of Those Things"   "Get Out of Town"
"You'd Be So Nice to Come   "I've Got You Under My Skin"
Home To"   "Night and Day"
"Easy to Love"   "It's De-Lovely"
"I Get a Kick Out of You"   "I Love You"
"All of You"   "What Is This Thing Called Love?"
"Love for Sale"
Reissues: ANITA O'DAY SWINGS COLE PORTER WITH BILLY MAY
    English World Record Club T-439 (mono) ST-439 (stereo)
    Japanese Verve 23MJ-3191 (stereo) (1982)

ANITA O'DAY SINGS THE WINNERS   4/58
Orchestras—Marty Paich and Russ Garcia   Los Angeles
Verve MGV-8283 (mono)/MGVS-68283 (stereo) (1958)
"Take the A Train"   "Sing, Sing, Sing"
"Tenderly"   "My Funny Valentine"
"Interlude"   "Frenesi"
"Four"   "Body and Soul"
"Early Autumn"   "What's Your Story, Morning Glory"
"Four Brothers"   "Peanut Vendor"
Reissues: ANITA O'DAY SINGS THE WINNERS
    Verve V-8485 (mono)/V6-8485 (stereo) (1962)
    Japanese Verve MV-2536 (stereo) (1977)

ANITA O'DAY AND BILLY MAY   6/60
SWING RODGERS AND HART   Los Angeles
Verve MGV-2141 (mono)/MGVS-62141 (stereo) (1960)
"Johnny One Note"   "Lover"
"Little Girl Blue"   "It Never Entered My Mind"
"Falling in Love with Love"   "Ten Cents a Dance"
"Bewitched"   "I've Got Five Dollars"
"I Could Write a Book"   "To Keep My Love Alive"
"Have You Met Miss Jones?"   "Spring Is Here"
Reissue: ANITA O'DAY AND BILLY MAY SWING RODGERS AND
    HART Japanese Verve 23MJ-3192 (stereo) (1982)

WAITER, MAKE MINE BLUES   8/60, 10/60
Orchestra—Russell Garcia   Los Angeles
Verve MGV-2145 (mono)/MGVS-62145 (stereo) (1960)
"That Old Feeling"   "Whatever Happened to You?"
"Angel Eyes"   "When Sonny Gets Blue"
"The Thrill Is Gone"   "Stella by Starlight"
"Detour Ahead"   "Mad About the Boy"

"Yesterdays"   "A Blues Serenade"
"Waiter, Make Mine Blues"   "Good-bye"
Reissue: WAITER, MAKE MINE BLUES Japanese Verve MV-2693 (mono)
    (1980)

COOL HEAT   4/59
Orchestra—Jimmy Giuffre   Los Angeles
Verve MGV-8312 (mono)/ MGVS-68312 (stereo) (1960)
    "Mack the Knife"   "It Had to Be You"
    "Easy Come, Easy Go"   "Come Rain or Come Shine"
    "Orphan Annie"   "Hershey Bar"
    "You're a Clown"   "A Lover Is Blue"
    "Gone with the Wind"   "My Heart Belongs to Daddy"
    "Hooray for Hollywood"   "The Way You Look Tonight"
Reissue: COOL HEAT Japanese Verve MV-2679 (stereo) (1980)

TRAV'LIN' LIGHT   1/61
Orchestras—Johnny Mandel and Barney Kessel   Los Angeles
Verve V-2157 (mono)/V6-2157 (stereo) (1961)
    "Trav'lin' Light"   "God Bless the Child"
    "The Moon Looks Down and   "If the Moon Turns Green"
    Laughs"   "I Hear Music"
    "Don't Explain"   "Lover Come Back to Me"
    "Remember"   "Crazy He Calls Me"
    "Some Other Spring"   "What a Little Moonlight Can Do"
    "Miss Brown to You"
Reissues: TRAV'LIN' LIGHT Japanese Verve MV-2582 (mono) (1977)
    English World Record Club T-600 (mono) ST-600 (stereo) (1966)

ALL THE SAD YOUNG MEN   10/61
Orchestra—Gary McFarland   New York
Verve V-8442 (mono)/V6-8442 (stereo) (1961)
    "Boogie Blues"   "Do Nothin' Till You Hear from
    "You Came a Long Way from Me"
    St. Louis"   "One More Mile"
    "I Want to Sing a Song"   "Night Bird"
    "A Woman Alone with   "Up State"
    Blues"   "Senior Blues"
    "The Ballad of the Sad Young
    Men"

TIME FOR TWO WITH CAL TJADER   2/62
Verve V-8472 (mono)/V6-8472 (stereo)   Los Angeles
    "Thanks for the Memory"   "An Occasional Man"
    "It Shouldn't Happen to a "The Party's Over"
    Dream"   "I Believe in You"
    "Just in Time"   "Mr. Sandman"
    "Under a Blanket of Blue" "Spring Will Be a Little Late This

"That's Your Red Wagon"   Year"
"Peel Me a Grape"   "I'm Not Supposed to Be Blue
                                       Blues"
Reissue: TIME FOR TWO WITH CAL TJADER Japanese Verve
       23MJ-3287 (stereo) (1983)

ANITA O'DAY & THE THREE SOUNDS   10/62
Verve V-8514 (mono)/V6-8514 (stereo)   New York
    "When the World Was Young"   "Whisper Not"
    "All Too Soon"   "(Fly Me to the Moon) In Other
    "My Ship"   Words"
                                  "You and the Night and the Music"
Reissue: ANITA O'DAY & THE THREE SOUNDS Japanese Verve
       MV-2629 (stereo) (1978)

INCOMPARABLE!   8/60
Orchestra—Bill Holman   Los Angeles
Verve V-8572 (mono)/V6-8572 (stereo) (1963)
    "It Could Happen to You"   "Easy Living"
    "Blue Champagne"   "Can't We Be Friends"
    "Avalon"   "Slaughter on 10th Avenue"
    "Old Devil Moon"   "If I Love Again"
    "The Party's Over"   "Speak Low"
    "Why Shouldn't I"   "Indian Summer"
Reissue: INCOMPARABLE! Japanese Verve 23MJ-3264 (stereo) (1983)

ANITA O'DAY with Rhythm Section   Late/60s
Anita O'Day Records AOD-1   Stockholm/Hawaii/Detroit
(simulated stereo) (1972)
    "Sunny"   "Bluesette"
    "So Nice Samba"   "Fly Me to the Moon"
    "My Funny Valentine"   "Quiet Nights of Quiet Stars"
    "Watch What Happens"   "Green Dolphin Street"
    "Walk on By"   "Street of Dreams"
    "Lush Life"
Reissues: ANITA O'DAY Glendale GLS-6001 (simulated stereo) (1974)
          Japanese TRIO PA-7100 (mono) (1975)

ONCE UPON A SUMMERTIME with Rhythm Section   Late/60s
Anita O'Day Records AOD-2   Hollywood/Stockholm/Hawaii/Detroit
(simulated stereo) (1972)
    "Sweet Georgia Brown"   "Is You Is or Is You Ain't My
    "Boogie Blues"   Baby?"
    "Tea for Two"   "A Nightingale Sang in Berkeley
    "Anita's Blues"   Square"
    "Honeysuckle Rose"   " 'S Wonderful"
    "Yesterdays"   "They Can't Take That Away from
    "Soon It's Gonna Rain"   Me"

"Once Upon a Summertime" "Night and Day"
"The Girl from Ipanema"
Reissue: ONCE UPON A SUMMERTIME
 Japanese Trio PA-6019 (mono) (1975) Glendale GLS-6000 (simulated
 stereo) (1974)

THE JAZZ STYLINGS OF ANITA O'DAY   1955–62
English Verve VLP-9125 (mono) (1965)

"Honeysuckle Rose"[1]	"Stompin' at the Savoy"[4]
"Four"[2]	"Take the A Train"[2]
"Trav'lin' Light"[3]	"Easy Living"[6]
"Four Brothers"[2]	"Old Devil Moon"[6]
"Sweet Georgia Brown"[4]	"A Night in Tunisia (Interlude)"[2]
"You're the Top"[1]	Medley: " 'S Wonderful" "They
"Fly Me to the Moon"[5]	Can't Take That Away from
"Tea for Two"[6]	Me"[7]
"Slaughter on 10th Avenue"[6]	"Under a Blanket of Blue"[8]
"Slaughter on 10th Avenue"[6]	

[1]from MGV-2000   ANITA
[2]from MGV-8283   ANITA O'DAY SINGS THE
            WINNERS
[3]from V-2157   TRAV'LIN' LIGHT
[4]from MGV-2043   PICK YOURSELF UP
[5]from V-8514   ANITA O'DAY & THE THREE
            SOUNDS
[6]from V-8572   INCOMPARABLE!
[7]from MGV-8259   ANITA SINGS THE MOST
[8]from V-8472   TIME FOR TWO

ANITA O'DAY—VERVE JAZZ NO. 11   1954–56
German Metro 2356 100 (mono) (1975)

"Pick Yourself Up"[1]	"Opus #1"[3]
"Don't Be That Way"[1]	"Boogie Blues"[3]
"Let's Face the Music and	"Let Me Off Uptown"[3]
Dance"[1]	"From This Moment On"[2]
"Stompin' at the Savoy"[1]	"Just One of Those Things"[2]
"Gypsy in My Soul"[2]	"Frankie and Johnny"[2]
"Anita's Blues"[2]	

[1]from MGV-2043   PICK YOURSELF UP
[2]from MGV-2050   AN EVENING WITH ANITA
            O'DAY
[3]from MGV-2008   DRUMMER MAN—GENE
            KRUPA

ANITA O'DAY—THE BIG BAND SESSIONS   1959–61
Verve VE-2-2534 (stereo) (1979)

"Up State"[4]	"Gone with the Wind"[6]
"Boogie Blues"[4]	"Crazy He Calls Me"[5]

"Night Bird"[4]
"A Woman Alone with the
Blues"[4]
"The Ballad of the Sad Young
Men"[4]
"You Came a Long Way from
St. Louis"[4]
"Trav'lin' Light"[5]
"Don't Explain"[5]
"If The Moon Turns Green"[5]
"I Hear Music"[5]
"Lover Come Back to Me"[5]
"It Had to Be You"[6]
"The Way You Look Tonight"[6]
"Hershey Bar"[6]
[4]from V6-8442
[5]from V6-2157
[6]from MGVS-68312
[7]from MGVS-62118

[8]from MGVS-62141

"Come Rain or Come Shine"[6]
"My Heart Belongs to Daddy"[6]
"Easy Come, Easy Go"[6]
"A Lover Is Blue"[6]
"You're a Clown"[6]
"What Is This Thing Called Love?"[7]
"Ten Cents a Dance"[7]
"Just One of Those Things"[7]
"Have You Met Miss Jones"[8]
"Easy to Love"[7]
"Get Out of Town"[7]
"Night and Day"[7]
"I Get a Kick Out of You"[7]
"Lover"[8]
"Johnny One Note"[8]
ALL THE SAD YOUNG MEN
TRAV'LIN' LIGHT
COOL HEAT
ANITA O'DAY SWINGS COLE
PORTER WITH BILLY MAY
ANITA O'DAY AND BILLY MAY
SWING RODGERS AND HART

ANITA O'DAY TOKYO '63   1963
Japanese Polydor 23MJ-3470 (stereo) (1985)   Japan
    "Trav'lin' Light"   "Sweet Georgia Brown"
    "Honeysuckle Rose"   "Tea for Two"
    "Avalon"   "Stella by Starlight"
    "Bewitched"   "Love for Sale"
    "You'd Be So Nice to Come   "Get Out of Town"
      Home to"   "That Old Feeling"
    "Night and Day"   "Four Brothers"
    "Let's Fall in Love"

SESSIONS, LIVE   1956-7
Stars of Jazz Telecasts   Hollywood
Calliope CAL-3021 (mono) (1976)
    "You're the Top"   11/12/56
    "The Man I Love"   11/12/56
    "Love Me or Leave Me"   7/1/57
    "My Funny Valentine"   7/1/57
    "A Cent and a Half"   7/1/57

THE SWING ERA: ENCORE   1970
Time-Life STL-351 (stereo) (1970)   Los Angeles
    "Boogie Blues" (recreation of Gene Krupa original)

THE SWING ERA: CURTAIN CALL 1970
Time-Life STL-352 (stereo) (1970) Los Angeles
"And Her Tears Flowed Like Wine" (recreation of Stan Kenton original)

DR. PEPPER: THE MOST 1974
ORIGINAL SOFT DRINK EVER Hollywood
Private LP: DP-1974 (stereo) (1974)
"Dr. Pepper" (commercial jingle)

RECORDED LIVE AT THE BERLIN JAZZ FESTIVAL 1970
MPS MB-20750 (stereo) (1973) Berlin
"Let's Fall in Love" "I Can't Get Started"
"Your Wings" Medley: "Yesterday"
"Soon It's Gonna Rain" "Yesterdays"
"Honeysuckle Rose" "On a Clear Day"
"Sunny" "Street of Dreams"
Reissue: ANITA O'DAY IN BERLIN Pausa 7092 (stereo) (1981)

ANITA 1975 4/75
Japanese Trio PA-7105 (stereo) (1975) Los Angeles
"A Song for You" "I Get a Kick Out of You"
"Undecided" "It Had to Be You"
"(What Are You Doing) the "Opus #1"
Rest of Your Life" "Gone with the Wind"
"Exactly Like You" "When Sunny Gets Blue"
U.S. Issue: A SONG FOR YOU Emily ER-83084 (stereo) (1983)

MY SHIP 6/75
Japanese Trio PA-7126 (stereo) (1976) Tokyo
"Satin Doll" • "After You've Gone"*+
"Mean to Me" • "A Nightingale Sang in Berkeley
"Why Shouldn't I"*+ Square"*+
"Body and Soul"*+ "The Man I Love"*+
"My Ship"+ "Penthouse Serenade" •
"Our Love Is Here to Stay"*+ "Come Rain or Come Shine"*+
"The Days of Wine and Roses"*+
U.S. Issues: *ANITA O'DAY Dobre 1014 (stereo) (1978)
+MY SHIP Emily ER-11279 (stereo) (1979)
•A SONG FOR YOU Emily ER-83084 (stereo) (1983)

ANITA O'DAY LIVE IN TOKYO, 1975 6/75
Japanese Trio PA-7140 (stereo) (1976) Tokyo
"Wave" "I Get a Kick Out of You"
"You'd Be So Nice to Come "I Can't Get Started"
Home To" "Anita's Blues"
"Honeysuckle Rose" "Sweet Georgia Brown"

355

"A Song for You"
"Exactly Like You"
Medley: " 'S Wonderful" "They
Can't Take That Away from
Me"

"Tea for Two"
"Wave"

U.S. Issue: ANITA O'DAY LIVE IN TOKYO, 1975 Emily ER-9579 (stereo)
(1979)

VOCAL SPECIAL (Unreleased Masters)   6/75
Japanese Trio TD-26 (Not for Sale) (stereo) (1978)   Tokyo
    "Is You Is or Is You Ain't My
    Baby?"
    "I Cried for You"
U.S. Issue: ANGEL EYES Emily ER-13081 (stereo) (1981)

ANITA O'DAY LIVE AT MINGOS   10/76
Japanese Trio PAP-9059 (stereo) (1977)   Tokyo
    "As Time Goes By"   "I Could Write a Book"
    "Stardust"   "Sophisticated Lady"
    "I Didn't Know What Time It   "I Hear Music"
    Was"   "I Cover the Waterfront"
    "The Very Thought of You"   "The Way You Look Tonight"
    "Anita's Blues '76"
U.S. Issue: LIVE AT MINGOS Emily ER-11579 (stereo) (1979)

THERE'S ONLY ONE   1978
Dobre 1029 (stereo) (1979)   Hollywood
    "It Don't Mean a Thing (If It   "Ace in the Hole"
    Ain't Got That Swing)"   "I Cover the Waterfront"
    "I'm Getting Sentimental Over   "Chicago"
    You"   "I Cried for You"
    "Old Folks"
    "What Is This Thing Called
    Love?"
Reissue: OLD FOLKS Japanese JVC VIJ-6370 (stereo) (1981)

SKYLARK—ANITA O'DAY LIVE AT SOMETIME   6/78
Japanese Trio PAP-9127 (stereo) (1978)   Tokyo
    "On a Clear Day"   "Lover Come Back to Me"
    "Candlelight and Wine"   "Skylark"
    "It Don't Mean a Thing"   "Like Someone in Love"
    "This Is All I Ask"   "I'm Getting Sentimental Over You"
    "Night and Day"

ANGEL EYES—ANITA O'DAY ON LIVE   6/78
Japanese LOB LDC-1012 (stereo) (1978) Direct-To-Disc   Tokyo
    "You'd Be So Nice to Come   "Send in the Clowns"
    Home To"   "Black Coffee"

"When Sunny Gets Blue"   "There Will Never Be Another You"
"Angel Eyes"   "Bewitched"
"Honeysuckle Rose"
U.S. Issue: ANGEL EYES Emily ER-13081 (stereo) (1981)

MELLO' DAY—ANITA O'DAY   Jan.–Feb./79
GNP/Crescendo GNPS 2126 (stereo) (1979)   Los Angeles
"Old Devil Moon"   "On the Trail"
"Lost in the Stars"   "You Can't Go Home Again"
"Meditation"   "When the World Was Young"
"You're My Everything"   "So Nice (Summer Samba)"
"You Could Have Had My   "Yellow Days"
   Baby"   "Limehouse Blues"
"Them There Eyes"

ANITA O'DAY LIVE AT THE CITY   9/79
Emily ER-102479 (stereo) (1980)   San Francisco
"Blue Skies"   "P-Town"
"What Are You Doing the Rest "Emily"
   of Your Life"   "Little Orphan Annie"
"In a Mellow Tone"   "Close Your Eyes"
"Hershey Bar"   "Shakin' the Blues Away"
"Four Brothers"

ANITA O'DAY LIVE AT THE CITY—THE SECOND SET   9/79
Emily ER-42181 (stereo) (1981)   San Francisco
"Wave"   "On Green Dolphin Street"
"I'm Getting Sentimental Over "My Funny Valentine"
   You"   Medley: "Tea for Two"
Medley: "Falling In Love with   "Wave"
   Love"
"Love for Sale"
"A Nightingale Sang in Berkeley
   Square"

MISTY—ANITA O'DAY DIRECT II   12/81
Japanese LOB LDC-1033 (stereo) (1981) Direct-To-Disc   Tokyo
"Misty"   "You Go to My Head"
"The Night Has a Thousand   "A Sleepin' Bee"
   Eyes"   "Bluesette"
"Am I Blue"   "I'm Old Fashioned"
"Afternoon in Paris"   "Speak Low"
"My Heart Belongs to Daddy"
U.S. Issue: THE NIGHT HAS A THOUSAND EYES Emily ER-32383
   (stereo) (1983)

ANITA O'DAY AO VIVO NO 150 NIGHT CLUB   8/84
Brazilian Estudio Eldorado 93-84-0454   San Paulo
     "Wave"   "P-Town"
     "It Had to Be You"   "The Man with the Horn"
     "A Sleepin' Bee"   "Body and Soul"
     "Time After Time"   "Lush Life"
     "Stompin' at the Savoy"   "The Song Is You"
     "Wave"

ANITA O'DAY CHRISTMAS ALBUM   10/84
Emily X-101C (cassette format only)   Los Angeles
     "One More Christmas"   "I'll Be Home for Christmas"
     "White Christmas"   "Jingle Bells"
     "Christmas Song"   "Have Yourself a Merry Little
     "Let It Snow, Let It Snow, Let   Christmas"
     It Snow"

SS' WONDERFUL—BIG BAND CONCERT 1985   5/85
(Live at Carnegie Hall)   New York
Emily ER-92685
     "Opus #1"   "I Can't Get Started"
     "Honeysuckle Rose"   "And Her Tears Flowed Like Wine"
     "Sweet Georgia Brown"   "Let Me Off Uptown"—duet with
     "Four Brothers"   Roy Eldridge
     "P-Town"   "Boogie Blues"
     Medley: " 'S Wonderful"   "I Get a Kick Out of You"
     "They Can't Take That Away   "I'll See You in My Dreams"
     from Me"

CARNEGIE HALL 50th ANNIVERSARY CONCERT—   5/85
THE QUARTET   New York
Emily 0685 (cassette format only)
     "Wave"   "Tea for Two"
     "You'd Be So Nice to Come   "Love for Sale"
     Home To"   "Lover Where Can You Be?"
     "I Cried for You"   "My Funny Valentine"
     "Falling in Love with Love"   "It Don't Mean a Thing"
     "A Nightingale Sang in Berkeley   "Lush Life"
     Square"
     "Tea for Two"

Section C
THE UNCOLLECTED RECORDINGS

(Recordings which remain unreleased in LP form or in any form.)

Part One—VOCALIST WITH STAN KENTON'S BAND

	RECORDED	ORIGINAL RELEASE
"How Come"	1/18/45	unissued
"I Can't Believe That You're in Love with Me"	1/18/45	unissued

Part Two—SOLO (1947-1975)

	RECORDED	ORIGINAL RELEASE
"It's Different"	9/47	Signature 15217
"Them There Eyes"	1/5/50	unissued
"Nice Dreaming"	1/5/50	unissued
"We Laughed at Love"	2/56	Verve 10014
"I'm with You"	2/56	Verve 10000
"The Rock and Roll Waltz"	2/56	Verve 10000
"Your Picture's Hanging Crooked on the Wall"	2/56	unissued

"I'm Not Lonely"	2/56	unissued
"Ivy"	12/56	unissued

ANITA O'DAY AND DAVE FRISHBERG   1975   unissued
"On the Sunny Side of the Street"   "The Sunshine of My Life"
"Old Folks"   "It Don't Mean a Thing"
"Beyond the Blue Horizon"   "Fools Rush In"
"Breaking Up Is Hard to Do"   "I'm Just a Lucky So and
"Hand-me-down Love"   So"

ANITA O'DAY SINGS BOB FRIEDMAN   1973   unissued
"Cookie Jar"   "All the Time"
"Once Upon a Happy Time"   "No Machine Can Take
"Rock N' Roll Rag"   Your Place with Me"
"How Could I Go On"   "Tender Loving Words"
"Fat Man"   "That's Love"
"Goodbye Old Dream"   "When It's Time to Tell"
"I Take It All Back"   "What's Wrong Clyde"

ANITA O'DAY ON COMPACT DISC

	RECORDED	ORIGINAL LP ISSUE	CD ISSUE
1. (THIS IS) ANITA	1955	Verve V-8483 (1963)	Japanese Polydor J33J-25009 U.S. Verve 829-261-2
2. ANITA SINGS THE MOST	1957	Verve MGV-8259 (1957)	Japanese Polydor J33J-25035 U.S. Verve 829-577-2
3. DRUMMER MAN— GENE KRUPA featuring ANITA O'DAY	1956	Verve MGV-2008 (1956)	U.S. Verve 827-843-2
4. SINGS WITH GENE KRUPA	1941–2 1945	Japanese CBS/SONY 20AP-1439 (1980)	Japanese CBS/SONY 32DP-567
5. LIVE IN TOKYO 1975	1975	Japanese Trio PA-7140 (1976)	Japanese APOLLON BY30-5140

Editor's Note: As this book is going to press, a new album is being recorded by DRG Records in Hollywood. It will include songs previously unrecorded by Anita. The new issue will be in Compact Disc, LP and Cassette formats.

THE FILMS OF ANITA O'DAY

1. *Let Me Off Uptown* * 1942 Soundie. (Black and White 3 min.)
   featuring Gene Krupa and his Orchestra
   "Let Me Off Uptown" (vocal by Anita and Roy Eldridge)
2. *Thanks for the Boogie Ride* 1942 Soundie. (Black and White 3 min.)
   featuring Gene Krupa and his Orchestra
   "Thanks for the Boogie Ride" (vocal by Anita and Roy Eldridge)
3. *Artistry in Rhythm* * 1944 Universal Name Band Musical.
   featuring Stan Kenton and his (Black and White, 20 min.)
   Orchestra
   "Tabby the Cat"
   "I'm Going Mad for a Pad"
4. *Cool & Groovy* 1956 Universal-International featurette
   "Honeysuckle Rose" (Black and White, 15 min.)
   (Anita accompanied by Buddy DeFranco Quartet)
5. *The Gene Krupa Story* * 1959 Columbia Pictures film biography
   starring Sal Mineo (Black and White, 101 min.)
   (Anita plays herself) (Don Weis, director)
   "Memories of You"
6. *Jazz on a Summer's Day* 1960 Galaxy Films (Color, 86 min.)
   "Sweet Georgia Brown" documentary of the 1958 Newport Jazz
   "Tea for Two" Festival
   (Bert Stern, director)
7. *Zigzag* (aka *False Witness*) 1970 Metro-Goldwyn-Mayer drama
   starring George Kennedy (Black and White, 105 min.)
   (Anita plays a nightclub singer) (Richard A. Colla, director)
   "On Green Dolphin Street"

---

* See Discography for long-play issue.

8. *The Outfit*
   starring Robert Duvall
   (Anita plays herself)
   "I Concentrate on You"

1974 Metro-Goldwyn-Mayer drama
(Color, 103 min.)
(John Flynn, director)

ANITA O'DAY ON VIDEO

1. JAZZ LEGENDS 1928–50   Adventures in Video, 1983
   1942 Soundie film short
   "Thanks for the Boogie Ride" with Gene Krupa Orchestra

2. BIG BAND BASH 1937–49   Adventures in Video, 1983
   1942 Soundie film short
   "Let Me Off Uptown" with Gene Krupa Orchestra

3. THE GENE KRUPA STORY   RCA/Columbia Home Video, 1987
   1959 Columbia Pictures feature

4. JAZZ ON A SUMMER'S DAY   SONY 0557 Home Video, 1987
   1960 Galaxy Film documentary

5. ANITA O'DAY TOKYO '63   SONY 6512-6 Home Video, 1985
   1963 concert

INDEX